Conspiracy Theories & Secret Societies

FOR DUMMIES®

by Christopher Hodapp
and Alice Von Kannon

WILEY

Wiley Publishing, Inc.

Conspiracy Theories & Secret Societies For Dummies®

Published by
Wiley Publishing, Inc.
111 River St.
Hoboken, NJ 07030-5774
www.wiley.com

Copyright © 2008 by Wiley Publishing, Inc., Indianapolis, Indiana

Published by Wiley Publishing, Inc., Indianapolis, Indiana

Published simultaneously in Canada

For general information on our other products and services, please contact our Customer Care Department within the U.S. at 800-762-2974, outside the U.S. at 317-572-3993, or fax 317-572-4002.

For technical support, please visit www.wiley.com/techsupport.

Wiley also publishes its books in a variety of electronic formats. Some content that appears in print may not be available in electronic books.

Library of Congress Control Number: 2008923595

ISBN: 978-0-470-18408-0

10 9 8 7 6 5 4 3 2 1

WILEY

About the Authors

Christopher Hodapp is a 32° Freemason and a member of the Masonic order of the Knights Templar. His first book, *Freemasons For Dummies,* has quickly become the most popular modern guide to the ancient and accepted fraternity of Freemasonry. He's also the author of *Solomon's Builders: Freemasons, Founding Fathers and the Secrets of Washington D.C.*, and co-author of *The Templar Code For Dummies.* He attended Indiana University, the University of Southern California, Los Angeles Valley Community College, and California State University Northridge. In 2006, Chris received the Duane E. Anderson Excellence in Masonic Education Award from the Grand Lodge of Minnesota. He has written for *Templar History Magazine, Masonic Magazine, The Scottish Rite Journal, The Indiana Freemason,* and *Indianapolis Monthly,* and he's a monthly columnist for *Living Naturally First* magazine. Chris has also spent more than 20 years as a commercial filmmaker.

Alice Von Kannon has been an advertising executive, a teacher, a writer, and even a greedy and villainous landlord. A history junkie beyond the help of an intervention since the age of 14, her studies of Near Eastern religious cults and sects led to her first book, *The Templar Code For Dummies,* co-written with Chris Hodapp. She's studied film production at Los Angeles Valley Community College and history at California State University Northridge, and she's worked for many years in advertising as a writer and broadcast producer. Alice has traveled widely in Europe and the Middle East and written on the subject of the Barbary Wars and the birth of the U.S. Navy. She's a member of Romance Writers of America and the Order of the Grail, the fraternal body of the International College of Esoteric Studies.

Both authors live in Indianapolis, Indiana.

Dedication

To Norma for her boundless help, support, confidence, and love.

To Charlie who was at Roswell before the aliens took over.

And to Bob and Vera, who somehow always knew.

Authors' Acknowledgments

Our deepest appreciation goes to the many friends and authors who unselfishly shared their knowledge with us.

To the unrelenting Ed King of www.masonicinfo.com for his kind assistance; and to Trevor McKeown and others who make the vast Web site of the Grand Lodge of British Columbia and Yukon such an invaluable resource.

To Nathan Brindle, Jim Dillman, Jeffrey Naylor, Eric Schmitz, R.J. Hayes, Stephen Dafoe, and all the "Knights of the North" for their constant support and input, and to Phillip A. Garver for his incredible knowledge of Gnosticism, Martinism, Catharism, and all things esoteric.

To Tom Atkins for making the Federal Reserve seem like a simple concept to understand. To Dr. William Moore for pointing us in directions we may not have otherwise looked; and to Mark Tabbert for pointing us at William. To Dave Pruett who graciously (and bravely) acted as the Technical Editor of this volume. To Carolyn Steele and Rex DeLawter for caring for our business when we weren't able to be there.

To Norma Winkler, without whose love and support our lives would be a much lonelier place.

To Tracy Boggier at Wiley Publishing for being a tireless champion of this book, and those that preceded it, through a long and sometimes tortured route to completion; to our patient and eternally unflappable editor Natalie Harris; to Carrie Burchfield for helping us cram a 500-page book into 348 pages; to Jack Bussell for his cheerful assistance, usually at the last minute with absolutely no notice whatsoever; to Rich Tennant, the great unsung hero of the *For Dummies* world; and to the entire *For Dummies* team that works behind the scenes to make this process simple.

Publisher's Acknowledgments

We're proud of this book; please send us your comments through our Dummies online registration form located at www.dummies.com/register/.

Some of the people who helped bring this book to market include the following:

Acquisitions, Editorial, and Media Development

Project Editor: Natalie Faye Harris

Acquisitions Editor: Tracy Boggier

Copy Editor: Carrie A. Burchfield

Editorial Program Coordinator: Erin Calligan Mooney

General Reviewer: Dave Pruett

Editorial Manager: Christine Meloy Beck

Editorial Assistants: Joe Niesen, Leeann Harney, David Lutton

Cover Photos: © Todd Gipstein/National Geographic/Getty Images

Cartoons: Rich Tennant (www.the5thwave.com)

Composition Services

Project Coordinator: Patrick Redmond

Layout and Graphics: Reuben W. Davis, Stephanie D. Jumper, Christine Williams

Proofreaders: Laura Bowman, John Greenough, Catie Kelly, Todd Lothery

Indexer: Potomac Indexing, LLC

Publishing and Editorial for Consumer Dummies

Diane Graves Steele, Vice President and Publisher, Consumer Dummies

Joyce Pepple, Acquisitions Director, Consumer Dummies

Kristin A. Cocks, Product Development Director, Consumer Dummies

Michael Spring, Vice President and Publisher, Travel

Kelly Regan, Editorial Director, Travel

Publishing for Technology Dummies

Andy Cummings, Vice President and Publisher, Dummies Technology/General User

Composition Services

Gerry Fahey, Vice President of Production Services

Debbie Stailey, Director of Composition Services

Contents at a Glance

Introduction *1*

Part 1: Conspiracy Theories and Secret Societies: The Improbable Wedded to the Inscrutable *7*

Chapter 1: Everything You Know Is Wrong 9

Chapter 2: Conspiracism and the Origin of Modern Conspiracy Theories 19

Chapter 3: Building the Perfect Beast: Secret Societies through the Ages 33

Part 11: A Colossal Compilation of Conspiracy Theories *45*

Chapter 4: Everybody Knows About It: The World's Most Common Conspiracy Theories 47

Chapter 5: JFK and Other Presidents: The Conspiracies Behind the Guns 67

Chapter 6: The World Ends Monday — Racial, Religious, and Apocalyptic Conspiracies 95

Chapter 7: Not of This Earth: Innocent Pawns in an Intergalactic Imbroglio 117

Chapter 8: Tracking the Evolution of the 9/11 Conspiracy Theories 137

Part 111: Secret Societies and Societies with Secrets *157*

Chapter 9: The Freemasons: The World's Longest-Running Secret Society 159

Chapter 10: Rosicrucians and the Evolution of Occult Secret Societies 183

Chapter 11: The Illuminati: The Bavarian Boogeymen 207

Chapter 12: Secret Societies of Terror and Death 219

Chapter 13: Frolicsome Fraternalism and Nefarious Foes of Freedom 249

Chapter 14: Thugs, Mugs, and Lugs: The Mafia and Other Underworld Societies 267

Chapter 15: Banks and Super Committees: Knowing All, Owning All, Controlling All...297

Part 1V: The Part of Tens *315*

Chapter 16: Ten Conspiracy Theories That Skirt the Edge of Madness.................317

Chapter 17: Ten Conspiracies That Were Absolutely True 329

Chapter 18: Ten Weirdest Secret Societies of All Time......................................343

Index *351*

Table of Contents

Introduction *1*
    About This Book...2
    Conventions Used in This Book 2
    What You're Not To Read 3
    Foolish Assumptions 3
    How This Book Is Organized..4
        Part I: Conspiracy Theories and Secret Societies:
          The Improbable Wedded to the Inscrutable 4
        Part II: A Colossal Compilation of Conspiracy Theories 4
        Part III: Secret Societies and Societies with Secrets 5
        Part IV: The Part of Tens..5
    Icons Used in This Book..5
    Where to Go from Here...6

Part 1: Conspiracy Theories and Secret Societies:
The Improbable Wedded to the Inscrutable *7*
    Chapter 1: Everything You Know Is Wrong **9**
        Living in the Age of Conspiracy Theories and Secret Societies..............10
        What's Worth Scrutinizing, and What's Not................................11
          Connecting the dots...11
          Being skeptical about speculative thinking 13
        The Conspiracism World Tour 13
          The birth of 20th-century U.S. conspiracism....................14
          Conspiracy theories aren't limited to the USA! 17
        A Word About Skepticism 17

    Chapter 2: Conspiracism and the Origin
    of Modern Conspiracy Theories **19**
        Defining and Recognizing Conspiracism....................................20
          Just what is conspiracism? 20
          Conspiracism and secret societies 21
        Understanding How Conspiracists Think 22
          Shall we dance to the left or the right?.........................23
          Lack of proof is the proof 23
          What the behaviorists say..23

Examining Types of Conspiracy Theories 24
The French Revolution and the Birth of Modern Conspiracism.............26
    Attitudes before the French Revolution 26
    Off with their heads!...27
    The birth of conspiracy literature..28
Dreck Alert! Dreck Alert!..31

Chapter 3: Building the Perfect Beast:
Secret Societies through the Ages **33**
Defining Secret Societies...34
The Difference Between a Secret Society and a Religious Cult.............35
    Examining the fine lines...35
    Examining the specifics 35
    Organizations that straddle the fence 37
The Second-Oldest Profession: Secret Societies in Ancient Times 38
    Egypt: Source of the first secret society?............................38
    Greece: Ancient cults and mystery schools..........................38
    Rome: Cults and paranoia 40
    Europe: Secret societies from the Middle Ages onward.................43
    United States: Societies and fraternalism 43
    A new interest in secret societies...44

Part II: A Colossal Compilation of Conspiracy Theories ...45

Chapter 4: Everybody Knows About It: The World's
Most Common Conspiracy Theories **47**
Technological Terrors 48
    Fluoridated water and the Cold War Communist Plot....................48
    Chemtrails 50
    Nikola Tesla and "free electricity".......................................51
    Peace ray or death ray?...52
    HAARP — The electromagnetic superweapon 52
    Philadelphia Experiment's vanishing ship 53
Dirty Work Down Below — Underground Government Installations 55
    Alleged underground bunkers 55
    Denver International Airport: The New World
        Order's subterranean HQ...57
Night of the Living Dead — A Conga Line of Corpses 59
    Elvis Presley still walks among us!..59
    "Paul is dead"..61
Stifling Innovations that Threaten Corporate Profits........................63
    Subliminal advertising...63
    The ten-wiener, eight-bun conspiracy 65

Chapter 5: JFK and Other Presidents: The Conspiracies Behind the Guns 67

JFK: The Very Model of a Modern Major Conspiracy Theory 68
    Just the facts, please...68
    Lee Harvey Oswald 69
    Examining the conspiracy background 70
    Taking style over substance...72
    Considering the source...73
    The pansy plot 74
    Okay, so why did Jack Ruby shoot Oswald? 80
Looking at Other Presidential Assassinations.......................................81
    Abraham Lincoln 81
    James Garfield...90
    William McKinley..91

Chapter 6: The World Ends Monday — Racial, Religious, and Apocalyptic Conspiracies 95

Picking on the Jews: History's Most Common Blame Game....................95
    Turning Jews into conspiracy scapegoats 96
    The Dark Ages get darker...97
    The Jews as moneylenders...99
    Extending the blame to the present day 99
Catholic Conspiracy Theories 101
    The 3rd secret of Fatima...102
    Pope Pius XII and the Nazis...104
    The Vatican Islam Conspiracy theory..105
Islamic Conspiracy Theories 106
African Americans and Conspiracy Theories...108
    COINTELPRO..108
    The King Alfred Plan 109
    The Willie Lynch Letter 110
    Memorandum 46...111
    Common urban legends...112
    Cocaine and the CIA 113
    The AIDS epidemic 114
Apocalyptic Conspiracies 115

Chapter 7: Not of This Earth: Innocent Pawns in an Intergalactic Imbroglio 117

Earth versus the Flying Saucers!..118
The Roswell Incident 119
    Unidentified debris discovered 119
    Roswell resurrected 121
    Tracking the government's paper trail...122

Area 51 124
   Strange aircraft 125
   The UFO connection 126
Government Investigations of UFOs 127
   Project Sign 127
   Project Grudge..128
   Project Blue Book 129
   The Brookings Report...132
   Britain's "Flying Saucer Working Party" 133
NASA's "Phony" Moon Landings....................................133

**Chapter 8: Tracking the Evolution
of the 9/11 Conspiracy Theories** **137**
September 11, 2001 138
Tracking the Origins of 9/11 Conspiracy Theories 138
   The 9/11 "Truth Movement" 140
Examining the Main 9/11 Conspiracy Theories.............141
   The terrorist pilots weren't trained well enough
      to do what they did 141
   Terrorists can't hold passengers at bay with simple
      plastic knives or box cutters........................144
   The Air Force was ordered to stand down.........145
   The Twin Towers were brought down by bombs,
      not the airplanes 148
   Fire can't melt steel!...149
   The gobbledygook over WTC 7 150
The Towers Struck an Iceberg..152
   The neocon menace 153
   The "proof" is in the poetry 154

Part III: Secret Societies and Societies with Secrets 157

**Chapter 9: The Freemasons: The World's
Longest-Running Secret Society** **159**
Examining the Origins of Freemasonry 160
   So what's the big secret? 161
   Dating back to the Old Testament.......................164
   Evolving into modern Masons: Operative
      and speculative periods................................165

Modern Mason Methods and Memberships..166
  Hints of suspicion...167
  The basic Masonic degrees of membership 168
  Aspiring to more and "higher" degrees 169
Worldwide Distrust of Masonry 170
Templars = Masons = Illuminati = Jews? 171
  How the Knights Templar got involved 172
  Mixing in the Illuminati...173
  How the Masons and Jews wound up controlling the world........173
  Who's in charge? Seeking Masonic authorities 175
  Looking at Masonic plots that were real 176
Popular (And Untrue) Masonic Conspiracy Theories...................178
  The satanic map of Washington, D.C. 180
  The Masonic dollar bill...181
  Scottish Rite 32nd degree rings..182

Chapter 10: Rosicrucians and the Evolution of Occult Secret Societies **183**

Before Rosicrucianism: Hermeticism versus the Enlightenment 184
The Rosicrucians...185
  The tale of Christian Rosenkreutz.....................................186
  Johann Valentin Andrae...186
  The birth of Rosicrucian societies 187
  Modern Rosicrucianism 188
Rosicrucianism and "Fringe Freemasonry" 189
  Societas Rosicruciana in Anglia (SRIA) 190
  Societas Rosicruciana in Civitatibus Foederatis (SRICF) 190
Martinism 191
  Martinism revived 191
  Synarchy hijacks Martinism...192
The 19th Century and Occult Societies.....................................192
  The Hermetic Order of the Golden Dawn............................193
  The influence of Spiritualism 194
  The Ordo Templi Orientis (OTO) 195
20th-Century Occultism and the Rise of the Nazis 198
  Madame Blavatsky's Theosophical Society 199
  German occultism, secret societies, and the Nazis 203
  Heinrich Himmler's Nazi Knighthood 205

Chapter 11: The Illuminati: The Bavarian Boogeymen **207**
  The Original "Illuminated Ones" 208
  The Bavarian Illuminati: Short Life, Long Legacy 208
    Adam Weishaupt...209
    Spartacus and the Areopagites...209
    The Masonic connection 210
    The Congress of Wilhelmsbad 211
    The Illuminati cracks up 212
  Illuminati in America?...213
  Building a Boogeyman: The Illuminati as All-purpose Evil 214
    The Illuminati and the occult...214
    Nesta Webster and the Illuminati's conspiracy
      against civilization...215
    The Illuminati today: All things to all people......................216

Chapter 12: Secret Societies of Terror and Death **219**
  The Ancient Brotherhoods of Death...220
    The Sicarii...220
    The Assassins 221
    The Thugs..226
    The ninjas 228
  Murder, Incorporated 231
  Hate Group Assassins..233
    The Knights of the Ku Klux Klan 234
    Birth of the first Klan 234
    "Birth of a Nation" and the rebirth of the Klan...................235
    The politics of change 236
    A nation of joiners 237
    Hijacking the Klan 239
    The Klan goes underground..243
    Mississippi burning...243
    The Klan today..245
    The spawn of the KKK 245
  Black Supremacism..246

**Chapter 13: Frolicsome Fraternalism and
Nefarious Foes of Freedom** **249**
  The Golden Age of Fraternalism..249
    The birth of the fraternalism movement..............................250
    What about women? 254
    The fraternal military orders 255

College Fraternities and Secret Societies.....................................255

Fraternities with a Masonic connection..255

Skull and Bones 256

Revolutionary Brotherhoods..258

Copperheads and the Knights of the Golden Circle.....................258

The Fenian Brotherhood 260

The Shield Society...261

Operation Werwolf..262

Al-Qaeda 263

Chapter 14: Thugs, Mugs, and Lugs: The Mafia and Other Underworld Societies **267**

Birth of the Mafia — Queen Mother of Criminal Secret Societies..........268

Sicily: Mafia's motherland 268

The birth of the Cosa Nostra 270

Vendetta!..271

The Mafia and Organized Crime in America...................................272

Tales of the Five Points gangs..272

Paddywhacked — The Irish Mafia...273

The Kosher mob 274

Shadow of the Black Hand..275

Prohibition and the birth of the Rackets.................................275

The FBI, RICO, and the Decline of the Mafia 282

The Big Five Families of the Commission 282

The Gambino Family 283

The Genovese Family 284

The Colombo Family 284

The Lucchese Family 285

The Bonanno Family 285

Welcome to the Family! Mafia Rituals..286

The Ongoing Struggle to Crush the Mafia.....................................287

Taking the fight back to Sicily...287

Two real "men of honor" 288

We're mad as hell, and we're not going to take it anymore! 289

Other Mafias, Lost and Found 290

Going Italian 290

Going International 292

The Impact of the Mafia on Popular Culture 293

Early gangster films...294

The Godfather myth cycle..295

Chapter 15: Banks and Super Committees:
Knowing All, Owning All, Controlling All 297

Bankers and Nefarious Banking Plots 297
Why do the Jews get the banking blame? 298
The Rothschild banking family 300
Perils of the Federal Reserve 301
Supersecret Committees 303
Cecil Rhodes and the Rhodes-Milner Round Table 303
Council on Foreign Relations 306
The Trilateral Commission 308
The Bilderberg Group 308
Bohemian Club and Bohemian Grove 309
The Committee of 300 312

Part IV: The Part of Tens 315

Chapter 16: Ten Conspiracy Theories
That Skirt the Edge of Madness 317

There's More than One Pope 317
Space Shuttle Columbia's "Deliberate" Destruction 319
Richard Hoagland and the Face on Mars 320
Polio Epidemic Spread by a Conspiracy Theory 321
David Icke, Reptilian Humanoids, and the
Babylonian Brotherhood 321
The "Murder" of Princess Diana 323
The Bombing of New Orleans's Levees 324
Scientology and the IRS 325
The Pentagon Cruise Missile of 9/11 326
Deniers of the Holocaust 327

Chapter 17: Ten Conspiracies That Were Absolutely True 329

The Aaron Burr Conspiracy 329
The Tuskegee Study of Untreated Syphilis in the Negro Male 333
The General Motors Streetcar Conspiracy 334
Project MKULTRA — The CIA's Mind Control and LSD Experiments 334
The Ford Pinto Memorandum 335
The FDR Putsch Conspiracy 336
The P2 Masonic Lodge Conspiracy 337
NATO, Nazis, and the Gehlen Conspiracy 338
The CAN Coverup 339
The Dreyfus Affair 340

Chapter 18: Ten Weirdest Secret Societies of All Time 343

Bohemian Grove..343
Carnation-Painted Eyebrows Society 344
E Clampus Vitus 344
Fils d'Adam (Sons of Adam)...345
The Khlysty...345
Los Hermanos Penitentes 346
Order of the Peacock Angel 348
The Skoptzy 348
The Vril Society 349
Worshippers of the Onion..350

Index *351*

Introduction

*N*apoleon said, "What is history but a fable agreed upon?" Of course, what nobody seems to remember is that Napoleon said a whole bunch of really questionable things. What's wrong with it is that it implies that history is just a matter of opinion.

Entering the world of conspiracy theories and secret societies is like stepping into another dimension — a distant, parallel, alternate universe where the images, words, and names that surround you are vaguely familiar, but where the laws of physics have completely changed: Black means white; up is down; do-gooders are really Beelzebub's Satanic waterboys; and the world seems to be viewed through a giant funhouse mirror.

We stepped into this alternate universe while Chris was working on *Freemasons For Dummies* (Wiley). In the alternate universe of conspiracy theories, the fraternity that he wrote about bore no resemblance whatsoever to the version found in stacks of conspiracy books and endless Internet information of anti-Masonic accusations.

Our exploration of the world of conspiracies and secret societies after working on the book about Freemasons led to extended discussions with Wiley's *For Dummies* folks, and the proposal for this book grew and grew as our research became more extensive.

Researching a book about conspiracy theories and secret societies is a frustrating experience, most notably because it's all *supposed* to be a secret. But it's a balancing act, as well. Too little skepticism risks falling down Lewis Carroll's rabbit hole into a twisted wonderland of circular logic, but too much skepticism risks overlooking something critical that may become tomorrow's tragic headline. We talk a lot in this book about secretive and suspicious groups that are at the center of conspiracy theories around the world, but we also let you know what you can do to spot truly malevolent secret societies and tell the real conspiracies from the fakes.

About This Book

For the millions of people who are true believers in their own favorite conspiracy theories, the type of information we cover in this book is all *very* important. Of course we feel that the material is important, but you don't have to read it in order. This book is intended to be a reference for you, so you don't need to read the chapters in order from front cover to back (even though we suggest it). So if you want to read about all the secret societies before you read about the conspiracy theories, or vice versa, that's fine with us. It's all interesting stuff!

Moreover, just because you may not believe the overwhelming majority of the conspiracies cited in this book, it doesn't make them all wrong. There have been *real* conspiracies in the world, as well as real secret societies that were seeking to accomplish real evil. Or amass power. Or money. Or both. We try to separate fluff, fear, and fantasy from the facts, and we endeavor to present them with a minimum of personal commentary so you can decide for yourself.

But there's a much more vital reason we've come to feel this book is important, and it's not because we believe the world is about to end in an ultimate showdown between the forces of Good and Evil. No, it's a lot simpler than that. It's a question of what can happen when the lit match of a fiery, professional conspiracist touches off the powder keg of a susceptible believer.

Conventions Used in This Book

This book is unconventional in a whole lot of ways, but we do follow a few rules:

- ✔ We *italicize* new terms, closely followed by an easy-to-understand definition. You also see names secret societies in italics.
- ✔ We **bold** important keywords in bulleted lists as well as the action parts of numbered lists.
- ✔ We use monofont for all Web addresses.

What You're Not To Read

This is a reference book, which means no one is going to whack your hands with a ruler if they catch you skipping ahead. In particular, anything marked with a *Technical Stuff* icon (more about those below) may make your eyes glaze over from information overload. Not that it isn't interesting, but feel free to skip ahead if you find yourself getting woozy.

Foolish Assumptions

We don't know most of you, but we make a few assumptions about you and why you picked up this book:

- ✔ **You're confused and want the unvarnished scoop on secret societies and conspiracy theories.** You've watched the History Channel documentaries on codes, conspiracies, and secret societies until your eyes have swollen shut. This book puts it all together for you. It gives you the tools to tell the difference between the big players, the small fries, the truly scary stuff, and the piles of pernicious piffle.

- ✔ **You're a complete skeptic.** All the rumors about the Illuminati, UFOs, and underground government bunkers beneath the Denver Airport strike you as balderdash from a weak *X-Files* episode. We separate fact from fiction and let you know when to really put on your tinfoil helmet.

- ✔ **You're a true believer.** You just know that at any minute black helicopters are going to land on your lawn and the Men In Black will bash down your door. We're here to help you sort through all the conspiracies. We'll help you come to grips with what's real, what's made up, who made it up, and why.

- ✔ **You're a member of what the rest of the world calls a "secret society" and you want to know why everyone is talking behind your back.** Does everybody shut up when you walk into the room? Is your daughter asking why people on the Internet claim you're the spawn of Satan. We examine the origins of secret societies and the more benign groups that have become the major suspects in the New World Order.

How This Book Is Organized

If you just plowed in here without bothering to look at the neatly organized Table of Contents, we don't mind. We prefer you to start at the top, but we won't call out the black helicopter guys if you don't. We're about to tell you all the important stuff about the way this book is laid out. It's chopped up into four neatly packaged parts, and you can read them in any order.

Part 1: Conspiracy Theories and Secret Societies: The Improbable Wedded to the Inscrutable

About 99.9 percent of all respectable conspiracy theories are tied hand and foot to some sort of secret society or organization. This part lays out easy-to-understand models, with no cryptic double talk about all the "theys" out there, and all the dark conspiracies behind them. Chapter 1 is an overview of the world of conspiracies and secret societies, while Chapters 2 and 3 get down to the nuts and bolts of defining and identifying them.

Part II: A Colossal Compilation of Conspiracy Theories

This part covers the best and the brightest in terms of conspiracy theories — from the sublime to the ridiculous. Chapter 4 discusses some of the most common theories, the conspiracies _so_ secret that _everybody_ knows about them. Chapter 5 is the hit parade of, well, hits — conspiracies related to famous assassinations. Chapter 6 covers the range of race, genocide, and apocalyptic doom, just to bring a little cheerlessness to your humdrum life. Chapter 7 covers conspiracies not of this Earth — from Roswell to the Moon-landing hoaxes. And finally, Chapter 8 covers the unsettling growth of the ever-wilder 9/11 conspiracies.

Part III: Secret Societies and Societies with Secrets

You can't tell the players without a program. This part exposes the major secret societies of the last century and a half — the ones that still haunt every conspiracist cubbyhole in the bookstore and on the Internet. Chapter 9 discusses the Freemasons, the world's least kept secret society, and Chapter 10 ventures into the world of Rosicrucian and occult groups, while Chapter 11 explores the origin and modern incarnations of the Illuminati. Chapter 12 delves into the tales of secret societies of assassins like the, well, Assassins, along with the Invisible Empire, the Ku Klux Klan, and other hate groups. In Chapter 13 you find a gallery of both frivolous and frightening secret societies, from the golden age of fraternalism and college groups, to a lineup of military and revolutionary cabals. And Chapter 14 rounds out the list with the criminal underground and the godfather of all secret societies, the Mafia.

Part IV: The Part of Tens

A *For Dummies* book wouldn't feel right without the Part of Tens — chapters divided into quaint lists of ten items of importance. In this part, we serve you ten conspiracy theories that skirted the edge of madness; ten conspiracy theories that really turned out to be true; ten secret societies with the goofiest names; and ten of the drop-dead weirdest secret societies of all time.

Icons Used in This Book

Throughout this book, you spot certain icons hanging around in the margins. They're there to help you navigate the conspiracies, conspiracists, and conspiratorial plots.

This icon indicates little-known or "unusual" information or facts that were originally kept secret. Consider the info in these icons to come from a legendary group or inner circle of an all-seeing, all-knowing Master within any number of secret societies. Think of him as the Mister Know It All on all things secret or conspiratorial.

This icon marks key points that are vital to understanding truly important topics. Don't skip them!

This icon highlights stuff like additional data or side trips with more detail than you may be interested in. They can be ruthlessly skipped without missing the really important topics of the chapters.

This icon gives you handy tidbits and helpful advice.

This book stinks with conspiracies. It's loaded with them. They're all over the place. This icon points out the ones that are the bedrock of conspiracy thinking — either the most important allegations, the best known, or in some cases, the most ridiculous.

Where to Go from Here

The best part of a *For Dummies* book is that you can start at page 1, or you can go all the way to the Part of Tens and read the book backwards. So, start with any chapter you want. Each chapter and section is pretty much self-contained, and if we think there's stuff you should've read about in order, we warn you and cross-reference other chapters as those instances pop up.

A *For Dummies* book isn't supposed to be the last book you pick up on a subject — it should be the first. But we hope that what you ultimately say about this book is that we've lifted the veil on topics you may have only vaguely heard of and presented you with enough facts to make up your own mind, or to study further. Or to just creep out your relatives.

Part I
Conspiracy Theories and Secret Societies: The Improbable Wedded to the Inscrutable

The 5th Wave   By Rich Tennant

MORRIS SPOTS ANOTHER SIGN OF THE ONE-WORLD GOVERNMENT CONSPIRACY.

In this part . . .

About 99.9 percent of all respectable conspiracy theories are tied hand and foot to some sort of secret society or organization. This secret society or organization is the *they,* as in "*they* hid the wrecked alien spacecraft in Roswell in 1947." This section lays out easy-to-understand models, with no cryptic double talk, about all the "theys" out there, and all the dark conspiracies behind them.

Chapter 1

Everything You Know Is Wrong

In This Chapter

▶ Believing the unbelievable: The age of conspiracy theories and secret societies

▶ Figuring out what's worth believing

▶ Touring the world, one conspiracy at a time

*J*ournalist H. L. Mencken once said, "The most costly of all follies is to believe passionately in the palpably not true. It is the chief occupation of mankind."

A conspiracy theory is the idea that someone, or a group of someones, acts secretly, with the goal of achieving power, wealth, influence, or other benefit. It can be as small as two petty thugs conspiring to stickup a liquor store, or as big as a group of revolutionaries conspiring to take over their country's government. Individuals, corporations, churches, politicians, military leaders, and entire governments can all be conspirators, in plots as evil as secretly developing nuclear weapons, as creepy as smuggling stolen human transplant organs, or as annoying as cornering the market on neighborhood $4-coffee joints.

The conspiracy theory is absolutely inseparable from the secret society. They go together like Minneapolis and St. Paul. Face it: Everyone hates secrets. You didn't like it when the kids kept secrets from you in gym class, and you've never gotten over it. Neither have we.

Secret societies are the repositories of the hidden knowledge that spins the conspiracy theory. But the term *secret society* covers a lot of ground — everything from college fraternities and the lodge your grandpa belonged to, to the lesser known, powerful groups that stay out of the eyes of the press, like the Bilderbergers, the Council on Foreign Relations, and the legendary Illuminati (if they really exist at all).

This chapter begins the process of teaching you how to tell the truth from the manure, at least where conspiracy theories and secret societies are concerned. Throughout this book, we also set out to simplify what at least sounds staggeringly confusing. We clarify conspiracy theories that are coming at you from all sides nowadays on everything from the Mafia running the Vatican to aliens landing in New Mexico (or is it the aliens in the Vatican and the Mafia in New Jersey?). Consider this chapter your warm-up exercise!

Living in the Age of Conspiracy Theories and Secret Societies

The popularity of the conspiracy theory as a way of explaining society and world events is a pretty recent phenomena, a product of the time since the French Revolution of 1789, which was the first real marriage of paranoia and the printing press. But it's just within the last 40 years that the philosophy of conspiracism has become like a wall of noise, an assault on the collective consciousness, and the most common way to explain complex world events. In many respects, conspiracies are a way of simplifying history into good and bad, right and wrong.

A *conspiracy theory* is a way of looking at a single event and postulating that maybe there's a lot more to it than can be seen on the surface, with darker forces behind the whole thing. *Conspiracism* expands on this, becoming an entire philosophy, as a way of viewing the world. For the professional *conspiracist,* a person who studies the conspiracies, there isn't much going on in the world that *doesn't* have darker forces behind it, from the price of a gallon of gasoline to the three ounces of hand lotion you can't ever seem to extract from the bottom of a 16-ounce bottle. Of course, in a way, even the term *conspiracism* is too respectable to apply to much of what is floating around the Internet and the tabloids these days. Since the middle of the last century, academic, postmodernist researchers have found it fashionable to refer to all psychological states and moods in German. It's a Sigmund Freud thing. Author Thom Burnett in the *Conspiracy Encyclopedia* (2005, Chamberlain Bros.) points out that the Germans have a great term, *Verschworungsmythos,* which means *Conspiracy Myth,* and in many ways, it has lots to recommend it as a descriptive label.

"Perhaps the conspiracy world is an updated version of ancient myths," Burnett says, "where monsters and the gods of Olympus and Valhalla have been replaced by aliens and the Illuminati of Washington and Buckingham Palace." In other words, the new wave of jitters over conspiracies and secret societies has beaten up the *zeitgeist* with their *weltschmerz* over *weltpolitik* (the spirit of our times has had the crap kicked out of it by anxiety over global domination). See, we can do the German thing too. *Gesundheit.*

What makes the study of conspiracy theories and secret societies unusual is, when boiled down to their most common elements, the overwhelming majority have grown or been adapted from the same few original sources. Historian Daniel Pipes has said that almost all conspiracy theories have as their origin the same two boogeymen — Jews and secret societies, most notably the

Freemasons. They have simply been recycled and renamed, again and again, as events have transpired over the last 250 years.

For example, if you take almost any conspiracy about the Jews from the 19th century, and erase "Jews" and substitute "military-industrial complex" or "neocons," you find that very same theory in dozens of books and on hundreds of Web sites about the sinister forces behind the 9/11 "conspiracy." In many ways, it shows a criminal lack of originality. On the other hand, conspiracists would claim, plots around the world and the evildoers who engage in them haven't changed much over the centuries. They've only gotten more ambitious.

What's Worth Scrutinizing, and What's Not

Between books, the Internet, and cable television, the average American comes into contact with a lot of ideas that are no longer sifted through "established media." A bigger and bigger chunk of these ideas challenges the status quo — the beliefs of stodgy academics and of society in general. Such thoughts also assert that organizations, from the government to the Illuminati (see Chapter 11), are in cahoots to make sure that no one yet knows the truth. But just because an appealing idea comes from the "alternative' media instead of the mouths of TV anchors or White House spokesmen doesn't always make it true.

As professional conspiracists write book after book, raking in the money faster than they can count it, most care very little about the confusion and fear they leave behind. Internet Web-meisters who peddle this stuff care even less. But we care about it, a lot. Don't fear — you can acquire the skills you need to digest it all and discern the information. In Chapter 2, in particular, we help you decide between information that's worth paying attention to and information you should ignore, and why.

Connecting the dots

There's a very important point about exploring conspiracy theories. It is not enough to just lay out facts or events, like dots on a page, and scream "aha!" at the mere "fact," for example, that over 100 people "involved" in the assassination of John F. Kennedy are dead. "Involved" often meaning as little as they were standing in the crowd in Dallas. It's been almost 40 years, and of the thousands of people peripherally involved in the case, it's not a *big* shock for more than 100 of them to have died. Now, if 75 of them had been wrapped in plastic and duct tape and dumped into a Dallas reservoir, you might have something.

What *is* proof?

Abraham Lincoln was assassinated on April 14, 1865. Since about 24 hours afterwards, the world has been trying to find out the details about the conspiracy behind it. (And there *was* a conspiracy — for more on that, see Chapter 5.) Interest in the plot has come and gone over the years, most recently in the 2007 film *National Treasure II: The Book of Secrets,* which prominently featured the discovery of the missing pages of assassin John Wilkes Booth's diary. And there really *are* missing pages — historians just aren't sure why.

One of the hundreds of books we consulted during this project was a bit nostalgic —*The Lincoln Conspiracy* (Schick Sun Classic Books) by David Balsiger and Charles E. Sellier. (This book was parent to the Sunn Classics film of the same name that did remarkably well in theaters in 1977.)

Like most conspiracy books, *The Lincoln Conspiracy* has many footnotes and an impressively long bibliography. But, also like most conspiracy literature, it's a *circular citing* process, with conspiracists endlessly referring to one another's work (see Chapter 2 for more on this phenomenon). Despite their abundant cribbing from an earlier conspiracist work from the 1930s by an Austrian chemist named Otto Eisenschiml, the authors claimed to be the *only* investigators in history who'd ever gotten the story of Lincoln's assassination right. They also seemed to have connected with an amazing number of documents to back up their version of events, papers, and diaries that had slipped past mere mortal historians.

The book's opening pages were touting these various miraculous discoveries, as well as the severe scientific methodology they had put to use in their quest. They claimed this was especially true of their discovery of the missing pages of Booth's diary, a set of documents "worth up to $1 million dollars." Wow! But when you read on carefully, you come across the following astonishing statement:

> *The authors acquired a full transcript of the contents of the missing pages and had the contents evaluated by historical experts, but have not been able to acquire copies of the actual pages to authenticate the handwriting.*

What these guys are saying is that they haven't even seen *copies* of the actual "million dollar" diary pages on which they've built just about the entire thesis of their book. It is this typical amateur detective work, backed up with hearsay, innuendo, and rumor that makes so many conspiracists so hard to take seriously.

The point we are making is that a box full of random dots is meaningless. To be a true theory worth considering, the dots have to be connected. And to be taken seriously, a conspiracy theory has to connect those dots convincingly and with some irrefutable proof.

Benjamin Franklin once said, "Three may keep a secret when two are dead." When you're confronted by a conspiracy that requires the military or the government or literally *thousands* of covert insiders around the world to keep a Very Big Secret for tens, or hundreds, of years, and just one lone "courageous" warrior steps forward with an outlandish tale that no one else backs up, it's time to turn on your alarm system again. Courage could be vanity, and honesty merely accusation or sour grapes or revenge.

Being skeptical about speculative thinking

Most theories, from the Kennedy assassination to Jesus-having-a-wife books, share the title of "alternative" histories, or "speculative" works. The word *speculative* is the key point here. Because once people start speculating, it becomes your job, to a great degree, to speculate, as well.

For example, in the mental gymnastics of the folks who love to tell you that ancient space aliens were responsible for the Egyptian Sphinx, or that the huge carvings called the Nazca Lines in Peru had to have been done by someone able to fly over the countryside, there's just a wisp of contempt for that most amazing of all tools, the human mind. There's an attitude that ancient man was just too, well, primitive (for primitive, read *stupid*) to have been able to build something on that scale.

The same sort of "speculative" thinking goes into more modern creations, like crop circles (see Chapter 7). Admittedly, many crop circles are astonishing as well as dramatic. But are they the watermarks of alien spaceships or superior extraterrestrial technology? All that's required to make a crop circle is a two-by-four and a rudimentary understanding of mathematics and geometry. Just as we were writing this chapter, a "crop circle" was discovered in New Jersey in the shape of a swastika. Somehow we doubt it was a message left to us from visitors from Alpha Centauri.

The Conspiracism World Tour

Where conspiracy theories are concerned, there's nothing particularly weird about our own time when you take a look back at history. Consider, for example, these items from the early years of U.S. history:

- George Washington, a Freemason, was edgy about the possible infiltration of the Illuminati (see Chapter 11) during his presidency.

- Many people believed Thomas Jefferson was secretly a member of the Illuminati.

- After killing former Secretary of the Treasury Alexander Hamilton in a duel, Vice President Aaron Burr really did hatch a conspiracy to wrestle control of the western territories away from the U.S. so he could be king of a new empire in the West (see Chapter 17).

- Economists and people nervous about financial dealings on a global scale have been shoveling grim and prophetic jeremiads about the privately owned Federal Reserve Bank, since its very creation, as being a hotbed of chicanery controlled by capitalist titans.

- The assassination of Abraham Lincoln (Chapter 5) resulted in a nationwide search for conspirators, both real and imagined, a lot of whom were hanged.

But, while there have been conspiracists throughout history, the 20th century seems to have been the biggest incubator for them. As we show you in the next sections, the 20th century was a particularly intense period that led to clammy hands over secret societies, coverups, and intrigues.

The birth of 20th-century U.S. conspiracism

During World War II, the U.S. government routinely hid secret missions and programs (along with military failures) as part of the war effort. It was vital to keep the national mood focused on winning. And the general belief of Americans was that government secrecy was a good thing: "Loose lips sink ships." Secrecy was patriotic. The government and the military were *supposed* to be keeping secrets.

After the war, the U.S. engaged in a nuclear stare-down with the Soviets, who were devouring countries all over Eastern Europe and had sworn to get around to us eventually. The stakes were very high.

Most Americans don't know how close the U.S. came to getting nuked by the Axis powers during WWII, when a sub with a dirty nuclear bomb, a joint German-Japanese endeavor, was literally on its way to San Francisco when the war ended. Then, less than five years after the explosion of the atomic bombs over Japan, Soviet scientists had their own full-blown nuclear bombs, and much of the technology had been stolen from U.S. laboratories and developed in Russia by former Nazi scientists.

While the notorious House Un-American Activities Committee (HUAC) and the bombastic Senator Joe McCarthy made headlines in the 1950s peering under the sheets for Commies in Hollywood, ferreting out the deep political thoughts of Gary Cooper, the truth was that there really *were* Communist agents across the United States, funding subversive anti-American groups, spying on military and scientific installations, and infiltrating U.S. intelligence organizations like the CIA.

 The Communist Party of the United States was no independent organization of starry-eyed idealists. By the 1970s they were receiving $3 million a year from the Soviet Union and had aided the Soviet Secret Police (KGB) throughout the 1940s and '50s in recruiting spies.

High-profile spying trials, such as the trials of Julius and Ethel Rosenberg and Alger Hiss (who were, in spite of claims to the contrary, all guilty of Soviet espionage), kept Americans looking *outward* for conspiracies. But that was about to change, drastically, and the threat to our way of life suddenly seemed to be from within.

JFK on secrecy

One of the most commonly printed quotes about secrecy and secret societies in the U.S. was made by President John F. Kennedy in 1961. It is frequently used by conspiracists to show that Americans distrust secret societies:

The very word "secrecy" is repugnant in a free and open society; and we are as a people inherently and historically opposed to secret societies, to secret oaths and to secret proceedings.

Of course, like any sound bite, the part that gets left out is that Kennedy was actually giving a Cold War–era speech *in favor* of secrecy. He was asking a ballroom filled with newspaper publishers to keep their mouths shut about U.S. government activities and to not print anything in their papers that might give "our enemies" an advantage. On the one hand, he blasted the Soviet Union for controlling its press with an iron hand. On the other hand, he sounded pretty envious of their power to do it.

The psychedelic '70s: Conspiracism peaks

To understand the explosion of conspiracism that has happened over the last four decades, you need to understand just a little of why the 1970s were the turning point.

While famous conspiracies were alleged in the deaths of Marilyn Monroe and John F. Kennedy in the early 1960s, most sociologists hang the modern growth and acceptance of conspiracy theories on the Vietnam War era and the Watergate-related events under President Richard Nixon. The government was starting to get caught engaging in old-fashioned, WWII-type secrecy to cover up military blunders in Cuba under President Kennedy and in Vietnam under President Lyndon Johnson.

Distrust peaked during the second term of Richard Nixon, stoked by his own infamous antagonism over the press and what he regarded as "subversive elements."

The Pentagon Papers

In 1971, *The New York Times* published a stack of reports leaked from the Defense Department, famously known as *The Pentagon Papers*. The top-secret reports were written in 1967 and outlined how the Johnson administration secretly expanded the Vietnam War, while lying to the public and pretending to seek strategic advice from diplomats, as well as engaging in "false flag" operations — staged raids supposedly from the Viet Cong.

The revelations came three years after Johnson had left office, but they helped turn the tide of public opinion against the war. This bitterness only worsened under his successor, Richard Nixon.

None dare call it conspiracy

Gary Allen and Larry Abraham's 1971 book, *None Dare Call It Conspiracy*, was a watermark for conspiracy "literature." Closely associated with the right-wing John Birch Society, they trace world events, from the Russian Revolution up through the Nixon administration and purport that history has been controlled by an elite cabal of international bankers.

This was the book that put the Council on Foreign Relations and the Bilderbergers on the conspiracists' map (see Chapter 15). All the suspects that have dominated the genre ever since were collected in this book — the Illuminati, the Freemasons, Jewish bankers, Cecil Rhodes, and the Rockefellers. It also raises the alarm over the printing of worthless paper money, fears over gun control, and puppet presidential candidates who are the willing stooges of the New World Order regardless of party affiliation.

In search of . . . conspiracies

After the Watergate scandals erupted in 1973, the general consensus of a once-trusting American public changed, drastically. The nation had seen their president spying on the opposition party and lying about it, and the military engaging in maneuvering war to their own ends. The vice president and the attorney general had been proven to be liars and crooks. The Vietnam War limped to an end, and U.S. troops were pulled out without achieving victory — the first loss of a war in American history. Suddenly, and sadly, the *Leave It To Beaver* TV universe of only 15 years before seemed absurd to a newly cynical nation.

Influenced by this almost universal sense of suspicion, the 1970s saw an explosion of books, movies, and TV shows about conspiracies. The first books about the purported UFO crash at Roswell, New Mexico, in 1946 appeared in the mid-1970s (see Chapter 7), 30 years after the fact. The film-makers at Sunn Classic Pictures were raking it in with over a dozen conspiracist films in that decade.

Even television got into the act, and the series *In Search Of . . .* covered similar topics, narrated by the most trusted, logical, and world-famous scientist of our time, *Star Trek*'s Mr. Spock (Leonard Nimoy). It was the generation that grew up with these influences that went on to create shows like *The X-Files* in the 1990s and to fashion for conspiracism an aura of brave and indefatigable truth in the face of powerful, dangerous enemies.

Conspiracy theories aren't limited to the USA!

America doesn't have the corner on the paranoia market when it comes to distrust of secret groups and the creation of conspiracy theories. Take a taste off the international menu:

- Canada has its own Roswell (see Chapter 7), called Shag Harbor.

- Israel has its own Kennedy assassination (see Chapter 5) in the killing of Prime Minister Yitzhak Rabin.

- The British believe that everyone from Princess Diana to UN weapons inspector David Kelly was murdered by the government.

- The Italians have their own Bilderbergers (see Chapter 15) in their Club of Rome.

- The French believe that the Freemasons (see Chapter 9) are behind *everything*.

- Throughout Central Asia and in parts of South America it is commonly believed that children are stolen from orphanages to harvest their internal organs for sale to the highest bidders in a bizarre medical "black market." Variations of the tale in India claim "thousands" of stolen human kidneys are shipped each year to rich patients in the Middle East.

- In some Islamic nations, conspiracy theories about Jews poisoning kids' bubble gum or tainting vaccines get printed on the front page of major metropolitan newspapers (see Chapter 6).

Such nervousness does seem to flourish best in democracies and free societies. Tyrants, fascist dictatorships, and totalitarian regimes lock down all information sources because they really *are* controlled by internal conspiracies and secret government agencies.

Writer Christopher Hitchens calls conspiracy theories "the exhaust fumes of democracy," and that's as good a phrase as any. It's the bad part of the free use of information, and that's the *abuse* of information.

A Word About Skepticism

There's an old bit of bumper sticker philosophy that says "just because you're paranoid doesn't mean they're not out to get you." In a post-9/11 world, conspiracies don't seem to be so far-fetched anymore. This real-life conspiracy played itself out on our TV screens. The result was the death of thousands of innocent civilians, and in the aftermath, everyone saw terrorist madman Osama Bin Laden take credit for it and the evidence unfold of the planning by his suicidal henchmen.

Then the conspiracy theorists stepped in and told everyone not to believe the evidence or common sense. The 9/11 conspiracy books started to come out, and dark hints of conspiracy showed up on various TV and radio commentaries. Somehow, right under our noses, the entire tone of the debate had changed.

In the world of the conspiracy theorist, loose bands of like-minded terrorists like Al-Qaeda can't possibly be smart enough, rich enough, devious enough, organized enough, or big enough to pull off such an attack, right? Besides, who's Al-Qaeda, anyway? No one had ever heard of them.

Many people thought someone else *must* be behind the 9/11 attacks, someone in the wings, someone bigger, someone pulling the strings as part of a vast, worldwide plan for global "control." So, according to the conspiracy theorists, why waste the most dramatic event of the century on a bunch of terrorists armed with 89-cent box cutters or on their handlers hiding out in a cave half a world away? It had to have really been the CIA. Or the president. Or the military-industrial complex. Or the Freemasons. Or the reptilian aliens of the ancient Babylonian Bloodline. . . .

Of course, there really *are* conspiracies out there. It's just human nature, the same human nature Chapter 3 discusses, that yearns to form secret societies. It's also human nature that some bully boy in Iraq, some artist in Vienna, or some revolutionary in Chile believes that he was destined to rule the biggest chunk of the world he can lay his hands on, or at least enthrall masses of adoring followers. In the hands of a dictator, conspiracies are great for blinding people while you grab power. It's like pointing and shouting, "Look over *there!*" while you steal all the poker chips. Yet, all the real conspiracies in the world may not have the potential for damage to culture that lies in believing that *everything* is a conspiracy. It's not a healthy world view.

Chapter 2

Conspiracism and the Origin of Modern Conspiracy Theories

In This Chapter

▶ Discovering the world of conspiracy

▶ Figuring out conspiratorial names

▶ Classifying conspiracy types

▶ Detecting the lies in theories

*I*n London's Hyde Park, there's a place called Speaker's Corner, where anyone can preach or shriek anything they like, as long as they keep it clean. There have been some famous and brilliant people who've made speeches there, and there have been an awful lot of cranks, wackos, and madmen in the park, too. Aye, there's the rub. How do you tell the difference between a cautionary reporter of impending calamity from a madman off his meds?

At one time, conspiracists, those who saw the dark hand of conspiracy in just about everything, were dressed in a white jacket that laced up the back with really, really long sleeves. Now, they have become respectable, even influential — or at least *New York Times* best-selling authors. There's no doubt that, apart from simply being a facet of human nature, conspiracy theories rise and fall in volume along with national tension.

This chapter examines the anatomy of conspiracy theories and the history of the first conspiracy theories to really catch on in a big way, and it delves into the tactics used by half-baked conspiracists to lead you to a conclusion that just isn't so. After reading this chapter, when some guy on TV tells you to just "connect the dots," in order to sell you his book, you should be able to determine whether this gentleman has oatmeal where his brains should be.

Defining and Recognizing Conspiracism

Simply put, a conspiracy theory is the notion that someone, or an organized group of people, is acting secretly with evil intent. Police and courts often charge criminals with conspiracy to commit a crime — a bad guy or a group of his buddies meet and plan to commit theft, kidnapping, havoc, or mayhem against other citizens. Conspiracy is a crime in and of itself.

The word *conspire* comes from the Latin word, *conspirare,* which literally means "to breathe together," and probably grew out of the idea of plotters whispering together — there were plenty of plots to go around in ancient Rome.

Boiled down to their simplest ingredients, conspiracy theories attempt to identify a struggle between good and evil, but on a much grander, and often worldwide, scale. Like bad guys in a James Bond movie, conspiracy theories can and often do go global and involve supercriminals, evil geniuses, megalo-maniacal trillionaires, satanic demons, or even alien invaders who are hell-bent on owning everything or controlling everything or destroying everything (society, religion, economics, racial groups, or a combination of all of them).

Conspiracies are thought to exist so a small class or category of schemers can create a situation — politically, militarily, economically, or just through sheer snobbery — that works solely to serve their own self interests.

One small point on terminology before going any further: Many writers have written books about conspiracy theories, and for many of them, the very term *conspiracy theory* is a put-down, as is calling someone a *conspiracy theorist.* We don't feel that way. "Tinfoil hat-wearing moon bat" is more our idea of a put-down. When we use the terms *conspiracism* or, when speaking of a single person, a *conspiracist,* we're talking about people who claim to identify conspiracies. The terms themselves don't imply whether we believe them or not.

Just what is conspiracism?

In the last two centuries, and particularly in the last 50 years or so, people the world over have embraced conspiracism. When we refer to a *conspiracy,* we mean an honest-to-goodness, old-fashioned conspiracy, as defined by the dictionary — a plot by some dark and nefarious characters to do something sinister or evil.

In its milder forms, conspiracism isn't too bad. You know what we mean — the kind of guy who's perfectly sane, yet he's absolutely convinced that the price of everything he buys is controlled by some tiny cartel of bankers in New York or Geneva. Or maybe he thinks that the United Nations wants to take over the U.S. government. Or that National Security Agency spies are tracking his movements through a microchip in his neck inserted when he had his tonsils out.

The problem is that, as this sort of thinking has become more and more common, it's spawned a new sort of social commentator and a new sort of world view, seeing every major world event through the dark filter of conspiracism.

The universe of conspiracism isn't a random place where things happen for no reason. As Michael Barkun puts it in his book, *A Culture of Conspiracy: Apocalyptic Visions in Contemporary America* (University of California Press):

- ✔ **Nothing happens by accident:** Everything that happens in the world is intentional, by someone's (or something's) Grand Design.

- ✔ **Nothing is as it seems:** Whoever or whatever is in control disguises their role and their identity. In fact, they go out of their way to look innocent, deflect blame, or just plain hide.

- ✔ **Everything is connected:** Because of an intricate, evil design that allows for no accidents, there's no such thing as a coincidence, and the patterns of evil forces are all interconnected with each other. Therefore, the right type of person can see these patterns of numbers, designs, events, or activities everywhere, once they know what to look for (see the sidebar "Fnord").

This last bit is important, because in most conspiracy theories a thread of insistence exists that only certain, truly enlightened people can see the truth behind the secret plots. Most conspiracies are, so the thinking goes, invisible to the vast majority of sheeplike citizens who go grazing through the pasture of life, never suspecting the evil wolves lurking behind the rocks of everyday occurrences.

In a way, conspiracism can be comforting to true believers, because it removes the scary notion of randomness from the universe. For some, conspiracies can seem like an extension of religious faith, with God and Satan locked in a struggle for supremacy on Earth. In fact, many conspiracists are strongly connected to a belief in the coming of the end of the world. After a specific series of world events happens, these "millenialists" believe, those events will usher in Armageddon, the final battle between the forces of good and evil on earth (more on this in Chapter 6).

Conspiracism and secret societies

Something else that's bound up hand and foot with conspiracism is, of course, the secret society. In fact, most of the popular conspiracy theories aren't as new as you may think, and they can be traced back either to a fear of the Jews or a fear of secret societies. We go into more detail about generalities involving these groups in Chapter 3.

It's important here to bring up secret societies' role in the majority of conspiracy theories, because wherever there's conspiracism, there's always the fear of some tightknit group of "theys" who really know the score. These groups can be anyone — the World Bank, the Bilderbergers, the Freemasons (all of whom have their own sections in this book — see the index). These groups are the very breath of life to conspiracism, and the one can't exist without the other.

Understanding How Conspiracists Think

In its most virulent forms, the fever of conspiracism can turn reality upside down. Dealing with the conspiracist, amateur or professional, is a lot like dealing with somebody who's part of a religious cult. In fact, if you keep it up, they'll probably accuse you of being part of the conspiracy.

A big part of the mindset of conspiracism is that all facts are malleable, all of them changeable in the right hands, none of them to be trusted. Like the cult member, conspiracists believe what they believe *because* they believe it, and they don't like to be challenged. In fact, challenges to this sort of thinking tend to bring out the worst in the conspiracist, which is why there's so little difference between a "conspiracist" and someone who's just plain paranoid.

To the conspiracy theorist, the world is locked in a battle between a good *Us* and a bad *Them,* whoever *They* happen to be. The battle may be spiritual, physical, economic, or philosophical — or a combination of all of them. The worst part is, *Them* is often portrayed as a small group, a tight group, who really knows what's going on, and *Us* takes the part of a herd of mindless cattle, being manipulated and too stupid to know they're being duped. Being a conspiracist doesn't require a love of mankind. In fact, the position is made to order for people who hate or mistrust humankind (called *misanthropes*).

As Daniel Pipes points out in his book *Conspiracy,* someone who indulges in conspiracism doesn't *necessarily* go off the deep end, but it happens often enough to give one pause. Question reality often enough, and you have no sense of it left at all. This loss of reality, combined with mild to severe paranoia, can make you see enemies everywhere. British conspiracist and anti-Semite Nesta Webster took a gun with her every time she answered the door; Joseph Stalin, by the end of his days in absolute power, had people shot just for looking at him the wrong way.

Oliver Stone, director of the 1991 film *JFK* (see Chapter 5), once said, "Paranoids have the facts." But he also said, "Who owns reality? Who owns your mind? I've come to have severe doubts about Columbus, about Washington, about the Civil War being fought over slavery, about World War I, about World War II and the supposed fight against Nazism and Japanese control of resources . . . I don't even know if I was born or who my parents were."

Shall we dance to the left or the right?

Conspiracists cross the political spectrum, and, in the process, sort of create their own party. In other words, from Holocaust deniers to Oliver Stone, they have the same *process* in their thinking. Now, Holocaust deniers tend to be right-wing and anti-Semitic, and would probably be deeply offended to be told they had anything at all in common with left-wing Hollywood director Stone. Yet, in the paranoid *pattern* of their thinking, they're one and the same.

Hates are justifiable and grudges eternal, evil embodied by anyone who denies the shining light of the truth they hold. For conspiracists, conspiracies are behind most of history's major events, even conspiracies involving so many people that they could fill the Seattle Kingdome. This, combined with an absolute allergic reaction to facts, is a dangerous combination. They trust no one apart from fellow travelers, and little enough in them.

Lack of proof is the proof

For the conspiracist, evidence is the hobgoblin of little minds. Looking for evidence is an annoyance, because for the true believer, the lack of proof *is* the proof of the conspiracy itself.

Lack of evidence proves that powerful forces are seeing to it that evidence never sees the light of day. But if evidence does come to light and refutes the claims of a professional conspiracist, he can turn it around to his advantage.

Such evidence is simply *more* proof that the conspirators are frightened of the conspiracists and are working overtime to cover their tracks by creating plausible, but utterly false, data. After all, so the argument goes, these evil forces control the media, business, banks, universities, governments, and all-you-can-eat buffets; obviously, the real truth will never come out. *They* will in vent and plant new evidence to make their accusers look discredited — or ridiculous — which is a waste of time, because they can do that all on their own.

What the behaviorists say

Psychologists, psychiatrists, and other people who study the pathology of conspiracy theorists have come up with a raft of behavior categories:

- ✔ **Apophenia:** This behavior looks at meaningless or unconnected images, numbers, words, or other data and finds patterns in them. It can be as harmless as gazing at clouds and seeing kittens or dragons or as bizarre as seeing shadows and craters in a picture from Mars and deciding that it's a gigantic face carved by some Martian Leonardo DaVinci.

✔ **Confirmation bias:** This habit is the tendency to develop a preconceived notion, then make all evidence conform to it, or to simply ignore the contrary evidence altogether.

Political arguments between members of opposite parties often degenerate into this type of selective, uncritical bias, such as "He's a tax-and-spend liberal," or "She's a country-club Republican." Any evidence to the contrary, such as him cutting a tax or her doing volunteer work in an inner-city church, is deemed either a lie or a complete aberration, because nothing can be permitted to interfere with this one's contention that all liberals love to tax and spend, or that one's contention that all Republicans love restricted country clubs. For many folks out there, this kind of thinking can be very comforting.

✔ **Cognitive dissonance:** "Cognition" is simply a knowledge you possess or something you know or learn. "Dissonance" means any two things that create tension by conflicting with one another. Therefore, *cognitive dissonance* is a state of mind in which a person has two thoughts or beliefs that are at odds with one another.

Examining Types of Conspiracy Theories

The various types of conspiracy theories can be broken down by what the perpetrators are supposedly up to. Author Michael Barkun classifies these types as

✔ **Event conspiracies:** These conspiracies are supposedly responsible for a specific event or chain of events, such as the creation of AIDS and "crack" by the CIA to wipe out inner-city African-Americans, or the claims that a U.S. military missile shot down TWA flight 800, with a subsequent coverup. The conspiracy exists to accomplish one limited, specific, well-focused objective.

✔ **Systemic conspiracies:** These broad-based conspiracies have ambitious goals such as gaining the control of a country, a region of the world, or the entire world, for that matter. Or maybe just everybody's money.

Naturally, to pull this off requires a massive organization, operating in secret, to infiltrate governments and institutions. These allegations regularly include the accusations that Jews control banks, the press, and Hollywood; Freemasons control governments and businesses; Catholics or Muslims want to take over all world religions; and, depending on who's weaving the conspiracy theory, either communists or world industrialists are taking over everything else. Unless, of course, you believe that the aliens have trumped the humans, and are just raising everyone to harvest people for food and/or sexual playthings.

✔ **Super conspiracies:** This notion comes back to the concept that everything is connected in one, vast, worldwide, super-duper plan of many conspiracies, all contained inside each other, like little Russian nesting dolls. All the event and systemic conspiracies (see preceding bullets) are merely tiny pieces of a giant puzzle, and their perpetrators are just pawns being controlled by one, great, all-powerful supergenius of evil, who's invisible to us all and completely secret.

In conspiracist literature, this category is often called "The Grand Conspiracy." For lack of a better or simpler example, Satan comes to mind for many, especially Christians who believe the end of the world is coming soon.

Applying Ockham's Razor

A maxim was devised by a 14th-century Franciscan friar named William of Ockham (or Occam, depending on who's doing the spelling) that comes up a lot in discussing conspiracy theories. The Latin version is, "Numquam ponenda est pluralitas sine necessitate," which means "Plurality ought never be posed without necessity." The more modern version is, "Keep it simple, stupid."

Ockham's Razor, when applied to a conspiracy theory, shaves away the really complex parts of the idea, just like a real razor does, and demonstrates that there's way too much that has to be interconnected and work perfectly, every single moment of every single day, to keep the entire world from discovering this horrid plot. It's just too complicated.

For example, it requires a complex, convoluted series of people, and of plans, to justify the belief that Princess Diana was killed by British agents, acting on orders from her royal ex-in-laws, who maneuvered her into a limousine, kept her from fastening her seatbelt, and arranged to have a series of motorcycles and cars goad her driver into rocketing down a Paris street at high speed and crashing into a concrete pylon, simply in order to hide the fact that she may have been pregnant by her Egyptian lover.

Ockham's Razor applied to the Princess Diana situation bears a more likely scenario: that her driver was drunk and, as drunks often do, was driving too fast; that paparazzi on motorcycles were irresponsible jerks and clearly trying to make a dangerous photo-op out of the situation; that the experienced English Royal Family and their own security people were better at taking care of her than the al Fayad family no matter how rich they are; and that Paris motorists are maniacs, which all resulted in a tragic accident.

The French Revolution and the Birth of Modern Conspiracism

Conspiracy theories appeal to something deep inside the human animal. In that respect, they're as old as man. For example, the chronicler William of Tyre made dark assertions about the behind-the-scenes power of the Knights Templar ten centuries ago. Yet the fact is that modern conspiracism, as experienced today, wasn't born; it was made. It was cooked up in the lab, just like Frankenstein's monster. And the laboratory was the French Revolution.

The *French Revolution?* Yes, it does sound as though we're taking a drunken loop off the beaten path. But it's necessary to understand a few of the uglier events of the French Revolution in order to understand the forces that sewed together the Frankenstein of conspiracism. The revolution was unlike anything that had come before, shaking civilization to the core. It destroyed the old society and the old culture overnight, replacing it with a completely new one, including a new religion, new forms of address, new forms of government, even new fashions and behaviors that were permissible in public, while the old ones were banned.

Attitudes before the French Revolution

Western civilization, after the fall of Rome, was built on kings and their courts and their system of justice, as well as the basic feudal system of peasant, knight, lord, and king. Along with the arrival of learning, extended to one and all by the printing press, the seeds of change began with the growth of an economically healthy middle class in Europe, as early as the 1500s.

By the time of the revolt in France, in 1789, the middle class was doing well. The state was nearly bankrupt, and what money it had came from taxing this class. Naturally, an idea took root pretty quickly — "If we're the backbone of the nation, then how come we get treated as if we're no different in social class from a peasant?"

In this period, called the Enlightenment, the buzzwords were "science" and "reason." Hot young philosophers were writing incredibly popular books that asked a lot of forbidden questions, especially, "How come the church and the nobles get to run everything, yet pay for nothing?" You'll see the Enlightenment referred to throughout this book, because it was a period of cataclysmic change philosophically, scientifically, religiously, and socially. And groups that pop up in other chapters — the Rosicrucians, the Freemasons, the Illuminati, and many others — were formed during the Enlightenment (roughly 1650 up through 1800).

This period led to tensions all over Europe, and even some violence, eventually creating a much better society. What it led to in France was the French Revolution. From 1789 until the rise of Napoleon in 1800, the richest, most populous (with even more people than Russia), and arguably the most powerful nation in Europe lost its collective mind.

Off with their heads!

French peasants were better off than most of the peasants in the world until America arrived on the scene. But several years of worsening crop failures caused one famine after another, and the government's response was pretty lackluster. All the free and easy criticism of the king got freer and ever more critical.

Storming the Bastille

The revolution erupted in the storming of the Bastille prison on July 14, 1789, a street riot that turned into a battle. The French still celebrate Bastille Day, like the United States' Independence Day. The battle led to years of unbelievable violence. Eventually, half a million people died, tens of thousands of them in the carnival atmosphere of the guillotine set up in the public square, so that their deaths could provide amusement for the crowds. This wasn't just in the Place de la Révolution in Paris but in every town and city across the nation.

In the beginning, both the middle class and the lower level of the clergy had been generally in favor of the revolution. Yet they were the first to die, along with the poor and the dispossessed. The violence was called "the Reign of Terror," because it was a far more horrifying bloodbath than most history books tell.

More than revolution: Terror!

Officially, the "Reign of Terror" began with the September Massacres in 1792. The royal family was held prisoner and eventually executed.

Jean-Paul Marat and his inner core of paid mercenaries were behind the September Massacres of 1792. Marat sent out death lists of priests, businessmen, and petty nobles suspected of being against the revolution, and the killing began. It didn't stop for days.

After they'd polished off their assigned lists, the rioters moved to the various prisons, on the assumption (not a true one) that the Assembly had parked people who were against the revolution there. They found a few nobles, but most of their victims were poor and powerless. About 1,500 people were killed in the spree. One 17-year-old boy was guillotined for forgetting the new form of address and calling a man "Monsieur" rather than "Citizen." All this was the kick-off to a national orgy of bloodletting. As for the church, Catholicism was banned. At least 25,000 priests fled the country, until Napoleon called a truce with the church 11 years later.

Eventually, Marat was stabbed in his bathtub by a young French girl from Normandy named Charlotte Corday, who traveled to Paris specifically to kill him, sickened by the savagery he'd inflicted on the opposing Girondist Party in the Assembly, many of whom were from her hometown of Caen.

Assigning blame

When Napoleon appeared on the scene in 1804 with a sword in one hand and a mop in the other, Frenchmen were left standing knee-deep in the blood-soaked rubble, dazed, wondering how on earth this had happened in the most civilized nation on Earth. "Cognitive dissonance" was about to afflict an entire nation. They couldn't deny that the cruelty, madness, and violence had occurred; the evidence was everywhere. And they couldn't face the fact that it had grown out of themselves.

Someone else had to be to blame. And so was born the first conspiracy literature, along with the identification of what have become the principal hobgoblins of the conspiracy world: the Freemasons, the Jews, and the Illuminati.

The birth of conspiracy literature

The books of conspiracy literature appeared slowly at first. Three books of major concern were

- ✔ *The Veil Withdrawn:* One little volume appeared in 1791 by a French priest named LeFranc. This book was *The Veil Withdrawn.* The veil LeFranc withdrew was the one surrounding Masonic ritual, when he accused the Freemasons of being behind the revolution.

- ✔ *The Tomb of Jacques Molay:* In 1792 came *The Tomb of Jacques Molay* by Cadet de Gassicourt. Jacques de Molay was the legendary last grand master of the Knights Templar, executed by French King Phillip IV in 1314. Cadet de Gassicourt made the claim that the Knights Templar were the founders of Freemasonry, and that they were *both* to blame for the revolution.

- ✔ *Proofs of a Conspiracy:* Next came an influential volume by an English Freemason named John Robison called *Proofs of a Conspiracy,* in which he praised noble and straightforward English Freemasonry for not causing bloody revolutions like their French brethren.

Augustin de Barruel and the Jesuits

Many French people were living in England at the time, having escaped from the Terror. One was an ex-Jesuit and abbot named Augustin de Barruel (sometimes referred to in writings as the Abbé Barruel). Barruel had been a member of the Jesuits (or Society of Jesus), a Catholic order of priests banned all over Europe by king after king (in France in 1766) until the pope caved and shut down the order in 1773. The ban wasn't lifted until 1814.

Jesuits were the cream of the crop in the church intellectually, and their missions were teaching, converting, and spreading Catholicism all over the world. The pope was fighting Protestants, and when the Society of Jesus was founded in the 16th century, the world-traveling Jesuits were sort of his shock troops in this effort, which was called the "Counter-Reformation." But the Jesuits came to be seen by the rulers of Europe as a secret society with way too much power and a dark Machiavellian hand in underground politics. And the fact is that a lot of people, during this "Who did it" period, were blaming angry, underground Jesuits for the revolution. But the Abbé Barruel had a better idea.

While living in England, this emigrant priest met the Englishman John Robison, and their meeting resulted in the most influential conspiracist work of all time. Inspired by *Proofs of a Conspiracy*, Barruel wrote a huge four-volume magnum opus entitled *Memoirs Illustrating the History of Jacobinism*.

We wouldn't recommend trying to read the whole thing, not unless you know how to prop your eyelids open with a pair of toothpicks. Augustin de Barruel does a lot of convoluted evidence building and also a lot of ranting, mostly about the anti-church Enlightenment thinkers like Voltaire. (Darn those Rationalists, anyway! Nobody was confused about what they believed until *they* came along.) What makes Barruel's rants important is that he attempts to trace the history of anti-clericalism and Rationalism, and comes to the dubious conclusion that there have been hives of both all down through the centuries, all of them hidden in various secret societies.

According to Barruel, it all started with the Knights Templar in the 11th century. The Templars were a brotherhood of warriors/monks, set up as an arm of the Catholic Church in the Holy Land during the Crusades. They'd been all but forgotten by most people until de Barruel got hold of them. Ever since then, the Templars have been a magnet for all sorts of conspiracy theories. (For a lot more on the Templars, pick up a copy of *The Templar Code For Dummies*, which is, in all due modesty, a book of ours.)

Barruel dug up all the old accusations that sent the Templars to be burned at the stake by the Inquisition; they were secretly against the church, they were magicians worshipping foreign gods they'd learned about from the Jews and Muslims in the Holy Land, yada, yada, yada.

The Templars-Freemasons-Illuminati-Jacobins were ultimately responsible!

What's more important for the history of conspiracism is that Barruel drew a connecting line between the Templars and the French Freemasons, who he claimed were originally founded by the Templars. All this anti-church rhetoric ran from the Templars to the Freemasons, and from the Freemasons to the Illuminati and the Jacobins (the radical group of French men who really *did* start the revolution).

Barruel said the Templars, the Freemasons, the Illuminati, and the Jacobins were one in the same. He made the case for his readers that the Templars, who'd been denounced by the French king and burned by the church in the early 1300s, had survived, hating both church and king, waiting for five centuries to have their revenge.

Over the course of the next two centuries, conspiracist literature came in waves. Yet, it's a testament to the influence of Barruel that his same theories still gallop through the books of many conspiracists today.

Barruel's ongoing modern influence

By the 20th century, the 1920s saw an enormous rise in conspiracist books, accompanied by the new interest in spiritualism and the occult. By the 1970s, other conspiracist books became even more popular — the kickoff was an underground hit that took the publishing world by surprise, called *None Dare Call it Conspiracy* (Lightyear Press) by Gary Allen, which told the "real" story of how the left-wing administration, rather than the right-wing administration of Richard Nixon, destroyed American liberty and sold children's futures to bankers and industrialists. Behind the whole conspiracy stood Barreul's old suspects — Jews, Freemasons, and the Illuminati.

Other books soon followed, on a wide range of subjects:

- Hugh Joseph Schonfield's *The Passover Plot* (1966; Random House) put forward the notion that Christ hadn't really been crucified and the phony crucifixion was part of a plot to gain power in Roman Judea.
- Charles Berlitz's *The Bermuda Triangle* (1974; Doubleday) suggested a government coverup of a rash of missing military and civilian planes in one highly charged area off the coast of Florida.
- Hal Lindsey's *The Late Great Planet Earth* (1970; Zondervan) launched a new wave of fascination with the biblical book of Revelation and the "End of Days."
- Erich Von Däniken's *Chariots of the Gods?* (1984; Berkley) put a new face on archeology by revealing the hand of aliens behind the history of mankind.

And so it went, rolling ever onward, right up to Dan Brown's *The Da Vinci Code*.

Dreck Alert! Dreck Alert!

Books, movies, TV shows, and coffeehouse arguments by conspiracists, when they're lucid, can be a lot of fun. Other times, sifting through the dreck can be like trying to get hold of the really good cashews in a jar full of mixed nuts.

Here are a few pointers to help you identify when somebody is stacking the deck in the conspiracy world:

- ✔ **Look at the sources.** One of the problems with conspiracist literature is that it can look just as scholarly and well researched as anything written by a respectable academic or investigative author. But take a glance at the list of books that are footnoted in the text (the bibliography).

  Pat Robertson, television evangelist and former presidential candidate, wrote a book called *The New World Order* that was absolutely littered with conspiracism. When questioned about his source material, he replied, "Well look! We have a seven-page bibliography!" But just what books was he citing?

  Conspiracists have a tendency to cite one another, so the same theories go round and round, with little in the way of cold hard facts to back them up. Likewise, when watching a documentary with a slew of "authors" and "historians" intoning solemn accusations, go look up who they are and what they've written (and as a side note, don't be fooled by researchers with British accents — they can be every bit as loopy as Yanks, in spite of their Cambridge diction).

- ✔ **No cherry-picking.** Conspiracists love to straddle the fence. Government reports, photos, and statistics can't be trusted because the government is usually part of the conspiracy — except when those same government reports, photos, and statistics back up their argument. And when such evidence is only partially favorable to the theory, conspiracists gladly use just what they need and ignore the rest.

- ✔ **Separate facts from emotional claims.** Often conspiracy theories are based on the passionate testimony of witnesses. Any good trial lawyer can tell you that, while eyewitness testimony is the most powerful to a jury, ironically, it's the *least* reliable evidence in reality. Stories can change over the years, especially when a witness feels the spotlight on him, and says what the listeners want to hear. And witnesses who don't come forward for decades until a famous incident might provide a lucrative book deal should be regarded with healthy skepticism.

- ✔ **Be alert for unsupportable statements.** Conspiracists have a tendency, some worse than others, to make completely unsupported and unsupportable statements. They're easy to spot: "John Doe claimed, of course, that he was at the airport at the time, *though that is questionable.* In the end, Irving Doe was *conveniently dead,* and John Doe moved ahead with his campaign for the Senate."

No proof is offered of any sort that John Doe is lying about having been at the airport; in fact, the very carefully phrased "that is questionable" implies that there may *be* evidence that he was at the airport, though this author wants to ignore it, so he calls it "questionable," explaining no further. In the end, it is hoped, the reader has picked up the dark suspicion that John Doe had Irving Doe bumped off in order to win the election. This is classic conspiracist style.

✔ **Examine how authoritative people are portrayed.** "Question authority" isn't a bumper sticker with a conspiracist — it's a way of life. If every famous name in a position of authority you come across, from J. Edgar Hoover to Pope John Paul II, is presented as grumpy, sullen, dark, evil, scheming, and completely untrustworthy, with his words treated like total lies and pulled out of the context of the statement, the style is conspiracist all the way.

Chapter 3

Building the Perfect Beast: Secret Societies through the Ages

In This Chapter

▶ Understanding secret societies

▶ Discovering cults and their entities

▶ Looking at ancient secret societies

*G*ang violence is tearing many cities apart. The larger gangs have moved out across the countryside, dealing crack in such unlikely places as Lincoln, Nebraska, and Appleton, Wisconsin. But wherever they are, they remain a society within a society, always underground, though they leave clues behind.

In Los Angeles, visitors are constantly assaulted by gang graffiti, the nonsensical lettering spray-painted over every available public surface, from highway bridges to park benches. But what seems to the casual observer to be nonsense as well as nuisance is in reality a language between gang members and rival gangs. It can only be read by the gang members themselves, apart from a few specialists in gang-related violence who work for police departments. For these young people who feel so impotent in the mainstream of society, it must cause an intoxicating rush of power to be painting that secret message 10 feet high, knowing that only your brothers in arms can understand it.

That moment, that rush, connects to one of the deepest satisfactions to be found in any secret society — the vague sense of superiority and pride, as well as a comforting feeling of *belonging* that's the very foundation of any self-perpetuating brotherhood. Apart from the need to feed himself and to procreate, one of man's most driving instincts has been the impulse to form groups, including tribes, sects, cliques, and cults.

This *we versus them* mentality seems to be encoded in human DNA. That's why the concept of the secret society is nearly as old as civilization. For the Greeks and the Romans, for Egyptian priests and Chinese hit men and medieval French knights, it's always been the same game. In this chapter, you get a better understanding of how psychologists, historians, sociologists, conspiracists, and the occasional cop work to understand just who and what makes up a secret society.

Defining Secret Societies

To begin defining secret societies, you must know that various types of secret societies exist (and are covered in this book). They are very similar — and closely related — to the classifications of conspiracy theories discussed in Chapter 2.

A secret society is

- An organization whose existence is known, and whose membership is public knowledge, but whose rituals and meetings are considered to be secret. The Freemasons are an excellent example of a secret society.

- An organization whose existence is known, but whose membership and objectives are a closely guarded secret. The Hellfire Club of 19th-century London is a good example of this type of secret society.

- An organization whose existence is rumored, but few, if any, concrete facts are known. Many times, this sort of organization gives birth to some of the wildest speculations of the amateur or professional conspiracy theorist, because their very existence is debatable, and in the end, impossible to prove. The modern-day Illuminati are a good example.

- An organization whose membership, traditions, and aims are completely open and above board, but whose meetings are conducted in private, and consequently are perceived by many in the public at large to be a focal point for something much more sinister, generally because of the high-octane political power of the membership. The Bilderberg Group is an excellent example of this sort of secret society.

- A certain high-level bureau within the federal government. They're listed here because they are, by their very nature, "secret societies," whether they admit it or not, and they have given rise to so many modern American conspiracy theories. While rumors abound, they may or may not exist, and their capabilities and missions may be very different from what the public believes — good or bad.

Historically, some intelligence agencies have actually grown out of a secret society. In Israel, for example, the famous Israeli intelligence bureau, the Mossad, grew out of an underground secret society formed to resist the British occupation of Palestine that was called the *Irgun,* as well as other secret offshoots of the British-recognized *Palmach,* the Jewish Army in pre-1948 Palestine. The easy transition from secret society to intelligence agency only serves to highlight how closely linked they are, in terms of their structure.

The Difference Between a Secret Society and a Religious Cult

Religion comes up on many occasions when discussing secret societies. Many societies are connected to a religious faith if only through the belief in that faith shared by their membership.

For example, the Ku Klux Klan was strictly a Protestant Christian organization, whether the Protestants claimed them as members of the congregation or not, while the Knights Templar was a Catholic organization, inseparable from the pope and the Catholic Church.

Examining the fine lines

So is a religious cult a secret society? The differences and similarities between the two can be a very fine line. Here are some very broad generalities:

✔ Most religious cults keep a great deal of their structure and their aims secret. Many are controlled by one messianic and powerful figure, a figure who often has an inner circle of trusted compatriots that can seem an awful lot like a secret society.

✔ Many secret societies are founded for a spiritual purpose that seems mighty close to a religion. (For example, a lot of the most conspiratorial of the secret societies in this book are occult in nature.) So, isn't occultism, or even Satan worship, a "religion?" It certainly is for some. And these occult beliefs are bound to spawn more secret societies than, say, the Congress of Anglican Bishops, simply by their very self-described mysterious makeup.

Look up the word *occult* in the dictionary sometime. You may think it means *supernatural,* or even *witchcraft,* but what it means is *hidden.* By their very nature of being groups that go against the grain of society, these organizations, such as Aleister Crowley's Ordo Templi Orientis, are going to qualify as "secret societies." So, in that respect, religion will be addressed, insofar as occult beliefs can be considered a religion.

Examining the specifics

In order to lend a little clarity to the cloudiness of the situation, here are a few points of difference:

✔ Generally, secret societies don't proselytize, while religious cults do little else. To *proselytize* means to get out there and find potential members by using high-pressure tactics. In general, secret societies get the wannabe members knocking on *their* doors and not the reverse.

✔ Secret societies usually set a bar high enough to keep out members they don't want. Religious cults, on the contrary, use their tactics on anyone standing nearby.

For example, cults often use a technique called "love bombing." This method usually happens in the period when the cult is still trying to get the potential convert to join. During this honeymoon period, everyone in the cult just *loves* you. They love the way you dress; they love your hair; they love your insightful comments; they love your bridgework. Meanwhile, in a completely opposite camp, a secret society is often spending this same "honeymoon period" testing potential members to see if they can make the grade.

✔ Religious cults are very often built around the absolute faith of the members in one messianic figure, as with Jim Jones in the People's Temple. Historians call this psychological effect the "Cult of Personality," and it works even in groups of millions, as with Soviet Russia under Joseph Stalin.

Religious cults often fade away or break apart into other cults when their leader dies, no matter how large they might've been (as in the case of the remnants of remaining Branch Davidians). Sometimes they go rolling on, with a second-in-command who keeps things going in the name of their dead messiah. Or worst of all, like Marshall Applewhite and the Heaven's Gate cult, the personality simply takes all the members with him when he goes.

As a rule (a rule with the occasional exception),noncultish secret societies may be founded by one man, like Adam Weishaupt and the original Bavarian Illuminati. Such societies are usually set up to be self-perpetuating and don't die away with their founder.

✔ The effect of membership on the relationship to a person's family is different. Religious cults often try to cut a person off from old friends and eventually from family members, particularly if the cults disapprove.

Many cults assign new members a sort of "keeper," an older and more trusted member of the group who accompanies the new member just about everywhere including the toilet, and this means tense and weird situations like coming home with the new convert for family events like holidays. Until the new convert can be trusted to have become utterly brainwashed and deaf to all criticism, the cult likes to keep him as near to hand as possible.

Generally, secret societies do little to damage a person's relationship with family and friends, although this rule isn't hard and fast. For example, a man may become deeply involved with an organization like Freemasonry, leaving home two or even three nights a week for Masonic events that don't include wives. Of course, Masons, seeing this potential for angry wives, long ago created many subsidiary organizations that get the wife and kids involved with the fraternity in order to ease any hurt feelings of being left out. But the dynamic is still there with many secret societies, and it can be far worse with some. For instance, if a man or woman is a member of the most clandestine offices within the CIA or NSA, they're not even allowed to tell their family what they do for a living. This, too, can create a strained distance in family relationships, though generally nothing on the scale of the home wrecking that cults can achieve.

Organizations that straddle the fence

Some secret organizations out there straddle the fence between a secret society and a religious cult. Because religions, cults, and secret societies don't always start with a well-designed road map, their purposes or methods can change over time. Everything from persecution or distrust by society to a change in the head of the organization can turn the tiller in a different direction.

In addition, people outside of the group can accuse it of different motives than what actually motivates the group internally. And then there are those that deliberately masquerade as one type of group, while they really are something else entirely.

One good example of this type of organization is the ancient Cult of the Assassins because "the Old Man of the Mountain" used the group's Ismaili faith to keep his men under his power. But their political ambitions and their various plots against the governments of the world put them fairly and squarely in the category of a secret society.

The Church of Scientology is perhaps the best modern case of straddling the fence. Their Religious Technology Center (RTC), one of the most powerful of the complex inner layers of organizations that govern the Church of Scientology, is a prime example of the fusion of cults and secret societies. Because Scientologists have a nasty habit of (allegedly) suing anyone who even sneezes in their direction, we speak only of the (alleged) inner secret society that governs over the (alleged) Pacific Area Command (PAC) Base Scientology Center in the (alleged) city of Hollywood, California.

Entire books and sequels to books, running feuds in print between present members and former members, have been devoted simply to the question of whether Scientology even *is* a religion, as well as whether it's a cult. Any organization that can go head to head with the IRS, blackmail its commissioner to obtain a special tax status, and *get away with it* is one to be deeply reckoned with.

The Second-Oldest Profession: Secret Societies in Ancient Times

Historians believe that the concept of the secret society is one that goes back to the concept of the tribe; in fact, one grew out of the other. Tribe members separated by war or disaster had to have signs with which to recognize one another. Many of the rituals of early adolescence, like the Jewish bar-mitzvah, grew out of tribal rituals that welcomed the young initiate into the group. That concept of being "initiated" is a bedrock of the secret society.

Egypt: Source of the first secret society?

Naming the first secret society that's similar to those in the current era is a difficult task. The Egyptians had innumerable secret fraternities — most having to do with their complex and ritual-drenched religion. But one secret society wasn't quite as much a priesthood as the others. The society grew up out of one of the first figures in history who wasn't a pharaoh or a king. His name was Imhotep, and he was the chancellor, or grand vizier, for the pharaoh Zoser (also spelled "Djoser") in the Third Dynasty of the Old Kingdom.

Apart from being a master builder of the first recognizable Egyptian pyramid, Imhotep was also a physician, the father of Egyptian medicine. And as if these laurels weren't enough, he was an astronomer, a sculptor, a poet, and a philosopher whose sayings were cherished 20 centuries after his death. Later, Imhotep was made a god, with a highly imaginative lineage from a mating between a mortal woman and the god Ptah. But for the men of the cult of Imhotep that developed in the city of Memphis, he wasn't a god but a man, and was revered as such.

This cult had an inner secret society, a *Brotherhood of Imhotep,* that worshipped his ability as a builder and that created a metaphor for god as an architect, making for a striking similarity with the Freemasons who don't come along for at least another 4,000 years.

Greece: Ancient cults and mystery schools

The Greeks had many closed and elite alliances, from factions of Spartan army officers to the private clubs of Athenian noblemen. The Kryptia, for example, was a secret organization of Spartan military men with a very rigid code by which the members lived.

The majority of the Greek secret societies grew out of the mystery schools. These schools were called mystery schools from the Greek word *myein,* meaning *to close,* as in close the eyes and mouth to receive the ritual secrets. The person taking in the young initiate was called the *mystag gos,* the leader of the mysteries, and his officer was called the *hierophant,* the "revealer of holy things."

Historians believe that, at one time, a couple thousand years before Christ, these mystery schools were made up of the entire tribe — initiation into the society and into the tribe were one and the same. Later, as their culture became more sophisticated, the original mystery schools that centered on the worship of mother-earth goddesses like Demeter broke apart into many mystery schools and many other forms of cults and sects, too.

The Dionysian and Eleusinian Mysteries

In their earliest days, the two most important mystery schools were the Dionysian and the Eleusinian.

- **The Dionysiac Mysteries:** An act of worship of the god Dionysus, god of fertility and of wine. In the Dionysian Mysteries, although they weren't exactly having orgies, a lot of sex was going on during these joyous, days-long, wine- and food-saturated festivals, and anthropologists believe that young men were initiated into their sexual manhood as well as their place in the tribe when they took part in their first mystery festival.

Animism

For almost all tribal religions, the name of the game is *animism* — the communication of human traits to animals and to elemental forces like the wind, the tide, and the seasons. To argue whether it's magic or religion has taken up a lot of room in scholarly books and papers, when there doesn't seem to be much point to it — it was simply what people believed.

A part of this belief was the secret society mystery schools — sometimes called sodality by the scholars. *Sodality* is the tight brotherhood (or sisterhood because many members were women) of a particular tribe. Many of the secret rituals of these sodalities had to do with the attempt to placate and control the forces of nature (which is why all the sex going on in so many of them made sense). Humans having sex led to fertility and either paid homage to the god's fertility that created the earth or perhaps even fired the gods up to a greater amount of sex and fertility, making for a bigger crop. Man was born, lived, procreated, died, and was buried in the earth to become a part of this process of enriching the land.

✔ **The Eleusinian Mysteries:** Celebrated the myth of Demeter, the great earth-mother and goddess of the grain, and the story of her daughter Persephone, or Kore, who was kidnapped by Hades and tricked into living with him for one third of the year. During this time the vegetation on the earth died. But each spring Persephone returned to her mother Demeter, and the land was reborn and fruitful once more.

Actually, Greece held festivals to honor the goddess Demeter, but the superspecial secret one, the one in which Demeter herself had imparted the ritual mysteries to the people, was only to be found at the festival in the city of Eleusis, which was eventually annexed to the city-state of Athens. These mysteries were open to any and all who wanted to attend, and huge numbers did just that. But strangely enough, as more and more Greeks attended to be initiated, it became less and less the initiation into a single tribe, and more simply a person's religious choice. This would help to lead, in Greece and her imitator Rome, to the secular mystery schools.

Greek secular schools

The secular schools retained an air of religion, but basically they were private social clubs and sometimes political clubs, too. Secret society mystery schools existed for those who followed the scientific quasi-religious teachings of Pythagoras. These clubs were known as the *Orphics.* Many people also followed the popular teachings of Plato.

The initiation rituals of these secular mystery schools remained the same, if not more dramatic and elaborate as time passed. But after the initiation was over, these societies focused on drinking together, eating together, and eventually, plotting together.

In the year 415 BC, the Athenian democracy was nearly destroyed by the conspiracy of several of these social clubs of powerful Athenian noblemen who got together and attempted to overthrow the state. Later on in Rome, similar attempts to overthrow the state happened several times until secret societies of any sort were outlawed completely.

Rome: Cults and paranoia

The Romans were a very sophisticated people, and they loved to band together into various societies and clubs, from groups of officers who served on the frontier under the same general, to organizations devoted to a particular trade or political party. These secret societies of a particular trade became the first powerful craft guilds in Europe in the Middle Ages. Many of these guilds were somewhat religious in nature and are often called religious confraternities, simply because particular laborers or craftsmen looked to particular gods or goddesses as their patrons.

But the rulers of Rome found the whole idea of secret societies to be unacceptable on the grounds of danger to the state. Before the reign of the first emperor, Augustus, they were, in fact, illegal. In ancient Rome, one of the reasons the odd new sect of Christians was perceived, in the three centuries before the conversion of Constantine, to be so dangerous was because the Romans saw them not as a religion so much as a secret society.

However, as the Roman emperors conquered the East, and the Mediterranean became their private lake, the influx of Eastern mystery cult religions was so overwhelmingly popular that no one could stop it. Besides, as the empire expanded, more and more people were cut off from hometowns and friends, and these cults filled a definite need. And so these various cults to Isis or Mithra or Bachus were allowed for a time, so long as it could be shown that their rituals were strictly religious.

They were also incredibly odd. Here are some examples:

- Some of the cults had priestesses, while others had priests who were eunuchs dressed in women's clothes and wore a lot of makeup.
- Ritual progressions consisted of people carrying sacred trees or plants.
- An initiate often fasted for a week or more before the ceremony that took him into the cult.
- Many cults had various levels or ranks through which a candidate could rise, like the Mithras cult, with its "Lions" and "Ravens" and "Couriers of the Sun."

Most of these cults had an initiation ceremony that mimicked death and resurrection, and as Rome became richer and more technically endowed, they relied on some great special effects for a ripping good show. The initiate may be closed up in a casket or a sarcophagus and then buried or shut away. Beforehand, he may be disemboweled in a phony play. The entrails of an animal were used in this play for greater blood spatter. The cults may also put on a show pretending to decapitate or to drown the initiate or to rip out his heart.

Instructions have survived that tell how to perform some of these tricks, which include

- How to put sulfur on a torch so it still burned when you drew it out of a pool of water
- How to make writing appear on a wall
- How to make a halo appear around a priest's head

After the initiate's "resurrection," the initiate may have a ritual with an officer of the cult, standing in for, say, Isis. All in all, it made for one great Saturday night.

The Vestal Virgins

The Romans had every sort of secret brotherhood, not to mention a sisterhood, in the form of the intensely guarded cloister of the Vestal Virgins, whose primary task was to maintain the sacred fire of Vesta.

For centuries an eternal flame burned within the Temple of Vesta on the Roman Forum. The Romans believed that the fire was closely tied to the fortunes of the city and viewed its extinction as a sign of disaster.

The Vestal duty brought great honor and privileges to women who served in the role. These women were the only female priests within the Roman religious system. Any woman who broke her oath or revealed the secrets of the order was led to the outskirts of the city, symbolically cast out of society, and promptly buried alive. But the Vestals were part of the state-approved faith, as old as Rome itself.

The rise of the gentlemen's club

In the fading days of the Roman Republic, the gentlemen's clubs on the Athenian model were very popular, until, in the consulship of Cicero in 63 BC, an aristocrat named Lucius Catalinus, or Cataline, attempted to launch a takeover of the government. The conspiracy was proved, and a warrant was issued for Cataline's arrest. He fled to his men outside the city, and many lives were lost to bring down him and his private army.

For the rest of the period of the Republic, and on into the later Empire period, forming a secret society in the Roman Empire was illegal, and the penalty for doing so was death. What makes this more remarkable is that the dynamics of the secret society haven't changed much since Cicero's day.

Within a few decades the Republic fell, but nervous-Nellie emperors didn't like the idea of secret societies any more than republican senators and consuls. Most emperors allowed all sorts of exceptions to the law, but it wasn't a good idea to push it. In fact, some emperors became absolutely neurotic on the subject of secret societies of just about any sort.

The Roman Emperor Trajan wouldn't allow the citizens of Nicomedia to form a club that would act as a citizen's fire brigade, and the most paranoid of emperors wouldn't allow associations whose objective was obviously charitable.

The Cult of Bacchus

Much of the Roman government toleration for the mystery cults came to a crashing end with the scandal of the Cult of Bacchus. The Bacchanalia, or the Festival of Bacchus, was officially suppressed in 186 BC because it had gotten completely out of hand, with public debauchery and lewdness of every sort, rape, drunkenness, murder, and worst of all, general drunk and disorderly conduct that resulted in more property damage with every year that passed.

The Cult of Bacchus drew more of the working-class folks than the aristocracy, and the Senate thought that the rowdy emotionalism of the festival made it particularly distasteful (meaning "frightening"). From that time forward, the Roman mystery cults lived with a sword over their head. (The festival still went on privately, out in the country, away from prying eyes.) Individual worship was fine — group worship and ritual was discouraged at every turn. Therefore, these "mystery rites" became more secret than ever, going underground so they could stay in business.

Europe: Secret societies from the Middle Ages onward

The relentless forming of alliances and fraternities continued through the Middle Ages, in every form from the secret fighting order of the Knights Templar, to the trade guilds of the prosperous merchant cities. By the late 19th century, Europe was drenched in secret societies, most of them having been formed in the period of the Enlightenment. Many had an anti-monarchial, republican, equality-of-mankind bent of belief, as well as the worship of the two new Enlightenment buzzwords — *science* and *reason*.

Of course, there were more than a few frivolous societies: drinking and dining clubs; groups that assembled secretly to read and discuss subversive literature or just dirty books; sex clubs like the infamous Hellfire Club; and of course, rabble-rousing political societies.

United States: Societies and fraternalism

In the United States at the end of the 1800s, belonging to a fraternal organization was nearly a necessity for any man who expected to be an upstanding member of the community. This was the golden age of American fraternalism with literally thousands of organizations like the Masons, the Knights of Columbus, the Knights of Pythias, the Maccabees, the Order of the Beavers, the Order of the Buffalo, the Red Men, the Sons of Italy, and even the Croatian Fraternal Union of America, just to name a very few.

Just about *everybody* had a society or fraternity. Most were patterned on the granddaddy of all fraternal secret societies, the Freemasons (see Chapter 9).

All this fraternalism lasted up until the 1950s. But the post–World War II generation, the baby boomers, prided themselves on not being "joiners." It just wasn't hip to become a Mason or a Moose, or anything else that smacked of the "Establishment." Men who belonged to such fraternities were incessantly mocked. Only a sap would ever consider such a ridiculous investment in time and energy. Masons wore stupid hats, the Scottish Rite had boring dances, and Rosicrucians advertised on matchbook covers. Now, just who in his right mind would search for spiritual fulfillment from a group that advertised on a book of matches?

A new interest in secret societies

At the dawn of the 21st century, America is undergoing a new wave of fascination with secret societies. And one of the most amazing aspects of secret societies is the large number of surviving groups from the "golden age" still around to greet them.

In our own time the dynamics behind the phenomenon are still the same. Whatever the baby boomers thought, breaking off into cliques and cults is a basic human trait, one that won't be left behind for long. After all, what was the hippie commune but just another kind of secret society, a breakaway sect feeling itself superior to the culture as a whole? Certainly, the murderous Charles Manson family, the dark underbelly of the hippie culture, qualifies as a secret society with its own symbols, rules, and mythology. It sure wasn't the Rotary Club. And heaven help the guy in a 1960s commune who decided that a wife, a couple of kids, and a split-level ranch house in the suburbs wasn't quite as "empty and futile" as his comrades had made it out to be.

Or, as the writer Eric Hoffer put it, "Woe to him inside a nonconformist clique who does not conform with nonconformity."

Part II
A Colossal Compilation of Conspiracy Theories

The 5th Wave   By Rich Tennant

In this part . . .

This part covers the best and the brightest in terms of conspiracy theories, from old reliables like Area 51 and Commie plots to fluoridating the water supply, to some lesser-known articles of faith for certain Americans, like the bizarre plots connected to every presidential assassination (and not just JFK's). We examine conspiracies — real and imagined — that are wrapped up with the flammable topics of race, religion, and genocide. And we discuss the eruption of post-9/11 conspiracy theories, from the sublime to the ridiculous, all in one easy-open package.

Chapter 4

Everybody Knows About It: The World's Most Common Conspiracy Theories

In This Chapter

▶ Surviving terrors of technology

▶ Suppressing geniuses and their inventions

▶ Searching out the living dead

▶ Uncovering corporate schemes

*I*t seems that we live in cynical times. No one and nothing can be trusted, when you get right down to it. Some conspiracies are *so* "secret," *so* "diabolical," and *so* "hidden from the public" that *everybody* seems to know about them. Like the evil corporate conspiracy that sees to it that hot dogs are sold in packages of ten, but hot dog *buns* come in packages of eight. Or that every time some backyard genius invents an engine that runs an automobile at highway speeds on nothing but water, the car companies buy him out, or "silence" him.

Likewise, there are long-held beliefs about secret underground government installations used for covert and probably evil purposes. Thanks to popular shows like *The X-Files,* every school kid knows about government labs dissecting space aliens, building sinister death rays, and testing mind-control weaponry on entire cities. With all this "secret" knowledge going around, it's amazing that the government can hide anything these days.

This chapter covers the classics of the conspiracy catalog, from fluoridated water to subliminal advertising that makes you uncontrollably consume at the retail trough. And you find a few folks who've been thought to be long dead, who may still walk among you.

TIP

Please note that a couple of the old favorites are missing from this chapter — namely items having to do with UFOs, space aliens, faked Moon landings, and the ever-popular "face on Mars." Fear not. Because these topics are so numerous, you find more information in Chapter 7.

Technological Terrors

"We're from the government, and we're here to help" — a phrase certain to send a chill through the heart of any citizen of the modern world (or at least through the hearts of conspiracy theorists). Some people believe that even when government wants to help, somehow it finds a way to get it wrong. And when it may involve introducing unknown chemicals into the water we drink, the air we breathe, and the very atmosphere that keeps us alive, we tend to get nervous. Or at least cranky.

Many of the conspiracy theories that we cover in this chapter can be traced back to one man: Nikola Tesla. Tesla was a fascinating scientist, possibly even the prototype for the classic Mad Scientist character of the sort usually played by Boris Karloff and Bela Lugosi. He's also a staple of the conspiracist's universe. Born in Croatia in 1856, Tesla came to the U.S. at the age of 28 with little more than the clothes on his back. His work in the fields of physics, electricity, and magnetism was groundbreaking, and probably everyday items like telephones, radios, televisions, X-rays, microwave ovens, and even the electricity in your home wouldn't exist had it not been for this eccentric inventor.

But conspiracy theorists believe that Tesla's greatest inventions — free electrical generation, an electrical "death ray," and a superweapon with enough power to "split the world in two," — have either been repressed by giant corporations or secretly developed by the military, or both. More on those in later sections.

Fluoridated water and the Cold War Communist Plot

In the 1964 Stanley Kubrick film *Dr. Strangelove,* a paranoid Army general, Jack D. Ripper, unleashes nuclear Armageddon over something most people have never heard of: fluoridation of water. As Ripper (played by Sterling Hayden) explains:

> *Have you ever seen a Commie drink a glass of water? . . . Fluoridation is the most monstrously conceived and dangerous communist plot we have ever had to face. . . . A foreign substance is introduced into our precious bodily fluids without the knowledge of the individual. Certainly without any choice. That's the way your hard-core Commie works.*

In 1909, a Colorado dentist noticed a curious development in some of the teeth of his younger patients. They were developing a strange stain on their teeth that came to be known as the "Colorado Stain." But what made the cases odd was that the children with greater evidence of the stain seemed to have markedly fewer cavities. Eventually, the discoloration was traced to large amounts of fluoride, a naturally occurring chemical found in the rocks of the famous Pike's Peak. As snow melted, water ran across mineral deposits of *cryolite,* which contained fluoride, and trickled into the water supply of the towns around the mountain. The surrounding folks might've had brown teeth, but at least they didn't rot.

Over the years, the U.S. government took on several studies to determine the safe level of fluoride in a water supply that would prevent cavities, without causing the ugly stain. At first the studies were to determine how much fluoride to remove from the Pike's Peak water supply to make it safe to drink, because fluoride in high concentration really is dangerous. But by the 1930s, dental and healthcare researchers were recommending the chemical be added to water supplies across the U.S. to prevent cavities.

At almost the same time, an anti-fluoride movement fought the proposals. At first, the argument was that adding the chemical violated a citizen's right to *not* be medicated against their will. Christian scientists said it was against their religion. Conservatives, who were watching the results of fascist forms of socialism in Mussolini's Italy and Hitler's Germany, claimed that fluoridation was nothing but socialized medicine.

Then an ex-Communist named Oliver Kenneth Goff testified in the House Un-American Activities Committee hearings in the late 1930s that Communist agents in the U.S. were in favor of fluoridation. Why? Their plan, according to Goff, was to take over water treatment plants and threaten to dump the large stockpiles of deadly fluoride into the nation's water supply if Americans didn't surrender.

Another tale was that the Nazis developed fluoride water treatment as a chemical means to sterilize women. And in 1954, research chemist Charles Perkins claimed, "Repeated doses of infinitesimal amounts of fluoride will in time reduce an individual's power to resist domination, by slowly poisoning and narcotizing a certain area of the brain, thus making him submissive to the will of those who wish to govern him."

Actually fluoride really is poisonous in very high doses over a long period of time — an accident in Alaska in the 1990s put excessive amounts of the stuff into the water of Hooper Bay, making almost 300 people sick and killing one. Nevertheless, close to 70 percent of the U.S. population drink fluoridated water every day. So do most of those former Commies over in Russia. But to this day there are conspiracists who believe that fluoridation really is a massive and evil plot.

Chemtrails

Look up in the sky on any given day. They seem to be everywhere across the blue canopy of the heavens — the white, tic-tac-toe lines known as *contrails*. They're the very natural byproduct of the very unnatural machines of human flight.

When moist air gets sucked through a jet engine, warmed up, expelled as exhaust, and hits the freezing temperatures found in high altitudes (somewhere around –40°F at between 25,000 and 30,000 feet), the result is the formation of tiny crystals of ice that dangle lazily in the sky before drifting apart and melting. If the air is too dry, contrails are short or even nonexistent. If the air is especially moist, they can hang around a long time and stretch from one horizon to the other. And if you live near Air Force bases that sometimes fire guided test missiles, the contrails left behind can sometimes look like drunken Etch-A-Sketch art.

Conspiracy theorists like William Thomas and others have stared up at the skies for a long, long time — maybe *too* long a time. And they see something more menacing:

- They've claimed that the government has really been spraying the population with chemical or biological substances, thus creating chemtrails.

- Other claims are that the military is attempting to devise either devious weather-altering weapons or desperate anti-global-warming programs (depending on if you think the military is evil or good).

- And still more have suggested that the military is seeding the skies with metal or other electrical conductive material as part of an alleged massive electronic weapon known by its acronym HAARP (see the section "HAARP — The electromagnetic superweapon" later in the chapter).

The Internet is rife with "spotter's guides" that depict the ways to determine whether that puffy streak in the sky is a harmless contrail or a deadly chemtrail. These seem to be almost comical in their hysteria as they pick out one cloud or contrail as being more suspicious than others.

Most scientists agree that spraying chemicals from planes at 25,000 feet and higher is a supremely dangerous, unpredictable, and worthless exercise, because high winds at those altitudes can carry airborne substances hundreds of miles in any direction, making studies of such activities — whether done by good guys or evil scientists — pretty useless at best, and at worst, liable to float down on the very heads of evil researchers themselves hundreds of miles away.

Nikola Tesla and "free electricity"

Nikola Tesla eventually worked for both of the giants in electrical development in the U.S.: Thomas Edison and George Westinghouse. When Thomas Edison developed the first commercially viable electric light bulb, he knew it would be worthless if communities had no way to power them. Edison's company, General Electric, built electrical generating stations using a power delivery system called direct current (DC). But Tesla had different ideas. Frustrated by Edison's methods, he quit and developed a competing generation system (alternating current — AC) for Westinghouse that still is the standard method of electrical delivery in the U.S. (and most other countries) today.

At the same time he was working for Westinghouse, Tesla had his own company and had much bigger ideas. What he envisioned was the transmission of "free" electrical power through the air without the need for wires. He invented what is still called the *Tesla Coil,* a device used to create bursts of extremely high-voltage electricity (they make massive lightning-bolt displays with exciting crackling noises and are often the centerpieces of modern day science museums). He believed that if he could create a coil big enough, electricity could be beamed to a receiver across town, with no need of anything in between.

Over the years Tesla set up research facilities in New York and Colorado Springs, where he built massive generators and transmission antennas to test his theories. Accidents occurred regularly:

- In New York, he created "harmonic resonance" that nearly knocked over buildings adjacent to his lab by vibrating them to pieces, and he feared he could create enough power to destroy New York and split the world in two.

- Later experiments at a more secluded lab near Colorado Springs resulted in sparks flying out of the ground and arcing from the city's fire hydrants. Still, his Magnifying Transmitter did manage to illuminate light bulbs from 25 miles away, without any wires.

Conspiracy theorists claim that Tesla's ideas about wireless electricity have been suppressed by giant electrical equipment manufacturers. Yet, his hundreds of patents and stacks of writings have been publicly available for over 100 years, and nothing has ever prevented anyone from attempting to re-create his experiments. Nothing, that is, but the danger of much death and destruction, since Tesla worked with thousands of volts of electricity.

There is an enthusiastic group of hobbyists and experimenters who regularly build their own Tesla Coils and attempt truly dangerous, deadly, and, in some cases, just plain stupid experiments with them.

Wardenclyffe Tower and Tesla's "World System"

Starting in 1901, Tesla assembled financial backing for his long-dreamed-of "World System." On Long Island he began to build a 187-foot tower, called Wardenclyffe Tower, with a domed top, looking like the world's biggest salt shaker. Tesla's ultimate plan was to build these towers all around the world to create a global radio broadcasting system, a way to synchronize the world's clocks, a global navigation system, and his greatest desire, the wireless transmission of free electricity to anyone with a special underground wire conductor and a dishlike antenna on their roof.

Tesla dreamed of free power for everyone, but financier J. P. Morgan wasn't so generous. When he finally heard of Tesla's "free power" plan, he demanded to know how investors would recoup their money if they couldn't sell electricity. "Where do I put the meter?" he famously asked.

When the inventor explained his humanitarian goal, Morgan and the rest of the finance team walked out. The tower was never completed and was torn down in 1917 during World War I because the government was afraid German submarines would use the landmark as a navigation aid.

Peace ray or death ray?

Tesla wasn't all hearts and flowers. He also recognized the destructive power of electromagnetic energy. In the 1930s he drew up plans for a Wardenclyffe-style tower that had a more deadly intent. He envisioned a particle beam weapon (what science fiction writers and comic books in those days called a "ray gun") that would narrowly focus a beam of energy strong enough to knock airplanes out of the sky. Tesla called it, ironically, a "Peace Ray," a weapon so horrible that it would end all wars. (Of course, every inventor of horrible weaponry has believed this, from Dr. Guillotine's beheading machine and Alfred "Peace Prize" Nobel's TNT, to the Gatling Gun and the atomic bomb.)

The ray gun was never produced, and when Tesla died, the most important diagrams of the invention were never found. The FBI claims that Russian spies broke into his apartment and stole the contents of his safe before U.S. authorities could get there.

HAARP — The electromagnetic superweapon

HAARP is the more manageable acronym for the *High Frequency Active Auroral Research Program* facility near Gakona, Alaska. Constructed in the 1990s, HAARP's official purpose is to study the effects of electromagnetic energy on the ionosphere. The way it accomplishes this is to direct 3.6

million megawatts of electricity into a transmitter, pump it out of an antenna straight up into the atmosphere, and take readings from satellites.

The effect seems to be that the ionosphere gets toasted by the beam of energy, similar to the effects of solar flares, albeit in a very tiny way (since 3.6 million megawatts is a pinprick compared to the electromagnetic energy hitting the Earth from the Sun). That's the 10-cent explanation of the official mission.

Conspiracists say that the military designed HAARP with a far more sinister intent. It is claimed that the facility is a weapon being developed to knock out enemy satellite and radio communication by bombarding the atmosphere with massive electromagnetic waves. Some have claimed that the 1993 power blackout in the northeast United States and Canada was triggered by a blast from HAARP.

In the 1980s, physicist Bernard Eastland proposed technology similar to what was built at HAARP as part of the so-called "Star Wars" defense shield (known in military circles as the less Hollywood-ish *Strategic Defense Initiative,* or SDI). Eastland built on the theories of famed electrical pioneer Nikola Tesla and proposed a high frequency, electromagnetic "shield" that could be used to electronically jam incoming Soviet nuclear missiles and knock out enemy satellites. When the government actually built HAARP, they claimed Eastland's patents weren't used, in spite of the similarity of the basic principles.

But critics who claim that HAARP is quietly sitting up in Alaska just waiting to be used by the military as a "death ray" aren't silenced. The belief is that the mild doses of electromagnetic pulses sent into the ionosphere are merely trial firings and tests, in anticipation of the really big jolt. A few of the very nervous have suggested that HAARP could direct its rays anywhere on Earth, and can be used to do anything from creating major weather catastrophes on demand or causing earthquakes, to causing mass brain damage on a global scale by frying brain cells.

HAARP isn't technically a U.S. military research site, and it has a large complement of civilians working on the property. However, the project is managed by a division of *DARPA* (Defense Advanced Research Projects Agency), the Defense Department's super-high-tech "gee whiz" office that works with industry and universities to develop sophisticated technologies that might have a defense application (like the Internet, before Al Gore claimed it for himself).

Philadelphia Experiment's vanishing ship

In October 1943, a U.S. Navy destroyer called the USS *Eldridge* was supposedly part of a wartime experiment that went terribly wrong. That is, if you believe in the *Philadelphia Experiment.*

The story goes that the Navy's Office of Naval Research (ONR) discovered a way to apply one of Nikola Tesla's concepts called the *Unified Field Theory* — a method of using electromagnetic energy in conjunction with gravity to "bend" light around a physical object, rendering it invisible.

In 1943, work began in the Philadelphia Navy Yard to install special equipment aboard the USS *Eldridge* to create what *Star Trek* fans would describe as a cloaking device. Supposedly, the first test in June did indeed make the ship disappear, but shrouded in an eerie green fog. When the experiment ended, the crew aboard the ship reported bouts with nausea. At that point, the Navy decided the process was too dangerous to use with a human crew, and altered the goal of the device to simply make the ship invisible to radar.

Four months later, the experiment was attempted again. This time, instead of just disappearing from sight, the USS *Eldridge* physically vanished and turned up briefly off the coast of Norfolk, Virginia, almost 400 miles away. Then, it mysteriously reappeared in Philadelphia. The scientists had accidentally discovered the secret of teleportation. Unfortunately, the experiment had a horrible effect on the crew. Many went mad. Five sailors were supposedly rematerialized within the steel walls or decking of the ship. Others kept fading in and out, appearing and disappearing. The psychological effects on the crew were so devastating that the Navy resorted to brainwashing techniques to get them to forget the entire experience. As can be expected, the Navy's ONR has always scoffed at the story, but true believers say the Navy is engaged in a coverup.

Actually, the entire story of the Philadelphia Experiment can be traced to the accounts of just one man, Carlos Allende. Allende claimed to be a crewman aboard a merchant ship in Norfolk when the USS *Eldridge* suddenly faded into view right before his eyes with no explanation. In 1955, Allende contacted a UFO researcher named Morris K. Jessup and told tales of seeing crewmen ashore wink in and out of sight and other effects of the experiment gone wrong.

However, Allende turned out to really be Carl Meredith Allen, a Pennsylvania man with a history of psychiatric problems. Allen created an elaborate manuscript of events, handwritten in different colored ink to look like three men had worked on it. When Jessup was unable to interest a publisher in his book based on Allen's writings, he became depressed, had a mental breakdown and committed suicide. Naturally, believers took it to be proof that Jessup and Allen had both been discredited by the government, and "gotten rid of."

Over the years, real Navy veterans of the USS *Eldridge* have attempted to debunk the tale. They point out that the ship wasn't even built in June 1943, but was completed in August of that year. And it wasn't built in the Philadelphia Naval Yards, either. The USS *Eldridge* was in New York from its christening until a shakedown cruise in the Bahamas in September of 1943. It never even docked in Philadelphia during the period in question.

Ships during the period really were often outfitted with massive electromagnet coils, used to demagnetize or degauss the hull to foil underwater mines and torpedoes with magnetic triggers. The process is still used today, and it's possible these giant coils were the inspiration for the story.

In 1979, Charles Berlitz and William Moore wrote the most famous account of the tale, *The Philadelphia Experiment: Project Invisibility* (Grosset & Dunlap). In 1990, Alfred Bielek came forward and claimed to have been a sailor who jumped off of the USS *Eldridge's* deck just as it winked out of sight. Bielek has since been exposed by several sources as a fraud who was never anywhere near the USS *Eldridge* during its supposed experimental mishaps.

Dirty Work Down Below — Underground Government Installations

The U.S. government over the years has built several survival bunkers to relocate officials or to run wartime operations from in the event of an atomic attack or other cataclysmic catastrophe. These have often been claimed by conspiracists to mean that a "shadow government" was in place and ready to take over — either for a U.S. government police state or the New World Order.

Most of these facilities protected critical operations of government during the MAD (Mutually Assured Destruction) days of the Cold War with the Soviet Union. President Dwight D. Eisenhower set many of these underground bunker plans into motion in the 1950s.

Alleged underground bunkers

President Eisenhower believed that, in the event of a nuclear attack on the U.S., the continuity of government had to be protected in case a large number of elected leaders were wiped out in the first blasts. As a result, a series of major underground installations were constructed, starting in the '50s.

The most famous underground bunkers include the following:

✔ **Greenbrier resort in White Sulphur Springs, West Virginia:** This facility is possibly the most famous, least secret, and most unusual underground government installation. Secretly built within a hidden wing of a luxury hotel and resort, the bunker was designed to safely hold members of Congress underground until the mushroom clouds passed by. No longer an operational top-secret site, public tours are now available.

✔ **Mount Weather, Bluemont, Virginia:** Another emergency government relocation site was constructed at Mount Weather, near Bluemont, Virginia. Technically a Federal Emergency Management Administration (FEMA) facility, Mount Weather has been around since the 1960s. Its location and purpose have been a loosely guarded secret almost since the beginning (serving as the inspiration for "Mount Thunder" in the 1962 novel, *Seven Days In May*).

Vice President Dick Cheney was brought to Mount Weather immediately following the 9/11 attacks, and it's one of the two "undisclosed locations" he and critical members of the administration have been taken to in times of emergency.

Mount Weather is believed to be the present underground relocation center for the government, with room and provisions for several thousand bureaucrats. The U.S. may be glassed over from falling nukes, but rest assured that your tax bill will be delivered come rain or shine or nuclear winter.

✔ **Site R:** The military has its own underground emergency operations center near Camp David, in the Pennsylvania hills. While places like Greenbriar and Mount Weather concentrate on protecting government bureaucrats during a nuclear attack, Site R is the temporary home of the Joint Chiefs of Staff and all branches of the U.S. armed forces.

Critics of the plans saw a *Dr. Strangelove* aspect to the idea, concerned that unelected officials or the military, safe in their bomb shelters, would take over the government, and that little or no provision was being made to protect the general public. There was also a sentiment that military "hawks" wouldn't be deterred from launching nuclear attacks if they thought they would survive in a cozy, multi-million-dollar hole in the ground with all their comforts provided for.

Fears of FEMA

The Federal Emergency Management Administration (FEMA) may be well known for passing out hot coffee during national disasters, but its primary (and less publicly known) mission is to see to the "continuity of Government" in case of national emergencies. Since its beginnings, FEMA has had a frightening laundry list of police-state powers to do much more than just provide an underground home for Washington politicians when D.C. gets nuked. Executive Orders over the years have given the agency the authority to round up U.S. citizens and detain them without charges if they are deemed to present a danger to the nation's security. Rumors have abounded for years about secret FEMA "concentration camps" existing all across the country.

In 2003 after the 9/11 attacks, FEMA was folded into the newly created, ever-expanding mega-agency, the Department of Homeland Security, which is now the third largest U.S. government agency.

As the former Soviet bloc fell apart and the Berlin Wall got knocked down, conspiracists started looking for different, more sinister reasons for underground installations. These have included secret detention facilities for thousands of military or political prisoners, underground labs for studying the remnants of crashed UFOs or alien bodies, or hangars for building advanced weapons and aircraft. Many of these supposed bunker locations are figments of the imagination, but some aren't.

Denver International Airport: The New World Order's subterranean HQ

Anyone who has flown since the 9/11 attacks knows that airports are Beelzebub's satanic stockyards, where passengers are treated like cattle. Communities can spend all the millions of dollars they like in an effort to fill these massive spaces with soothing artwork and soaring terminal designs, packed with wall-to-wall retail shopping and fast-food Valhallas, but it doesn't matter. Air travel has been made miserable, and airports are places to be avoided.

But one airport in particular has attracted the attention of a wide range of conspiracists who see something sinister there, and it's even worse than TSA cavity searches over forbidden shampoo bottles, corkscrews, and nail clippers.

When Denver, Colorado, outgrew its old Stapleton Airport, the city and county government decided to think and build big. They went 25 miles out of town and built a facility that takes up twice the landmass of Manhattan. The airport was designed with the future in mind and is the largest airport in the U.S., the third largest in the world. As with any project of this size, there was much consideration given to the decoration and design of the terminal, and its unique roof line was made to represent the conical peaks of the Rocky Mountains.

But it was the artwork inside the airport that first attracted curious groups of the very, very nervous. And then more accusations started pouring in. Here are some of the peculiarities noted by researchers:

- **Evil words:** Some conspiracists have pointed to words cut into the floor as Satanic, Masonic, or just some impenetrable secret code of the New World Order: *Cochetopa, Sisnaajini,* and the baffling *Dzit Dit Gaii.* It turns out that these words are actually Navajo terms for geographical sites in Colorado. The other creepy terms often pointed to as evil references include *Braaksma* and *Villarreal,* which are actually the names of Carolyn Braaksma and Mark Villarreal, artists who worked on the airport's sculptures and paintings.

✔ **Creepy murals:** We don't know art, but we do know that a soldier wearing a gas mask, stabbing a dove with a scimitar, and waving a gun over a river filled with women carrying dead babies isn't really the sort of thing to uplift our spirits while dashing for a far gate on a short layover Other bizarre images include a scene with caskets featuring a dead Navajo woman, a dead Jewish woman, and a dead African-American woman. Artist Leo Tanguma wrote explanations of his personal, if odd, inspirations for the paintings, describing them as depicting scenes of violence and tragedy being overcome by peace and harmony.

✔ **Masons and the New World Order:** There is a dedication marker in the airport that's clearly inscribed with the square and compasses of the Freemasons, along with listing the involvement of the two Grand Lodges of Freemasonry in Colorado. All this is mounted over a time capsule sealed during the dedication of the airport. Some claim that this is a futuristic "keypad" with some unknown purpose. Spookier to them is the notation of an organization called the *New World Airport Commission*.

The New World Airport Commission, says Denver Airport officials, was a group of local businesses that organized the opening ceremonies of the facility, and they chose the name because Denver was aiming to create a "new, world-class" city and airport. The Freemasons participated in laying the "capstone" (the last, finishing stone) of the airport project. This is by no means unusual. Masons have been laying cornerstones, capstones, and memorial markers for public buildings for almost 300 years. On the other hand, we don't hear people grousing about the new wave of Feng Shui "space clearing" ceremonies popping up everywhere these days, consecrating everything from municipal buildings to nail salons.

✔ **Masonic Great Hall:** Another claim is that the large portion of the terminal is called the Great Hall and is named after a room found in Freemason lodges. There may be Masonic buildings in the world with assembly rooms or dining areas referred to as Great Halls (London's comes to mind), but it's by no means a common term in the overwhelming majority of Masonic buildings. It's frankly a more common term in castles, from Chinon to Disneyland.

✔ **Nazi runways:** Most modern airports wishing to utilize the most efficient runway designs are built these days with two parallel runways. Not so in Denver. Looked at from above, there's no denying that the runways radiate like twisted spokes from the terminal building, and they do seem to resemble a *swastika*. Conspiracists claim this is either a fascist message to secretly show off the totalitarian power of the New World Order, or that it's an occult depiction of the old Germanic rune for power.

✔ **Secret underground base:** This is the most common charge against the Denver Airport, that it is built over the top of a massive, secret, underground military base. The airport was budgeted to cost $1.7 billion, but came in closer to $5 billion when all the dust cleared. While it was built on a site chosen for its flat setting, millions of tons of earth were moved around the property, giving credence to the claim that something huge was being built underground.

Bear in mind that the airport was overdesigned to be flexible for decades, to be easily expandable, and to use the very latest in technology, which created a nightmare of technical glitches throughout the first years of operation. Miles of tunnels were dug for underground trains between terminals and for a troublesome subterranean baggage handling conveyor system that took years to get operating properly.

In addition, there are other tunnels for a huge fuel pipeline system to pump jet fuel to gates instead of relying on tanker trucks. Part of the justification for all this underground infrastructure is because Denver gets whacked with major snowfall for much of the winter, and the more that can be handled underground instead of dealing with snow, the more efficient it will be.

Conspiracists cry balderdash. They say there is a multilevel, subterranean base run by the New World Order, or the government, or both. Author Alex Christopher claimed to have worked in the tunnels under the airport, and described what appeared to be vast holding areas for prisoners, strange nausea-inducing electromagnetic forces, and caverns big enough to drive trucks through, presumably filled with helpless political prisoners.

Night of the Living Dead — A Conga Line of Corpses

Over the years, one of the regular types of articles in supermarket tabloids has been the dead celebrity rising from the grave to be spotted shopping in Wal-Mart or working in a gas station. Up until Oprah Winfrey's weight loss and gain and Paris Hilton's video debut changed the tabloids' editorial vision, the tale of the walking dead was the most popular story to tell. John F. Kennedy was supposed to be alive and well and living in Switzerland. Hitler was goose-stepping along the beach in Rio de Janeiro. And, of course, there was Elvis.

Elvis Presley still walks among us!

Throughout the 1950s and '60s, Elvis Presley was legitimately a superstar. His breakthrough combination of rockabilly, gospel, pop, rock-and-roll, and traditionally black rhythm and blues made him a universally beloved figure in the music business. But by the late 1970s, to many people, Elvis had become a parody of himself, and only the truly faithful fans still flocked to his concerts. When Elvis died in 1977 at the age of 42 of a heart attack brought on by obesity and drug use, one wag famously quipped, "Good career move."

However, claims that the King of Rock and Roll had cheated death began to appear almost before his alleged corpse was allegedly cold in its alleged grave. The most commonly cited evidence that he wasn't really dead was a discrepancy between the spelling of his middle name that appeared on his birth certificate, *Aron,* versus what appeared on his grave, *Aaron.* Believers say that Elvis's family knew that he really wasn't in the grave, so they spelled the name wrong on purpose. But there are many more reasons why true believers say the King is far from dead:

- ✔ There are inconsistencies between witnesses as to when Elvis's body was found, what he was wearing, and when his death was actually declared.

- ✔ Photos from 1977 of the corpse taken by Elvis's third cousin and sold to the *National Enquirer* don't seem to match up with last-known photos of Elvis when he was alive.

- ✔ The coffin weighed too much. The King was unquestionably of a portly circumference when he joined the Choir Invisible, but witnesses say the coffin tipped the scales at 900 pounds. Conspiracists say it was full of bricks.

- ✔ A strange, Elvis-looking man bought a ticket to Argentina and left Memphis the day before Elvis "died." Some say it was really the King getting out of town before the staged "death."

- ✔ Elvis's longtime creepy manager, Colonel Tom Parker, said at a press conference shortly after Elvis's demise, "Elvis didn't die. The body did. We're keeping up the good spirits. We're keeping Elvis alive. I talked to him this morning and he told me to carry on."

- ✔ And then it could've just been that he was sick of the adoration and his inability to walk down a public street without getting mobbed — the curse of superstardom.

Perhaps the most curious belief of all stems from a bizarre meeting that really happened between Elvis and then President Richard Nixon in December 1970. The King had written to Nixon offering his services in fighting drug use and "hippie elements" and was hoping to be made some sort of "Federal Agent at Large" in the Bureau of Narcotics and Dangerous Drugs. After having lunch in the White House Dining Room, Elvis was indeed presented with his badge. Surely a curious development for a man whose body would be found with at least 14 significantly dangerous drugs in his system.

Believers say Elvis was really working undercover for the Bureau (precursor to the Drug Enforcement Agency) on a supersecret case and was so recognizable that he was compelled to live out the rest of his days with a secret identity under the Witness Protection Program.

After several star-struck ghouls attempted to steal his body from its original public gravesite at Memphis's Forest Hills cemetery, Elvis's coffin and marker were dug up and replanted at his Memphis estate, Graceland. Meanwhile, the Elvis Sighting Society keeps track of reports of the King's postmortem activity: www.elvissightingsociety.org.

"Paul is dead"

One of the forces that knocked Elvis off his rock-and-roll throne was the arrival of the Beatles on the '60s music scene. And one of the strangest events surrounding the Beatles was the rumor in 1966 that band member Paul McCartney was dead. Not only dead, but replaced with a double. More amazing was that the band seemed to be putting clues in their music and album covers to leak the truth — although the Beatles always denied any part in promoting the rumor.

The most famous elements were contained on the *Abbey Road* album cover. The four Beatles are shown walking across the pedestrian "zebra crossing" on London's Abbey Road, but there are curious clues. McCartney is in a suit, barefoot and out of step with John Lennon (dressed as a priest), Ringo Starr (dressed as an undertaker), and George Harrison (dressed in work clothes, like a grave digger). A Volkswagen Beetle is parked on the road, with the license plate "LMW281F," implying McCartney would have been 28 "if" he had lived, while LMW supposedly stood for "Linda McCartney Weeps."

In 1969, a Detroit disc jockey named Russ Gibb received a phone call from a listener named Tom, who announced that McCartney was dead, and for clues, to play the Beatles song "Revolution #9" backwards. In reverse, the words that are repeated over and over, "number nine, number nine" sort of sound like "turn me on, dead man."

The rumors continued to spread from University of Michigan students and became a worldwide urban legend when a WABC disc jockey in New York rambled on about it on an overnight show that was heard over the clear channel AM station in two-thirds of the U.S. and halfway around the world. Afterwards, there wasn't a campus radio station in the country that wasn't running a weekend-long "Paul-a-thon," with listeners calling in their favorite clues as they poured over the albums and fan magazines until their eyes fogged over. Grade-point averages plummeted all over the U.S.

Conspiracists pieced together a hodgepodge of lyric lines from several albums to create the story. Supposedly, McCartney had a fight with the other members of the band during the recording of the *Sgt. Peppers Lonely Hearts Club Band* album and stormed out of the studio. He hopped into his Austin-Healey at about 5:00 a.m. on November 9, 1966, drove into the dark morning, crashed into a light pole, and was killed. Following the accident, a secret funeral was held, and the news was withheld from the public. A quiet search was quickly made for a McCartney look-alike/sound-alike — named Billy Shears — who finished the recording of *Sgt. Pepper*. It was Billy Shears who went on to record all subsequent Beatles albums and launch his own band, Wings.

Of course, all this started in the creative minds of a small group of college students who went cherry-picking through the lyrics of wildly different Beatles songs to invent the story. Unquestionably, the band was bewildered at first by the story, but John Lennon in particular seemed to enjoy playing along, while never exactly commenting on it openly.

The ageless everyman: Count de St. Germain

Just in case you think sightings of the "walking dead" are purely a modern phenomenon, consider this: In 1742, a curious man appeared in Europe. He claimed he had just arrived from Persia, and he seemed to be well acquainted with the customs of the East. He also claimed to be an alchemist, who'd learned the art of fusing jewels like diamonds to make larger stones. To all who met him, he looked to be in his 40s, and he was fluent in the major European languages, as well as Sanskrit, Latin, Arabic, and Chinese. He was a virtuoso violinist, a painter, and he seemed to possess incredible wealth, with no real source for his endless funds. He was known in social circles as the Count de Saint-Germain, and many believe that he discovered the secret elixir to eternal life.

Many sources claim that St. Germain was hundreds, if not thousands, of years old. Voltaire said he was "a man who never dies and who knows everything," and the legendary Casanova overheard the Count say that he was more than 300 years old. Variously, he's been identified as a high priest of Atlantis; the biblical character Samuel; the Greek philosopher Plato; Joseph, husband of Mary and father of Jesus; St. Alban, fourth-century English martyr; Merlin the Magician; Christen Rosenkreuz, legendary founder of Rosicrucianism; Christopher Columbus; and Francis Bacon.

During the Enlightenment period of the 18th and 19th centuries, he became a world-famous alchemist. Some have claimed that he was a secret advisor to Freemasons George Washington and Benjamin Franklin during the formative years of the founding of the United States, and it's been said that he tended to Franklin's painful gout while the aging diplomat was in Paris. Today, he's a regular figure in fantasy novels, frequently appearing as a vampire.

In the 1740s, St. Germain became a diplomat to France's King Louis XV. In the 1760s, he was in Russia as part of a plot to install Catherine the Great on the throne. And after warning France's Louis XVI and Marie Antoinette of the impending French Revolution nearly 15 years before it occurred, he managed to traipse in and out of Paris during the Terror in the 1790s without losing his head.

Some records claim that he died in Germany in 1784. Yet, France's Comtesse d'Adhémar saw him many times between 1789 and the 1820s, and he never looked older than his 40s. Madame Helena Petrovna Blavatsky claimed to know him in the 1870s, and French singer Emma Calve said she knew him as late as 1897.

A French magician named Richard Chanfray appeared in Paris in 1972, claiming to be the ageless Count, and briefly made a name for himself on television by transmuting lead into gold. Money troubles led him and his girlfriend to take massive amounts of drugs and lock themselves into a garage with their car running in 1983, so questions about this suicidal final appearance of the Count throw questions on his immortality.

As it turned out, it was bad timing to be claiming subliminal messages on their albums. The Charles Manson trial was going on in Los Angeles in 1970, and prosecutors claimed Manson had heard what he believed were hidden messages on the Beatles's *White* album to instigate the mass killings that he thought would set off "Helter Skelter," a race war between blacks and whites. But John in particular was determined not to let that take the fun out of it. So remember when looking into the dead man's tulips through a glass onion, that "here's another clue for you all, the Walrus was Paul."

Stifling Innovations that Threaten Corporate Profits

For years, many people have claimed that corporations regularly prevent public access to "free" technology in order to prevent their profits from dropping. A favorite conspiracy theory is that the major automakers have long suppressed a wave of new engine technologies that would let everyone drive water-powered cars. Ditto with the electric car, the hydrogen car, the salad oil car, and the solar car. Unfortunately, there's no need for a conspiracy in these cases. The real culprit is economics, public demand, and really jittery stockholders.

Fair or not, corporations, far more than government, are a favorite paranoia magnet for conspiracists. In prime time TV, the most common character to turn out to be a murderer isn't a drug dealer or a thug, but a businessman.

Subliminal advertising

When 1979's horror classic *The Exorcist* premiered in theaters, news articles reported people running screaming from their seats, vomiting uncontrollably, and other seemingly out of proportion reactions. While the movie was scary and had its gross moments, it didn't seem horrible enough to cause these strange reactions in audiences.

Slowly, reports emerged that *The Exorcist*'s filmmakers had done something manipulatively sneaky. They'd added single frames, seen onscreen for just 1/48th of a second, of horrific demon faces, cut at random into the scariest scenes. Almost completely imperceptible to the eye, subconsciously it supposedly had the effect of making the scenes unbearable. At least, that was the hype.

The Exorcist hadn't done anything new. In the 1950s it was claimed that certain enterprising theater owners were using a device known as a *tachistoscope*, a machine that flashed words or images onto a screen for mere fractions of a second, with helpful messages like "Buy a Coke!" or "Hungry? Buy popcorn!"

Researcher James Vicary became famous for a 1957 study that supposedly induced audiences to run to the snack bar and buy popcorn, drinks, or candy, increasing sales by more than 50 percent. Vicary's study was hyped in a 1957 bestseller, Vance Packard's *The Hidden Persuaders,* a book that told lurid tales of psychological manipulation by advertisers, and even politicians, based on subliminal messages.

While the book sold millions, perplexed researchers were unable to replicate its claims, and Vicary's theater study actually turned out to be a hoax and publicity stunt. Nevertheless, the notion of subliminal suggestion in advertising became a popularly accepted urban legend.

It resurfaced in the 1970s with the publication of Wilson Bryan Key's equally disputed *Subliminal Seduction,* which actually led to a somewhat hysterical Federal Communications Commission (FCC) hearing over the topic. The FCC decided that subliminal advertising was deceptive, contrary to the public interest, and was banned on television. Not that many people were actually doing it anyway.

Sex sells, apparently

Print ads were another matter. Especially between the 1960s and 1980s, ads that featured tendrils of cigarette smoke, liquor pouring over ice cubes, swirling hairstyles, and even puffy white clouds in a blue sky were frequently airbrushed to include suggestive images or words.

"Sex" was a favorite, and seemed to appear everywhere:

- Pepsi Cola was compelled to stop production of a '70s pop art can that clearly said "sex" on the label.

- Shadowy outlines of genitalia and various sexual positions would show up in the most innocuous ads, as a subliminal way to make you look at them.

- An early '80s Christian Dior ad featured a cartoon representation of a woman in a multicolored coat, and almost every thread of it spelled out words that would make your cousin in the Navy blush.

- A Coca-Cola ad featuring a sweaty bottle of the soft drink was headlined "Feel The Curves," and buried in the ice cubes below it was a blatant drawing of what one might genteelly refer to as similar to Monica Lewinsky's most infamous contribution to Bill Clinton's presidency.

Backmasking

The other famous application of subliminal encoding of messages was first made famous when the Beatle's placed reversed recordings within songs on their 1966 *Revolver* album. John Lennon claimed he got the inspiration while smoking marijuana, and their experiments with the effect contain pretty harmless, not to mention mellow, references. However, other groups climbed on the bandwagon and used the effect.

The technique became popular enough that by the 1970s, alarmed evangelical Christian groups began protesting that bands were hiding Satanic messages in their music. The claims were often little more than an audio Rorschach test (you know, those ink blots that look like all sorts of things), and perfectly normal lines of lyrics were imagined to be something quite horrible in reverse.

One notorious rumor was that even the theme song to the talking horse comedy *Mister Ed* when played backwards said, "I am Satan," although efforts to actually hear the message required much imagination.

The hysteria became so bad that in 1974, Congressional hearings were held, and warning labels on albums were proposed. The publicity had the opposite effect that the critics were seeking because more and more bands began inserting silly, insulting, or blatantly provocative "satanic" messages into songs, all in reverse. For example, Pink Floyd notoriously included a backwards message in the group's 1979 song "Empty Spaces" that said "Congratulations. You've just discovered the secret message. Please send your answer to Old Pink, care of the funny farm, Chalfont."

Laws recommended by Congress were never passed, and the switch from vinyl albums that could be easily spun backwards to CDs that couldn't seemed to kill off the mania. The messages have been rediscovered in recent years because computers can play back music tracks in reverse with the click of a mouse. But the terror over subliminal messages seems to have died off. In retrospect, compared to the straightforward lyrics of Ice-T's "Cop Killer" or Cannibal Corpse's "Meat Hook Sodomy," it all seems so trivial.

The ten-wiener, eight-bun conspiracy

Here we cover the most devious corporate conspiracy and the question that has confounded mankind for a century. Why do hot dogs come in packages of ten, but hot dog buns in packages of eight? If you believe in no other conspiracy in this chapter, believe this one.

The meat-packing business has been pricing its products by the pound since the days of Ancient Rome, so it makes sense that the average package of hot dogs weighs one pound. At the generally accepted wiener length of 6 inches with a 1-inch circumference, that works out to ten dogs in a one-pound pack. That is, of course, ignoring foot-longs, jumbos, and other recent innovations that muddy the computations and needlessly detract from the seriousness of this issue.

Bakers, on the other hand, are less transparent in their thinking. Some have proposed that bakers' fondness for dozens, or numbers more easily divided by four, make packs of eight buns because of the mathematical functions of the power of four. Others say it is because an eight-pack of buns fits more comfortably on a grocery shelf than ten. Whatever the justifications may be, we cry foul and see a clear conspiracy at work.

If you're the sort of consumer that abhors waste, or you have obsessive/compulsive disorder, there's just no getting around the fact that you'll have to buy four packs of hot dogs and five packages of buns before you have an equal matchup of 40 of each. It's a big conspiracy. Everybody knows about it.

Chapter 5

JFK and Other Presidents: The Conspiracies Behind the Guns

In This Chapter

▷ Investigating the queen mother of assassination conspiracies

▷ Swimming in the Bay of Pigs

▷ Getting the lowdown on plots against presidents

*O*n November 22, 1963, America's young and handsome 35th president, John F. Kennedy, was assassinated, riding in an open limousine in Dallas, Texas. Another passenger, Texas governor John Connally, was injured in the shooting. Americans were shocked and grief-stricken over the brutal and senseless murder of a beloved president who embodied the youthful optimism of the 1960s.

These bare facts of the case are the only ones not debated by conspiracists concerning the death of JFK. Recently, the accusations against the Bush administration of being behind the 9/11 attacks have, for the first time in over four decades, pushed the Kennedy assassination off its pedestal as the most talked-about and debated event in the last hundred years. Whether the 9/11 conspiracies remain at the forefront of the conspiracists' world view is some-thing only time will tell.

But for the time being, the handful of books that have been written about 9/11 can't hope to compete with the over *2,000* books that have been written about the Kennedy assassination, most from a conspiracy point of view. Countless documentaries have featured it, and countless films have used the assassination as a shorthand symbol for the murder of innocence by corrup-tion. To be a true Kennedy assassinologist, you'd have to give up your day job.

In fact, for baby boomers, those people born roughly from the end of World War II in 1945 until the heyday of suburban America in the 1950s, the Kennedy assassination is more than just another historical event — it's the ultimate symbol of the smashing of their utopian dreams by The Establishment. And the conspiracist writers and filmmakers of the baby boom have crafted a truth that is not to be questioned — that JFK was the victim of a massive conspiracy to be rid of a president boomers think of as representing their generation.

But was John Kennedy in truth the victim of a dark and complex conspiracy? And another question, just as important: Were all the other American presidents who've been assassinated really the victims of a straightforward "lone nut gunman" in the way that history tells us? Both these questions are explored in this chapter, which covers the conspiracies surrounding the death of JFK, and the equally suspicious but not so well-known conspiracies behind the murders of other American presidents.

JFK: The Very Model of a Modern Major Conspiracy Theory

The assassination of John Fitzgerald Kennedy has become the classic "event conspiracy," dosed with superatomized growth hormone, creating a many-tentacled, 40-foot monster. Most people know the bare facts of what happened that day; the images are woven into the very fabric of our culture. But in case your knees don't creak and you still have all your own teeth, here's a brief outline of the facts. Skip over it if you know it all, and meet us at "Taking style over substance."

Just the facts, please

President John F. Kennedy arrived at Love Field in Dallas around 11:40 on the morning of November 22, 1963. He was making a goodwill tour, preparing for the next election, and trying to shore up support amongst some renegade Texas Democrats. He was scheduled to give a speech at the Dallas Trade Mart. The route of the presidential motorcade had been published in the newspapers.

At about a minute before 12:30, as the open limo cruised down Elm Street, shots rang out from the eight-story Texas School Book Depository as the motorcade passed. Eight stories was the limit on building height in Dealey Plaza, and the Depository was the highest building in the area. Chaos and screaming erupted.

Three shots were fired. The first was the one that probably missed, causing a shard of concrete to cut the face of bystander James Tague; the second passed through the president's back, out of his neck, and into Texas governor John Connally; and the third struck the president in the back of the head, exiting on the right side, horrifically blowing out blood and tissue in a cloudy red mist as it did so, all of which is captured on a famous 8mm home movie shot by Abraham Zapruder. The motorcade rushed to nearby Parkland Memorial Hospital, but it was, for Kennedy, hopeless. Governor Connally survived, but the president was pronounced dead at 1:00 p.m.

Vice President Lyndon Johnson, who'd been farther back in the motorcade, was rushed aboard Air Force One and flown to Washington, D.C. In the wake of the Cuban Missile Crisis, there was fear in Washington that this was only the first blow in a Russian attack. Responding to this aura of national emergency, Johnson was sworn in as the new president almost at once, while the plane carrying him, as well as Kennedy's body and his widow, was safely in the air.

Lee Harvey Oswald

Many witnesses who heard the shots claimed having seen the shooter through the sixth-floor window of the Book Depository. Cops arrived at once. The supervisor said that only one employee was missing, a man named Lee Harvey Oswald. Soon afterwards the rifle used in the shooting was found carelessly hidden behind some book boxes that had been set up into a sniper's nest. An APB went out at 12:45 for a slender white male seen leaving before the area was cordoned off.

At about 1:15, a Dallas police officer named J. D. Tippit spotted Oswald and stopped to question him, as he fit the description. Emerging from his car, he was shot by Oswald with a .38 pistol. Oswald hit him three times in the chest, then purposely walked toward him to fire a final shot into the downed officer's head. Twelve people witnessed the shooting, so Oswald would not be free for long. He ran from the scene, ducking into the nearby Texas Theatre cinema without paying; the ticket clerk phoned the police. He was arrested at the theatre for the Tippit murder by a large number of cops, one of whom he attempted to shoot.

Police didn't realize at first that this was the same man who'd shot the president. Oswald was taken into custody on suspicion of having shot Tippit; later that night he was questioned about the assassination. Over the course of two days he denied everything, including eyewitness reports that had seen him with a rifle-sized package that morning at work, a package that he claimed contained curtain rods.

Once Oswald's identity was established (he'd had two different sets of ID on him with different names), his story began to emerge. Lee Harvey Oswald was a loner, a loser, an ex-Marine, and a passionate Marxist who'd lived in Russia for three years and had a Russian wife. He'd garnered a little newsprint for that, and for his work for a pro-Castro organization called the Fair Play for Cuba Committee. After his arrest, he was arrogant and cold as ice. Oswald liked big, important-sounding words. But when he was paraded in front of the press, his Gomer Pyle accent and his lack of a formal education (he never got past the eighth grade) gave a "jailhouse lawyer" tone to his bland protests that he hadn't done anything except suffer police brutality.

Why didn't anyone believe the Warren Report?

A fair question — why didn't anyone believe the Warren Report? The answer's pretty simple — virtually nobody actually *read* the Warren Report. Or very few did, anyway. But lots of people read the ever-increasing number of conspiracist books that said the report was garbage, and if you say something's garbage often enough, people begin to believe it.

The Warren Commission that delivered the report was made up of squeaky-clean and powerful men, and was named for its head, Supreme Court Chief Justice Earl Warren. It was commissioned by President Johnson with the best intentions. Many people, including Johnson, felt there was a probable conspiracy behind the shooting, and it might lay at the doorstep of the KGB, Russia's far-more-powerful-than-ours version of the CIA. But Johnson played politics, wanting it done in ten months, before the next election. That disappointed a lot of people, who felt that the admirably bipartisan committee should be above such things as elections. If they're not, why have a bipartisan committee? On the other hand, ten months is a long time for hundreds of people to work on an investigation; it seems absurd when its critics say it was slapped together.

The Warren Report is extremely valuable because it's contemporary to the events. In other words, it says in black and blue exactly what the witnesses said after the shooting, rather than what the witnesses were saying 20 years later. That's important, because as conspiracism took the assassination for its own, there were absolutely tectonic shifts in the stories of many witnesses. The more attention they got, the more colorful their story became.

In the end, the report is nearly 900 pages long, with many other volumes relating to evidence — 26 volumes in all. But it's an excellent piece of police work, with examinations of over 3,000 pieces of evidence, and over 25,000 interviews. In the end, you should read The Warren Report before passing judgment on it. Okay, it's not exactly a Tom Clancy novel. It reads like what it is, a police report, one with elephantitis. But it shouldn't be dismissed out of hand, especially since the major government investigations since have never disproved the basic facts of the report.

Two days after the shooting, on national television, the assassin was assassinated. Oswald was handcuffed to an officer, Detective Jim Leavelle, to be moved to the Dallas county lockup, when Jack Ruby, a strip club owner who regularly hung out with the cops at the station, stepped forward and fired once; he was taken down to the ground before he could fire again. It was the first murder ever seen live on national television. Oswald died at Parkland Hospital a little after 1:00 p.m.

Examining the conspiracy background

Almost immediately, public opinion was fixed that there had been some kind of conspiracy surrounding the shooting. The assassin had been "silenced" before he could talk, and Jack Ruby *must* have had a secret motive. To understand, in the perspective of time and place, what that motive might have been, it's necessary to look at the backdrop of the various conspiracies.

Lots of important things happened during the three years of JFK's presidency; this wasn't a boring administration, like say, the Calvin Coolidge years. The president had appointed his brother Robert as attorney general, and together they'd gone after the Mafia and organized crime. But of all the national and world events, the overthrow of the government of Cuba, an American protectorate, by a Marxist revolutionary named Fidel Castro in 1959 would define the Kennedy years. Two key events may well have led to JFK's assassination:

⮡ **The Bay of Pigs,** the name for a failed attempt on the part of the CIA and anti-Castro Cubans, in April of 1961, to lead a small invasion force into Cuba and free it from Castro's iron rule. John Kennedy, newly elected, had promised to follow through on what had been a plan of President Eisenhower's, and give the Cuban rebels the air and naval support they needed. But unwisely, at the last minute, Kennedy chose not to, fearful of what the international community would say. Without the air support they'd expected, the Cubans were left to die on the beach or be captured and dumped into Castro's prisons. After years of conspiracist accusations, the CIA has recently admitted that they drafted the Mafia into helping with the invasion, since the mob had contacts on the ground and a vested interest in getting the gambling casinos back that Castro had confiscated (sorry — *stolen*). Kennedy's desertion of the small Cuban force made him many bitter enemies in the CIA as well as in the Mafia. Kennedy also made enemies when he had the FBI come down hard on paramilitary groups of anti-Castro Cubans in America who were running weapons to the island.

⮡ **The Cuban Missile Crisis**, the name for a terrifying two weeks at the end of October 1962. There were several close calls during the Cold War, but this was the nearest the world ever came to all-out nuclear war. Ever since the Russians had gotten the nuclear bomb, a Cold War had raged between America and the Soviets. There may not have been shots fired, but fingers were on the triggers. On October 14, a U-2 reconnaissance plane, flying at 7 miles above Cuba, got photographs of nuclear ballistic missiles on launch sites being built by the Russians, Castro's allies. They were pointed at the U.S. – 36 missiles, with 250 times the power of the Hiroshima bomb, now 80 miles off our coast, with all the cities of America's eastern seaboard, including Washington, less than ten minutes from potential annihilation. It was an intolerable situation, and on the night of October 22, President Kennedy addressed a frightened public to say that Cuba was to be ringed in by a tight naval blockade. It was a game of nuclear chicken, and finally, on October 28, Nikita Khrushchev, Stalin's successor, capitulated, getting a secret promise in return from Bobby Kennedy that our missiles near the Soviet Union in Turkey would be dismantled, helping Khrushchev to save face in Russia.

These two events would form the backdrop, along with the growing war against the communists in Vietnam, for decades of Kennedy assassination conspiracies.

Taking style over substance

The speculative books written about the Kennedy assassination are the absolute ultimate in conspiracist literature. Three thousand years ago, Greek playwrights loved to do plays about tragedy growing out of revenge. The Greeks were very big on revenge. But in the killing of John Kennedy, there was enough potential revenge for a hundred Greek tragedies.

In the end, out of the darkness of chaos, comes . . . more chaos. So, to save you having to read a couple thousand of these tomes, here is a brief list, by no means complete, of the most common conspiracy theories out there:

- ✔ **There was more than one assassin.** Oswald did not shoot alone; there was another, or several other, shooters. More than one means a conspiracy.

- ✔ **Oswald was not really Oswald.** He was framed. A political assassin simply "borrowed" Oswald's identity, perhaps before his return to the U.S. from Russia, and left clues that led to the real Oswald. When Oswald was arrested, he had no idea why.

- ✔ **Lyndon Johnson wanted Kennedy dead so he could be president.** Johnson was in danger of Kennedy dropping him as his vice-presidential running mate in the 1964 election. And the murder happened in Johnson's home state of Texas, which spiced the conspiracist stew.

- ✔ **The Military Industrial Complex wanted Kennedy dead so they could escalate the Vietnam War.** And presumably make millions of dollars.

- ✔ **The CIA wanted Kennedy dead out of revenge.** Cheeks still red over the Bay of Pigs, they wanted payback.

- ✔ **The Communist Cubans wanted Kennedy dead out of revenge.** The U.S. had tried to invade Cuba, and the CIA had tried to kill Castro. It seems logical they might have wanted Kennedy dead before he could pull anything else on them.

- ✔ **The anti-Communist Cubans in exile in America wanted Kennedy dead out of revenge.** If he had properly backed the Bay of Pigs operation, they would have gotten their homeland back. Also, Kennedy was cracking down on freelance paramilitary operations of the anti-Castro set. This really burned them up, after his "betrayal" at the Bay of Pigs.

- ✔ **The Russians wanted Kennedy dead out of revenge.** Kennedy had won the nuclear standoff with Kruschev and humiliated the Soviet Union.

- ✔ **The Mafia wanted Kennedy dead out of revenge. So did the labor unions.** JFK's brother, Attorney General Robert F. Kennedy, had spent two years going after the Mafia bosses and organized crime, along with their links to powerful labor leaders like Jimmy Hoffa. Killing Kennedy would get both men off their collective backs.

✔ **Sam Giancana wanted Kennedy dead out of revenge.** Giancana, the heir of Al Capone and head of the Chicago Mafia, otherwise known as "the Outfit," said that Joe Kennedy, JFK's father, who had Mafia contacts from his prohibition days as a rum-runner, drafted him into helping get his son elected. And, when Giancana was called before the Kennedys' congressional committee on organized crime, he felt personally betrayed.

✔ **Richard Nixon wanted Kennedy dead out of revenge.** JFK and Nixon had run against each other in the 1960 presidential election. Nixon lost by the tiniest margin in history at the time, and he believed what lots of historians believe, that he only lost because Kennedy looked better than he did on TV. In fact, Nixon had been in Dallas the morning of the shooting, attending a Pepsi Cola board of directors' meeting with actress Joan Crawford (who was a member of the board).

✔ **The Jews did it out of revenge.** Always a favorite. Kennedy opposed Israeli nuclear programs, and was using former Nazi rocket scientist Werner Von Braun as part of the NASA space program, which enraged Jews. "Jewish bankers" were also upset because of Kennedy's tinkering with the Federal Reserve. Oswald assassin Jack Ruby's real name was Rubenstein, which was proof enough of a Jewish conspiracy for groups like the racist John Birch Society.

In the months after Kennedy's death, roughly two-thirds of the American public believed it had all been part of a conspiracy. Now, decades later, more Americans believe this than ever before. In fact, as Gerald Posner points out in the preface to his book *Case Closed* (1994, Anchor), the conclusion that both Oswald and Ruby were glory-seeking nut cases who acted on their own has become far more controversial than anything in the 2,000 books on Kennedy conspiracies.

Considering the source

There's no question that the most influential of all conspiracism related to the Kennedy shooting came late to the party — Oliver Stone's Oscar-winning 1991 film *JFK*. The most remarkable thing about this murky melodrama is that it manages to incorporate all the above theories, and even more, in a confusing melding of fiction and fact served up with an aura of documentary truth. It was based on two books: *On the Trail of the Assassins,* the memoirs of New Orleans district attorney Jim Garrison, and *Crossfire: The Plot That Killed Kennedy,* by assassinologist Jim Marrs. No book that did not take a conspiracist viewpoint was given credit.

If we took the time to tear apart every deception, fib, whopper, misrepresentation, obfuscation, misdirection, or artful piece of propaganda, we'd all be here until Oprah gets cancelled. But we would like to address some of the real humdingers, because so much of what is in the film has become "common knowledge" and is taken as fact — when it is anything but factual.

Director Oliver Stone chose to build his story around the disastrous prosecution of businessman Clay Shaw in New Orleans in 1967 by "crusading" district attorney Jim Garrison, on the charge of conspiring to assassinate President Kennedy. This all happened in New Orleans, the Big Easy. But even in a city that prides itself on colorful and shady public figures, District Attorney Jim Garrison was over the top. Considering the flimsy evidence, the whole thing played more like the Salem witch trials. It bankrupted Shaw and blackened his name forever. Yet Garrison failed, big time, to get a conviction. (The jury was out for less than an hour — one juror said they could have gotten back faster, but several had to go to the bathroom.)

The pansy plot

The most distasteful aspect of Garrison's prosecution had to do with his feelings about gay men. Homosexual panic, perhaps, since several people in New Orleans, and even columnist Jack Anderson, spoke of Garrison's secretive passes at young boys. After his arrest of Clay Shaw, Garrison told newspaperman Jim Phelan of *The Saturday Evening Post* that, since David Ferrie was gay, and so was Clay Shaw, it was obvious they knew one another. (Don't all gay men know one another?) He said it was obvious as well that both Ruby and Oswald were gay. Then Garrison made the incredible statement that the murder of Kennedy was a gay thrill-killing, like the infamous Leopold and Loeb case. It was only later, when he discovered that calling them "fascists" played better in the press, that Garrison accused the men of being part of a CIA/military industrial complex-conspiracy instead. However, he had no evidence against Clay Shaw either way; he once told Jim Phelan that Shaw wasn't the first man he'd arrested, and *then* built the case. Really scary.

As the investigation progressed over the course of two years, Garrison suspected just about everybody, and came to believe that his own gut instincts were all the evidence he needed. Even before he had Clay Shaw arrested, Garrison claimed that he had solved the case. He then spent two years promising a trial that would shake America to its foundations. In the end, the trial was a rather embarrassing flop.

None of Garrison's stirring speeches as delivered up by Kevin Costner in the movie-land courtroom are real; they were scripted by the screenwriters.

The film *JFK* accomplishes one thing beautifully; it efficiently piles just about every major conspiracy theory about the Kennedy assassination into one easy-open package, which makes our job of analyzing those theories a whole lot easier. So here, in no particular order, are some of the worst of the delusional piffle in *JFK:*

✔ **New Orleans district attorney Jim Garrison was a hero for getting to the bottom of the real conspiracy.** Jim Garrison was many things, but a hero wasn't one of them. Yet, in the film *JFK,* the carefully crafted image of Garrison, as played by Kevin Costner, is the all-American "aw, shucks, ma'am" innocent, crusading against evil, beloved by his staff, shy with reporters, disdainful of fame, fixed only on the ideal of justice. The real Jim Garrison, according to many who knew him, was a hellion with his staff, a paranoid, an opportunist who *loved* publicity, and a man obsessed with the Kennedy assassination to the point of mania. Not content with the dull and ordinary "second shooter on the grassy knoll" conspiracy theory, he finished by claiming at least 16 gunmen in Dealey Plaza, which would have looked more like D-Day than an assassination.

✔ **There is overwhelming evidence that three men in New Orleans were part of a right-wing CIA plot to oust Fidel Castro and were behind the assassination of President Kennedy.** There is no evidence whatsoever to back up this assertion. The three men, David Ferrie, Guy Banister, and Clay Shaw, were never proven to have CIA ties, or to have known Oswald. None of these three men were *anything* like they're portrayed in the film. The shocking truth is that Garrison's entire case rested on a couple of half-baked witnesses who claimed to have seen the men partying together with Lee Harvey Oswald, and to have overheard them discussing the assassination of Kennedy.

✔ **New Orleans businessman Clay Shaw was the mastermind of the whole Kennedy plot.** Clay Shaw was in fact a highly decorated World War II veteran, the founder of the International Trade Mart for the Port of New Orleans that brought the city a business renaissance, and the force behind the historical renovation of the French Quarter. The fact that he did some intelligence work for the OSS (the precursor to the CIA) during the war in the 1940s hardly proves that he was some sinister spy for rogue elements of the CIA.

✔ **David Ferris, one of Garrison's "witnesses," is portrayed as having been murdered.** He died a natural death of a brain aneurysm, which was proved again with a new autopsy in 1992. His aneurysm could not have been in any way induced by murderers. Nor did he commit suicide. However, he had been in poor health, and more than one of his friends felt that the stress of Garrison's persecution of him contributed to his death.

✔ **Oswald never owned the rifle; it was mail-ordered by the people who set him up.** As proof, a famous photo of Oswald holding the rifle with which he killed the president was claimed in *JFK* to have been a phony. Not true. The photograph is genuine. Dozens of scientists with no political axe to grind have proven the photo genuine. Oswald's wife Marina also testified to having taken it. Oswald used the same post office box to order the .38 caliber revolver that was used to kill Dallas police officer J. D. Tippit.

✔ **Oswald was a far right-winger.** Stone makes every attempt to pry Oswald away from the Left Wing, which Mr. Stone admires, and glue him to the right wing, which he despises (as if there's any difference). But Oswald's Communism was very real; there's no evidence at all that it was a front for right-wing beliefs. He'd been a Marxist since the age of 15. He loved the way telling people shocked them, in those Cold War anti-communist days. Also, at 15, Oswald was sent to a shrink, Dr. Hartogs, who noted at the time that Oswald was cold, arrogant, and incapable of getting along with others, a deeply disturbed boy with a "vivid fantasy life" that could easily erupt into violence.

✔ **Oswald's defection to Russia for three years was only a ruse — he was sent there as a CIA operative.** This sounds logical, but there's no evidence whatsoever to support it. It's a complete lie to state that the Marines taught Oswald Russian — Oswald taught himself Russian, and not very fluent Russian, either. As he grew more unhappy in the Marines, unable to stand the discipline (Oswald always had problems with authority), he told all his Marine buddies of the glories of Russia, and how he was going there someday. They all thought he was nuts, but, once again, Oswald enjoyed the attention it got him. The Marines didn't love him any more than his mother had — he was court-martialed twice.

✔ **Oswald was allowed back into the country quickly and easily because he was working for U.S. intelligence.** It wasn't quick or easy for Oswald to come back after defecting to Russia. But the fact is, he had never given up his American citizenship; the American consulate wouldn't let him, feeling he was too young and dumb to make such a decision. Oswald, disenchanted with life in Russia, was grateful. This meant it only took him a year to get back, about average for the few cases there were like his.

✔ **Oswald wasn't violent, and had nothing whatsoever to do with shooting Kennedy, but was an innocent patsy, pure as the driven snow.** Stone completely omits any mention of the fact that Oswald had already attempted one assassination, that being the shooting of the rabidly right-wing major general Edwin Walker. Hardly the actions of an innocent patsy. Walker was shot at through his dining room window by Oswald while working at his desk; he miraculously survived when the bullet missed the target of his head because it glanced over the edge of the window frame.

✔ **On the day of the assassination, a man fell down in Dealey Plaza with a phony epileptic seizure, in order to act as a diversion for the police, then disappeared.** The man who had the seizure was named Jerry Belknap, an epileptic since childhood. He was taken to Parkland by ambulance, but was never admitted because, like most epileptics, he felt weak but better after the seizure, and saw no reason to be admitted over a routine for epileptics.

- ✔ **To believe in a lone gunman means the "magic bullet" that hit Kennedy and Connally did impossible acrobatics.** In the film, during the trial of businessman Clay Shaw, Costner/Garrison's speech about the "magic bullet" uses two men as models for Kennedy and Connally during the shooting. But the two are seated at the same level, with the model for Connally directly in front of the president. Actually, Connally was seated on a jump seat, farther inboard, lower down, his body turned far to the right to look over his shoulder as he reacted to the sound of the first shot (which can all be seen in the Zapruder film). Bullets have a tendency to ricochet, skim, and go where they will. But when the two men are shown seated as they really were, there's nothing at all unusual about the trajectory of the "magic" bullet — it went straight through them both.

- ✔ **"Back, and to the left. Back, and to the left."** Garrison/Costner makes much of this general direction of the president's body after he was shot, repeating it over and over to prove the shot came from ground level to the president's right, on the so-called "grassy knoll." If the Zapruder film is slowed way down, there *is* a short and violent lurch forward of the president's head, before it falls backwards. Real bodies react violently to being shot, and the Zapruder film shows the body of the president reacting as if to an electric shock, in a contortion that's called a "neuromuscular spasm." The president then slowly falls over into his wife's arms. Also, Kennedy had long suffered terrible back pain, and he was wearing a stiff back brace, which probably helped to keep his spine erect, explaining the strange way he fell over but didn't seem to slump.

- ✔ **"The guy couldn't do the shooting. Nobody could."** Not true. Oswald's view from the sixth-floor window was not "through heavy foliage." For about two seconds, while Oswald reloaded, the limo drove under the tree outside the Depository window. Oswald had probably already taken one shot, and when the car reappeared, he took two more. The Mannlicher-Carcano rifle (really just a "Carcano") Oswald used was not "the world's worst shoulder weapon." On the contrary, the Italian Carcano is similar in design to the efficient German Mauser bolt-action rifle. The sight on the rifle was not broken, as Stone claims. It had a bad scrape on the side, and a slight mis-alignment that could have happened when it was dropped by Oswald behind some other boxes, or while it was in custody. It's doubtful this would have ruined Oswald's shot, assuming that he used the sight at all. Ballistics tests of the rifle showed it to be in perfectly good working order, and an accurate weapon.

- ✔ **The president was really caught in crossfire from three different directions, which Stone calls "a turkey shoot."** If that were true, then the president's car would have resembled the Ford in the finale of *Bonnie and Clyde*. But it doesn't. There is no evidence that more than three bullets were fired, or that the fire came from more than one direction.

✔ **The parade route was changed at the last minute in order to make it easier for the assassins to do their evil deed.** There was no last minute route change. Period. The map Jim Garrison cites as "proof" from the front page of the *Dallas Morning News* is simply too lacking in detail to show tiny Elm Street. It follows the route all the way from Love Field. But in both the *Dallas Morning News* and the *Dallas Times Herald,* the route that was laid out in the fine print, street by street, is the one JFK's motorcade took.

✔ **The bullet found on the stretcher of Governor Connally at Parkland Hospital was "pristine."** Not true. It was battered and flattened at the nose, just as one would expect for the journey it had taken through two men. The bullet was also a ballistic match for a test bullet fired from Oswald's rifle. In the film, Jack Ruby is shown planting this "pristine" bullet on the governor's stretcher in order to frame Oswald. But fragments from the bullet were found in the governor's wrist. How did Ruby manage to plant those?

✔ **President Kennedy's brain disappeared after a sneaky and under- handed autopsy.** No. Two technicians at Bethesda Naval Hospital, where, at Mrs. Kennedy's request, the autopsy was performed, alleged that the president's body had no brain when it arrived there from Dallas. Ghoulish nonsense. They made this claim many years later, but neither of them was part of the team that removed the body from its casket. The doctors on that team have stated categorically that the president's brain was where it belonged when his body arrived in Washington. However, it's true that the president's body was buried while autopsy doctors still had his brain and some other tissue samples. It was given over to Admiral Burkley, Kennedy's personal physician, preserved in formaldehyde. The family wanted it to be buried with the body, and Bobby Kennedy's biggest concern was that it would never be displayed publicly. When JFK was re- interred in 1967 in a new memorial at Arlington cemetery, the president's brothers quietly had the brain put back with the body.

✔ **Oswald was not only innocent, but he tried to warn the FBI about the assassination!** Unbelievable hogwash. He hand-delivered a note to an FBI agent who'd questioned his wife Marina about his trip to Mexico, when he tried to get a visa to go to Cuba. He said he wanted to fight for Castro. The note said to leave his wife alone and talk to him if they wanted to know anything. It takes a vivid imagination to turn this inci- dent into a warning from Oswald that JFK was about to be killed. There is no shred of evidence to support it.

✔ **Oswald was a lousy shot.** This is the most brazen lie of all. Oswald was an excellent shot. He killed the president from about 89 yards. His Marine firing range scores, which are still on file, show him getting 48 and 49 of a possible 50 in a rapid-fire test range where the target was at *200 yards,* over twice as far away. These results were with an M-1 that didn't even have a telescopic sight. The film says Oswald had less than six seconds to fire the three "impossible" shots. It also states that FBI sharpshooters could not re-create his shots. This simply isn't true. And if you'd like something more public than the FBI, look for a CBS documentary from 1975 in which 11 volunteer marksmen made the shots in times ranging from 4.1 to 6 seconds, all without even practicing with the Carcano. Also, a closer examination of the Zapruder film with modern computer technology reveals that the first shot was probably fired at frame 162, the last at frame number 313, leaving a generous total of over eight seconds, plenty of time to do the job. On film for the documentary "Beyond Conspiracy," historian John Lattimer pulled the shots easily at less than 8 seconds. He was 82 years old at the time.

Oliver Stone, we suppose, had no more obligation to put exact history on film than Cecil B. DeMille did back in the 1930s. But everyone knew DeMille was making escapist fun. In *JFK,* the conspiracist view of history is presented as irrefutable fact, no matter what movie magic Stone whips up to present it. For example, when Stone couldn't get any gun he could find to create the "large puff of smoke from a gun" that his favored witnesses claimed to have seen coming from the grassy knoll, he had a special effects guy create the smoke with a bellows. 'Nuff said.

If you want some more on the film *JFK,* but don't want to take the time to read one of the major heavyweight tomes out there, check out `www.jfk-online.com/jfk100menu.html`. The site was put together by historian and researcher David Reitzes, and is an exhaustive collection of every conceivable assassination fact and allegation.

ABC proves the single-bullet theory

Oliver Stone claimed in more than one interview that there was nobility in his distortion of fact in *JFK,* for if it opened public debate, it was a good thing. Yet, Mr. Stone wasn't too happy with the reaction of one viewer who wanted to reopen the debate; namely, newsman Peter Jennings. Disturbed by the distortions of fact in Stone's film, Jennings and the ABC team put together a powerful two-hour documentary entitled "Beyond Conspiracy" that would win the prestigious Edward R. Murrow Award for best documentary. It also put a sharp burr under the saddle of professional Kennedy conspiracists like Oliver Stone.

Over the years, as conspiracists controlled the debate, the words "magic bullet" became an American idiom for a clumsy lie and a coverup. But using modern computer technology, in the skilled hands of Dale Myers, a computer animator who'd studied the assassination for 20 years, it proved to an overwhelming majority of viewers that the much-derided "magic bullet" theory was all too true. The second bullet passed straight through Kennedy's neck, into Connally's chest, then on through Connally's wrist, embedding in his thigh. It's a bullet kind of thing to do. The documentary also points out many other blatant errors of fact in Stone's film.

Okay, so why did Jack Ruby shoot Oswald?

Jack Ruby is the lynchpin of the Kennedy assassination conspiracy. Because in every other presidential assassination, nobody ever shot the shooter. No matter what Jack Ruby was, no matter what the circumstances were, it's nearly impossible to convince a conspiracist that there's even a *possibility* that Jack Ruby did not shoot Oswald because he wanted to shut him up.

Jack Ruby thought he would be a hero for killing Oswald. He was a strip club owner, and he loved hanging out with cops. He had a hair-trigger temper, which earned him the nickname "Sparky," and he may well have had petty Mafia ties, but he was no player. He loved to hang out at the police station; it made him feel important, at the center of things. That's why he was there the day before, on the day of Oswald's arrest — that was a big day in Dallas. Though of course, conspiracists make much more of his presence.

But Ruby had begun to fall apart psychologically; we have statements of his ramblings and wild outbursts of temper after the shooting of his beloved President Kennedy, from his friends, his roommate, his employees, and even his rabbi. The fact is that Jack Ruby simply doesn't fit the persona of a Mafia hit man — ruthless, coolly efficient, virtually invisible. On the contrary, Ruby would have made an unimaginably lousy choice, because he was the ultimate loose cannon, all mouth and "Look at me!" bravado. If Ruby killed Oswald for the Mafia because Oswald was a loose cannon, then the Mafia would have had to send out another assassin to kill the loose cannon assassin. History does not record this. History records, instead, that the pathetic Jack Ruby rotted away in a Texas jail, dying of cancer in 1967.

Although Jack Ruby was the first assassin of an assassin in American history, he was far from the first potential one. After John Wilkes Booth shot Lincoln, the whole country went a little bonkers, grieving hysterically, and searching for the killers. In dozens of ugly episodes all across the nation, men were beaten or even lynched, simply because they fit the description of Booth. And as for other presidential assassins, by that time law enforcement was a little more organized. Nevertheless, both Charles Guiteau, Garfield's assassin, and Leon Czolgosz, the murderer of President McKinley, had to be kept under constant, well-armed guard to prevent any frontier justice.

Ruby thought he'd get a light sentence; instead, he got life. It was only as the years passed and he became ill, and the attention was on him no longer, that he liked to hint darkly of the forces behind his deed. But no names were forthcoming, maybe because there were none to give. As a matter of fact, on December 19, 1967, he made the deathbed statement there was no one else behind his act, and that there was nothing to hide.

Does all this mean that we don't believe it's possible that there was a conspiracy to kill Kennedy? No, that's not what we're saying at all. And proving a single shooter in Dealey Plaza, as well as proving it was Oswald, doesn't mean there was no conspiracy here. Really, what we're saying is that the evidence for the "two lone nuts" theory is every bit as compelling as the evidence for a broad conspiracy.

If you would like to know more about the Kennedy assassination, especially if you feel yourself being sucked into conspiracist obsession, read Jim Marrs's *Crossfire* for the conspiracist side, then Gerald Posner's *Case Closed* for the other side. Amidst the literally thousands of books, films, and Web sites on the subject, these two are the most exhaustive and best researched.

Looking at Other Presidential Assassinations

Perhaps, when our Founding Fathers decided that what the world needed was a new kind of government, with no king, they also thought they had left the problem of revolutions and assassinations behind them in Europe where they belonged. After all, if you have an election every four years, what's the point in killing somebody? You can just wait him out.

And for nearly a century, their logic was right on the money. America didn't suffer the shock of a presidential assassination until 1865, with the death of Abraham Lincoln. After his death, Lincoln was seen as a Christ-like figure, a sacrificial lamb whose blood healed the wound between North and South. John Wilkes Booth assumed that he would be a hero in the South for killing Lincoln. He was not. Instead, he was admired by some, but despised by many others for his cowardice, shooting an unarmed man from behind, and for bringing back the ugliness and bloodshed that was finally coming to an end.

Other murdered presidents didn't really get elevated to permanent sainthood, not until John Kennedy was killed. Yet, whatever you've heard about the Kennedy assassination, there are far more potential "assassins behind the assassin" in the death of Lincoln than that of Kennedy, not to mention our other martyred presidents. The last half of this chapter takes a look at the morass of lies and dark intrigues surrounding them all.

Abraham Lincoln

Abraham Lincoln was the first American president to be assassinated, and however it went down, it really was the result of a conspiracy. Just how broad that conspiracy was is the only question left to history. Afterwards, there was apparently no one left in the entire District of Columbia who hadn't said, "Mr. President, maybe you shouldn't go to the theatre tonight." Yet, there was other blood spilled that night — assassin John Wilkes Booth had accomplices spread over Washington, and they were trying to take out the most important men in the government in one blow. Mr. Lincoln died at 7:22 a.m. the morning after he was shot. The conspiracy theories started about ten minutes later.

The plot thickens

It had begun as another conspiracy entirely, to kidnap Lincoln and hold him for the release of Confederate prisoners. This scheme was hatched by several people, including actor and Confederate agent John Wilkes Booth, along with two of his childhood friends, Samuel Arnold and Michael O'Laughlen. Booth met Confederate messenger and agent John Surratt in 1864, who was taken with the plan, and then things began to jell, or so it seemed. Others were soon drafted into the plot. All this was supposedly in revenge for an attempt the year before by the Union to kidnap (and perhaps kill — it's debatable) Confederate President Jefferson Davis and two key members of his cabinet.

So Lincoln was to be kidnapped, ferried across the Potomac into Virginia, then held for the release of thousands of Confederate prisoners of war. But then, after months of failed and foiled kidnap plans, Robert E. Lee surrendered at Appomattox Courthouse. An embittered Booth, apparently on his own, turned the kidnapping plot to assassination. His co-conspirators didn't find out until that very day, April 14, that Booth had decided that Lincoln's appearance at Ford Theatre that night was the perfect opportunity to kill. Booth had played the theatre many times; he even picked up his mail there. The location seemed a godsend. But the squeamishness on the part of some of the other conspirators to commit political murder caused the night of April 14 to unfold as a series of blunders.

The only conspirator who didn't blunder was the determined Booth himself, of the renowned Booth theatre family. He entered the Ford Theatre with a loaded, .44 caliber, single-shot Derringer pistol, crept like a wraith to the president's box, and fired an iron ball into the back of Lincoln's head. Like his fellow conspirators, he also had a Bowie knife; when one of the Lincolns' guests in the box, Major Rathbone, attempted to grapple with Booth, he was stabbed in the arm.

The president's single guard that night was a lazy incompetent named John Parker. He'd picked up his chair from outside the entrance to the box and moved it far away to see the play; eventually he actually took a gallery seat. He was never punished for this, which is grist for the conspiracy mill. We have no record of the proceedings that freed Parker without punishment, but he *was* freed, in an atmosphere that could only be called a hanging mood. It's been suggested that his defense might have been that Lincoln *told* him to take a seat and enjoy the show — this would have been very much in character for the president.

Afterwards, Booth leapt from the box to the stage, catching his leg in the flag draped there, and falling, landing in the worst position for any actor, with his back to the audience. But he leapt up at once to shout dramatically, "*Sic semper tyrannis!*" It's Latin, the state motto of Virginia, and it means "Thus ever to tyrants!" Dramatic, huh? This is what happens when actors get involved in politics. Meanwhile, his co-conspirators were stumbling and bumbling in their attempts to kill Vice President Andrew Johnson and Secretary of State William Seward.

"This last was not a wrong, unless God deems it so"

The above quote is from John Wilkes Booth's diary. Actually, to call it a "diary" is essentially misleading. It's not long, and is more than anything else a manifesto, and a bit of a whining one at that. The diary is simply an 1864 calendar-memo book, which Booth used to jot down notes. It tells us a lot about the man that no less than five photographs of lovely ladies were tucked inside it — Booth was not only secretly married, he was apparently engaged, as well, not to mention his other numerous liaisons. He was the handsomest actor of his day, and the women were nuts about him.

But conspiracists are far more concerned about the fact that there are 18 pages (or perhaps more) missing from the diary. Certain of impending immortality, Booth had composed a long declaration on the day he shot Lincoln, sealing it and stamping it, with the intention of mailing it to the *National Intelligencer,* Washington's oldest and most influential newspaper. In one of those quirks of historical fate, about 3 p.m. he met in the street a friend and fellow actor, John Mathews, who was appearing in "Our American Cousin" at Ford's Theatre that night. Booth gave the letter to him instead, to be delivered the next morning to the newspaper. Booth

may have thought that the letter wouldn't arrive until Monday, denying him his manifesto appearing just after the Friday night shooting; or maybe he feared it might be lost in a shuffle of gas bills and other, unimportant letters to the editor. Mathews thought it a bit strange, but promised solemnly. Then, after the assassination, and the rage that followed it that night, Mathews panicked, fearful he might be arrested. He read the letter through, then burned it.

Meanwhile, on the run, Booth scanned the newspapers every day, looking for his manifesto on the front page. It never appeared, and he knew something had gone wrong; in the diary he states that he assumes the government was keeping it from being published. And so, in agonizing pain, hiding out in swamps and barns, he jotted some of these same thoughts down in his little memo book, hoping that at least it might survive for posterity. Alive or dead, fame is all that counts for an actor. Although Booth was once seen tearing out a page to give someone a note, the missing pages are still one of history's great mysteries. But Booth's diary is no secret. Anyone can see it on public display in the Ford's Theatre Museum in Washington, D.C.

The passionately unhinged patriot

Every school child knows that Lincoln was a saint; but it does seem fair to point out a few of Booth's motivations. History has often passed him off as a loony, even if he wasn't a patsy. But emotional and unstable as he was, for Booth, this was a legitimate act of war. After some time to get organized on both sides, the Confederates had consistently out-generaled the poorly led Union army, until generals Grant and Sherman were put in charge. Robert E. Lee was not a messianic figure in the South for nothing — he was ten times the general that McClellen or Burnside could have hoped to be. Even General Grant was awed to meet with him at Appomattox, and it was his respectful reverence for Lee that made the surrender go without a hitch. But only Lee had surrendered. General Joe Johnston's army was still fighting Sherman in North Carolina. (Johnston would finally surrender on April 26, aligning himself with Lee against the orders of the increasingly irrelevant Confederate president.) And Lee had just surrendered, on April 9, less than a week before the Lincoln assassination.

Of course, as commander of the Confederate army, he had this right. Lee understood that the South was beaten, that she did not have the men or the resources to do anything but achieve complete self-destruction if the war continued. But President Jefferson Davis did not agree. He was on the run that April, with wild plans of guerrilla warfare and counter-attacks, the very thing that Lee was praying to stop. Whether or not Booth was an agent of Davis's, he was very much in the Davis camp — Lee might have surrendered, but the South wasn't beaten yet. (If you're interested in this pivotal moment in history, pick up a copy of *April, 1865 – The Month That Saved America,* by Jay Winik.)

For Booth, as for many Southerners, Abraham Lincoln was a tyrant, attempting to deny them the right to secede that is guaranteed in the Constitution. He was a tyrant, suspending the heart of all judicial order, *habeas corpus,* which enabled the War Department to arrest and jail thousands of suspected Confederate sympathizers, without evidence and without trial. Worst of all, Abraham Lincoln was the man who had ended slavery, a system which Booth believed to have been the natural order ordained by God. According to Booth, it was when he heard Lincoln's last public speech, on April 11, in which he promised the vote to freed slaves, that Booth decided the president had to die. The thought of a black man with the right to vote was, for him, simply intolerable. Also, it was a shock for some, because extending the vote hadn't been part of Lincoln's policy. In a chilling photograph from that day, Booth can be clearly seen on the balcony above Lincoln during the speech.

The evangelical white abolitionist John Brown led a famous raid on the U.S. armory at Harper's Ferry, Virginia, in 1859, attempting to arm a slave uprising. Robert E. Lee led a force of Marines to put down the rebellion that is often seen as a prequel to the Civil War. John Wilkes Booth was so outraged by Brown's actions that he volunteered for the militia squad guarding him. When John Brown was hanged on December 2, Booth was standing at the foot of the scaffold. Although, as everyone knows from the Union marching song, "Battle Hymn of the Republic," "John Brown's body lies a'mouldering in the grave, but his truth is marching on."

Conspiracy theories galore

Historians, amateur and professional, have been trying to unravel the conspiracies behind the night of April 14 for a century and a half. Before the Kennedy assassination, it was the holy grail of conspiracists everywhere. There are many minor theories, some from outer space. Conspiracist David Icke believes it's even possible that an opium-addled Mary Todd Lincoln shot her own husband. 'Nuff said. But there are many theories that have been with us from the beginning:

- ✔ Lincoln was assassinated by Jewish bankers like the Rothschilds, for issuing "greenbacks," government notes to fund the war, robbing them of high-interest loans.

- ✔ Lincoln's murder was part of a Catholic plot, particularly a Jesuit plot, that is clear from the fact that Booth's co-conspirator, John Surratt, hid out under an assumed name in the pope's Swiss Guard after the assassination.

- ✔ Several books accused the Knights of the Golden Circle, a secret society of Northerners on the side of the South. (Northern sympathizers were often called "Copperheads.")

- ✔ There were numerous theories that Booth had not been the man killed in the burning barn at Garrett's farm, but that he survived into old age. Some claim that Secretary of War Stanton, in on the plot, had a look-alike hastily buried in the Arsenal prison, and sent the real Booth to India. *India?*

Are we all taking note of the similarity here with many of the Kennedy conspiracy theories listed above? Good. We knew you were on the ball!

The whole Booth family would carry the burden of hatred and suspicion for years; Edwin Booth, John's brother and the most respected actor of the family, got used to being booed off the stage in the early years after the shooting. But Robert Todd Lincoln's favorite story to tell in later years was how, by sheer chance, Edwin Booth had saved his life at a New Jersey rail station in 1863, pulling him out from in front of a moving train after he'd slipped and fallen from the platform.

For historians, there are three key theories that are the most popular:

The Jefferson Davis theory

Although it's a plausible theory, it may not seem important whether or not the long-gone Confederate president, Jefferson Davis, had a hand in Lincoln's death. But for moderate Northern Republicans, who were trying to keep Stanton from unleashing a scorched-earth policy on the defeated South after Lincoln's death, it was *very* important. It's also important simply from the standpoint of understanding history. If Booth was an agent of the Confederacy, then other conspiracy theories either gain or loose momentum. And Booth quite possibly was.

He'd already been to Montreal, Canada, a few months before. This city was a hotbed of clandestine meetings for the Confederates and their Secret Service. Booth also apparently made a large deposit, nearly $20,000, in his bank account afterwards. For the Confederates, Booth would have been an ideal spy. He'd already proven his loyalties to the South in many ways, including smuggling quinine and medical supplies past the tight Northern blockade. Besides, many actors were spies; their movements from town to town in theatre troops made excellent cover.

The Andrew Johnson theory

This one claims that Lincoln's vice president, Andrew Johnson, was behind the assassination, a not very plausible theory. In the climate after the assassination, no Southerner was safe from suspicion. It seems absurd looking back, but Lincoln was barely cold before the finger was pointed at Andrew Johnson of Tennessee. Johnson had survived the night unscathed, as well as unguarded. He'd been a Democrat, the party of the South, and the elected Tennessee governor. When he took an anti-war, pro-Union stance, Lincoln appointed him military governor of Tennessee. And when Lincoln ran for a second term, Johnson seemed the perfect running mate to reach out to southern Democrats.

Astonishingly, one of the chief proponents of the Johnson conspiracy theory was the widowed First Lady. Mary Todd Lincoln hated Andrew Johnson, and this lady really knew how to hate. The First Lady was an intemperate person, at times to the point that she seemed emotionally unbalanced. Mary actually wrote to friends that she suspected Johnson, which seems remarkably irresponsible. She also wrote that a calling card Booth left on the afternoon of the assassination (Booth and Johnson knew one another socially) was proof Johnson was in on the whole thing. Actually, it seems pretty clear why Booth left the calling card — he wanted to know if Johnson would be home that night, so that he could send George Atzerodt to kill him.

An investigation ensued into whether or not Johnson could have been behind the assassination. Despite the fact that he was deemed a Southern sympathizer for wanting to carry on Lincoln's policy of a civilized peace, and conversely was trying to backpedal on the Emancipation Proclamation and erode the rights of "Free Blacks," both of which enraged Radical Republicans, no evidence was found against him.

But the Radicals still despised him, and in 1866 they gained control of the Congress. They tried twice to cook up an impeachment, and the second one, in 1868, looked like it would get him tossed out of office. The charges were trumped up over the fact that Johnson had fired the top dog of the Radicals, Secretary of War Stanton. The impeachment failed, by one vote, that of Kansas senator Edmund G. Ross. A century later, John Kennedy would devote a section of his book *Profiles in Courage* to Ross.

The most compelling evidence presented to clear Johnson's name was the fact that, although Johnson was not attacked, one of the conspirators, George Atzerodt, had been assigned to kill him, and admitted it. Atzerodt, a native of Germany, had been brought into the plot because he had experience ferrying rebels back and forth across the Potomac. One of those rebels was John Surratt. The lumbering Atzerodt was taken to meet the charismatic Booth, and he was hooked — he would be the ferryman to take the president into Virginia.

But Atzerodt had not come on board for a murder. When the kidnapping seemed to be going nowhere, Booth proposed blowing up the White House. At this point, it should have been clear that Booth was erratic, vain, and just plain nuts. But Atzerodt followed along, until, literally at the last minute, he was assigned to kill Vice President Johnson. About ten minutes after Lee's surrender, the Confederate agent Surratt fled for Canada, and Atzerodt's original contact was long gone. Still, he grudgingly followed Booth's orders and moved into the hotel where Johnson lived, the Kirkwood House. The assassination night, he began quizzing the hotel bartender about Johnson's habits, which got Atzerodt arrested.

But the fact is, there really wasn't anything, apart from conspiracy, to arrest him for; he chickened out completely. In his confession, he said he never really believed that Booth would go through with killing anybody, and that he couldn't work up the nerve to kill Johnson. Instead, he stayed in the hotel bar, got roaring drunk, and wandered the streets of Washington the rest of the night, too frightened to return to his room.

The Edwin Stanton theory

As for the Edwin Stanton theory, much is made of the fact that the secretary of war supposedly talked General Grant out of attending the theatre with the Lincolns that night. The general had already given a tentative yes to the invitation, even though his wife was anxious to move on to New Jersey to see their children. Stanton suggested that the situation was still too unstable for the general to safely appear in public; he'd intercepted assassination threats. When Grant replied that this was certainly more true for the president, Stanton dismissed it with an airy hand, saying that he was tired of warning the president.

In all fairness, Stanton *had* warned Lincoln away from appearing in public. But conspiracists say that the real reason Stanton wanted Grant to stay away was that the general never went anywhere without a military guard. Actually, the real reason that Grant was just as happy to get out of going that evening was not because he was acting under Stanton's "orders," but because his wife, Julia, had had several unpleasant scenes with Mary Lincoln, and wasn't looking forward to spending an evening with her. The First Lady strikes again! And so Rathbone was invited in the Grants' place. In a rather creepy and little-known epilogue, someone attempted to break into the Grants' compartment on the train that night. This, too, might indicate a much broader conspiracy than is known to history.

The first book to take the Stanton-was-behind-it theory was written by Otto Eisenschiml in 1937, called *Why Lincoln Was Murdered.* Many others, including *The Lincoln Conspiracy,* followed in his wake. But to tell the truth, much of the "evidence" against Stanton in these sources is pretty circumstantial:

- The fact that Stanton wasn't targeted that night.

- The fact that Stanton had the most effective communications and spy network in the nation. Many have put forward the theory that he probably had some knowledge of the assassination beforehand.

- The fact that Stanton refused Lincoln's request that his powerfully built second-in-command, Major Thomas Eckert, accompany them to the theatre that night; he said he had business that evening and needed Eckert.

- The fact that Stanton had Booth buried secretly and without ceremony in the Arsenal Prison yard. But his reason given, that he wanted no mourners or potential hero's monument for the murderer, seems reasonable. (Later, the body was exhumed and proven to be Booth's.)

The fate of all the rest

With Booth dead, four conspirators were hanged on July 7, 1865:

- **Mrs. Mary Surratt:** Although Maryland was officially Union, this slave-holding border state was loaded with Confederate sympathizers. This is partly what got Mary Surratt hanged, though her execution is commonly seen today as a miscarriage of justice. While her husband was alive, the Surratt tavern was ground zero for local Confederate agents. It was only 13 miles from Washington. After being widowed, Mary moved to one of her last remaining assets, a townhouse in Washington, and turned it into a boarding house. However, there *is* evidence against Mary. There's no doubt that her boarding house was a meeting place for all the conspirators, and little doubt she knew what was coming. Also, when Booth and Herold fled Washington, they met at the old Surratt tavern, now run by one of Surratt's creditors, a John Lloyd, who gave them weapons, whiskey, and field glasses left with him earlier that day by Mary, according to his testimony. It should be noted that much testimony at the tribunal was rather ruthlessly coerced. Mary Surratt was the first woman ever hanged by a federal court. Yet, even the brutal Paine (see next bullet) insisted until his death that Mary was innocent, pleading for her life.

- **Lewis Paine:** It seems bizarre that Mrs. Surratt would die next to a man like Lewis Powell (aka Lewis Paine, the name under which he was executed), whose brutality that night was worse than anyone's. Paine was a former soldier and probable agent of the Confederate Secret Service who was assigned by Booth to kill the influential secretary of state, William Seward. Seward was 64 and bedridden at the time, recovering from a carriage accident. The hulking Paine talked his way into Seward's home a little past 10 p.m. holding a large medicine bottle, claiming to have been sent by Seward's doctor. He pushed his way into the house and assaulted several servants as well as the Seward family; he stabbed a servant and one of Seward's sons, and tried to shoot Seward's other son. When his gun jammed, he pistol whipped the young man nearly to death, before diving onto Seward's bed and stabbing him repeatedly and viciously. Only the fact that the old man's broken arm and jaw were in a brace saved his life; Paine thought that he'd cut Seward's throat. The attacker then stumbled out into the street, amazingly having killed no one.

✔ **David Herold:** Considered Booth's chief henchman, he was supposed to oversee the night's other two assassinations. Herold had been a schoolmate of Confederate agent John Surratt, Mary Surratt's son. Herold was a pharmacist, and may have met Booth when the actor was smuggling quinine into the South. He knew the city of Washington well, and on the night of the assassination, he was supposed to escort Paine to Seward's house and see that the job was done. Then he was to help Paine escape across the Potomac. But in the end he chickened out, too. When all the screaming started, from the whole Seward household, Herold bolted and left Paine to fend for himself. Later he met up with the injured Booth on the road to Surrattsville, the town in Maryland named for John Surratt's grandfather. (It's now called Clinton.) Together the two men went on the run.

✔ **George Atzerodt** was an unlikely conspirator. Atzerodt had been brought into the plot to begin with simply because he was such a strong rower, and knew the Potomac well, traits that would come in handy in the original kidnapping scheme. Atzerodt was a German immigrant who'd once been a carriage repairman. He was described by his friends as good natured, and most important of all, a coward. His own defense lawyer tried to claim that it was clear Atzerodt was a coward, because he'd killed no one, and with a lawyer's inverse logic, the fact that everyone knew he was a coward should be proof enough that Booth wouldn't have assigned him such an important task. The tribunal didn't buy it, and the pathetic Atzerodt died with the rest.

Conspiracist fever gripped the North after Lincoln's assassination, and many innocent people were arrested — they were lucky they didn't hang. Men who'd known Booth, like his two boyhood friends with whom he'd planned the kidnapping, Arnold and O'Laughlen, were imprisoned, as was the man whose guilt or innocence has always caused the most debate — Dr. Samuel Mudd. Many books and films (and descendants) have portrayed the good doctor as an innocent victim of fate, just an upright Maryland man of medicine who cared for a stranger with a broken leg and ended up being sucked into the maelstrom.

Nonsense. Booth knew Mudd, of that we're certain. In fact, it was Dr. Mudd, a passionate supporter of the South, who first introduced Booth to his key co-conspirator, John Surratt. There's a great deal of conflicting evidence, but a good guess might be that Mudd knew about the kidnap plan, but nothing about an assassination. In a document discovered in 1976, part of George Atzerodt's confession, he stated that Booth told him he had sent supplies on to Dr. Mudd two weeks before, in order to aid them in their planned escape.

Mudd was sentenced with O'Laughlen and Arnold to life imprisonment, but all three were pardoned in 1869 (O'Laughlen had died of a fever by then), the same year John Surratt was captured, tried, and set free by a hung jury. The conspiracist fever had waned by then, and apparently, the nation just wanted to put the whole bloody mess behind them. As for Dr. Mudd, despite being a slave-owner and Southern sympathizer, there was greatness in the man. In fact, after the prison doctor died of the same yellow fever epidemic that killed O'Laughlen, Dr. Mudd took over, and his work was so selfless that the guards in the prison especially petitioned President Johnson for his release.

James Garfield

The 20th president was the second to be assassinated. He served only from March to September of 1881. The history books tell us that he was shot by the classic lone gunman, a madman named Charles Julius Guiteau, on July 2, 1881. Guiteau was the "disgruntled former employee" type, along with being a religious fanatic. He had expected a post that he didn't deserve in the new administration, and when he didn't get it, he stalked Garfield until he got his opportunity at the Sixth Street Railway Station in Washington. He approached the president, who was standing with his secretary of state and, ironically enough, his secretary of war, Robert Todd Lincoln, son of the assassinated former president. (Incredibly, Lincoln was also present, though not an eyewitness, when President McKinley was assassinated.)

Guiteau shot Garfield twice; one bullet struck the president in the arm, the other, the fatal shot, lodged in his spine. As Guiteau was fought to the ground and arrested, he shouted, "I am a Stalwart of the Stalwarts! I did it and I want to be arrested! Arthur is president now!" This is pretty interesting, conspiracy-wise.

The "Stalwarts" were a powerful faction within the Republican Party, the faction that had kept Ulysses Grant in power, as well as causing the sad legacy of his corruption-filled administration. Grant himself wasn't on the take, but just about everyone around him was, and they all got off scot-free.

In those days, federal jobs and lucrative appointments were handed out according to a "spoils system," as a reward to supporters, whether they were qualified or not. Unfortunately, it's a system still in place in many counties and states. The "Stalwarts," whose day was passing, wanted to retain that system. When Rutherford B. Hayes beat Grant for the presidency, he had promised to end Reconstruction and pull Northern troops out of the South, and to reform the civil service. He was successful at the first, but at the second, his attempt to give civil service jobs to Southerners outraged his opposition and tabled reform.

Garfield had promised to pick up the gauntlet. Chester A. Arthur, Garfield's vice president, had not been chosen as a running mate because they were political soul mates — Arthur was chosen to placate the Stalwarts and keep the Republican ticket from splitting. The upright Garfield actually disliked Arthur, knowing he'd been fired from his lucrative position as Collector of Customs for the Port of New York, for, *surprise!*, graft and taking bribes. So the greatest irony is that Arthur went down in history as a good president, especially because of *his* civil service reform.

Garfield didn't die for an agonizing two and a half months, because his bungling physicians couldn't find the bullet, although just about everyone but the cook came in and tried. Even Alexander Graham Bell designed a metal detector to find it, but later realized he'd been foiled by the metal frame of the presidential bed — it hadn't occurred to him, since most bed frames of the period were wooden.

When the reason for Garfield's assassination hit the papers, there was suddenly an enormous surge of protest over the spoils system. Arthur had no choice but to back the new "merit" system in Ohio senator George Pendleton's Civil Service Reform Act, which created the Civil Service Commission. No more handing out federal jobs as if they were giveaway key chains. He smiled through it all, because if politics had taught Chester Arthur anything, it was how to make the best of a bad bargain. Yet, there are still some historians who believe it's entirely possible that Arthur was in some way connected to the assassination.

William McKinley

McKinley was the 25th president, and the third to be assassinated. Like Rutherford Hayes and James Garfield, he was another clean-as-a-whistle Ohio Republican. He was quite liberal in many of his beliefs, including tariffs as a more fair form of taxation, and an attitude that diversity in the nation and government was a great thing; his presidency is considered the opening of the Progressive Era.

The similarities to Garfield of the actual assassination are eerie (see the preceding section). McKinley was speaking at the Pan-American Exposition in Buffalo, New York, on September 6, 1901; he stepped down to greet the public, and standing in the line was one Leon Frank Czolgosz, an anarchist, with a pistol hidden in his right hand. When McKinley reached out to shake his hand, Czolgosz fired, striking the president in the shoulder and, like Garfield, through the internal organs to lodge in his back. Strangely enough, the first X-ray machine was being shown at the Exposition, but this set of bungling doctors forbid it for fear of horrific side effects from the newfangled machine. McKinley died a week later, of gangrene.

Once again, the assassin of McKinley would eventually be termed a "lone gunman," and once again, the likelihood of that is pretty low. Czolgosz may have been alone on the day he shot McKinley, but to think that he planned it alone is a little naïve.

Okay, so what's an anarchist?

The name comes from the word "anarchy," which means, along with "disorder and confusion," a political state in which no one is running the government — and this is just what anarchists wanted. Its use as a political term dates to the French Revolution, although the peak of the anarchist movement was between about 1880 and 1930. Anarchists were initially a secret society in Russia, called "Nihilists." The illogic of the movement is staggering, because most anarchists of that time were also socialists or communists, which means they wanted to see a forced redistribution of wealth. And if you think people are going to voluntarily give up their income and belongings without the force of a very *powerful* central government, you're living in a dream world.

It's a strange movement to understand, especially because the classic Anarchist Movement rose quickly, burned hot, then died out just as fast. At its height, it was a worldwide terrorist problem, with other assassinations, including the Tsar of Russia and the King of Italy.

Leon Frank Czolgosz had been a follower of the notorious American anarchist Emma Goldman, portrayed by Maureen Stapleton in Warren Beatty's film *Reds* as a sort of lovable, curmudgeonly earth-mother. But anarchists were anything but lovable. Their tactic, wantonly killing anyone in power, was called by them "Propaganda of the Deed," and they were intent on killing every world leader who stood in the way of their dreamland anarchist paradise where there was no government and all belongings were held in common. But anarchist violence was often a series of flubs, utterly pointless, winning them no friends whatsoever. Except, usually, it killed a lot of innocent people. In fact, an anarchist group in Russia called the "People's Will" invented the suicide bomber, taking out dozens of people before they finally got the Tsar.

Anarchists also invented the car bomb. In their worst attack on the American people, they set off a massive carriage bomb on Wall Street in 1920, killing 38 people and injuring over 400; it was the Oklahoma City bombing of the 1920s, and the public was just plain fed up. The movement died quickly in part because many anarchists drifted into socialist and communist organizations to escape the heat, but there are still some around today. Their symbol is a giant "A" in a circle.

The difference between the Garfield assassination and McKinley's is that, as with the assassination of Kennedy, the American people were convinced that it had been an anarchist plot, despite the assassin's claims he acted alone. The cops came down like gangbusters on every nest of anarchists they could find — they even arrested Emma Goldman, who claimed never to have met Czolgosz, despite the fact that witnesses had seen her speaking to him a few weeks before the shooting. But apart from supportive articles in anarchist newspapers, they could find no evidence to prove a conspiracy. Of course, that doesn't mean there wasn't one.

So, those are some of the bare facts on our other dead presidents. Not one shooting doesn't stink to high heaven of some sort of conspiracy. So why is it only John Kennedy who gets the 2,000 books written about him? Why is it only Kennedy's assassination that gets supposedly normal people to watch four-hour conspiracist documentaries that spend 15 minutes on a virtually blacked-out Polaroid that claims to be a photograph of the shooter on the grassy knoll? And why, after four decades, aren't people just plain sick to death of hearing about it?

For the boomers, the assassination of JFK was a national disaster. But any presidential assassination is a national disaster, a shared shock and a shared grief. Perhaps this is why the world will always be plagued with terrorists and dark societies of political murderers — it's just too easy for the disaffected to assault the security and peace of an entire nation with one bomb or one bullet.

Chapter 6

The World Ends Monday — Racial, Religious, and Apocalyptic Conspiracies

. . . .

In This Chapter

▶ Blaming the Jews: Holy writ for conspiracists

▶ Common conspiracy theories of Catholicism

▶ Conspiracy theories of Islam

▶ African Americans and conspiracy theories

▶ Discovering why some want to hasten The End

. . . .

*I*n this chapter, we move to the deadly serious (and very touchy) subjects of race and religion. Throughout history, men and women have suffered because of their faith or their race, and the grim facts don't seem to allow for a whole lot of debate. But in the hyperactive, feverish world of conspiracism, race and religion can give birth to the most outlandish of conspiracy theories, the ones with the biggest dose of drama. We're dicing with dementia here, from the CIA inventing crack to kill African Americans, to those small but loud collections of folks who contend that the Holocaust was a figment of the imagination of Jews working hand in hand with Hitler. This chapter opens with an examination of the world's most universal neuroses.

Picking on the Jews: History's Most Common Blame Game

The modern conspiracy theory and conspiracist mind-set, laid down in influential books and essays, is relatively new, having grown up since the French Revolution in 1789, which was often blamed on the Jews and the Freemasons. This nicely illustrates that all conspiracy theories have grown out of hatred and fear of the Jews, or hatred and fear of secret societies, initially the Freemasons (see Chapter 9). In fact, often both, because Freemasons were many times perceived as the willing tools of "World Jewry."

All conspiracy theories, right up to the present-day 9/11 ones, are the same recycled theories that grew from this original source. Only the names of the accused get changed. And if you accept this as being so, then it leads inevitably to the next logical question: Why the Jews?

Turning Jews into conspiracy scapegoats

The nation of Israel (divided in two in ancient times, with Israel in the north and Judah in the south) was conquered many times over the centuries. The last major conqueror was Rome. In the century before Christ, Rome set up a puppet state called "Judea," with a royal Jewish family, the Hasmoneans. In the year 6 AD, Judea went from a client state to a Roman province, ruled by a viceroy called a "procurator." But Judea was in a constant state of turmoil, and very difficult to govern.

Eventually, in 68 AD, the future emperor Titus, son of the Emperor Vespasian, led his legions, totaling about 60,000 men, into Judea to subdue it. Jerusalem was put under a long and bloody siege, and by the year 70, Titus breached her walls, and the whole city was destroyed. Two more major wars of Jewish rebellion followed this one, until, in the year 135 AD, the Romans simply banned the Jews from their homeland. Jerusalem was renamed Aelia Capitolina by Emperor Hadrian, and for Rome, the problem was solved.

Anti-Semitic semantics

Anti-Semitism is, according to some, a misused word because Arabs are a Semitic people, as well. Much of the propaganda in Nazi Germany used this scheme to deny the persecution of the Jews — "How can we be anti-Semites, when we're so fond of the Arabs?" And it's true that some of the most powerful Arabs of the 1930s were close allies of the Nazis. Of course, the tie that bound them together was hatred of the Jews. And the other reason for the Nazi "affection" for the Arabs is because Germany had an unquenchable thirst for Arab oil to feed its ever-hungrier battleships and war planes.

But this is just "semantics," playing with words to blow a fog over the issue. Nowadays, the same sort of people, on the Far Left and the Far Right, from Louis Farrakhan to Pat Buchanan, say that they're not anti-Semitic at all. How could you say such a thing? They're only "anti-Zionists," meaning that they have nothing against the Jews, they just hate the nation of Israel — a free nation and American ally made up of Jews. See the difference? But in this book, anti-Semitism means hatred of the Jews, period. We see no reason to muddy the waters.

For the Jews, the problem was just beginning. This was the wellspring of what came to be known as the "Diaspora," the scattering of the Jews to the four corners of the earth. As a people, they became like the myth of the Flying Dutchman, always on the move, always ready to be expelled from one country and refugeed to another. But it's important to remember that, despite Roman decrees, a Jewish presence would always be in Jerusalem and the surrounding countryside. Jews in the Middle Ages made pilgrimages to the Holy Land, just as the Christians did, and many Jews asked to be buried there upon their death, if their family could afford such a journey. It was more than just empty ritual when Jews finished every Passover Seder, as well as the ritual for the holy day of Yom Kippur, with the words, "Next year in Jerusalem." Yet, despite this love that burned for 2,000 years, the days of a Jewish homeland surrounding the sacred Temple Mount were over.

A love of Jerusalem and refusal to give up their ancient faith kept the Jews a people apart. But the upshot of the Diaspora was that just about every country had at least *some* Jews. And this is part of the key here. Just about everybody has some Jews. And it's that very *universality* of the Jewish community that has been one of its greatest assets, and one of its greatest handicaps. *Everybody* could gripe about the Jews. And once a really good conspiracy theory about them took hold in one country, it could easily move to the nation next door, without even bothering to erase "Jews" and substitute "Estonians."

Actually, the very fact that they seem to be everywhere becomes one more point of paranoia in the conspiracist playbook. The communal Jewish experience has been pretty much the same the world over, and this very sameness has made Jew baiting an international pastime. There's a story of the visit of the Japanese war minister to Germany, just before the signing of the Tri-Partite Pact in 1940 that allied fascist Germany with Japan and Italy. As the Japanese minister was shown the capital of Berlin, seeing its rebirth from the ashes of defeat and economic disaster after World War I, and seeing how the new Aryan nation had united beneath the banner of racial superiority, he's purported to have said, "I agree, it's a wonderful system. The problem is, we don't have any Jews."

The Dark Ages get darker

During the 1100s, a superstitious Christian Europe began to believe that the Jews were more than deniers or killers of Christ; they were downright sinister. The "blood libel" was born, which is the belief that Jews murdered Christians, especially babies, and used the blood in their "rituals." In towns across France and Germany, whole communities of Jews were burned at the stake by hysterical Christians. Anything from a plague of locusts to a cholera epidemic could get blamed on the Jews. Christians were dying of fever because the Jews desecrated the communal host eaten in the mass, putting a curse on it. (Of course, people were really dying of fever because their sewage contaminated their own water supply.)

Jews were famous for their knowledge of medicine, but this, too, was turned against them, twisted into knowledge of alchemy and witchcraft. All it took was a bunch of drunks in a tavern claiming that someone's baby had a withered arm because the midwife had been a Jewess and that started a riot that got hundreds, and sometimes thousands, of Jews killed.

Straining for righteousness in their cause, some rather absurd anti-Jewish spectacles grew up in this period. Several times in the medieval world, the Talmud, a holy book for the Jews, was put on trial. No, not the Jews. Just the book. The Talmud, of course, always lost and was promptly burned in an equally symbolic circus. This nonsense began to happen, slowly at first, worsening in the years of the Crusades (11th to 13th centuries), as anti-Semitism became more entrenched in the European mind-set. Of course, in Spain they weren't burning the book — they were burning the Jews.

By the 16th century, it was common to force the Jews of any city to live in a separate area, called a *ghetto*. The word itself is Venetian slang for "their own Jewish Quarter," which was near the slag heap for the iron foundries of the city — thus, ghetto, from *gheta*, Venetian for "slag." The Germans called it the *Judengasse,* the Arabs the *mellah,* but it's all the same prison: a section gated off from the rest of the community where the Jews were allowed to live.

In the ghettos Jews were forced to endure all sorts of humiliating edicts. They had to wear special clothes or badges; they had to have passes to travel, and they had to jump through other hoops, like making themselves scarce around various Christian holidays, especially Easter, when Christians paid homage to the crucifixion of Christ that they openly blamed on the Jews.

In the earlier centuries of settlement, many Jewish merchants became wealthy. But by the 12th century, as Jewish oppression worsened, Christians began to pass laws forbidding the Jews to take part in the normal economic life of the community. They were banned from the various powerful guilds, each of which controlled particular professions. If you couldn't get into the guild, you couldn't be a draper, a carpenter, a stone mason, or a vintner. Less prosperous Jews settled in the artisan trades, such as gold- or silversmiths, producing and selling their own works; many others became small, pushcart tradesmen. But for the men with a little capital, pushed out of the guilds, there weren't that many ways to make a living left open to them. Being merchants made it easy for them to slip into both pawnbroking and moneylending (see Chapter 15).

During this period there were many mass evictions of the Jews, from cities, duchies, and entire countries. The worst was the expulsion of all the Jews from Spain by the rabidly anti-Semitic Ferdinand and Isabella in 1492. It's a sad irony that many of these Jews fled to the nearest refuge, Islamic North Africa, where later anti-Semitic crusades on the part of the Muslims there decimated those communities, as well. But it happened just about everywhere in Europe; the English did it twice.

The Jews as moneylenders

Much of 20th-century anti-Semitism harps incessantly on the subject of Jews as the "world's bankers," controlling the world's economy and following the deranged Ku Klux Klan (see Chapter 12) mythology of the "five Jew bankers" who run everything except pay toilets in airports. We talk much more about the specifics of these allegations in Chapter 15, but it's important to know where these kinds of claims first came from.

The early Catholic Church, based on a very small passage in Luke that's about loaning money and not expecting to get it back out of Christian generosity, interpreted that to mean that they should forbid what they called *usury,* the making of money by loaning money. But people from kings to innkeepers still needed to borrow money.

The Jews, however, didn't arrive in the Rhine valley and start setting up ATMs. As early as the sixth century AD, Jews expelled from Judea and pushed out of the Near East and began to immigrate into Western Europe. In those first, quiet centuries, no organized form of anti-Semitism in Europe existed. The two faiths, Christianity and Judaism, often eyed one another with emotions from distrust to distaste. But apart from that, early medieval kings had too much trouble hanging on to their property to worry about tension between religious faiths.

Jews worked side by side with Christians, in every profession from masons to laborers to farmers. Because they could count on the help and support of the Jewish community scattered the world over, many Jews became merchants. But they moved down the roads and bought and sold without facing any special taxes or burdens simply for being Jewish. The 6th-century pope, Gregory I, even forbade the forced conversion of Jews, as well as any attempt to interfere with their free practice of their faith.

Extending the blame to the present day

There's been a great rebirth recently of anti-Semitism and conspiracy theories blamed on the Jews in Europe, Russia, and the Middle East. It's still a universal tie. In the U.S., it isn't hard to sniff out the obsessive Jew baiting in many of the "alternative conspiracy theories" offered up by the "Truthers," for example, who believe that 9/11 was an atrocity committed by the government (see Chapter 8). Many common leaders who've predominantly associated themselves with white supremacist groups, like David Duke of the Ku Klux Klan, have switched over or broadened into anti-Semitism, the scheming Jewish bankers, and Holocaust denial, which is becoming dangerously popular.

Protocols of the Elders of Zion

One of the most infamous pieces of propaganda ever devised is known as the *Protocols of the Elders of Zion*. In it, a secret meeting is described of a group of Jews who discuss their world takeover plans, with the Freemasons (see Chapter 9) as their accomplices. The document first According to the *Protocols,* Jews are behind a plan for world conquest, and the Freemasons are their willing stooges. Jews and the Masons control the press and the courts, and Jewish revolutionaries use liberalism to weaken Christianity and the State. They use their international banking power to destroy the economy by taking countries off the gold standard. Jews and the Masons control governments from behind the scenes by blackmailing politicians. And during times of war, Jews suspend civil liberties and then secretly make the measures permanent. The Protocols outline the use of brainwashing, pornography, alcohol, and drugs to subvert society, and the careful manipulation of the illusion of individual freedom to mask society's destruction from behind the scenes.

Here's the twisted path of the *Protocols* from inspiration to current incarnation:

✔ The *Protocols* were inspired by Abbé Barruel's *Memoirs,* in which he blamed the Freemasons and the Illuminati for the French Revolution. In the early 1800s, Barruel re-wrote his thesis, shifting the blame to the Jews.

✔ In the 1840s, the French author Eugène Sue trotted the exact same conspiracy story out again, rewriting it to make the Jesuits, a Catholic order with an intellectual and internationalist bent, into the villains.

✔ In 1864, Sue was plagiarized by another French author, Maurice Joly, in a pamphlet called *Dialogues in Hell Between Machiavelli and Montesquieu.* Joly's version of the story alleged a conspiracy between the Devil and Napoleon III, not Freemasons, Jews, or Jesuits, but it was all the exact same dialog with a different cast of bad guys.

✔ In 1890, a Russian named Mathieu Golovinsky, living in France, wrote what became the modern version of the *Protocols.* His family was aristocratic members of Russian society but lost their fortune. Golovinsky apparently blamed the Jews for his family's fate, and embellished the Protocols, expanding the story to detail how the Jews control banking, wars, and the world.

✔ The Czar's secret police, the Russian Okhrana, finally picked up the tale and made the enemies both the Jews *and* the Masons, circulating the Protocols as propaganda. It was even ordered to be read from the pulpit after Orthodox church services. In their version, the Jews supposedly dangle the hope of political freedom in front of silly, stupid Gentiles to encourage revolution, but have no intention of delivering on their promise.

✔ A Russian monk named Sergei Nilus republished the *Protocols* in 1905 and announced after the Russian Revolution in 1917 that they were really part of the minutes of the 1897 Zionist Congress at Basel, Switzerland. The congress was actually attended by a number of Christian clergy and political figures. What was really discussed at that famous meeting was the creation of a Jewish organization to purchase land in Palestine for a Jewish homeland. Nevertheless, the Russians used the fictional *Protocols* as justification for slaughtering Jews after the Russian Revolution in 1917.

✔ In 1919, American industrialist Henry Ford purchased the *Detroit Independent* newspaper for the specific purpose of presenting his personal anti-immigrant, anti-Jewish, and anti-labor messages to the public. In 1922, he brought the Protocols to the American public in serial form. The series, The International Jew, was widely reprinted around the world, and some say it's how Adolph Hitler became acquainted with them. He even gave copies away with new cars. Curiously, Henry Ford was a Freemason, and edited out unflattering references to Masons.

Not long afterwards, when the Nazi party came to power in Germany, Adolph Hitler used the Protocols as justification for his plans to exterminate the Jews and the Freemasons. A popular Nazi slogan was *"All Masons Jews — All Jews Masons!"* The Protocols have been circulated for over 100 years, and today they can be found all over the Internet, posted by a wide range of conspiracist groups. The Protocols remain very popular in Islamic countries, including Egypt and Saudi Arabia, where they're handed out as texts for school children to study. Groups as wildly divergent as the African-American Nation of Islam, white patriot militia groups, the Palestinian terrorist group Hamas, and the American Nazi Party still peddle the Protocols as fact. Others simply remove the words "Jew" and "Freemason" from the allegations and substitute words like *Neocons, globalists,* or *International bankers.* And the truly bizarre David Icke believes that the Protocols are describing neither Jews nor Masons, but actually 12-foot tall, shape-shifting reptilian aliens.

One of the most curious developments in the history of the Protocols is a comic book version of their forgery by celebrated artist Will Eisner. Called *The Plot: The Secret Story of the Protocols of the Elders of Zion,* it details the twisted path of the Protocols in a truly unique presentation.

And without a doubt, anti-Semitism as part of conspiracism had its harmonic convergence in the most important forgery of all time. With the birth of the Protocols of the Elders of Zion (see the nearby sidebar, "*Protocols of the Elders of Zion*"), conspiracy theories that grew out of hatred of Jews and of secret societies merged, becoming one single conspiracy dogma of unprecedented proportions. That's because, at that point in history, the Jews *became* a secret society, bent on nothing less than world domination.

Catholic Conspiracy Theories

No organization that has been around as long as the Roman Catholic Church could possibly escape accusations of conspiracies. The church has engaged in its share of wrongdoings and persecutions over the last 19 centuries or so, and after dominating the Christian world up until the growth of Protestantism, the church didn't take encroachment on their spiritual and secular monopoly lying down.

The flip side was a movement of anti-Catholicism. In the original 13 British colonies that became the United States, only Maryland allowed Catholics a degree of freedom to worship freely and own land. Public distrust of Catholics in America lasted openly until the election of President John F. Kennedy. In France, arguments that started during the French Revolution over the influence of the church over government still are hotly debated today.

Nevertheless, there are more than a few Catholic conspiracy theories that dive off the deep end. Here are some modern accusations still making the rounds:

- The church has supposedly suppressed evidence that proves Jesus and Mary Magdalene were actually married to each other, and had a daughter. After Christ's crucifixion, Mary and the child fled to France, where Jesus' bloodline was nurtured for centuries and hidden from the public, by groups like the Knights Templar, the Priory of Sion, and the modern Opus Dei. If you haven't read Dan Brown's *The Da Vinci Code,* we just ruined the end for you. For much more than can be covered in this book, see *The Templar Code For Dummies* (Wiley) for the complete lowdown.

- On November 5, 1605, Englishman Guy Fawkes and a group of Catholic supporters were caught in London just before attempting to blow up Parliament and murder King James I. The Gunpowder Plot was seen as a church-sponsored attempt to restore Catholic rule to a Protestant nation, and many Catholic priests who had no clue about the plot were imprisoned.

- Abraham Lincoln was supposedly assassinated by the Jesuits because of an 1856 court case in which Lincoln arranged a settlement between a priest and the friend of a bishop. During the height of the anti-Catholic movement in the U.S., a book written in 1897 by a member of the Assassination Commission alleged that the Vatican was pro-slavery.

- The Vatican is purportedly dominated by Satanists or Freemasons, or both, who support a one-world government. The European Union is just the first step in this church-backed scheme.

- Jesuits are really secretly Freemasons who are out to destroy the church from within.

Besides these, there are a few more serious accusations involving the church from recent years, which we explore in the following sections.

The 3rd secret of Fatima

Between May and October 1917, on the 13th of every month, three young Catholic girls claimed to have been visited by a vision of the Virgin Mary in Fatima, Portugal. Lucia Santos and her cousins Francisco and Jacinta Marto insisted that on July 13, 1917, the image of Mary gave them three prophecies, which remained secret for more then 20 years. The location of their vision instantly became a holy shrine among Catholics, known as Our Lady of Fatima.

Lucia was the oldest child, and just 10 years old at the time. The Marto girls both died in a flu epidemic in 1919, but Lucia went on to become a nun and lived until 2005. In 1941, Sister Lucia revealed the first two prophecies as part of the documentation needed for the canonization (bestowing sainthood) of her cousins, but told church authorities that Mary had told her to keep the third a secret.

✔ The first secret was a vision of hell, with demons and souls in human form blackened by fire. The vision of Mary assured the girls they'd be taken up to heaven.

✔ The second secret predicted the end of World War I, but it also predicted the beginning of World War II, if Russia didn't end its persecutions and convert to Catholicism. (Bear in mind that the prophecy wasn't divulged until WWII had already begun.)

In 1943, Sister Lucia was gravely ill, and her local bishop suggested that she write down the third prophecy so it could be revealed in case of her death. It was sent to Rome, only to be seen by the pope. Lucia recovered, and later granted permission for the secret to be revealed after 1960. Yet, the church kept the prophecy a secret until 2000.

The third secret was an image of an assassination attempt against the "Holy Father." Many believed it referred to the attempted shooting of Pope John Paul II on May 13, 1981. But almost immediately, suspicion arose about the third prophecy.

✔ The church refused to release the text of the third prophecy in 1960, even though Sister Lucia approved it. It took 40 more years before it was made public.

✔ Cardinal Ratzinger, later Pope Benedict XVI, said in 1984 that the release of the secret dealt with the "end times," and would cause a sensational reaction with the public if it became known. Given the attempt on John Paul II occurred three years before Ratzinger's statement, it's hard to understand his claim.

✔ The Vatican had a longstanding policy forbidding any Catholic who'd seen sacred visions from making public statements without the specific approval of the church. This was rescinded in 1966 — except for Sister Lucia. She was sworn to secrecy until her death in 2005, forbidding her to even discuss what had been officially released by the church.

"The Fatima Crusader," a newsletter published by a fringe group led by Father Nicholas Gruener, has long alleged that Sister Lucia died in the 1950s and was replaced by an imposter. The group believes that the church's reforms in the 1960s, known as Vatican II, were engineered by Communists and Freemasons within the church, and that these evil insiders have purposely hidden the true third prophecy that would've exposed their nefarious schemes.

Pope Pius XII and the Nazis

One of the most common conspiracy theories of the 20th century concerning the church is that Pope Pius XII supported the Nazis during World War II, and aided Nazi war criminals in fleeing Europe by using the worldwide network of Catholic Relief Services. While the war was raging, Catholic priests were tossed into concentration camps, and the pope in Rome was surrounded by fascist Italy, Hitler's allies. Pius XII attempted to keep the church politically neutral, but in 1939 was threatened by Mussolini over communication with leaders of nations invaded by the Nazis. In response to the threats, he told the dictator's foreign minister that he was ready to be deported to a Nazi camp, rather than violate his own conscience.

Throughout the war, Pius XII generally refused to make public statements against Axis policies and activities. Even when faced with incontrovertible evidence concerning Nazi atrocities against Jews, gypsies, homosexuals, Freemasons, and others, the church's public policy was usually one of silence, as a matter of self-preservation. Privately, however, this was another issue.

- In 1939, the pope personally arranged for 3,000 visas for "non-Aryan Catholics" to leave Germany for Brazil, as a way to smuggle Jews out of the country. Brazilian authorities cancelled the program a year later once they discovered the truth.

- Within Rome itself, the pope secretly ordered all convents and monasteries to hide Jews.

- The church instituted a policy of quietly baptizing orphaned Jewish children as Catholics to save them from deportation to the camps.

- In 1943, when Germany occupied Northern Italy, the pope offered to use church gold to ransom Jewish-Italian hostages.

- In 1944, the pope privately appealed to 13 Central and South American countries to accept "emergency passports" from Jews fleeing Europe.

- When the war ended, the church assisted in resettling 6,000 Bulgarian Jewish children into Palestine, while publicly declaring that the Vatican wasn't a supporter of Zionism.

After the war ended, there is evidence that some Nazis and Nazi sympathizers really were shielded by the church, especially in countries that were swallowed up by the Soviet Union. And it's assumed that Pius XII looked the other way because the officially atheistic Soviets were considered a greater threat to Christianity and Catholicism than the defeated Germans and their Eastern European helpmates. Meanwhile, Pius XII became an immediate advocate for the release of all war criminals and the commuting of all death sentences against Axis officials. Nevertheless, Israeli diplomat Pinchas Lapide stated in the 1960s that Pius XII saved between 700,000 and 860,000 Jews during the war.

The Vatican Islam Conspiracy theory

Fundamentalist Christian comic-book artist Jack Chick has become infamous for his "Chick Tracts," tiny comic booklets that get slipped onto grocery shelves, under windshield wipers, into airliner seatbacks, and into every other nook and cranny that his many fans can find. Each one tells a little morality tale on a wild variety of subjects, with an evangelical message. He is a strong purveyor of a wide range of conspiracy theories, and in many cases, he is the source of a few popular ones. One of the most notorious is the Vatican Islam Conspiracy.

Chick's tract "The Prophet" alleges that the Roman Catholic Church invented the Islamic religion by manipulating events that swirled around its founder, the prophet Mohammed. The goal was to use the followers of Mohammed's new religion to eliminate Jews and non-Catholic Christians. Because the church supported Mohammed, so the tale goes, it was supposed that he and his armies turned over control of Jerusalem to the Vatican, as the pope's willing stooge. But Mohammed's victories were too swift and great, and he rebelled against his Catholic masters. The medieval Crusades were an attempt to crush the forces of Islam and bring them back under Catholic control, but Christian forces were unable to beat the Muslims. Exciting, isn't it?

Of course, there is absolutely nothing to back this story up, historically or archeologically, on paper or anywhere else. It all seems to have sprung from the mind of Alberto Magno Romero Rivera, a purported ex-Jesuit priest. Rivera was a Spanish anti-Catholic who claimed to have left the priesthood in the 1960s when he "discovered" that the church was controlled by Freemasons. Investigation of Rivera and his biography revealed him to have a long history as a swindler and a colossal liar. There is no record of him ever being a priest, much less a Jesuit, and his supposed degrees in theology were mail-order ones. He claimed that the Jesuits threw him into a secret Vatican madhouse and tortured him, before he escaped and rescued his own sister from a London convent where she was near death.

It turned out that none of his story was true. Nevertheless, his biggest supporter, Jack Chick, believed every word and featured Rivera as a character in many of his comic tracts. Meanwhile, the Vatican Islam Conspiracy has taken on a life of its own and is widely circulated in the evangelical Christian community.

Islamic Conspiracy Theories

The overwhelming number of conspiracy theories within the Islamic community involve Jewish or Israeli plots against Muslims. The list is virtually endless, but here are some highlights:

- ✔ AIDS has been spread into the Muslim community via World Health Organization polio vaccines. This one has been perpetrated by Muslim clerics in Nigeria and elsewhere, resulting in the spread of a Nigerian strain of polio (see Chapter 16).

- ✔ Israeli scientists created hormone-laced chewing gum to make Palestinian children sexually promiscuous.

- ✔ The 2004 tsunami (tidal wave) in the Indian Ocean that caused thousands of deaths was created by the explosion of an Indian nuclear device, engineered by Americans and Israelis to kill Muslims.

- ✔ The Iranian press service reported in 2006 that 10,000 Russian women are kidnapped every year and brought into Israel, where they are sold for as much as $10,000 apiece.

- ✔ Western products are continually criticized for bringing non-Islamic ideas into Muslim culture. Most recently, the film *Pirates of the Carribean*, McDonald's, Levi's, and Coca-Cola have been singled out as evil influences. Pepsi, in particular, is alleged to hide within its name the slogan *"Pay Each Penny, Save Israel."*

- ✔ Television networks and newspapers in numerous Islamic countries continue to report the protocols of the Elders of Zion are authentic documents that outline Zionist treachery against the Muslim world.

- ✔ The 9/11 attacks in the U.S. weren't made by Osama bin Ladin, but by the Israeli secret service, masterminded by Henry Kissinger.

- ✔ Egyptian cleric Hazem Sallah Abu Ismail, a former Islamic lecturer in America, appeared on Saudi Al-Risala on April 14, 2006, and proclaimed that United Nations's studies concluded, "Eighty-two percent of all attempts to corrupt humanity originate from the Jews."

The Nation of Islam

Since the 9/11 attacks, Americans have taken a heightened interest in the Islamic faith. Most have heard of Minister Louis Farakhan and the *Nation of Islam* (NOI). The NOI is known for its doctrine of black separatism, as well as its members' strong commitment to service within the African-American community. What isn't commonly known is the group's UFO cosmology.

The Nation of Islam was formed in the 1930s by Wallace D. Fard, who proclaimed the origin of the white race was an experiment by an evil scientist named Yakub, of the Tribe of Shabazz. According to Master Fard, the Original Man was an "Asiatic black man." Apparently Yakub, it's claimed, created a race of white devils by grafting a black germ and a white germ together in his lab on what's now the Greek island of Patmos (where the New Testament's apocalyptic book of Revelation was written). The experiment's result was the white race, who were destined to rule the Earth for 6,000 years until the black race regained power, beginning in 1914.

The NOI also teaches that visions described in the book of Ezekiel 1:15–18 are actually portraying a UFO and extraterrestrial beings: "Now as I beheld the living creatures, behold one wheel upon the earth by the living creatures, with his four faces. . . ."

According to Minister Farakhan's description of his own immediate predecessor Elijah Muhammad's teachings, Ezekiel saw a giant wheel in the sky called a Mother Plane, originally built on the island of Japan in ancient times. This massive, flying wheel is a half-mile in diameter, containing 1,500 smaller wheels, with three huge bombs originally used for the creation of mountains by alien terraforming engineers. "That Mother Wheel is a dreadful-looking thing," says Farakhan. "White folks are making movies now to make these planes look like fiction, but it's based on something real."

Most other sects of Islam consider the Nation of Islam heretical. The NOI teaches that Allah came down to Earth in the person of W. D. Fard, a claim that could get you stoned to death in some parts of the Muslim world where just drawing a cartoon of the prophet Mohammad is blasphemous. Indeed, it was a trip to Mecca and discussion with Muslim scholars in Africa and the Middle East that helped to turn former NOI leader Malcolm X away from the teachings of Elijah Muhammad in the early 1960s. Malcolm X started his own more traditional Sunni mosque before his murder by members of the Fruit of Islam, an internal NOI paramilitary group.

The NOI's widely circulated newspaper, *The Final Call,* has been the recurring source of many outrageous urban legends and conspiracy theories perpetrated as fact. While the NOI gets a lot of press and public attention (often for Farakhan's notorious anti-Semitic rhetoric), it should be pointed out that a split schism in 1978 resulted in the formation of a far more traditional Sunni-styled group that is much larger. The *Muslim American Society* was created by former NOI leader Elijah Muhammad's son, Warith Dean Muhammad, and doesn't contain the NOI's more extreme and unorthodox Muslim teachings. It's bereft of NOI's flying saucers, not to mention its virulent anti-Semitism and wild conspiracy theories about mad Jewish scientists inventing AIDS, and other followers of the Jews' "dirty religion" being the biggest group of slave owners in the South.

African Americans and Conspiracy Theories

African Americans in the U.S. have plenty of reasons to be suspicious and downright distrustful of government officials, going back to the earliest days of the colonial slave trade. Very real and oppressive conspiracies have been perpetrated on African Americans over the centuries, from the slave business itself, to disenfranchisement, Jim Crow laws, the infamous Tuskegee syphilis experiments (see Chapter 17), and up to the very creepy FBI program COINTELPRO (see the following section).

COINTELPRO

One of the most infamous U.S. government operations against its own citizens was a secret FBI program known by its acronym COINTELPRO (Counter Intelligence Program). Starting in 1956 during the height of the Cold War, the program was initially designed to discover and disrupt the activities of the U.S. Communist Party. The Soviet Union funded Communist Party activities in America, as well as supported an expanding list of organizations considered "subversive" by the government. Unfortunately, as time went on and the program grew, little distinction was made between groups advocating the violent overthrow of the U.S. government and those that conducted nonviolent protests of government policy. This put the growing civil rights movement of the 1960s square in the FBI's sights.

COINTELPRO targeted all sides of the political spectrum by the mid-1960s, from the Socialist Workers party, the Ku Klux Klan, and American Indian groups, to the Nation of Islam, the Student Nonviolent Coordinating Committee, the Black Panthers, and African-American leaders like Malcom X and Dr. Martin Luther King, Jr.

There's no question (based on declassified, decoded intelligence documents, as well as information from former Soviet agents) that the Russian KGB was manipulating many subversive groups within the U.S. to create what might euphemistically be called "domestic unrest."

Nevertheless, the FBI engaged in illegal wiretapping, infiltration, legal and illegal harassment, assault, break-ins, propaganda planted in the news media, and other "dirty tricks" to subvert, confuse, or otherwise disrupt the groups it was investigating.

Little, if any, good came out of the activities of the COINTELPRO program. Some believe that the assassinations of Malcolm X and Dr. King may have been the result of COINTELPRO activities. Neither allegation has ever been proved, but there were many cases of blatant and often deadly criminal activities conducted by the FBI or its embedded informants during the COINTELPRO years.

In 1971, one of the groups took matters into its own hands and turned the tables on the FBI. A burglary was staged by a group calling itself the *Citizen's Committee to Investigate the FBI,* in an FBI field office in Pennsylvania, and files were stolen and leaked to the press that outlined the agency's illegal COINTELPRO activities. FBI director J. Edgar Hoover was forced by public opinion to disband the program. The worst of the already sordid details were made public in Senate hearings chaired by Senator Frank Church (D-Idaho) in 1976, commonly called the Church Committee. The committee's final report concluded that the FBI's activities would've been intolerable even if every single group investigated was involved in the worst possible violent and subversive activities — which they weren't.

Issues brought to light by the end of the COINTELPRO period have been resurrected in the wake of the 9/11 attacks, and especially over broad powers granted to domestic intelligence agencies by the Patriot Act, which are seen by many detractors to be every bit as unconstitutional as the FBI's activities between 1956 and 1971. Nevertheless, everything old is new again, because the Internet has allowed terrorist organizations like Al-Qaeda to easily inject propaganda videos and recruitment efforts into African-American and Islamic controversies on the Web — often, unlike the old KGB, without bothering to hide their motives of encouraging terrorist acts against the U.S. and European nations.

The King Alfred Plan

Conspiracy theories can spread in curious ways. In 1967, African-American novelist John A. Williams promoted his book, *The Man Who Cried I Am* (Thunder's Mouth Press), by photocopying passages of his story and anonymously leaving them on subways around New York City. The circulated pages described a fictional conspiracy called *The King Alfred Plan,* a government program to round up and exterminate people of African origin (it's named after Britain's King Alfred the Great). In a matter of weeks, the rumor made its way around the city and was regarded as true by a growing number of worried blacks. Even when it was later exposed as being a fictional account, taken from an acclaimed novel by a respected author, the rumor lingered. It can still be found 40 years later, presented as an authentic series of documents on the Internet.

Some Web sites connect the *King Alfred Plan* to a very real FEMA government readiness plan called REX-84 (Readiness Exercise 1984), a joint military/intelligence service simulation held in April 1984. REX-84 presented a chilling scenario that combined all military and federal intelligence and law enforcement agencies to test cooperation between these agencies to "round up" subversive groups, terrorist cells, and other gaggles of citizens deemed worrisome by the government, and throw them into detention camps — under emergency circumstances only — of course. While the methods outlined in REX-84 were never carried out, there's no denying that the plans still exist, along with the vast military and intelligence means to do what was planned.

FEMA has been absorbed as part of the many tentacles of the giant government squid known as the Department of Homeland Security, which, even though brand, spanking new, the branch is the second largest U.S. government agency after just six years of existence.

The Willie Lynch Letter

In 1712, along the banks of the James River, a British slave owner from the West Indies named Captain William "Willie" Lynch stood before a crowd in Virginia and gave a speech on how to control black slaves. Lynch was called to the colony to help plantation owners keep slaves from revolting, and he presented an insidious method to create distrust between blacks based on their degrees of light or dark skin. Dark-skinned blacks were to be confined to manual labor in the fields, while light-skinned blacks were given supervisory duties, or jobs in the plantation owner's house. The result would be hatred between house and field slaves, which would deflect their hatred of their white masters.

Lynch warns the slave owners to keep their slaves in ignorance, and to never speak to them "man to man. If you teach him all about your language," says Lynch, "he will know all your secrets, and he is then no more a slave, for you can't fool him any longer, and being a fool is one of the basic ingredients of any incidents to the maintenance of the slavery system." It's a shocking speech. Except that it never happened.

The *Willie Lynch Letter,* as it came to be known, is a hoax that has been widely circulated ever since 1993 when the letter appeared literally out of nowhere. The text of the "document" surfaced strictly on the Internet, without proof of evidence or origin. Reputable historians who've studied the letter have long denounced it as a complete fake. And there is, by the way, no record of a William Lynch in records of the West Indies as a British landowner, nor any verifiable record of such a person coming to Virginia for such a mission.

Some folks have claimed that the term "lynching" came from the William Lynch cited in the letter. Most scholars agree that the term derived from the "Lynch Law," possibly named after a real William Lynch, a Virginia resident who convened vigilante tribunals from 1776 through 1782 during the American Revolution. The Virginia Assembly supposedly allowed such irregular trials without due process because the war with Britain made regular, formerly English courts impractical. Another candidate is a Virginia planter named Charles Lynch, who punished British loyalists during the revolution by whipping, tarring, and feathering, confiscating their property, and even forcing them to join the Continental Army — everything, it seems, *except* hanging.

Lynching didn't become a common term for hanging until the early 1900s and the resurfacing of the Ku Klux Klan (see Chapter 12).

Some people have defended the continued repetition of the hoax by saying its origin is unimportant, because of the underlying truth of the application of what was described in the letter. Historians strongly disagree. When something is an intentional hoax, it needs to be properly labeled as such. And this one is a howler.

Memorandum 46

In the late 1970s, President Jimmy Carter's national security advisor Zbigniew Brzezinski allegedly drafted a document known as *National Security Council (NSC) Memorandum 46: Black Africa and the U.S. Black Movement.* In it, he proposed a devious plan to undermine black leadership in the United States, and referred to strategies being developed by the National Security Council's (NSC) Political Analysis Committee and the NSC Interdepartmental Group for Africa.

For more than 30 years, this document has made the rounds as endlessly photocopied handouts, and later, Web sites. More damaging is that it has been discussed on African-American radio talk shows, in black-oriented newspapers, and as factual evidence of government-sponsored racism before the Congressional Black Caucus, and even the United Nations.

Like the Willie Lynch Letter (see preceding section), Memorandum 46 is a complete fake. The *real* NSC Memorandum 46 is available at the Jimmy Carter Library and Museum Web site. (It's a numbingly boring review of U.S. policy toward Central America, and has precisely zero to do with African-Americans; nor is it really subtitled *Black Africa and the U.S. Black Movement.*) Brzezinski himself has vehemently denied the authenticity of the forged document, pointing out that in many versions his name is misspelled, on a document he's alleged to have written himself! The Carter administration in 1980 made a specific point of denying the alleged document's contents. And there has never been an NSC Political Analysis Committee or an NSC Interdepartmental Group for Africa.

In 1982, the CIA presented the document before the Senate Select Committee on Intelligence as part of a stack of 100 forgeries that were intentionally circulated by the Soviet KGB as part of their ongoing disinformation operations against the U.S. In short, overwhelming evidence exists that the endlessly circulated Memorandum 46 isn't genuine. Nevertheless, in June 2007, XM Radio talk show hosts Eliot Morgan and Casey Lartigue, Jr., both African Americans, were fired by Radio One, they claimed, for daring to question the validity of the document on the air.

Common urban legends

Urban legends are one thing, but when they start to affect the daily behavior of people, they're out of hand. And when, with absolutely no basis in truth, they're used to damage personal and businesses reputations, based merely on Internet accusations, they're downright libelous. Here are some of the most common, and hurtful, ones:

- ✔ In the 1980s, it was widely claimed that Church's Fried Chicken was owned by David Duke, former Grand Wizard of the Ku Klux Klan, or at least that one-time owner Al Copeland gave large amounts of money to Duke's political campaigns. But the most enduring myth was that Church's used either saltpeter or another chemical to sterilize black men, or at least render them impotent.

  Variations of the story substitute Kentucky Fried Chicken, malt liquor brewers, and Tropical Fantasy soft drinks as the evil, potency-robbing culprit. Of course, this was a common claim around high school cafeterias in the 1970s, too — but saltpeter has precisely zero effect on the male libido, teenaged, African-American, or otherwise.

- ✔ The "K" appearing on food labels, one claim goes, identifies the food manufacturer as being owned by the Ku Klux Klan. In actuality, the K stands for *kosher,* so observant Jews can plan their religious dietary restrictions accordingly.

- ✔ Snapple iced tea was originally labeled with an antique image of the Boston Tea Party, showing rebellious Bostonians hurling tea into the ocean from the deck of a ship. Rumors began to spread among blacks that the vessel depicted was actually a slave ship. The theory was so widespread that Snapple redesigned their label in 1994 and eliminated the ship.

- ✔ In 1992, film director Spike Lee told an interviewer for Esquire magazine that clothing designer Liz Claiborne appeared on the *Oprah Winfrey Show* the previous week and proclaimed "she didn't make clothes for black people to wear." Lee recommended that blacks immediately go to their closets, throw out Claiborne's tags, and never buy from the company again. Unfortunately for Lee's story, Claiborne retired from her company in 1989 and never appeared on the *Oprah Winfrey Show*. A similar hoax was circulated about Tommy Hilfiger, who also never appeared on *Oprah*.

✔ The Timberland logo depicts a tree as part of its design. A poem called "Clothes" circulated on the Internet and was deliberately misrepresented as the work of African-American poet Maya Angelou. The poem claims that the tree represents one from which blacks were lynched. The poem also alleges famed designers Tommy Hilfiger, Donna Karan, Versace, and Liz Claiborne, along with Guess and Nautica, all disdain selling their wares to black people. None of these rumors has any basis in fact. Angelou, one-time poet laureate of the United States, has emphatically stated on her Web site that the poem isn't her work.

Cocaine and the CIA

Between 1982 and 1999, the CIA made an agreement with the Department of Justice that drug trafficking by "non-employees" and "assets" working for the Agency didn't have to be reported (there was a long, detailed list of criminal activities by intelligence assets that *did* have to be reported, but drug trafficking was left off the list). As a result, Columbian drug lords, Nicaraguan Contras, and Afghan rebels who agreed to provide intelligence info to the CIA were free to import cocaine into the U.S. without being ratted out. If police or the DEA or the FBI caught them, it was fair game. But the CIA wouldn't tattle.

In 1995, *San Jose Mercury News* reporter Gary Webb wrote a three-part article about the CIA's program, the Contras, and cocaine. Later published as a book called *Dark Alliance: The CIA, the Contras, and the Crack Cocaine Explosion* (Seven Stories Press), Webb wrote that CIA-backed Nicaraguans spread crack cocaine across Los Angeles and sent the profits home to the Contras. Further, Webb believed that the CIA's actions were responsible for the spreading epidemic of crack cocaine use, especially in inner cities. Critics countered that the CIA couldn't be held responsible for simply knowing that the Contras were financing their military activities with drug money, but it became quick and easy, headline-grabbing shorthand that the CIA itself was importing cocaine. The truth was complex, hard to explain, and ugly no matter what the justification was. Then, nine months after breaking the story, the *San Jose Mercury News* backed off Webb's reports.

The African-American community reacted with outrage. The story recounted by Webb quickly morphed into the accusation that the recipe for making crack was created by U.S. government scientists and deliberately designed to turn the inner-city African-American community into addicts. The allegation was clear — it was a government plan for genocide. The accusations spread rapidly on black-oriented talk radio and in newspapers like the Nation of Islam's *Final Call*. The story became so widespread that then-CIA director John Deutsch made the historically unprecedented move of flying to

California and holding a town hall meeting in South Central Los Angeles. His attempts to stamp out the fires of public distrust were a colossal failure.

Webb's story resulted in public exposure of the CIA's role in looking the other way at drug operations sending dope into the U.S. In 1998, an internal report by the CIA itself confirmed that the Reagan administration's secret involvement in the Nicaraguan Contra War resulted in the protection of at least 50 Contras and other drug importers, a situation that the National Security Council (NSC) was made aware of. Money made directly from importing cocaine into the U.S. was used by the Contra rebels to fund their war against the Communist Sandanistas. Since the Contra operation was secret — and illegal — the NSA saw no reason to pass the news along to the DEA.

It's important to remember that Webb didn't accuse the CIA of direct involvement in smuggling drugs to the U.S. The CIA simply didn't bother to stop it or inform anyone else. But he also fell under criticism for overstating the CIA's responsibility and effects on U.S. drug imports, as well as playing fast and loose with who and what constituted a CIA "agent." Still, the core allegations he made that were denied by the government turned out to be true after all. Nevertheless, after a series of career setbacks, Webb was found dead in December of 1999 from a double shotgun blast to the face — purportedly a suicide. That's what they say, anyway.

The AIDS epidemic

Since the early 1990s, conspiracy theorists have claimed that the AIDS (Acquired Immune Deficiency Syndrome) epidemic is the result of either a government germ warfare experiment gone horribly wrong, or a deliberate government creation to eliminate homosexuals and African-Americans from the population.

The generally accepted origin of the Human Immunodeficiency Virus (HIV) that causes AIDS is that the very similar SIV (Simian Immunodeficiency Virus) "jumped species" from chimpanzees to humans. Researchers have traced the probable origin to the African country of Cameroon, and the virus is widely believed to have come from an infected chimp biting a human, or transmitted through a cut while a human was butchering a chimp. While many conspiracists like to claim such species jumping is almost nonexistent in medicine, that's simply not true; both the terrifyingly deadly Ebola and Marburg viruses have done just that in recent memory.

Rumors abound that the virus was created at the U.S. Army Medical Command labs at Fort Detrick, Maryland. While there has never been any credible evidence to back up this allegation, Ft. Detrick *has* been the site of medical experiments on human subjects involving germs and viruses (see the sidebar "Operation Whitecoat").

Operation Whitecoat

Between 1954 and 1973, Operation Whitecoat was a secret program to test the effects of antibiotics on germ warfare agents. Volunteers were recruited (from a pool of conscientious objectors to the military draft who were mostly members of the Seventh Day Adventist Church) to be infected with yellow fever, hepatitis, the plague, and others, and treated with antibiotics and vaccines. Of the 2,300 volunteers — many of whom were Operation Whitecoat researchers themselves — none appear to have died from the effects of the diseases, just in case you wanted to send a card or flowers.

Apocalyptic Conspiracies

Remember the Y2K scare — the belief that when everyone's clocks, computers, and VCRs clicked over to January 1, 2000, we'd all be plunged into a disastrous reign of electronic techno-terror of cataclysmic proportions? Cars would stop dead in their tracks. Nuclear missiles would launch on their own. Power plants would shut down. Riots would erupt all over the world, and woe to any unprepared, witless, doubting boob who hadn't purchased a year's supply of freeze-dried food, a 55-gallon drum of drinking water, plenty of ammunition, cyanide pills, and an emergency generator. Then, as you may recall, nothing happened.

The approach of the millennial year packed an emotionally foreboding wallop, and while the year 2000 was an anti-climactic dud as far as Earth-shaking cataclysms go, the year 1000 AD was also a cause for major alarm all across Europe. Christians were largely convinced that the End Time, foretold in the Bible's book of Revelation (more properly *The Apocalypse/Revelation of John*), was at hand. Of course, January 1, 1000, came and went, and nothing changed. Even an attempt to cheat a bit and shove the date to 1,000 years after Christ's crucifixion — 1033 AD — still didn't result in the arrival of the End Times. All it did was give Christians another 33 years to sweat it out.

At the heart of Millenialism is the description of Armageddon in the biblical book of Revelation, the final battle on Earth between God and Satan. Popular belief is that the Antichrist will reveal himself, and Christ will return to the Earth to take the good and the righteous up to heaven in an event known as "The Rapture," leaving Satan behind to rule the Earth for 1,000 years. The philosophy and theology surrounding these "End Times" is called *eschatology*.

There are variations in the way Christians interpret Revelation, and it's without question the hardest book of the Bible to understand. Even the author, "John," is disputed by scholars — no one can say with authority whether this John is an apostle or an otherwise unknown author. These difficulties have resulted in wildly differing viewpoints:

- ✔ **Revelation is a future prophecy.** Its many visions and descriptions can be laid over past, present, or future events, but readers of all times and places tend to think Revelation is describing the prelude to the Apocalypse as being right now. Of course, this has been done for 1,950 years, give or take, and every evil dictator has been nominated by doomsayers as the Antichrist, right down to Napoleon, Hitler, Libya's president Muammar al-Qaddafi (a big candidate in the 1980s), and Osama bin Laden.

- ✔ **Revelation already happened during the Roman Empire.** Some biblical scholars argue that Revelation isn't about some future apocalyptic cataclysm at all. They say that the Beast referred to in Revelation is really the Emperor Nero, and that 666 refers to Hebrew numerology of Nero Caesar's name. This is the Nero who famously fiddled while Rome burned, but more important, he was the first emperor to order official Roman persecution of the Christians.

- ✔ **Revelation is a road map that tells how to trigger Armageddon and the Second Coming of Christ.** The formation of the Jewish state of Israel in 1945 was the first step to arming the cosmic trigger. Now that the Jews have come back to Jerusalem, all that's left is for them to flatten the Islamic mosques currently occupying the Temple Mount and to rebuild the Hebrew Temple for God to set the Final Conflict in motion. This reason is why fundamentalist Christians strongly support Israel — helping them will bring Christ back that much faster. It's also a partial reason why Islamic authorities who are in charge of the Temple Mount categorically refuse to allow Israeli excavation under the mosques on the Mount, or to even publicly admit that there was ever *any* Jewish Temple up there to begin with.

- ✔ **Revelation is an allegory, and you need to always be prepared for The End in your heart.** Some Christian sects hold that Satan is being held in the wings by God, where he can be dragged out onto the cosmological and ecclesiastical stage whenever God chooses to bring about the End Times. So the best way to prepare isn't to look for signs of The End in headlines or warring nations, but to live every day like it's the last one.

And there are a lot of variations in between. There's big money being made in eschatological opportunism, and there's a big difference between prophets and profits.

Chapter 7

Not of This Earth: Innocent Pawns in an Intergalactic Imbroglio

In This Chapter

▷ Separating fact from fiction in Roswell, New Mexico

▷ Discovering more info about Area 51

▷ Getting to the bottom of government UFO investigations

▷ Examining claims of NASA shenanigans

The tale has become part of the fabric of culture. A flying saucer crash-landed on an isolated ranch near Roswell, New Mexico, in 1947. The recovery of the debris made headlines for just one day before the U.S. military stepped in to silence the chatter, but rumors persisted throughout the 1950s that the bodies of alien occupants were discovered, autopsied, and then packed off to a secret hanger at Wright Paterson Air Force Base outside of Dayton, Ohio. Meanwhile, the Roswell spacecraft, along with other UFOs captured over the years, was taken to a top-secret Air Force installation in Nevada known only as "Area 51," where government scientists have spent the last 60 years "reverse-engineering" the propulsion and weapons technology found on the alien ships.

Depending on whose poll you look at, somewhere between 70 and 85 percent of Americans believe that Earth has been visited at some point by extraterrestrial forms of life, and the overwhelming majority believes that the U.S. government has been hiding it. But if so many people believe it to be true, why would the government hide it? What are they afraid of?

Space really is the source of an infinite number of unknowns, which is a conspiracist's playground. In this chapter, we discuss the truth, rumors, and unknowns about UFOs, Roswell, Area 51, and the many admitted government operations to find the truth and then hide it. And we examine allegations that the Moon missions of the 1960s and '70s may have been faked.

Earth versus the Flying Saucers!

Starting in the late 1800s, reports of mysterious "airships" periodically cropped up across the U.S., Europe, Australia, and New Zealand. The earliest known photo of an Unidentified Flying Object (UFO) was a stereoscopic picture of a cigar-shaped object in the clouds over Mount Washington, New Hampshire, taken in 1870. Just as in modern UFO sightings, some of these 19th-century sightings turned out to be hoaxes, some hallucinations, and some real and explainable phenomena, leaving a small handful that couldn't be explained.

The Schulgen Memo

A real Air Force memo was issued in October 1947 on behalf of the Secretary of the Air Force, Brigadier General George F. Schulgen. Commonly called the Schulgen Memo, it appears regularly as "proof" that the Air Force was secretly afraid of interplanetary UFOs.

In the light of UFO sightings beginning in June 1947, military intelligence quickly turned its sights on the Soviet Union with much suspicion. Declassified Air Force documents clearly show just how nervous the military was. Soviet spies stole the technical secrets to the U.S. atomic bomb almost as quickly as they were developed, and the Russians exploded an A-bomb just four years after the war. The U.S. intelligence community was truly spooked by the unknown capabilities of our former ally.

Nazi aircraft engineers Walter and Reimar Horten were self-taught aircraft enthusiasts who developed revolutionary "flying wing" designs during the war. Just as the hostilities in Europe came to a close, the Hortens designed and built the world's first jet-powered flying wing, the *Horten Ho 229*. A jet/rocket-propelled hybrid, as well as a much larger, intercontinental bomber to use against the U.S., were designed just as the war ended, and the U.S. Air Force was concerned that what was being spotted in the summer of 1947 was a Soviet flying wing, based on a captured Horten design. The Schulgen Memo outlined in detail specific fears that the Hortens were directly helping the Russians and that the Soviets were rumored to be building 1,800 intercontinental, jet-powered bombers based on Horten designs. The fears weren't unfounded. U.S. intelligence was well aware that the Germans came very close to developing the atomic bomb, the Japanese came within days of dropping a dirty nuclear device on the California coast, and now the Russians were close to having their own nukes.

In June 1987, a forgery of this memo was circulated in books by British researcher Timothy Good, altering a critical passage and making it appear that the Air Force believed saucer sightings may actually be interplanetary aircraft. A comparison of Good's version with the actual Air Force document makes it clear that the military's sole belief was in a Soviet source for the aircraft, and an inquiry into the whereabouts of the Horten family members. Just one sentence of the memo was altered (by Good or by his source for the memo), and in context, it's clear that an "interplanetary source" isn't talked about at all in the real letter. It's just one of the many hoaxes perpetrated by some so-called UFO researchers.

Throughout the early 20th century, science-fiction stories laid the groundwork for tales of flying machines from outer space. During World War II, Allied pilots reported many sightings of what came to be called *Foo Fighters* — erratic UFO sightings, usually of bright lights, that have never been sufficiently explained. A wide variety of possible causes were proposed, from ball lightning, St. Elmo's Fire, and anti-aircraft targeting flares to unknown secret weapons. None of which were ever explained.

On June 25, 1947, a highly respected pilot named Kenneth Arnold was flying over Mt. Rainier, Washington, when he spotted something he couldn't identify. He described a group of objects that flew like geese, and moved "like a saucer would if you skipped it across the water." Thus was born the term *flying saucer,* and a wave of UFO sightings occurred almost immediately across the U.S. and Canada.

The Roswell Incident

The Roswell Incident is the most famous UFO story on record and is the cornerstone of an alleged government conspiracy to hide alien visits from the world. The initial discovery of a suspected UFO crash site in 1947 played out over a three-day period, then almost completely vanished from view for 30 years, before being resurrected in the 1970s by UFO researchers.

The biggest problem facing anyone who steps into the Roswell/UFO arena is telling truth from fiction. For every account of the event, someone debunks it. For every so-called fact, there's a dispute over it, and even eyewitness accounts and deathbed confessions can't be trusted. And, according to most dedicated ufologists of course, nothing officially released by the government can be trusted at all. Nevertheless, this section covers what's generally known or alleged and what can be verified — or at least generally agreed on.

Unidentified debris discovered

Just one month after pilot Kenneth Arnold's publicized sighting of a UFO over Washington State, a curious report came out of the little town of Roswell, New Mexico (see Figure 7-1). On July 4, 1947 — Independence Day — a violent thunderstorm swept through the area. The next morning, a sheep rancher named Mac Brazel, who was employed at the J. B. Foster ranch, set out across the property to look for damage from the storm. What he found was unusual debris that he couldn't readily identify, stretched out across a large area. After showing it to a neighbor, he took some of the pieces into Roswell, about 70 miles away, and presented them to the local authorities, wondering if it might be wreckage of one of the flying saucers recently reported in the news. (It may have helped motivate him that the press was offering a $3,000 reward for physical evidence of a flying saucer.) Brazel was interviewed by a local radio station, whose reporter contacted the 509th Bomb Group of the 8th Air Force at nearby Roswell Army Air Field for a comment.

The base sent Intelligence Officer Jesse Marcel into town and then to the Foster ranch to investigate. Marcel gathered up some of the pieces and took them home for the evening, where he showed some of them to his family. The next morning, he took the debris to the base, and Colonel William "Butch" Blanchard ordered the debris site cordoned off so it could be recovered, then issued a press release about the discovery.

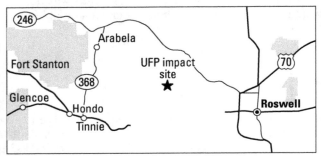

Figure 7-1: Location of the alleged UFO impact site near Roswell.

Newspapers and network radio reports appeared quickly, announcing that the Air Force captured a flying disc, but by the next day, a correction was issued changing the story to say that the debris came from a weather balloon. A press conference was held, and debris was displayed that seemed to verify that what was recovered was, in fact, a large rubber balloon and other pieces covered in silver foil.

Brazel himself was dismayed over the publicity. He'd found pieces of weather balloons on the ranch in the past, but this find had unusual composition. Still, the rancher never claimed that what he found was metal. When it was all collected, the wreckage consisted of foil, rubber, wooden sticks, paper, and tape.

Over a period of three days, the remaining debris was collected and flown to the 8th Air Force Headquarters in Ft. Worth, Texas, where it was examined. On July 9, the Air Force issued a press release from Ft. Worth identifying the wreckage as a high altitude balloon carrying a radar target made of wood and reflective aluminum. And within several weeks of the incident, the whole event slipped from the public memory for 30 years.

Roswell resurrected

In 1978, UFO researcher Stanton Friedman was contacted by retired intelligence officer Jesse Marcel, and at this point, the Roswell story was resurrected and it becomes difficult to separate fact, fiction, faulty memory, and fraud. Bear in mind that all the following events, cast of characters, and recollections from the Roswell incident have only come forth since 1978:

- **Jesse Marcel** claimed the wreckage he collected was part of a flying disc and not a balloon. The foil-like material was unlike anything he'd ever seen before, and there were strips of purple tape that contained symbols that looked like either flowers or hieroglyphics. He said that photographs of himself posing with balloon debris were taken after the real pieces were replaced with balloon parts by superior officers. Marcel, however, couldn't remember the month or year of the events.

- **Frank Kaufman** claimed to have been a radar specialist at White Sands Proving Grounds. He stated that he was ordered to the White Sands facility where he tracked incoming UFOs the night of the fabled crash. He was then sent to Roswell, where he witnessed the retrieval of at least one alien occupant — except that Kaufman was really nothing but a civilian clerk in the Roswell Army Air Base personnel office. And there was no radar at White Sands. After his death in 2001, analysis of letters, memos, and other documents show that Kaufman really was an expert at forgery, records falsification, and spectacular lying, but not radar.

- **Glenn Dennis** was a local funeral director in Roswell and claimed he'd been contacted by the air base's "mortuary officer" about caskets and the proper treatment of bodies recovered from the desert. Later, he "stumbled" into an autopsy being performed on one of three alien corpses. He further claimed that a nurse at the Roswell air base named Naomi Maria Selff (or Naomi Sipes — it varied) told him details of the top-secret operation and gave him sketches of the aliens. Dennis said the nurse suddenly disappeared, but there's no record of any such nurse ever having worked at the base or living in Roswell. His story had enough inconsistencies that he was eventually labeled a fraud by many UFO researchers.

  The film, *Alien Autopsy,* was shown on the Fox television network in 1995, purportedly showing the dissection of these Roswell bodies. The footage was later exposed as a hoax, although London filmmaker Ray Santilli claims it was actually a re-creation of authentic footage. The original film footage has never been handed over by Santilli or anyone else.

- **Gerald Anderson,** who was 5 years old in 1947, claimed that he and his family discovered a crashed flying saucer with four aliens on July 5. Two of the creatures were dead, one barely alive, and one unhurt. Anderson later provided a forged diary supposedly kept by his uncle Ted Anderson, written in ink that didn't exist before 1970.

✔ **Jim Ragsdale,** a truck driver living in nearby Carlsbad, claimed that he and his girlfriend (the perfectly named Trudy Truelove), witnessed the actual crash, and came back the next morning to check it out, before seeing a convoy of 200 military vehicles coming towards them in the desert, scaring them off. Over the years, his tale has changed dramatically as to the location of the site (35 miles north of Roswell, then 55 miles west of town), pieces of wreckage that he and Trudy supposedly recovered before the military arrived, and other important details. Ragsdale claimed there were four alien bodies and that he removed several golden helmets from the UFO, but couldn't remember where he buried them. As to other debris he claimed to have in his possession, all has been lost or stolen over the years.

Over and over again, so-called Roswell witnesses have been exposed in major inconsistencies or outright lies. So what could the motive for all these, and literally a hundred others, have been to make these tales up?

Aliens aren't just big business in Roswell — they're the town's number-one source of income. There are no less than three UFO museums in the town of only 50,000 people. True believers flock to Roswell, and it has become a UFO mecca. They sell T-shirts, dolls, coffee mugs, inflatable balloons, tours of the competing crash sites, and literally anything else you can think of — raking in an estimated $5 million a year in revenue to the town and nearly 20 percent of its income. The military base has been closed, there's no interstate close by, and there's not a lot of economic opportunities for the town of 45,000. Aliens are very big business.

Tracking the government's paper trail

UFO researchers and debunkers have both been noisy attack dogs and have made ceaseless requests for reports to be declassified and released to the public under the Freedom of Information (FOI) Act. A cataclysmic, earth-shaking event like capturing a real flying saucer and its alien occupants would change the course of civilization. At the very least, a military culture that's governed by a strict code of procedures and conduct would document such an event with a mountain of paper, photographs, and other physical evidence. Every step in the investigation of alien conduct would be painstakingly chronicled, if for no other reason than to cover the backsides of career officers terrified of making a misstep and bringing down the wrath of angry superiors on them, or worse, the wrath of an angry invading fleet of a superior intergalactic force.

Out of literally thousands of pages of FOI-released documents, there isn't even the hint of evidence of any such authentic events. In 1995, the General Accounting Office (GAO), at the request of New Mexico congressman Steve Schiff, conducted a search of all documents relating to the Roswell Army Air Base and the events of July 1947. As a result of the GAO investigation, the Air Force was directed to make an internal investigation and to report its findings.

The Air Force released reports about two formerly top-secret programs: 1994's *The Roswell Report: Fact Vs. Fiction in the New Mexico Desert,* identified a program called *Project Mogul;* and 1997's *The Roswell Report: Case Closed* described *Operation High Dive:*

- **Project Mogul:** This program was designed to detect Soviet nuclear bomb tests by using very high altitude balloons loaded with sensitive microphones and reflective boxes that could be tracked by radar. Several balloons were clustered together for extra support in case some broke, as well as to assure a constant, standard altitude position. A string of radar targets was tied to the end of the balloon clusters like a long kite tail. The targets were needed to track the experiment because the rubber balloons themselves were invisible to radar. The target boxes were mass-produced, under contract by a toy manufacturer, out of special foil, balsa wood, and tape. The tape, it was claimed, was left over from a line of holiday items and contained gold flowerlike patterns on a purple background, which accounted for the claims that the so-called saucer debris had hieroglyphics on it.

  The reason for the high security involved in recovering Mogul's debris in Roswell was that it was a closely guarded, top-secret program, whose complete details weren't even known by the civilian scientists involved in developing its technology. Likewise, the Roswell Air Base personnel would've had no idea what they were looking at. The balloon flights were conducted between 1947 and 1948, and based on the physical description, these may very well have been the objects spotted by pilot Kenneth Arnold the week before the Roswell Incident. The Soviets really did set off their first nuclear blast in 1949, based on secrets stolen from the U.S. program (see the sidebar "The Schulgen Memo" earlier in this chapter).

- **Operation High Dive:** This is a little stranger, but the Air Force alleges that this project was the genesis of claims of seeing military personnel recovering bodies from the desert. It was a top-secret program carried out in the 1950s to test extremely high altitude human parachute jumps, primarily in case U2 surveillance plane pilots had to bail out from 70,000 feet or higher. The tests themselves were done on early crash test dummies in an effort to make design changes in parachutes that prevented uncontrolled and fatal spinning. The Air Force believes that witnesses saw these strange-looking dummies being collected in the desert by military crews, who kept the public away because of the secret nature of the experiments (the Air Force didn't want word to get out to the Russians that they had spy planes that flew so high).

Predictably, the Air Force and the GAO's reports, along with a subsequent CIA investigation and report, all raised new accusations of a government coverup. Nevertheless, the overwhelming majority of UFO researchers have begrudgingly accepted that the Roswell Incident is, in all probability, nothing more than a colossal hoax.

Majestic-12

In the early 1980s, a series of documents appeared throughout the UFO community that resurrected belief in government coverups of alien visits. They described a secret government panel, authorized by President Harry Truman in 1947. The committee was known as the Majestic-12, MJ-12, and several other variations. Supposedly, the group was assembled to study the recovered Roswell spacecraft. The members were referred to as the Majestic-12 because the dozen affiliates were very big noises in the military, intelligence, and scientific communities, headed by Rear Admiral Roscoe Hillenkoetter, first director of the CIA. Later additions to the group reportedly included Albert Einstein, rocket scientist Werner Von Braun, and nuclear scientists Robert Oppenheimer and Edward Teller. Other documents have been produced that allege that President Eisenhower was briefed by MJ-12 members in November of 1952 about Roswell and a later 1950 New Mexico UFO crash. This was on the same day that the president really was briefed by the Joint Chiefs of Staff, and the documents relating to that briefing remain classified to this day. Which only adds to the mystery about MJ-12.

Documents relating to MJ-12 were leaked anonymously and under questionable circumstances to several members of the UFO research world throughout the 1980s, and ufologists seem to be split over whether they're authentic or not. If they are what they appear to be, they contain records of government officials clearly discussing UFO incidents as being very real. Unfortunately, there's also evidence that the papers are forgeries — that they've been retyped from other non-UFO-related documents with some paragraphs changed; that they contain errors in military titles of members that government stenographers probably wouldn't have made; that they use modern phrases that wouldn't have appeared in the 1940s; and most important, the unconventional and suspicious way in which the documents have turned up. They haven't come from the government as part of an FOI request. But if they're a hoax, events have been meticulously researched, and the MJ-12 papers contain much factual background. Like so much in the UFO world, finding the truth is nearly impossible.

Area 51

Even if Roswell wasn't the site of an alien spacecraft crash and military recovery mission, that hasn't stopped speculation over one of the most top-secret government installations in the world. Known by its secret designation, Area 51 (see Figure 7-1) is a highly classified military base northwest of Las Vegas in the Nevada desert. It's actually located within the sprawling Nellis Air Force Base, adjacent to the Nevada Testing Site, where the military and the Department of Energy test nuclear weapons.

During WWII, the so-called "Las Vegas Army Airfield" was the primary gunnery school for the Army Air Corps and was the home to more than 15,000 people between 1943 and 1944.

Area 51 itself is centered on a dry lake bed called Groom Lake and was used during WWII for bombing practice. In 1955, the Lockheed Corporation was looking for an isolated place to test and develop the U2 spy plane. The testing site needed to be in the middle of nowhere, easily restricted to outsiders, and far from the interested eyes of Soviet spies.

The name "Area 51" comes from the way sections of the Nevada Testing Site were designated in early internal maps. The area is highly restricted — the airspace is protected, photography is strictly forbidden, and trespassers can be fined or even shot. The perimeter is guarded by surveillance cameras, guards, and buried motion detectors. For many years, you could see the runway of Area 51 from a nearby hilltop known as "Freedom Ridge," but recently, the government expanded the land around the base by thousands of acres, and all easy views into the facility have been effectively cut off. (The closest public vantage point is now the very hard to hike to Tikaboo Peak, some 25 miles from the base.) In addition to widening its "no-spy" zone, the Groom Lake runway has been lengthened to six miles, twice as long as a conventional runway. Something very fast is still landing there.

Prior to the mid-1990s, the public never heard of Area 51, and it's clear from the reaction of the military that they aren't happy that everyone knows about it now. Its very existence was classified until 1997, and even military pilots who stray into its protected airspace are still risking major trouble. Many buildings on the base are constructed without windows, and both civilian and military workers are required to sign an oath not to reveal what goes on there.

Another deterrent to spies, snoops, and sightseers is Area 51's location next door to the principal nuclear testing range in the U.S. Is it worth it to sneak a peek at exotic technology if you're going to absorb enough radiation to glow in the dark for the rest of your shortened life?

Strange aircraft

So, now that the Cold War is over, what are they hiding today? Groom Lake and Area 51 have been used since the 1950s to test many of the Air Force's most revolutionary aircraft designs, including the F-117 Nighthawk Stealth fighter. The military keeps such aircraft development a secret by providing millions of dollars each year for "black projects," development programs that don't appear in annual budgets by name or description. Today, rumors abound on the Internet over a new Mach 6 aircraft that can fly at 130,000 feet, code named *Aurora*. Military sources say it doesn't exist, but that's just what we'd expect them to say. It's these and other unconventional aircraft that many believe are the source of supposed UFO sightings around Area 51 and elsewhere. Face it: Until the official public announcement of the B2 Spirit Stealth Bomber back in 1988, anyone seeing its extraordinary silhouette flying overhead would've figured Batman — or maybe a flying saucer — was in town.

The UFO connection

Area 51 has an authentic and vital role in the military's development of "secret weapons," but that's not really why most Americans know or care about the place. As you drive the three hours north of Las Vegas on State Highway 375, the helpful signs put up by the Nevada highway department tell the story most people want to know about. It's been officially named the "Extraterrestrial Highway." The story goes that Area 51 is the location of the wreckage of the UFO that purportedly crashed at Roswell, New Mexico, in 1947, along with the bodies of its alien occupants (see the section "The Roswell Incident" earlier in this chapter).

In 1987, Robert Lazar claimed to have worked at a base next to Area 51 called *Sector 4* (S-4). Lazar maintained that S-4 had nine UFOs, and that he was hired to help "reverse-engineer" alien technology from them. He also said that he was briefed about the origin of the UFOs — they came from the Zeta Retuculi 1 and 2 star system, 37 light years from Earth, and the aliens are referred to as *Zeta Reticulians*.

Lazar described the aliens as 3 to 4 feet tall, gray, with large heads, almond-shaped eyes, and possessing telepathic, mind control power. According to his accounts, the reverse-engineering program began in 1979, and the aliens themselves were actually in charge of the program.

Unfortunately, Lazar's incredible story is undermined by his claims that he has a master's degree in electronics Technology from Caltech and a master's in physics from MIT. Investigators have never been able to find any record of Lazar attending either institution, which only scratches the surface of the lies he has told over the years (false employment claims, incorrect details about Area 51, misrepresentation of Site 4's real-life role as a simple radar installation, and many more). Lazar counters that the government has completely removed all public records of his education and employment as either a security measure or a sinister effort to discredit him. They even removed his name from hundreds of Caltech and MIT yearbooks in libraries all around the country. Once again, a story that has become a cornerstone of the UFO movement turns out to be an elaborately embellished hoax, and no serious UFO researchers believe Lazar's claims anymore.

Meanwhile, UFO enthusiast Richard Boylan tells tales about Lockheed's X-22A "Dark Star" Anti-Gravity Fighter Disc, based on alien technology and armed with a "neutral particle beam" weapon. According to Boylan, the X-22A is deployed out of a secret underground base hidden underneath King's Peak, outside of Salt Lake City, Utah, which he believes is the new Area 51. Others have claimed (perhaps a little more realistically) that Area 51's location and activities have been compromised by all the publicity in recent years, and that the military has taken its creepy, covert aircraft business elsewhere, to Utah's Dugway Proving Ground (see Figure 7-1).

Nevertheless, tales of UFOs flying in and out of Area 51 continue to be reported. If you're truly determined, head three hours north of Las Vegas on Nevada 375, and look for a white mailbox owned by rancher Steve Medlin — it's supposed to be the best vantage point on the flight path. Pull over, be patient, and watch the skies.

Government Investigations of UFOs

At the end of 1947, the Air Force was sufficiently concerned about the growing list of UFO sightings across the country that it ordered an investigation, called *Project Sign.* Over the years, there was a series of studies made by the Air Force, along with records being kept by the FBI and the CIA on UFO sightings. We cover those studies in the following sections.

Project Sign

Project Sign was conducted between 1947 and 1948 out of the Air Technical Intelligence Center at Wright-Patterson Air Force base in Dayton, Ohio, to investigate the flurry of flying saucer sightings that began before Kenneth Arnold's famous report over Mt. Rainier (see "Earth versus the Flying Saucers!" earlier in this chapter).

The memos leading up to the formation of the investigation make it clear that the Air Force took such reports very seriously, that they believed people really were seeing flying disks of some kind, and that they were afraid the objects were using advanced technology being developed by the Soviets. They also considered the possibility that another top-secret military or civilian project, unknown to the Air Force, may be constructing these objects.

An often-repeated story about Project Sign is that the investigation team ran into enough unexplainable cases that they issued a preliminary "Estimate of the Situation" prior to the final report, stating flying disks had a "non-earthly source." Such a document has never been found and there is disagreement as to whether it ever existed. Whether it did or not, superior officers at Wright-Patterson found flying saucer claims to be ridiculous and that any suggestion of an extraterrestrial source translated as bias and sloppy intelligence work on the part of Project Sign's investigative team.

Because of the argument between superiors and the investigators, Project Sign was shut down in 1949, and its official conclusion was inconclusive.

The real X-files

FBI director J. Edgar Hoover took an interest in the reports of UFOs, Roswell, alien abductions, cattle mutilations, and other related topics. Over the years, he amassed these reports into one large collection that is sometimes referred to as the X-files. To see the 1,600 pages of FBI X-files released under the Freedom of Information Act, go to `http://foia.fbi.gov/foia index/ufo.htm`.

Project Grudge

Project Grudge was a code name deliberately chosen by anti-UFO officers within the Air Force. It immediately replaced Project Sign in 1949, and was given the directive to discredit any and all reports of flying saucer sightings.

While Project Sign expressed the opinions of investigators that the overwhelming majority of saucer sightings could be explained by natural phenomenon and misidentification, Project Grudge went out of its way to completely discredit even unexplainable sightings. The report's conclusion added mass hysteria, wartime jitters, hoaxes, and nut cases as additional causes of UFO reports. In addition, Grudge provided "assistance" to newspapers and magazines by writing UFO debunking articles.

News of the anti-UFO bias within Grudge's organization reached Major General Charles P. Cabell, the head of Air Force Intelligence at the Pentagon, who was furious that serious investigations were no longer being carried out, in favor of slapdash reporting and simply ridiculing the UFO subject. Cabell literally ordered Grudge's staff to have an open mind!

The general realized that public opinion of the military on the UFO subject was a double-edged sword: If it really turned out that UFOs were authentic, he wanted the Air Force to be able to produce a serious, scientific analysis of any potential threat; on the other hand, if they were simply figments of wild imaginations, he didn't want the Air Force to be guilty of looking too credulous. Most of all, he really didn't want the word to get out that he personally believed in the things himself.

In 1951, Project Grudge was shut down, and a new program with a new staff was formed that was intended to be as open-minded as Cabell had ordered.

MIB: Men in Black

Throughout the UFO investigations of the 1950s and '60s, a persistent rumor began to accompany sighting reports. Witnesses began to claim that strange men, often dressing in black suits and wearing dark sunglasses, appeared and attempted to intimidate them into clamming up about UFO reports. Descriptions varied wildly, but these MIBs were said to know personal information about UFO witnesses, leading to the conclusion that they were government agents, sent to silence UFO sightings.

Over the years, the tales were embellished. The MIBs were described as either dressing in suits that were years out of date, or in high fashion, and old Cadillacs seemed to be the car of choice. Some have claimed that the MIBs were actually aliens themselves, and much of the folklore about them was woven into the popular film *Men In Black* (1997) and its sequel. A centerpiece of the film was a device used to wipe the memory of a UFO sighting from the mind of witnesses. Those who claim the MIBs are real say they remove UFO crash site evidence, then erase the memories of witnesses — a handy way to explain fuzzy recollections and lack of evidence.

Researcher Bill Moore believes that the MIBs are part of the very real *U.S. Air Force Office of Special Investigations* (AFOSI), an internal security department started in 1948 and patterned after the FBI for investigating criminal activity within the Air Force and its weapons contractors. Because one of the missions of the AFOSI is to protect Air Force technology, programs, and personnel on a global basis from "external threats," it would frankly be astonishing if the MIB *didn't* exist, especially if UFOs are real.

Project Blue Book

Project Blue Book is perhaps the best known and most famous of the Air Force UFO studies. Opened in 1952, the original director of the program was Captain Edward J. Ruppelt, who was the first to actually coin the phrase "Unidentified Flying Object." The project had the blessing of General Cabell (see previous section), who was encouraged by a member of his own staff — General William Garland, who'd witnessed a UFO himself!

Project Blue Book is widely considered to be the last and best government effort to seriously study UFOs in an unbiased and comprehensive manner, and Ruppelt assembled a team of both military experts and civilian scientists. Anyone who was found to be too obviously pro or con was fired.

Blue Book standardized the way UFO sightings were investigated, with a questionnaire that allowed the data to be analyzed statistically. Additionally, Ruppelt issued regular reports and press releases concerning the ongoing investigation. The result was a growing public interest in UFOs, along with an increase in reported sightings.

The Robertson Commission: Debunking Project Blue Book

Not long after Project Blue Book was established (see the preceding section), the CIA got involved in the UFO investigation business. The Agency was concerned that the swelling number of UFO reports were starting to tax the abilities of the Air Force to investigate them all (UFOs had become such a public-relations hot potato that the other branches of the military didn't want to go anywhere near the subject).

In February 1953, the CIA assembled the Robertson Commission, made up of respected civilian scientists (including future Nobel prize–winner in physics, Luis Alvarez, and an Einstein colleague, Samuel Gaudsmit), along with skeptical military officers. After studying the issue for just a few weeks, their conclusions were as follows:

- All UFOs could be explained by known scientific means.

- Even if they couldn't be scientifically explained, the UFO controversy was overwhelmingly dominated by natural events, explainable phenomenon, or hoaxes, and took up way too much of the Air Force's time and effort.

- An enemy (presumably the Soviet Union) could use bogus UFO reports and mass hysteria to immobilize or otherwise preoccupy military resources in order to mask an invasion.

- The Air Force and other government agencies should, therefore, begin a public relations campaign to debunk UFO sighting claims and to teach the public how to identify natural phenomena that could be mistaken as UFO sightings. The panel went on to suggest getting Walt Disney to make public education films on the subject.

- The CIA being the CIA, they also recommended investigating UFO-sighting clubs and other pro-UFO civilian groups because of their potential to whip up public hysteria or other subversive activities. Based on this recommendation, the FBI quickly shut down the *Civilian Saucer Investigations,* a California-based flying saucer club with an impressive list of scientists as members.

As a result of the Robertson Commission report, Captain Ruppelt was reassigned, Blue Book's staff was severely reduced, and its budget was hacked to pieces. With Ruppelt gone, the Air Force changed Blue Book's mission to see to it that reports of truly "unidentified" objects were kept to a minimum. Investigators weren't to speak to the press unless an event was neatly explained.

The new shift in Blue Book's stance wound up wrecking its credibility with the public, and its official explanations were increasingly seen as just plain ludicrous. In one incident, four UFOs tracked by several radar installations and seen by police in Oklahoma in 1965 were passed off as misidentification of the planet Jupiter. In another notorious case, Ohio and Pennsylvania police chased a UFO across 85 miles in April 1966, and watched it descend as low as 50 feet. Project Blue Book explained it as a communications satellite, and then the planet Venus. Another famous incident, seen by several hundred civilians and police officers in Michigan over several days in 1966, was explained away as "swamp gas."

The Condon Committee: Closing the Book

As a result of the growing public ridicule of Blue Book's explanations, a Congressional hearing was held in 1966, followed by yet another investigative panel, the Condon Committee. Named for respected physicist Edward U. Condon, the committee stacked the deck in its investigation of some of Blue Book's reports so that unexplained UFO sightings never even came up for review. The investigation was held by the University of Colorado after a long list of more prestigious universities and organizations turned it down — no one wanted to touch the UFO question with a ten-foot pole.

The committee concluded that UFOs weren't extraterrestrial, were completely explainable, and posed no danger to national security. These findings brought immediate catcalls and hoots of derision from almost every corner of public and professional opinion.

In 1967, word leaked that a memo had been circulated at the start of the committee's investigation, known as the "Trick Memo." In it, committee member Robert J. Low suggested that the University of Colorado could save its reputation from ridicule if the committee's final report only *appeared* objective, but came to the predetermined conclusion that UFOs were natural phenomena, misidentifications, or figments of feverish imaginations. The memo went on to suggest that if the conclusions were suitably dismissive and if they painted UFO spotters as four-alarm loons, "the scientific community would get the message."

The final report was released in 1968, and true to the Trick Memo's suggestion, any case that had been studied that couldn't be explained was eliminated from the final version, including a puzzling sighting by U.S. astronauts during a Gemini mission. It effectively brought an end to Project Blue Book and the government's official investigations of UFOs. The only conclusion that most everyone agreed with was that the Air Force spent 21 years looking into UFOs, and almost no scientifically useful information ever came out of it.

Project Blue Book was officially closed in January 1970. Unofficially, almost 22 percent of the cases reported remain unsolved. Project Blue Book's documents have all been released to the public and can be seen at www.bluebook archive.org.

Close Encounters

Astronomer J. Allen Hynek was a consultant with all three Air Force studies, along with presenting evidence to the Robertson Commission. He started out in the beginning as a near total skeptic, but as he investigated more and more sightings, too many events were unexplainable, and his views changed. In his 1972 book, *The UFO Experience: A Scientific Study,* Hynek proposed a scale to describe the experiences of people who'd witnessed a UFO. The terms were made famous by the 1977 film *Close Encounters of the Third Kind.* While subsequent authors have added to and embellished Hynek's original terms, most UFO researchers stick with his list:

- **Daylight Disks:** UFOs more than 500 feet away, seen during the day

- **Nocturnal Lights:** UFOs more than 500 feet away, seen at night

- **Radar/Visual Reports:** Visible UFOs also spotted on radar

- **Close Encounters of the First Kind:** Visual observation of a UFO closer than 500 feet (flying saucers, odd lights, or flying objects that defy known human technology)

- **Close Encounters of the Second Kind:** Observation of a UFO closer than 500 feet, combined with physical effects (heat, radiation, radio interference, or damage to terrain or property)

- **Close Encounters of the Third Kind:** Observation of animate beings in association with a UFO, closer than 500 feet

The Brookings Report

In 1960, the Brookings Institute was commissioned by NASA to report on the future of space travel and exploration. The official title of the report was *Proposed Implications of Peaceful Space Activities For Human Affairs,* and it was submitted to Congress on April 18, 1961. The Brookings Institute is the oldest public policy think tank in the U.S., and its reports are regularly submitted to the government on a wide range of issues.

The 1961 report discusses a wide range of topics about space and NASA's role, but two sentences in particular are the subject of controversy in the UFO conspiracy universe. There is a section of the paper called *The Implications of a Discovery of Extraterrestrial Life,* and the authors surmised that "face-to-face" meetings between humans and aliens wouldn't likely occur within 20 years (through the 1980s). However, it was expected that NASA would discover artifacts or other evidence of alien life on the Moon, Mars, Venus, and other planets. The report doesn't advocate covering up such discoveries, but it does explore the possibly harmful effects such a discovery could have on society, disrupting some cultural and religious groups. Conspiracists see within the language of the Brookings Report a motive for official government coverups of alien contact to save the world from culture shock.

Britain's "Flying Saucer Working Party"

The United Kingdom's Ministry of Defence followed the same line of reasoning that the U.S. military did, waffling back and forth over the official origin or existence of UFOs, depending upon who was in charge at the time. A study team was formed in 1950 based on the recommendation of Sir Henry Tizard (the pre–World War II pioneer of radar), who felt that UFO reports shouldn't be dismissed without proper scientific investigation. Known by the unintentionally comical name, the Flying Saucer Working Party (FSWP), the directorate did work similar to Project Sign (see earlier in this chapter). After less than a year, the conclusion of the team was that UFOs weren't extraterrestrial. In 1952, Prime Minister Winston Churchill inquired about government investigations of UFOs, asking if they were real. The reply from the directorate was dismissive and made it clear that the FSWP saw no evidence whatsoever for believing in alien spacecraft.

In September 1952, NATO was holding a 12-day joint military exercise called "Operation Mainbrace" near Norway, involving 80,000 troops from nine different nations. Between September 19 and 22, at least four major UFO sightings of "spacecraft" were reported by many pilots, as well as the crew of the USS *Franklin D. Roosevelt* aircraft carrier. It was almost like a deliberate attempt by intergalactic pranksters to deflate the ego of the Ministry of Defence's dismissive report to Churchill. The result of the embarrassing incident was new British military policy that no report of UFOs would ever be made public. Service personnel weren't to discuss such sightings with the press, and internal investigations were classified as secret.

The Ministry of Defence publicly denied they'd ever looked into the UFO question for almost 50 years, which should've struck the British people as a criminal lack of curiosity on the part of their military. The FSWP files were classified by the British government as "Secret Discrete" until the 1990s. They were released to the public in 2001.

NASA's "Phony" Moon Landings

On July 20, 1969, the whole world stared into their television sets and watched blurry, flickering, black and white images as Apollo 11's lunar excursion module, nicknamed "The Eagle," descended from orbiting around the Moon and touched down on the Sea of Tranquility. In 1960, deep in the heart of the Cold War with the Soviet Union, President John F. Kennedy upped the stakes in the "space race" between the two superpowers by proclaiming that the U.S. would land a man on the Moon "before this decade is out." Apollo 11 managed to pull it off with just four months to spare.

ASK THE UNSEEN MASTER

Crop circles

One thing we've learned over the years is never to attack someone's religion. And in some circles, UFO belief has become the next best thing to a religion. No matter what evidence comes to light to contradict their claims, true believers just won't be shaken.

A case in point has to do with crop circles. To "croppies," these strange, mathematical designs stamped down in flattened crops in the middle of farm fields are proof positive that aliens are visiting Earth. To them, crop circles are either the result of UFO propulsion systems knocking down wheat and barley plants, or messages from aliens that we just don't understand yet. They've even developed a name for the study of crop circles: *cereology*. Of course, this phenomenon is a matter of hilarity to a growing group of people who regularly go into fields armed with a board, some string, and wire to make complex crop circles.

Appearing first in England in the early 1970s, crop circles fascinated the public and the press as they materialized overnight in the region around Stonehenge. As the public became convinced they were of extraterrestrial origin, the strange designs started showing up around the world.

In 1991, Doug Bower and Dave Chorley came forward and admitted they started the commotion 20 years before after planning their first crop circle in a pub. They'd intended the circles to be a hoax from the beginning, and wild tales of UFO origins only egged them on. Since then, groups of crop-circle artists have sprung up around the world. Crop circles have become major tourist attractions, and the designs have even been used for advertising in recent years — there are professional groups like Circlemakers in England.

To true believers, these artists are heretics and hoaxers, who obscure the real source of the strange designs. They believe crop circles are created by balls of light (BOLs) emitting electromagnetic energy from alien spacecraft.

It was truly the technological achievement of the century, and perhaps the greatest milestone in the annals of mankind. And yet, the day after astronauts Neil Armstrong and Buzz Aldrin left the first human footprints on another world, there were those who didn't believe it was possible. One woman interviewed by *Newsweek* proclaimed that she didn't believe it because she didn't think her TV set could pick up a transmission from the Moon. A rumor began to spread across the countryside: Maybe the Moon landings had been staged.

Various claims have been made over the last three decades about ways in which the Moon landings may have been faked, and why. Some of the more common ones include:

- ✔ NASA's first manned test flight of the Apollo space capsule and Saturn-series rocket resulted in a tragic fire that killed astronauts Gus Grissom, Ed White, and Roger Chaffee. In a test on January 27, 1967, fire broke out in the oxygen-rich cockpit, and the three men died within 17 seconds. The claim goes that the fire set the program back so badly that the

Moon landings had to be completely or partially fabricated in order to make it look like the U.S. had achieved its goal on time.

✔ Some have claimed that the Van Allen radiation belts that surround the earth were far too deadly to allow Apollo spacecraft to pass through without killing the astronauts inside. Most scientists (including their discoverer Dr. James Van Allen) reject this claim, because radiation poisoning is dependent upon the amount of time a person is exposed, and Apollo astronauts passed through too quickly to have received a dangerous dose.

✔ Conspiracists claim that the astronauts were launched into low Earth orbit, and that the Moon landing was videotaped in a studio. Then, after the appropriate amount of time, the orbiting Apollo spacecraft splashed down, all on international television.

✔ According to conspiracists, Stanley Kubrick, hot on the heels of directing the 1968 film *2001: A Space Odyssey,* which contained the first realistic and convincing special effects depicting spaceflight ever put on film, was brought from England to direct the Apollo 11 telecast. Anyone who knows anything about the famously temperamental and perfectionist director knows how impractical this claim is. Some claim that special effects were created by *2001* effects artist Douglas Trumbull in a studio in Huntsville, Alabama, home of NASA's Marshall Space Flight Center.

✔ A variation on the claim is that only *some* of the six successful Moon landings were faked, while NASA had extra time to work on its faulty technology. Apollo 13's almost fatal accident was staged in order to refocus a bored public on NASA's need for greater funding. And Apollo 17, the final mission to the Moon, was the only authentic trip, because it had a civilian crew member who couldn't be threatened or bought off.

✔ The 1978 film *Capricorn One* added fuel to the hoax claims, by telling a fictional story of NASA faking a landing on Mars, while filming the events in a studio — using spacecraft virtually identical to the Apollo missions.

✔ The International Flat Earth Society, as their name makes clear, believed (and still does) that the Earth isn't round, but flat as a pancake. That being the case, as far as they were concerned, the Moon landings could be nothing but a hoax.

There's too much evidence and far too many participants in NASA's Apollo program to convince the overwhelming majority of people that the Moon landings were anything but authentic. The Apollo missions involved $30 billion in federal dollars and 400,000 employees, with nary a squealer in the bunch. That hasn't prevented a small cottage industry of authors from crying "hoax." The 842 pounds of lunar rocks returned to Earth by Apollo astronauts over the course of six missions isn't proof to them. Conspiracists claim unmanned NASA missions brought the rocks to back Earth before Apollo 11 ever launched, or they were simply cooked up artificially in a high-temperature kiln.

In spite of piles of photographic and physical evidence, this conspiracy theory hangs on, largely promoted by late author Bill Kaysing. He was a librarian at Rocketdyne, an early NASA supplier, and claimed (without proof) that the space agency never had the expertise needed to actually land men on the moon. He further alleged that the Apollo 1 astronauts (and later the Challenger Space Shuttle crew) were murdered because they were about to reveal the "truth" about NASA. Kaysing claimed that the astronauts were actually in the Nevada desert putting on the "moonwalk show" during the day, and hanging out with strippers and Las Vegas showgirls at night — requiring years of psychological therapy before they could get over the guilt of duping the public.

Amateur filmmaker Bart Sibrel has taken a more confrontational approach to the issue. In 2002, he accosted Buzz Aldrin in front of a Beverly Hills hotel, demanding answers to his questions about the so-called Moon landing "hoax," calling the astronaut a "coward, a liar, and a thief." Aldrin reacted in a less than Socratic method over the controversy and punched Sibrel right in the kisser. Other Apollo astronauts have characterized Sibrel as a "stalker."

The first time men from Earth stepped onto a new world had a profound effect on Neil Armstrong and Buzz Aldrin, and both men grappled long and hard with their public and private reactions to an event that the whole world was watching. There are two little-known items about Aldrin, in particular. Professional atheist Madalyn Murray O'Hair sued NASA for violating church/state separation by allowing government-employed astronauts to read from the book of Genesis during Apollo 8's Moon-orbiting mission in 1968. So, on his own, Aldrin (a Presbyterian) privately gave himself Communion when Apollo 11's Eagle landed. Aldrin is also a Freemason, and he carried a special document proclaiming the moon as being under the jurisdiction of the Grand Lodge of Texas of Free and Accepted Masons, which means the Masons control not just the world, but the moon!

Chapter 8

Tracking the Evolution of the 9/11 Conspiracy Theories

In This Chapter

▷ Seeking out the origins of 9/11 conspiracies

▷ Exploring the well-known theories of 9/11

▷ Weighing in on the theory that the Jews did it

*T*hey call themselves *Truthers*. Charles Dickens, that master of mirth in monikers, couldn't have come up with a more ironic name. "Truthers," people who are involved in the "Truth Movement," believe that 9/11 was "an inside job," something that, in intelligence circles, is called a *false flag* operation. That comes from an old naval term, because ships of all countries, including pirate ships without a country, usually carried with them flags of several nations, so that they could tactically hide their identity if necessary.

Truthers believe that 9/11 was a false flag operation and that the real face behind the false flag was the CIA, the Bush administration, and the "military-industrial complex." Or worse. Everyone saw it happen on national television. Everyone heard the chilling tapes of flight attendants describing the Middle Eastern hijackers and what they were doing. Everyone saw the tape of Osama bin Laden crowing about how he didn't dare to hope the buildings would actually come down, and how thrilled he was that they did. Everyone saw every horror unfold before them in real time. It's become the ultimate event for which everyone can remember exactly where they were, and exactly what they were doing when it happened.

The unprecedented tragedy of 9/11 has been a gold mine for the conspiracy-minded. In a 2006 Scripps-Howard poll, an astonishing 36 percent of Americans considered it "very likely" or "somewhat likely" that government officials either allowed the attacks to be carried out or carried out the attacks themselves. This chapter explains where and how these theories started, and just how many facts, if any, are contained in the contentions of these peddlers of what they call the "unofficial," rather than the "official," conspiracy theory.

September 11, 2001

On a sunny and crystal clear Tuesday morning, September 11, 2001, commonly abbreviated as 9/11, America suffered a shocking and appalling terrorist attack on our own home ground, for the first time in our history. Nineteen dedicated and highly-trained Islamic terrorist commandoes, under the leadership of Mohammed Atta, smoothly and efficiently spread themselves into four tactical units and hijacked four American commercial aircraft, all from the east coast headed west, all carrying maximum fuel load, all taken within the space of an hour. Coolly and deliberately, the first aircraft, American Airlines Flight 11, was flown into an icon of American capitalism, the north tower of the twin World Trade Center Towers in Lower Manhattan, in New York City. It struck the 110-story building at 8:46 a.m., passing completely through the 94th to 98th floors.

Before America could catch its collective breath, before the nation could realize that the attack wasn't an accident, the second aircraft, United Airlines Flight 175, crashed into the other tower, through the 78th to 84th floors, at 9:02 a.m. News cameras all over the country were fixed on the already burning North Tower, and, as planned, the entire world witnessed the horror of the second crash live on television. In a very short time, the towers collapsed, reducing both skyscrapers and 2,750 people to a pile of wreckage and dust that smoldered for three months. This was no accident; it was an attack.

This was made abundantly clear when, at 9:37, American Airlines Flight 77 crashed into the Pentagon in Arlington, Virginia, a suburb of Washington, D.C. It's been the symbol of our military since its construction in 1948. By the time of this final blow, phone calls alerted the passengers of the fourth hijacked plane, United Airlines Flight 93, that this was no ordinary hijacking, but a suicide mission. It's probable their target was the White House or the Capital Building. The passengers attempted to overcome the hijackers, and in the ensuing battle, the plane crashed outside Shanksville, Pennsylvania, killing all 44 passengers and crew aboard. The numbers weren't higher, on any of these four jets, because they hadn't made stops across the country to pick up more westbound passengers. Nevertheless, nearly 3,000 Americans were dead, and the rest of America was frightened, stunned, and caught utterly unaware.

Tracking the Origins of 9/11 Conspiracy Theories

A group of professional terrorists, called Al-Qaeda, living in the sympathetic nation of Afghanistan and led by a dangerous fanatic Saudi millionaire named Osama bin Laden, brought the most powerful nation on earth to its knees with 19 commandoes and a bunch of box cutters. News cameras recorded the Mardi Gras joy in the streets of Gaza over the attacks. There was just no way

Americans could understand it. We'd been dumping billions of dollars in foreign aid into the Palestinians, indeed the whole Middle East, for decades, while president after president worked to bring peace to the region. Why on earth did they hate us?

The shock and confusion were there in part, at least, because in the past 40 years, Americans have seemed far too willing to shrug off terrorist attacks on our citizens, so long as those citizens were abroad. Since the birth of the militant Black September terrorist group in the 1970s, we'd seen Americans shot on board hijacked planes, we'd seen helpless elderly Americans kidnapped and beaten, one even thrown overboard in a wheelchair, and we'd seen Americans of all ages blown out of the sky by terrorist bombs. All these acts were the product of a blind, almost maniacal hatred of the United States.

Yet, right up to the most recent Al-Qaeda atrocities in the year 2001, so long as it didn't happen on American soil, we've seemed far too willing to look the other way. As long as everyone had their TVs and SUVs and credit cards, they didn't really want to know about the madness in the Middle East, or the blind hatred for the U.S. Even the first bombing of the World Trade Center, in 1994, though a big news story, didn't seem to make the nation as a whole feel vulnerable. The attacks of 9/11 was the logical outcome, the crash that will inevitably happen when you're asleep at the wheel. Though no one could've predicted the horrific details of 9/11, many analysts were surprised that an attack in our own back yard took as long a time in coming as it did.

Not long after the events of 9/11, a widely disparate group of people began to reject what they disparagingly refer to as the "official version" of the attacks, or the "official conspiracy theory." Like those who believe FDR engineered the attack on Pearl Harbor (see nearby sidebar), a belief has developed over the events of 9/11 that the attacks were either allowed to happen or that the U.S. government intentionally staged the attacks in order to justify war in Afghanistan and Iraq. While these folks are a statistically tiny portion of Americans, they're also quite noisy, and they've used the modern technology of the Internet and other nontraditional media to get mainstream media attention. Apparently, some of what they claim has resounded with the public, because, after all this time since the attacks, more than 100 million Americans think there may be something to it.

According to the Truthers:

- ✔ **Al-Qaeda didn't plan and execute the attacks on the World Trade Centers and the Pentagon.** The government did it. They staged the plane crashes and filled the twin towers and other buildings in the World Trade Center complex with explosives to bring them down. (See the "Al-Qaeda" sidebar later in this chapter.)

- ✔ **The Pentagon wasn't hit by an airplane.** A 757 has a 124-foot wingspan, but there wasn't a 124-foot hole in the building. The hole was created by a cruise missile. You'd think the literally hundreds of eyewitnesses who saw the plane crash, many of whom were sitting in rush-hour traffic, would put this dog to sleep, but no such luck. (For more details on this, see Chapter 16.)

- ✔ **Flight 93 didn't crash in Pennsylvania after its passengers tried to rush the cockpit.** It was shot down by military jets. Because the military was given permission to shoot down Flight 93 (17 minutes too late), nobody seems able to say why the government would hide this if it were true.

- ✔ **The government and especially the 9/11 Commission can't be trusted.** But a statement on September 20, 2001, by bin Laden originally denying involvement in 9/11 can be.

The 9/11 "Truth Movement"

The so-called 9/11 "Truth Movement" is essentially divided into two schools of thought:

- ✔ **LIHOP:** "Someone" Let It Happen On Purpose
- ✔ **MIHOP:** "Someone" Made It Happen On Purpose

Pearl Harbor Syndrome: The government knew

Devious conspiracy theories about causes of war are nothing new. Controversy still rages over whether the USS *Maine*, whose sinking in Havana in 1898 set off the Spanish-American War, was blown up by an accidental coal bunker fire or intentionally destroyed by a Spanish mine. In 1915, the RMS *Lusitania* was sunk by a German submarine, killing 1,195 people — 128 were Americans. Almost immediately, accusations flew that the British Navy intentionally let the ship be hit in order to turn public opinion against Germany and goad President Woodrow Wilson into entering World War I.

And then there's the long-rumored theory that President Franklin Delano Roosevelt provoked the Japanese into attacking the U.S. Navy in the Pacific, and that Pearl Harbor was no sneak attack. Suddenly, Roosevelt had everything he'd dreamed of, our military, our industry, and our civilians fully behind him, with a healthy boost to the economy to finally put an end to the Depression. Who wouldn't think he might've planned it, or at least known the attack was coming and let it happen? In spite of overwhelming evidence to the contrary, people of sane and moderate political beliefs continued through the years to keep faith with the notion that Roosevelt knew about Pearl Harbor ahead of time, or even caused the attack as part of his own evil plan. It's true that Naval Intelligence was jittery over several decoded Japanese messages. In fact, all America had the jitters, and we had every right. But the massive sneak attack was a surprise to everyone. Whether we should've been better prepared is another matter entirely.

The "someone" in each camp, of course, was President George W. Bush, or the New World Order, or the Illuminati, or the Jews. Anyone was responsible, it seems, except a group of Islamic terrorists who left an evidence trail of their planning behind them and whose organizers claimed victory over the U.S.

The Truthers don't seem to have one central thesis or theory, and the LIHOPs and MIHOPs often seem to be at odds with each other. The movement as a whole assembles a bizarre mixture of the Far Right and the Far Left to quibble over details. The two things they do seem to agree on are

- ✔ The "official version" of 9/11 is a lie.
- ✔ George W. Bush had *something* to do with it.

Those folks who do believe the official version of 9/11 are contemptuously labeled "sheeple."

Among the first and crankiest of the Truthers was Austin, Texas, talk radio personality Alex Jones. He has long claimed that he "predicted" the attack on 9/11, that Osama bin Laden would be blamed, and that any future terrorist attack in the U.S. would actually be perpetrated by the Bush administration. Of course, Jones regularly made vague but dire predictions that there would be terrorist attacks sometime in the future — not a big stretch of the imagination, with regular footage of angry Islamic radicals waving banners and screaming "Death To America!" on the news. It's like playing roulette and always betting on 23; sooner or later he was bound to be right. A stopped clock is right twice a day.

Examining the Main 9/11 Conspiracy Theories

If we start getting into every single thing that conspiracists see in fuzzy photos from weird angles, we'll all be here till next St. Swithin's Day. However, in this section we address the most common 9/11 conspiracy theories — the ones that are the bedrock of the genre.

The terrorist pilots weren't trained well enough to do what they did

All nervous, neurotic, terrified-to-fly types know that the most dangerous moments in any plane are during take-off and landing. These are the moments in which a plane is in the most jeopardy. Taking off, landing, dealing with severe turbulence, and handling minor or major emergencies require the skill of a pilot. But cruising is so easy that there's a movement in aviation to allow pilots to sleep on miserably long flights, so they'll be fresh for the important part. The rest of the time, the copilot can handle things; the *plane* can handle things, practically by itself. In short, it only takes brains to command a plane. It doesn't take brains to crash one.

Al-Qaeda

Al-Qaeda was born in a very different world — bin Laden cut his teeth, militarily, on the Russians who'd invaded Afghanistan late in 1979, and remained until 1989. Bin Laden's organization, founded in 1988, made up a very small and powerful minority of Saudi Arabians who helped the Afghan rebels to drive the Russians, and all other foreigners, out. The CIA gave them help, and assumed they'd be grateful to America. But for Al-Qaeda, the West was still hated, whether they were Russians or Americans or Belgians, for that matter. Like the Taliban, Al-Qaeda has been a threat to regional Middle Eastern security for years but was a name hardly known in America. It was hard enough to get a response to the name Osama bin Laden, unless you prefaced it with, "You know, that millionaire Saudi nut who's a terrorist living out in the desert." Both Hamas and the PLO were far more well-known Islamic terrorist organizations. But while the PLO was shattering internally and Yasir Arafat was hiding in a bunker from Israeli bombs, Al-Qaeda's attacks on the West, and America in particular, grew bolder and closer all the time, the worst being the two that occurred in this lead-up period:

- The first were the brazen, dual, American Embassy bombings of August 7, 1998, one in Dar es Salaam, in Tanzania, the other in Nairobi, Kenya, which took 225 lives and wounded over 4,000 people.

- The second was the bombing of the American destroyer USS *Cole* as it was docked for refueling at the port of Aden in Yemen, in October of 2000. Seventeen sailors were killed, and 40 more wounded.

But most important, and totally discounted by the 9/11 "Truth Movement" is the undeniable fact that Al-Qaeda proudly claimed responsibility for attempting to blow up the North Tower of the World Trade Center on February 26, 1993, hoping to make it topple over and take down the South Tower with it. Six people were killed in the failed attempt. How is it a leap of the imagination to believe that the terrorist group would try again, seeking out a more foolproof way to bring down the towers?

So, as for the Truthers who contend that bin Laden and Al-Qaeda are innocent, we have only this to say: Bin Laden's coy denials in videotapes released to the Arabic Al Jazeera TV network were deliberate messages to the West. In statements to Middle Eastern henchmen, bin Laden took full credit. Meanwhile, as Al-Qaeda cells were busted in Europe and the Middle East, ample proof of his involvement was uncovered. He was, for awhile, playing the game out of the Yasir Arafat playbook that helped to make the Palestine Liberation Organization almost respectable — deny it in the media of the West, but proudly take the credit in the radical mosques of the Middle East. But that game has fallen by the wayside. In a November 2007 videotape sent to Al Jazeera, bin Laden criticizes America's war on the Taliban in Afghanistan by stating that only he and Al-Qaeda were responsible for 9/11.

As for finding their target, especially on a day as clear as September 11, someone could do that with a map and a two-dollar compass. Or are we to assume that a terrorist military operation planned for two years didn't involve even a glance at a map of the United States? There are even flight simulation software packages for less than a hundred bucks that teach you, on your computer, terrain and landmark recognition and basic navigational skills. This would've helped them to learn the terrain they were flying over.

A lot of the Truther stuff about the hijackers seems not just patronizing, but almost racist, as if they denied the ability of these Middle Eastern men to do what they did. But this wasn't done on the spur of the moment, or in an emotional fit of anger or despair — this commando operation had all been carefully planned, to the most minute detail. Each of the four teams had one man who was the pilot, and it was the job of what the 9/11 Commission termed "the muscle hijackers" to keep them alive and get them into the pilot seat. As for the terrorist pilots, take a look at the training that they *did* have:

✔ All four of these terrorist pilots obtained a license to fly private planes, the easiest one to earn, which alone gave them basic aeronautical skills.

 • Three went on to get FAA commercial pilot's licenses for smaller multi-engine aircraft, logging at least 250 hours in the air; the fourth had this training, but hadn't yet gotten his license.

 • They all enrolled in flight simulation classes for large commercial jets.

✔ Just before the hijacking, they'd flown on these same flights before, up in first class, where they could monitor the routine of the crews, and so on.

 • Ghoulish or not, the fact is that each hijacker practiced not only overcoming passengers in the aisles, but also slitting the throats of animals with their small knives and box cutters.

 • And, the icing on the cake — at least two of the pilots requested and received training flights down New York's Hudson Corridor, while another took one over Washington, D.C.

   For historians, the Hudson Corridor is the channel cut out of New England by the Hudson River. It's been said that it was a great feat of navigation for the planes that left Boston's Logan Airport to find New York from western Vermont or New Hampshire. Unfortunately, that's not so. Clear from Lake Champlain on the U.S.-Canadian border, this path of water that becomes the Hudson River points like an arrow directly southward, down the eastern portion of New York State, ending in an arrowhead that is the joining of the Hudson and Long Island Sound; in the V sits the island of Manhattan. Historian Colonel David Fitz-End calls the Hudson Corridor the "same old invader's road to war." This is the route that the British used, not once but twice to invade America, in the Revolutionary War and the War of 1812. This route delivered up both the British and the 9/11 terrorists directly to the heart of New York City.

✔ Apart from their knowledge of basic navigation, all four men purchased and practiced with Global Positioning Satellite (GPS) systems. If you take this little GPS box and stand in front of, say, the World Trade Center, it will tell you your exact coordinates in longitude and latitude within 20 feet.

✔ These terrorists were also trained to use the autopilot. The autopilot is connected to a computerized navigation system. After taking over the cockpit, all they had to do was reset the navigation computer for the coordinates of their targets that they'd already obtained if they got disoriented.

But none of the pilots needed to fly on instruments to locate their enormous and singular-looking targets — it's estimated that the Twin Towers could be seen at least 50 miles away on such a clear day. One Truther accusation is correct; none of the terrorists did great in flight school. They weren't there to have a career in aviation. But there isn't little doubt here; there's *no* doubt at all that the flight tasks they performed were perfectly within their abilities.

One thing more, on the subject of skill. The two planes that hit the WTC were Boeing 767-200s. The other two planes were Boeing 757s. The two planes are similar, but there can be minor differences from one model to the next, just like cars. Also, modifications can be made by the airline that buys the plane from Boeing. The terrorists trained in cockpits that were similar to these two planes. But nothing short of the day of the hijacking could actually put them in those pilot seats, which caused the terrorists' only mistake.

Part of the terrorists' plan was brilliant — they were to turn off their "transponders," which are navigational devices that send a message to air traffic controllers on the ground. This message displays their plane's flight number and altitude on its individual radar blip being monitored by the controllers. The terrorists were also told not to reply to any radio contact from the ground. These two things made it very difficult for the controllers to figure out what was going on before it was too late. But it was the flub on the part of two of the pilots, who thought they were only on the plane's PA system talking to the passengers, but who were in fact speaking to the ground, that let the air traffic controllers in on the fact that it wasn't a technical problem, but a hijacking of some sort.

Terrorists can't hold passengers at bay with simple plastic knives or box cutters

Some of the most distasteful remarks of the conspiracists have been made over the assertion that the terrorists couldn't have kept control over the passengers who greatly outnumbered them with the weapons they possessed. Now try some truth.

First of all, only one of the sets of terrorists used box cutters, and they, like all the others, had knives as well, sharp 4-inch blades such as Swiss Army knives, that were allowed at the time to be carried in hand luggage. When the takeovers began, the slightest resistance resulted in an immediate and bloody killing, to terrorize the other passengers. Also, in the same way that the 300 Spartans were able to hold off a quarter of a million Persians, the hijackers were only guarding a narrow aisle, a corridor up which the passengers had to come no more than two at a time. This made the defense of the cockpit against a larger force a lot easier for the terrorists.

There are two other facts ignored by those who say these so-called "muscle hijackers" couldn't have subdued the passengers:

- First, they claimed to have bombs, and wore body-wrapped phonies that looked real.

- Second, and far more powerful, is the fact that, for 30 years, all hijackings, with only a couple of notable exceptions, have gone down the same way; everybody stays quiet, they end up on the tarmac in Cuba or Beirut, and the government bargains them out. This is *exactly* what the hijackers told them — to remain quiet and calm, they were being returned to the airport, and so on — on the announcements to passengers that air traffic controllers weren't supposed to hear.

The terrorists knew that everyone knew what they were supposed to do in a hijacking. Attacking the terrorists seemed foolish in the extreme. But by the time Flight 93 was over Pennsylvania, the passengers got news from the outside world and realized that Flight 93 was a suicide mission. Then they attacked the hijackers at once.

The most heartbreaking part of Flight 93 is that they came so close to succeeding. Despite the narrow aisle, the passengers obviously managed to overcome the muscle hijackers, then used a drink cart as a battering ram, along with anything else they could lay hands on. The passengers actually made it into the cockpit when the terrorists decided that if they could only kill 44 people, that would have to do. The first thing the pilot did was to turn the plane over, thereby throwing off his attackers, before he deliberately took the plane down.

The Air Force was ordered to stand down

Thruthers say that it's obvious, due to their lack of a successful response, that the Air Force was ordered to "stand down" on 9/11 by either the president or the vice president. They also claim that annual war games were deliberately scheduled for September 11 in order to draw fighter planes away from the East Coast.

The conspiracy theory of having the Air Force stand down doesn't wash because the country was in peacetime. Now, maybe these conspiracy theorists have just seen too many war pictures, but this nation doesn't live under a constant umbrella of fighter protection in peacetime — it isn't necessary. Besides, hijackings are considered an issue that falls, for the most part, under civilian rather than military authority, so discussing this as a profound military failure is a little pointless, anyway.

As for the annual war games, the most important one was called "Northern Vigilance," an exercise to simulate a potential Russian threat, that was taking place up north, in Alaska and close to Canada. (The Russians were having their own games at the same time in the same area, and also pulled out when word reached them of the 9/11 attacks.) The Air Force has claimed the higher state of alert during these games actually made their response speedier, while the Truthers say it caused a failed response. The truth is, it didn't have much effect one way or the other. The same 14 planes were on call to be deployed over the East Coast that were there in 2000, 1999, and 1998. It was just standard peacetime operating procedure then.

The only difference the war games made was to cause a few moments of confusion. In calls to NORAD (the North American Aerospace Defense Command) from air traffic controllers, the recorded conversations have pilots asking questions like, "Is this real world?" Of course they were momentarily confused, and probably hoping it was just a new wrinkle to the war games someone cooked up. However, overall, there's no evidence that the war games of that day were some deep, dark plot, or had much effect on events one way or the other.

In a normal emergency, if an air traffic controller's supervisor has confirmed a hijacking, the report goes up the FAA ladder to a hijack coordinator, through layers of FAA and Department of Defense procedures, and then NORAD is contacted by telephone, which simply wasn't quick enough for that unprecedented day. After receiving a phone call, NORAD scrambles jets to *escort* — not to shoot down — the hijacked plane. This is the only thing the military does in a hijacking. No U.S. military plane has ever shot down an American civilian aircraft before. They're there to supply information and to enter the fray in case of an emergency or a search and rescue.

On the day of September 11, 2001, 14 fighter jets were on standard alert across the continental U.S. By the time the hijackers were tracked down, even though at the bitter end, the pilots, once airborne, were given permission to go supersonic (normally forbidden in civilian airspace), it was too late for them to actually intercept the hijacked planes. And there was so much confusion that day, it was difficult for the military pilots to be absolutely certain that what they were headed for was a definite hijack. It was all happening too fast in too many different places, just as the terrorists planned.

Much is made of the fact, by Truthers, that the military response was suspiciously faster in the Payne Stewart case. It wasn't. In this 1999 case, one of the famous incidents of this sort of military escort, golfer Payne Stewart's private jet decompressed at 39,000 feet, killing or knocking out all on board, but the plane was still in the air because the autopilot was on. Truthers report that controllers lost contact with Stewart's Learjet at 9:33 a.m., and that a military F-16 jet reached the plane by 9:52, 19 minutes later. But they don't bother to tell you that the 9:33 loss of contact was at 9:33 *eastern* daylight time, while the 9:52 was *central* daylight time. This was two different time zones. In actuality, it took the jet one hour and 19 minutes to reach Stewart's plane, Also, this plane didn't have to scramble — it was already in the air on a training flight, although in fact, it had to refuel. If it hadn't, it could've reached the plane in about 50 minutes. But remember, on Stewart's plane, the transponder was still operating, making the plane easier to track. And it was one plane, not four. Considering that, on 9/11, there were only 104 minutes from the first report of a hijacking until the final crash of Flight 93, it's time to admit that the Air Force did the best they could on that incredible day.

As for the controllers being alert, even despite the accepted chain of procedures, the supervisor at Boston's Logan Airport smelled something funny, and contacted NORAD directly. Two F-15s were immediately scrambled from Otis Air Force Base in Massachusetts. But they couldn't get any coordinates, so they had no real idea where they were going. Things were just happening too fast. Before they were even in the air, Flight 11 hit the North Tower. Hijackers attacked so soon after take-off not only because the fuel tanks would be full, but because they could turn about and hit their targets before anyone could figure out what was going on. So the Otis-based fighters took off at 8:53 and were given a standard vector to fly out over Long Island and await exact coordinates.

Meanwhile, Flight 75 was hijacked, while *the same controller* was still trying to find Flight 11. Never before in aviation history had a controller dealt with more than one hijacking at a time. At 9:03, 10 minutes later, New York Center reported this second hijacking to NORAD, just as the plane was hitting the South Tower. It was only afterwards that the scrambled jets were informed that two planes hit the World Trade Center. At that point, they did the only thing that they *could* do, which was to establish fighter cover over Manhattan, circling over the ocean out of busy commercial flight paths, in case there was another incoming plane.

And incidentally, if the Air Force was told to stand down that day, as the Truthers allege, then why did so many thousands of witnesses see the fighter jets fly over the city? Was it some sort of mass hallucination?

The Twin Towers were brought down by bombs, not the airplanes

Some conspiracists believe that the Towers were brought down by bombs that were planted in anticipation of the attack and were set off in a series of explosions after the planes crashed. One of the events they love to bring up is the crash of a B-25 bomber into the Empire State Building on a foggy day in July of 1945. Incredibly, just 14 people were killed — 3 crew members and 11 office workers. But the two events weren't nearly as similar as the conspiracists would have you believe.

A B-25 isn't a 757

First, a B-25 carries, if it's loaded with optional extra fuel tanks, less than 1,000 gallons of fuel. A standard load was more like 600 gallons. A fully-loaded 757 carries 24,000 gallons of jet fuel to get from New York to California. Second, the bomber made a dead-on collision on the 79th floor of the Empire State Building, just to the right of a load bearing column, thereby, luckily, taking out none of them, which helped to minimize damage.

All the 9/11 terrorists were told to bring their planes in at an angle, which can clearly be seen on the footage of the disaster. That way, they took out as many floors as possible. (Remember that Osama bin Laden grew up in the construction business and is a civil engineer — he knew what he was doing.) Third, the B-25 bomber was going about 200 miles an hour, while the jets were going over twice that fast, and the bomber was about a tenth of the weight of a 757.

The Empire State Building versus the World Trade Center

The most important difference between the two events is in the essential structural differences between the Empire State Building and the World Trade Center:

- The Empire State Building is a web of thick steel girders, holding up a limestone fortress. It's a man-made Rock of Gibraltar, and comparing it to the Twin Towers is like comparing Belgian lace to a brick.

- The World Trade Center was a revolutionary design, the culmination of a whole new kind of construction for high rises. It was built to be flexible. Because of its great height and its glass curtain exterior, it needed to flex in high winds. That's what these buildings were *constructed* to do. Several employees of the Towers have said it took them awhile to get used to the sensation; it's somewhat like getting your sea legs.

  The chief building support was a central core of steel girders that protected elevators, heating and AC systems, and other essential building operations. This lack of the Empire State's girder system gave the Twin Towers 40,000 more square feet of office space *per floor*. Everything on the outside was just glass, concrete, drywall, and lightweight steel trusses. These steel trusses were load-bearing, as well, but to a much lesser degree. In a way, they were simply a framework from which to hang the windows. This made the buildings incredibly lightweight. The Empire State Building weighs 38 pounds per cubic foot; the Twin Towers were just 9 or 10. The structure, though huge, was downright airy, a central core supporting a glass box for show.

The men who built the World Trade Center did design the structure with a potential "worst-case scenario" in mind, the worst at that time being an accidental collision of a Boeing 707, the largest passenger jet in the mid-1960s. Of course, they were also assuming the plane would be attempting to *evade* the building once it appeared in front of them. But even the structural engineers who worked on the building admit that the fuel load of the plane wasn't something to which they gave much thought.

Fire can't melt steel!

Many conspiracists believe that the fires started by the planes couldn't have brought these buildings down. This is our very favorite conspiracy theory, though it's usually delivered up as fact. Fire can't melt steel. Right.

A fireman will tell you that fighting a fire in a high rise is like being inside a chimney. Exactly like a chimney. Think about that. It's the same method used, even by primitive man, to get fires hot enough to melt down metal.

After the two planes crashed into the World Trade Center, the windows on both sides of the towers shattered, and the high altitude wind was roaring in off the ocean like an Olympian set of bellows, feeding the flames from the thousands of tons of combustible materials in the buildings. The thousands of gallons of fast-burning jet fuel burst into flames, creating, in effect, the world's biggest commercial-grade smelter, a blast furnace. You know — *the kind they use to melt steel into girders.* Yes, in spite of the scientific research conducted by bombastic amateurs, fire really *does* melt steel. Girders don't come gift-wrapped from the pig iron fairy.

The point here is that the fire didn't *have* to get hot enough to melt the girders into a puddle. It only had to soften and weaken them. Combined with the catastrophic damage to the building, fireproofing was blown away and sprinkler systems cut off, leaving nothing to lower the temperature. The final reports estimated that the fires reached at least 1,000 degrees Celsius, or 1,832 degrees Fahrenheit. Steel begins to loose its structural integrity at about 600 degrees Celsius, and by 1,000, retains only about 10 percent of it. No, they didn't melt into a liquid pool. They bent, buckled, and could no longer bear the load. This sent the weight to the outer truss beams that were never intended to carry the weight to begin with.

Apart from the usual handful of opportunistic grumblers, most structural engineers contend that it was the skillful design of the Twin Towers that allowed them to stand for as long as they did, which enabled thousands to escape.

Unfortunately, the "pancake effect" of the collapse plays right into conspiracists' hands, because it *looks* just like a controlled implosion done by demolition experts, who've removed the building's main supports, planted explosives on key floors, and then brought the building down in just such a fashion, in order to avoid damaging surrounding properties. For a minute there, even a lot of civil engineers were shocked at the way the Twin Towers came down in such a, well, an almost *orderly* fashion.

Again, this was an unprecedented event. When they thought about it, they realized that the buildings couldn't have come down any other way; they couldn't have tipped over onto Broadway. They were reacting to the damage according to the immutable laws of gravity and physics. As each floor collapsed onto the floor below, mountainous gusts of air were pushed out of that floor, creating a visual impression of an explosion going on below the collapse, at least to the eyes of conspiracists. But it is simply a force of nature, as each floor hit the one below, collapsing the next and then the next. Despite what conspiracy Web sites tell you, this isn't unprecedented in a building collapse — it's simply extraordinary on such a dramatic and catastrophic scale.

The gobbledygook over WTC 7

The World Trade Center was a complex of seven buildings in total. World Trade Center 3, the Marriott Center, was crushed when the North and South towers collapsed. The four other nearby buildings — WTC 4, 5, 6, and 7 — suffered horrific devastation. But the collapse of WTC 7 seven hours later is a particular conspiracist favorite. In fact, it's become their banner. Why? Come now. Don't be naïve. It's because the CIA and the Secret Service had offices there, that's why! But the most damning "evidence" stems from an offhand remark made by property owner Larry Silverstein, who told firefighters, "Pull it," when told of WTC 7's imminent destruction.

Structural engineers are still studying what happened at WTC 7, but there are some things we know for certain. The wreckage from the North Tower collapse put a 20-story gash into the south side of WTC 7, but the image was drenched in smoke and away from where most cameras were placed. This gash helped to create the same chimney effect mentioned above. Large fires were also burning in the rarely-if-ever-mentioned buildings of WTC 5 and 6. Initial FEMA reports (like all initial reports, issued when confusion still reigned supreme) were seized upon by conspiracists, because they said that they couldn't understand exactly why the building came down.

But in the FEMA photographs used to slap together the initial report, you can't see much of anything for all the smoke, much less a detailed study of what was happening in those buildings. Later, when the National Institute of Standards and Technology began a massive study, they came to the conclusion that the building was far more compromised by falling debris than initially supposed.

Tower 7 also had several other things going against it. It was built straddled over a Con Edison substation, which may have caused a flaw in the design that helped to speed its demise, compromising proper support in that area. Also there were two 6,000-gallon diesel fuel tanks in the basement pumping pressurized fuel to auxiliary power generators in the building, because this was, by chance, the emergency command post for the City of New York — it had to stay running if the lights went out. After a six-hour uncontrolled burn, it was clear that the building was facing imminent progressive collapse. When the building exterior began to visibly bulge, three different fire officials ordered their people out. The slumping east side of the building went first, the penthouses were swallowed up, and the west side collapsed as well. Nobody *pulled it* – which sounds like possible slang for taking down a building with explosives, but isn't. It was simply an unfortunate choice of words in the final order of the building's lease holder, Larry Silverstein.

Later, during the cleanup of ground zero, demolition teams attempted to "pull" buildings 5 and 6, which in this instance means literally wrapping cable around the sadly annihilated buildings and trying to safely pull them down so that they can be dismantled. They couldn't manage it, even with those far smaller buildings. Building 7 was *47 stories tall,* and nobody, no-how, was going to try to "pull it."

The intent of Mr. Silverstein's words was simple — pull your people out of there ("pull it" being common slang for this with firefighters, by the way). Pull out of the effort to save it. Let it go. Stop fighting the fire, and don't risk any more lives. But the conspiracists have turned those two little words into a conspiracy, as well. How would you like for every single word you said, in a sentence in which your words may have gotten tangled up underfoot, especially while under great emotional stress, to be taken apart for years to come? We wouldn't.

Also, the initial FEMA report on building 7 made the mistaken and misleading statement that they'd never seen a building of this structure taken down by fire alone. Later, trained fire investigators and historians found a welter of similar situations in which similar structures completely collapsed under similar circumstances.

Debunking, debunkers, and the science of debunkation

In the afterward to his popular bestseller *Debunking 9/11 Myths,* James B. Meigs, editor-in-chief of *Popular Mechanics,* said:

> On February 14, 2005, I became a member of the Bush/Halliburton/Zionist/CIA/New World Order/Illuminati conspiracy for global domination. It was on that day the March 2005 issue of *Popular Mechanics,* with its cover story debunking 9/11 conspiracy theories, hit newsstands. Within hours, the online community of 9/11 conspiracy buffs ... was aflame with wild fantasies about me and my staff, the magazine I edit, and the article we had published.

He later adds, "We had begun our plunge down the rabbit hole. Within hours, a post on www.portland.indymedia.org, a Web site which claims to be dedicated to 'radical, accurate, and passionate tellings of truth,' called me 'James Meigs the Coward and Traitor.'" Well, that's subtle. According to Mr. Meigs, the invective and threats began to pour in, calling the magazine a front for the CIA, evil scum, puppet of the Mossad (Israeli intelligence), yada, yada, yada.

This is a favorite "Truthers" tactic — don't address the facts, just demonize the opposition. It's an old ploy, but these guys have given it a dangerous new razor's edge. In fact, Mr. Meigs's afterward essay on "The Conspiracy Industry" is a neatly written and brief but thorough guidebook on the tactics used by conspiracists: demonizing the enemy, argument by anomaly (if there's one tiny fact we don't yet understand, then none of it is true), ceaseless echoing of the same ideas from one book and Web site to another, and of course, upping the ante on the ever-expanding number of people who are obviously in on the conspiracy or who've been silenced by it, as one by one experts and organizations find not a shred of reason in their arguments.

However, we'll risk life, limb, and reputation by saying that of all the books out there on the conspiracies of 9/11, you won't find a more informative one than *Debunking 9/11 Myths.*

As for the absurd contention that, even if the Twin Towers came down the way they said, building 7 was taken down on purpose in order to destroy incriminating documents within the offices of the CIA and others, it's so stunningly stupid it almost defies a reasonable reply. It makes sense to these conspiracists to involve hundreds, if not thousands of people in a conspiracy to take out the building with airplane crashes and preplanted explosives in order to destroy some paperwork? So, these guys never heard of a paper shredder?

The Towers Struck an Iceberg

There's a lousy joke that's about a century old. Some guy says the Jews were behind the sinking of the Titanic, and when the other guy says he thought it was an iceberg, the guy replies, "Iceberg, Goldberg, what's the difference?"

Some things never change, and one of them is the existence of the kind of person who blames the Jews for everything. From the price of toilet paper to the hassle of daylight saving time, it's all a Jewish plot. No, all Truthers aren't anti-Semitic. But it does say something about the movement as a whole that so many anti-Semites have found a haven there.

While America was still grieving, still trying to come to grips with what happened, the first and perhaps the ugliest conspiracy theory began to hit the Internet. Like a number-one song on the pop charts endlessly droning in your ears, the first theory dredged up that age-old sentimental favorite of jack-booted thugs everywhere — *the Jews did it.* Did you notice that over 4,000 Jewish workers in the World Trade Center didn't show up for work that day, after receiving a warning phone call about the attacks? Yeah. We didn't notice it, either.

The neocon menace

Here's how this conspiracy theory goes. Apparently, barbeque-mad, Western, boot-and-hat-wearing George Bush, son of Texas oil money, is really controlled behind the scenes by a small cabal (they love that word for a sinister little group) of evil Jews called *neocons*. Heard the term before? It's short for "neoconservatives," and in very broad, general terms, it means former liberals, from "red diaper babies" to 1960s campus radicals, who've become conservatives — a new kind of conservative. And yes, many of them in places of power are Jewish. In the case of this conspiracy theory, neocon is a code word, meaning "the bunch of Jews running the administration who only care what happens to Israel."

According to this theory, George Bush is an accommodating boob who was tricked by his Jewish handlers into looking the other way, while they set up 9/11. And why would they do that, you ask? Because Afghanistan and Iraq, both peace-loving nations, were certainly no threat to America, but they *were* a threat to the conniving Zionist Jews in Israel that are the sinister comrades-in-arms of the Zionist, Freemasonic, Illuminati plotters in the White House. And the only way that they could dupe powerful America into doing their dirty work for them and creaming these two countries is by crafting an attack so vicious, so diabolical, that Americans would never forgive and forget, and never look the other way as they have at so many embassy bombings and kidnappings and regular, standard-issue hijackings in the past.

Look, we don't write 'em, we only report 'em.

An organization of neocons that's most particularly in conspiracist gun sights was founded by Bill Kristol and Robert Kagan, and called the *Project for the New American Century.* Both men are Jewish, so it's always big on the paranoia hit parade. On the other hand, many neoconservatives, from Rupert Murdoch to Donald Rumsfeld, aren't Jewish. What the Jewish portion of neoconservativism really represents are former influential liberal Jewish intellectuals who slowly changed into influential conservative Jewish intellectuals. Men like publisher and TV pundit Bill Kristol, son of the ultimate neocon Irving Kristol, decided that liberalism of the 1970s and 1980s had drifted so far from basic American principles that it no longer constituted a "viable and cohesive set of ideals on which to run a country." And, as far as Jewish liberals are concerned, them's fightin' words.

The "proof" is in the poetry

Arguably, the starting point of this conspiracy theory can be traced to the poet Amiri Baraka (born Everett LeRoi Jones). He was the poet laureate of New Jersey. (The poet laureate of *New Jersey?*) In his ode *Somebody Blew Up America,* he wrote:

> *Who knew the World Trade Center was gonna get bombed/Who told 4,000 Israeli workers at the Twin Towers/To stay home that day/Why did Sharon stay away/Who know [sic] why Five Israelis was filming the explosion/and cracking they sides at the explosion?*

Well, it's not exactly Tennyson. All artistic merits aside, it blatantly helped to spread two completely absurd lies:

- ✔ 4,000 Jewish workers didn't show up at the World Trade Center on 9/11.
- ✔ Israeli prime minister Ariel Sharon was scheduled to speak in Manhattan that day and cancelled at the last minute.

This whole grim fairy tale got started when Syria's government-owned newspaper, *Al Thawra* (now there's an unimpeachable source), reported from nowhere on September 15 that 4,000 Jews hadn't shown up for work that day at the World Trade Center. It seems that they twisted this fantasy out of a statement in an article in the *Jerusalem Post* that the government was attempting to find 4,000 Israeli nationals who were in the Manhattan area on the day of the explosions. Many foreign governments were doing this, since hundreds of, for example, British and French nationals were killed on that day.

Of course, it's sheer lunacy. If you're the sort that finds any comfort in figures regarding dead people, it's provable lunacy. A total of 2,071 occupants of the World Trade Center were killed that day. Of that number, based on the word of family members and the records of the medical examiner's office, at least 400 victims were confirmed to have been Jewish. That represents roughly 15 percent of the total victims, which is in line with the percentage of Jews in the population of New York City and the state; actually, it's a shade higher.

Probably the most dangerous part about the Jewish 9/11 conspiracy theories is the way that they're so enthusiastically embraced by our enemies in the Middle East. While most really wild and wooly conspiracy theories only make it to the Internet in America, or sometimes into self-published books, they make the front pages of the major newspapers in the Islamic world, reported as gospel (pardon the expression) truth. And probably the most depressing part about this conspiracy theory is that, even though it's the one that got going first, it's proved to be the one with the most staying power. It still plays a key role in a huge number of Truther and conspiracist accusations.

History is truth. The people who study the history of a past event, whether it's ten or ten thousand years in the past, are patient sojourners after truth, because they know that truth is mankind's only life preserver, and so it's our most precious possession. Truth is the only hold we have on reality. A famous maxim states that those who don't remember history are destined to repeat it. But those who twist the truth beyond recognition are destined not just to face a repeat performance of history, but to become its first victims.

Screws loose in *Loose Change*

One of the most spectacular, and unexpected, successes of the "Truth Movement" has been a college-made video by three 20-something Truthers: Dylan Avery, Korey Rowe, and Jason Bernas. Like the Hardy Boys on crack, they set out to do their own scathing investigative journalism into the "lies" about 9/11. The video, *Loose Change,* was made on a laptop computer by using footage cobbed off the Internet. (Tellingly, the project started out as a fictional story.) Sometimes rising far above its limitations in quality, it plays right out of the Jolly Joe Stalin Handbook for Propaganda, filled with unsupported assertions, scurvy intimations, and some out-and-out lies. They use simplistic, unscientific arguments to prove their points, and they go cherry-picking for quotes from government officials, to juxtapose unrelated statements in order to make it sound like the government knew ahead of time. Some of their claims include the following:

✔ **The fires in the Towers weren't hot enough to melt steel.** Quite the contrary — they were plenty hot enough to weaken the girders, causing them to structurally fail under the weight of the floors above.

✔ **The Empire State Building wasn't knocked down when it was hit by a B-52, so the WTC Towers should've survived the smaller plane hits.** The Empire State Building wasn't hit by a B-52. It was a much smaller, lighter, slower B-25.

✔ **Terrorist hijackers couldn't have been flying the planes, because the moves they executed were unsafe.** What part of "they were intending to crash them" do these boys not understand?

✔ **The South Tower was hit by an unmarked, gray jet, with no airline markings.** Maybe it looks unmarked when played back on an iPod, but the United paint job is undeniable in frame enlargements.

✔ **$167 billion in gold was stored under the World Trade Center and was secretly removed.** It was really $230 million — not chump change, but considerably less than their outrageous claim, and all of it was recovered and accounted for.

✔ **Flight 93 didn't crash in Pennsylvania.** They claim the *real* Flight 93 was loaded with some 200 passengers from all four planes and landed in Cleveland, where the

continued

passengers were taken off and, presumably, "disposed of." The problem with this one being that the total manifest of all four planes couldn't fit onboard Flight 93. At other times they claim Flight 93 *did* crash in Pennsylvania, but after being shot down by the military.

✔ **A mysterious "pod" was mounted under the fuselage of one of the planes, clear evidence that it's a massive bomb.** Both planes that hit the Trade Towers were 767-200s. Comparisons with 767s under the same lighting simply show a bulge where the wings join the main body of the jet. This reckless claim was so loudly debunked almost immediately that the boys quickly edited it out of subsequent versions.

Probably the worst claim was in their first version of the film, which is hard to get your hands on. Not surprising, since they've retreated from so much of the garbage in it. In their original film, they asserted that the phone calls from loved ones onboard the hijacked planes were phonies. Because pilots have never allowed passengers to use cell phones in flight (they have the potential to interfere with the cockpit radios) this "documentary" (or maybe "mockumentary"?) was able to get away with saying that cell phones don't function between 30,000 and 40,000 feet. Actually, most of the calls were made from onboard telephones. However, when the scientists working for *Popular Mechanics* were able to easily disprove their assertion about cell phones, one of these shrewd journalists said in a recent documentary on 9/11 conspiracy theories, "Well, we're editing that out in our new version, because we don't want to loose our credibility."

When the documentary claimed that these phone calls, the last words of wives to husbands and sons to mothers, were phonies created by the federal government as part of the plot, it was too much for even the nuttiest of Truthers. Subsequent versions of the video had the disgusting assertion edited out. New edits of the video continue to be released, as one by one their most appalling claims get blasted out of the water (www.screwloosechange.com).

Each version of the video will probably be more slick and convincing than the one before, but we give you fair warning. The politics of these three is a little more than just edgy. Recently the perpetrators of *Loose Change* were interviewed by Eric Hufschmid, an all-purpose rabble-rouser who is also a devout Holocaust denier. (For more on the phenomenon of Holocaust denial, see Chapter 6.) When Hufschmid accused them of not spending enough time in their documentary making it clear that the Jews were behind 9/11, this was the lucid response of Jason Bermas:

> "Take our word for it; we're well aware of the Illuminati and the New World Order, and we're well aware that there are people who want an all-Jewish state. We realize that all these things exist, but that's not what we're about." Bermas later added, "We're hoping to get to the bottom of this Zionist criminal network you're talking about."

There's a reason that *Loose Change* was seen in the vast, jumbled ocean of the World Wide Web, rather than on, say, CBS. The wild and wooly, and often fact-free world of the Internet is sort of a sandwich board for the alienated, a place where they can say what they like without being answerable to anyone. Most television shows won't even interview the *Loose Change* triumvirate, for fear of giving them a forum to spread their views. Or, as comedian Bill Marr said, "Will you people stop asking me to do a show on this subject, and start asking your doctor if Paxil may be right for you?"

Part III
Secret Societies and Societies with Secrets

The 5th Wave   By Rich Tennant

"Yes, I recently joined the Mystic Order of the Noble Yam. How'd you know?"

In this part . . .

Starting a secret society goes back to ancient Egypt and Rome. This part exposes the major secret societies of the last century and a half, the ones that still haunt every conspiracist cubbyhole in the bookstore and on the Internet. Here you meet the Freemasons, the Rosicrucians, the Illuminati, the Ku Klux Klan, the Mafia, and the rest of the rogue's gallery that lurk in the shadows of secrecy. You can't figure out the players without a program. Let this part be your guide!

Chapter 9

The Freemasons: The World's Longest-Running Secret Society

In This Chapter

▷ Investigating the Masonic fraternity

▷ Discovering the practices of the Freemasons

▷ Uncovering Masonic conspiracies, real and unreal

*I*f you're over the age of 60, you probably know who the Freemasons are — you might be one, or your dad or a relative may very well have been a member. At its most basic level, Freemasonry, or just Masonry, is the largest, oldest, and best-known gentlemen's fraternity in the world. Like college fraternities, this group binds its members together into a brotherhood by providing a shared initiatory experience (without the binge drinking, wedgie fights, pink bellies, and depantsing). Initiation into the Freemasons is a serious and solemn ritual ceremony, and that ritual unites its members everywhere in the world.

In 1900, one out of every four adult American men was a member of some kind of fraternal organization, and the Masons were the premiere group to join. When they were in their heyday in the 1950s, there were more than 4 million Freemasons in the U.S. alone. That number has declined to just under 2 million today, with about 5 million worldwide.

The baby boomer/Vietnam-era men, who rejected anything that sniffed of "The Establishment," brought a long decline in interest and membership, but Freemasonry seems to be on the upswing again. Popular references in movies, television, fiction, and even comic books generated buzz on the Internet. In the past, prospective applicants needed to ask a known Mason for a petition or be referred by existing members, today's new petitioners pound on lodge doors electronically, via Masonic Web sites.

Even Dan Brown's original *Da Vinci Code* book cover contained a clue for his long-anticipated sequel that implied it was about the Freemasons and Washington, D.C. Freemasonry seems to be everywhere.

With new popularity has come new — or in most cases, resurrected — notoriety and suspicion. With one notable period in the 1820s and '30s, Freemasons in the United States have historically been regarded as pillars of their communities, upright, clean-living, trustworthy, and charitable. That hasn't been the case outside of the U.S., where the Masons were accused of a wide range of crimes, from petty deceptions to world domination, and everything in between. Depending on the country, Masons were ridiculed, hounded, arrested, imprisoned, and even executed, right up into the 21st century.

This chapter explains who the Masons are, why they attract conspiracy theories to themselves like Angelina Jolie attracts tattoos and tabloid paparazzi, and why so many groups copy their rituals and their structure. For even more detail about the Freemasons than we can go into in the context of this book, see *Freemasons For Dummies* (Wiley) by Christopher Hodapp.

Examining the Origins of Freemasonry

The Freemasons are arguably the world's best-known and least hidden secret society, and they've been portrayed as an object of ridicule as well as a dark and sinister force since the early 1700s. The modern fraternity of Freemasonry began in Scotland and England throughout the last half of the 1600s, but its legendary origins go back to the stonemason guilds of the tenth century in the English town of York. And its mythical beginnings are said to date to 1,000 BC with the building of King Solomon's Temple in Jerusalem.

Boiled down to its simplest philosophy, the modern day Freemasons are based on the cathedral builders of the Middle Ages, and they use the terminology of the stonemasons to teach their members allegorical lessons about morality, charity, and honor. Instead of building cathedrals out of stone, the Masons say they're building cathedrals in the hearts of their members.

Very briefly, Freemasonry is a great big club, primarily for men, that uses symbolism and ritual to initiate its members and to teach them allegorical, moral lessons. The stated goal of the fraternity is to take good men and improve them morally, spiritually, and emotionally, by encouraging them to cultivate brotherly love, charity, honesty, and integrity. Masons believe they can improve society by making men better husbands, fathers, sons, and citizens.

Freemason lodges can be found in nearly every country on Earth. Certainly their existence is no secret. In the United States, Masonic lodges are listed in the phone book, and their activities are frequently covered by local newspapers. Masons wear rings, hats, and belt buckles sporting the organization's well-recognized symbol: the square and compasses, usually with the letter "G" appearing in the middle (which stands for the combination of geometry and God, referred to as the Great Architect of the Universe). They have Web sites and blog sites and have even recently started advertising for new members on television.

So what's the big secret?

The Masons themselves often use the somewhat coy expression, "We're not a secret society — we're a society with secrets." In recent years to help increase their membership, they've gone out of their way to throw open the doors of their lodges, invite the press in, and declare, "We have no secrets, apart from passwords and funny handshakes." And, indeed, on the surface, taken very literally, that is so. The distinction is in how you perceive the concept of secrecy.

The Freemasons have three different levels in the initiation of their members, called *degrees,* which are based on terminology from the medieval stonemasons' guilds from which the Masons are ostensibly descended (there are additional degrees in associated Masonic organizations, and we discuss them later in this chapter):

- ✔ New members are *initiated* and made **Entered Apprentices.**
- ✔ Next, they're *passed* to the degree of **Fellow Craft (or Fellows of the Craft).**
- ✔ And finally, they're *raised* to the third degree, the **Master Mason.**

The Masons weren't the first to have such trappings. There have been initiatory ceremonies in Ancient Rome, Greece, Egypt, and long before (see Chapter 3). But for some reason, when the Freemasons started performing them shortly after their public formation in London in the early 1700s, their detractors immediately piled on, both with hoots of derision and dire warnings of evil doings.

We're going to let the cat out of the bag right now and tell you the Very Big Secrets of the Freemasons. Sort of. The secrets of Freemasonry are (cue the eerie organ music):

- ✔ **Passwords:** These are part of the methods of recognition used to keep non-Masons from entering a lodge meeting. Nobody gets in without knowing the password, and it's different depending on what part of the world you're in and on what "degree" the meeting is being opened on.

- **Grips:** These are the different handshakes used, in conjunction with the password, to be admitted into the lodge. Again, depending on the degree, there are different ones. Grips may also be exchanged in social settings outside of the lodge to quietly determine if another person is a Mason. Masons do this all the time, and it really creeps out wives and girlfriends.

- **Signs:** These are specific hand gestures used in a lodge meeting as a salute between members and officers. Again, there's a different one for each degree. You may have heard your great aunt Matilda say, "Granddad's car broke down once. He went out and made some funny signal and three Masons pulled over to help us." *That's* what she was talking about. It still works.

- **Steps:** These refer to a specific placement of the feet, which are accompanied by the signs as part of a salute.

- **"The secrets of a Brother Mason, when communicated as such":** This is when the truly nervous types get truly nervous. Masons obligate themselves to keep a brother's secret if asked to do so — *murder or treason excepted.* Conspiracy lovers and secrecy haters, please feel free to leap from your reading chairs at this point and scream, "Ah-HA!" Except that this directive is really not about secrecy, but about honor and keeping your word. Much of what goes on in Masonic rituals deals with that somewhat quaint, old-fashioned, out-of-date concept of honor. But this obligation doesn't mean Masons lie or cover up for each other.

- **The particulars of the three degree ceremonies:** Okay, we won't be telling you a lot about these, because the point of initiatory ceremonies in any given group is to not ruin the surprises for the initiates. But it's another aspect of honor. The degree rituals of Freemasonry have been available in bookstores, written by eavesdroppers, former Masons, and other opportunistic weasels, almost since the fraternity was publicly formed in 1717. Masons know that non-Masons can find out anything they really want to know. But a new Mason promises to keep these secrets, even if the whole world knows them, as a token of his personal pledge of honor to his fraternal brothers. It's a symbol of his integrity, which is why Chris won't show his mom the handshakes.

The Internet is rife with examples of the literally dozens — if not hundreds — of symbols used in the many different branches of Freemasonry (see Figure 9-1). These aren't secrets at all, and are used by Masons as part of their allegorical lessons, or at times, to help Masons memorize their rituals (Masonic ceremonies are usually recited by officers from memory). It's no exaggeration to say that there are enough books available to fill an entire library about interpreting Masonic symbols, and every Masonic author (and every anti-Masonic author, for that matter) has his own opinion of what the symbols of Freemasonry mean.

Figure 9-1:
An 18th-century visual aid, called a Tracing Board, showing some of the many symbols used in Masonic rituals.

Dating back to the Old Testament

Some of Freemasonry's legends claim that the group was descended from the great builders of the Old Testament — the Tower of Babel and King Solomon's Temple. By making such claims, Freemasons figured they gave themselves a more "ancient" and impressive pedigree. Other legends of the origin of Freemasonry have been advanced over the years. Here are a few that some Masons and historians have speculated about, with very little (if any) proof. Most modern Masonic scholars regard them as balderdash:

- ✔ Freemasonry may have been founded by the ancient Egyptians, who created the pyramids — the pinnacle of geometry, architecture, and the building arts.

- ✔ Masonry may have descended from the ancient Greek mystery schools (discussed in Chapter 3), especially the Pythagoreans (named after the creator of the Pythagorean theorem that was drummed into your head by your 7th grade math teacher). This theory accounts for the preoccupation the Masons have for geometry in their ceremonies.

- ✔ Masonry may have been created out of the *Rosicrucians,* possibly by alchemists. Many of the early speculative Masons like Robert Moray and Elias Ashmole were also students of Rosicrucianism, and they may have brought a lot of those philosophies with them into their Masonic lodges.

- ✔ Freemasonry may have been created by the medieval Knights Templars, who had been excommunicated and disbanded between 1307 and 1314.

The problem with these and other legendary origins is that non-Masons take them as fact, or at least as being worthy of strong speculation. In most cases, these theories were created by wishful thinkers and speculative Masons who sought a more ancient origin. Just seeing similarities in organizations, societies, philosophies, and words that came before Freemasonry's big change in the late 1600s ignores the strong probability that the new Enlightenment-era organizers of the fraternity borrowed from many sources to create something new.

There were certainly influences from many of these earlier groups, and philosophies were added to Masonic ritual, degrees, ceremonies, and vocabulary over the years, but it isn't credible to believe that Freemasonry itself has a clear line of descent from Egypt, Greece, or even the Templars of the 13th century. Most important, modern Freemasonry was developed by Enlightenment thinkers, who specifically *rejected* superstition and the occult — which is what makes allegations that Freemasonry is occult somewhat comical.

Evolving into modern Masons: Operative and speculative periods

In their history, Freemasons speak of two periods:

- *The operative period,* when they were actual stonemasons building churches, castles, and bridges

- *The speculative period,* when operative Freemasonry evolved into a philosophical fraternity

So today, here's what's really known about the origins of modern day Freemasonry:

- The first stonemason guilds appeared in England in 926 AD under King Athelstane, grandson of Alfred the Great. They were essentially trade unions, charged with training their members, setting wages, and guaranteeing a level of quality for their work.

- Guild members formed themselves into lodges — the equivalent of today's union locals, centered around specific construction projects. *Lodge* became a word both for the group of members, as well as for a cabinlike structure on the construction site where the members gathered for education, meals, initiation of new apprentices, socializing, and sometimes even sleeping.

- Written records of the Mason guilds that detail their rules, activities, and organization have survived. The earliest is the *Regius Manuscript,* from 1390 AD. Modern Masons would later use these records as inspiration to create their own rules, rituals, and practices.

- The first records of speculative, non-stonemasons joining operative stonemasons' lodges were Robert Moray in 1641 in Scotland and Elias Ashmole in England in 1646. Both men were members of the *The Royal Society of London For The Improvement Of Natural Sciences* after its formation in 1660, and started what would be a regular association of Royal Society gentlemen joining Freemason lodges. Between Moray's and Ashmole's initiation into Freemasonry, and its official founding in 1717, the nature of the fraternity completely changed, and no one fully understands how or why. Over the next 50 years, London lodges began admitting nonlaboring gentlemen as speculative or "accepted" Masons. And the groups also began meeting in pubs.

- In 1717, four London lodges, named after the taverns in which they met, held a joint meeting at the Goose and Gridiron Pub near St. Paul's Cathedral and announced the formation of the "premiere" Grand Lodge of England. The first grand officers elected at the meeting were all "gentlemen," and not operative Masons. The Freemasons were now officially, wholly speculative and visible to the public.

Modern Mason Methods and Memberships

Modern Freemasonry was created during the time of the Enlightenment in Europe, largely in Scotland and in England. Both countries suffered through centuries of internal wars, many of them motivated over the struggle between Roman Catholicism and Protestantism. The English Civil War seemed to be the final powder keg that led to the Enlightenment. The philosophy of the Enlightenment was to put an end to superstition, magic, and surmise, and replace it with rational thought and the scientific method — a bold goal at a time when a belief in witchcraft and the religious persecution of heretics were all still in full force. At the time of Freemasonry's beginnings, people were still being burned at the stake or having their feet roasted off in ecclesiastical dungeons over the question of whether there were five holy sacraments or just two.

The Freemasons brought the ideas of the Enlightenment into their lodge rooms and put them into practice. The lodges were places of true equality. Two topics — politics and religion — were forbidden to be discussed in open meetings. Out in the street at the time, such discussions in the company of the wrong types of people could get you killed, or at least worked over by unsympathetic men wielding hot, pointy, uncomfortable devices.

Freemasons meet in a building called a Masonic Temple, a Masonic Center, or simply a Lodge. Throughout most of the world, a lodge has a name and usually an identifying number assigned to it by the state or country's governing Grand Lodge (for example, Ancient Landmarks Lodge No. 319).

The neighborhood lodges you find around the world are referred to by several descriptions. In everyday usage, they're interchangeable:

- ✔ **Symbolic Lodge:** This term was taken from the many symbols used as part of the Masonic ritual ceremonies.

- ✔ **Craft Lodge:** Because Masonry is believed to have come from the medieval craft guilds, the fraternity is often called the Craft, and the lodge is a Craft Lodge. This term does *not* mean witchcraft.

- ✔ **Blue Lodge:** This term is the most common one for a local lodge and may come from a line in the ritual ceremony of the first degree referring to the canopy of heaven, meaning the sky. It may also have to do with the traditional color decorating English Masonic aprons, which is light blue.

Hints of suspicion

It wasn't long after the Freemasons formed that they spread literally around the world, by way of the colonizing ships of the English, French, Dutch, and other European powers. The 18th century saw Freemason lodges open in major cities and even minor outposts, and it wasn't long before the important men in a given area wanted to be a member. While on paper Freemasonry talked of universal brotherhood and the equality of Man, in reality it was one of the first, biggest, and most influential private clubs in the world, and the lodges were always happy to have the mayor or the banker or the principal churchmen or the successful businessmen ask for membership. And that, of course, is where the first whiffs of suspicion came from.

The Masons were bringing the concepts of the Enlightenment out of the lofty, utopian-minded salons of the philosophers and putting them into practical use. Its origins in the mid-1600s occurred while Europe's nations were busy making war on each other, and even on their own citizens — over the so-called "divine right of kings" to have a guaranteed job for life, and over whose church was the most properly Christian. What the Freemasons did was to take the Enlightenment notions of scientific knowledge, reason, equality, freedom, and "natural law" and apply them to the operation of their new fraternity. And that's where the seeds of suspicion first came from.

Royal objections

Kings didn't much care for Freemasonry because Masonic lodges let all their members vote for their officers. This was a drop-dead terrifying notion for a king, because if his subjects got the idea that they could actually vote for or against someone in authority, his Majesty may have an open rebellion on his hands. And, of course, the Masons met behind closed doors, where plots could be hatched.

Kings in France and the German states, in particular, were wary of the growth of Masonry in their countries. English Masons, on the other hand, made a shrewd move early on — they courted members of the English royal family. Since the mid-1700s, a royal (usually the prince of Wales) has generally served as the Grand Master of the Grand Lodge of England.

Papal objections

The Catholic Church didn't care for the Masons either, because the lodges had a strictly ecumenical, nonsectarian arrangement. Britain's citizens, where Freemasonry began, had spent more than two centuries killing each other over religion, so the founders of Freemasonry established a nonsectarian rule: A man could become a Mason, so long as he believed in a "supreme being" and an afterlife. What church he attended — Catholic, Quaker, Protestant, Anglican, Calvinist, even Jewish — didn't matter (as long as he attended *some* church). His private beliefs could remain private.

That didn't set well in an age when governments were intertwined with official, established religions, and keeping one's job (or at times, one's head) depended on your personal declaration of the "right" church as yours. In addition, all those ideas about voting could affect the Catholic Church in particular. Disgruntled faithful may get it in their heads to "replace" a pope.

Public perceptions

The public, on the other hand, seemed to quickly embrace the reputation the Freemasons were quickly creating for themselves — of honorable, upstanding men who were the leaders in their communities. Freemasons made up a large number of the Founding Fathers in the U.S., including George Washington, Ben Franklin, John Hancock, Paul Revere, and many others. And Freemasons performed public cornerstone dedication ceremonies for many projects, including the White House and the U.S. Capitol building.

The Freemasons weren't the first secret society to have passwords, secret handshakes, rituals, initiation rites, special clothing, and other hallmark practices. But they were, perhaps, the best-known group that actually came out into the open. The Masons quickly became popular enough that, even if the public didn't actually know the details of what went on in the lodge room, they came to hear about the basics.

It was that popularity that would lead to literally thousands of clubs, societies, and other groups that would copy the practices of the Masons over the next 300 years, up through today. Organizations as diverse as the Odd Fellows and the Catholic Knights of Columbus, to college fraternities and the Boy Scouts' Order of the Arrow, would all base their ceremonies and infrastructure on the format created by the Freemasons in 1717.

The basic Masonic degrees of membership

As we say earlier in this chapter, in the Symbolic lodge (the average neighborhood lodge), new candidates progress through the three most basic levels of initiation (called degrees) to become a full, voting member: the Entered Apprentice, the Fellow Craft, and finally, the Master Mason degrees. In U.S. lodges, progressing through these degrees can take weeks or months, and some state Grand Lodges will even have large events and confer all three in one single day. In other parts of the Masonic world, the progress through the degrees is much slower, and can take up to a year.

In the early 1700s, Masons conferred just two degrees on their members: the *Entered Apprentice* degree was the initiation of a new member, and the *Fellow Craft* was the second degree ritual that made the man a full member.

Between 1725 and 1738, a third degree — called the *Master Mason* degree — was created and introduced into the London lodges that quickly spread throughout the rapidly growing fraternity. This degree tells the story of the building of King Solomon's Temple in 1000 BC in Jerusalem and its principal architect, Hiram Abiff. The story of the third degree was an immediate hit throughout most of the fraternity, and it became so popular as an additional degree conferred in lodges that by 1738 it was officially made part of the full lodge rituals by the Grand Lodge of England.

Aspiring to more and "higher" degrees

If one new degree could be added in 1738 (see the preceding section), the door was now open to adding even more degrees. Over the next 150 years, literally hundreds of degrees associated with Freemasonry were created by an ever-expanding list of side organizations (known as appendant bodies), along with unauthorized pseudo-Masonic groups that walked, talked, and quacked like Freemasonry. These different developments and influences are covered in the following sections.

Chevalier Ramsay's Oration

In 1730, a Scottish expatriate in France, Chevalier Andrew Michael Ramsay, presented a paper to *Le Louis d'Argent Lodge* in Paris. Known today as "Ramsay's Oration," he claimed that Freemasonry had originated before the days of ancient Egypt, and that its mysterious secrets (whatever they were) had been lost. He claims that these secrets were rediscovered by the knights of the Crusades in the Holy Land and brought back to Europe. He didn't mention the knights by name, but it was quickly surmised that he meant the Knights Templar (he had meant the Knights of St. John, actually), and the secrets they found must have been buried under the site of King Solomon's Temple.

A flurry of French degree inventions

French Freemasons in particular went wild over Ramsay's story, and set off inventing a whole *casserole* of new degrees. What particularly appealed to France's middle- and upper-class joiners was the notion that Freemasonry may have had a more noble and heroic origin than just a scruffy old labor union of rock carvers. Everyone could now have a title of nobility, even if it was just in the lodge.

The new degrees pulled material from all kinds of sources: biblical, historical, and even the fresh discoveries of Napoleon in Egypt in the early 1800s. Some degrees told stories that extended the tale of Hiram Abiff and the building of Solomon's Temple and some were sequels or prequels to his story. Other degrees flashed forward to the age of crusading knights. But all of them told some allegory of charity, fidelity, honor, and brotherhood.

Baron Von Hund

Sometime between 1742 and 1751, a German with the unwieldy name of Karl Gotheif, Baron Von Hund, und Alten-Grotkau (or just Baron Von Hund to his friends) was initiated into a French lodge (or claimed he had been, anyway) that centered around a Knights Templar legend. Baron Von Hund said he had been received into this lodge by a very mysterious and unknown, "Knight of the Red Feather." In 1751, he went home to the town of Unwerde (near Dresden, Germany), and started a lodge that conferred degrees called the *Rite of Strict Observance*. While Von Hund's version of Freemasonry with a Templar twist only lasted 60 years before dying out, if helped to firmly plant the Templar myth into the minds of Masons throughout Europe.

The other curious contribution of Von Hund to Masonic lore is that his *Rite of Strict Observance* was named after the oath he took in France to swear obedience to what he called "Unseen Superiors." Even though his Rite had died out by 1811, modern day conspiracy theorists claim that Masons today still take such an oath.

The York Rite

The York Rite degrees came to North America via Scottish and Irish military lodges in the years just before the Revolutionary War. The York Rite system in the U.S. is a series of degrees that revolve around more stories of King Solomon's Temple. They include the Royal Arch degrees, the Cryptic Council degrees (named after the "crypt" or vault under Solomon's Temple, not for being obscure or creepy), and the Masonic Knight Templar Orders. The degrees of the York Rite are progressive, meaning that they must be taken in order.

The Ancient Accepted Scottish Rite

The other big appendant Masonic organization is the Ancient Accepted Scottish Rite, which is more simply known in the U.S. as just the Scottish Rite. (No, you don't have to be Scottish to join, and the degrees originally came from France.) The Scottish Rite confers degrees that are numbered 4 through 32. Additionally, a 33rd degree is awarded to Scottish Rite Masons who've given extraordinary service to the Rite or to their community. Because of these higher numbers, many non-Masons are confused into thinking they're of higher rank.

Worldwide Distrust of Masonry

If you ask the average North American Mason about his plot to take over the world, the typical reply would be, "Right, just as soon as we decide what night to hold the fish fry." The U.S. Masonic lodges are clearly marked on the outside. Masons themselves wear rings and lapel pins and have Masonic bumper stickers on their cars. But in other parts of the world, Freemasonry isn't so public, nor are the members considered to be mostly harmless.

English society has had a longstanding mistrust of Freemasonry, and in the 1990s Britain held hearings over accusations of Masonic influence in the judicial system. No evidence of any kind was ever found of institutional favoritism among Masons who were police officers or officers of the courts. Nevertheless, police, judges, and others in the government across the United Kingdom today are now required to disclose their membership in the Masons, simply because there *might* be something sneaky going on. No other group is singled out in this way.

The British media today goes out of its way to point out if an accused criminal is a Mason, and can't seem to resist mentioning in any article about Freemasonry "dodgy" handshakes and the custom of initiates being required to "roll up their trouser leg." It seems to be part of the British journalism handbook.

Other parts of the world have at various times treated Masons with more than just ridicule. Here are some examples:

- ✔ Fascist or other authoritarian governments have good reason to distrust groups that meet in secret. Mussolini's Italy and Hitler's Germany outlawed Freemasonry, and the Nazis sent Masons to the death camps.

- ✔ Many Islamic countries that are governed by strict Sharia law, based on passages in the Koran, demand jail or even death for Freemasons.

- ✔ Masonry was also outlawed in the Soviet Union and Soviet bloc countries. After the fall of the Iron Curtain, Freemasonry began to rebound in the former Soviet republics, but distrust remains.

- ✔ Zealous members of the Ukrainian parliament recently recommended jail sentences for citizens who joined Masonic lodges, with especially harsh terms for members of the government found to be Masons.

Templars = Masons = Illuminati = Jews?

The Knights Templar, the Illuminati, and the Jews are supposedly linked with the Freemasons, mostly because the alleged combination of the three in connection with the Freemasons became the very first conspiracy theory hatched during the modern age. And the most enduring one.

Keep in mind the upheavals going on in the world when this conspiracy was first alleged. The American Revolution had concluded in 1783, showing the rest of the world that it was possible to shuck off a king and create a democratic republic, where the governed decided who would govern them. But the French Revolution in 1789 put all Europe into near total panic. The French beheaded their king and most of his family, along with thousands of members of the nobility and the clergy, before it even turned on its own leaders. The French executed 40,000 people, and as many as 600,000 would die before the revolution limped to an end. Monarchs everywhere worried that rebellion was just around the corner in their own countries.

When the carnage in France ended, the survivors — and others outside of France — looked for a reason for the savagery of the revolution. Three different writers built connections off each other that culminated in a grand conspiracy theory that endures to this day. We'll get to them shortly, but first you need to see the pieces of the puzzle and how they were put together.

How the Knights Templar got involved

Early in the formation of Freemasonry, a rivalry existed over who had the first Masonic lodges and who had the right to create, or *charter,* new ones. The first group set themselves up as a Grand Lodge in London in 1717. But earlier groups felt they had just as much right to claim governing authority over Masonry, if not more. Much of the controversy centered in Scotland, where lodges had existed as far back as the 1400s. Antiquity became something of a bragging right.

In 1737, Chevalier Ramsey's "Oration" (see "Aspiring to more and 'higher' degrees" earlier in this chapter) claimed that the skills of Masonry were lost during the days of Ancient Egypt, but had been rediscovered in the Holy Land by crusading knights in the 1100s, and brought back to Europe. He didn't mention them by name, but enthusiastic Freemasons glommed on to the tale with vigor, and believed Ramsey was talking about the legendary Knights Templar. Enthusiastic Masons fell in love with the idea and began to create *side orders* (additional Masonic degrees) based on, among other things, the Knights Templar.

A legend appeared in Scotland that the medieval Knights Templar had fled to the north of the country when they were hunted down by France's King Phillip IV in 1307. Myths grew up that the Knights, now excommunicated by Phillip's handpicked puppet pope, Clement V, hid out in Scotland and developed the secret handshakes, passwords, and other trappings that eventually turned into Freemasonry.

In the late 1700s, stories suddenly appeared that the Templars had done all kinds of heroic deeds in Scotland — from saving King Robert the Bruce's bacon by riding out onto the battlefield at the Battle of Bannockburn and terrifying the English troops, to building the legendary Rosslyn Chapel near Edinburgh (seen at the end of the book and film of Dan Brown's *The Da Vinci Code*).

Valiant as these legends seemed, and as often as they're trotted out to this day, these legends were probably created by Scottish Freemasons simply to claim a more ancient pedigree than their upstart English brethren in London, who claimed themselves to be the "premiere" and "Mother" Grand Lodge of the world.

To read the whole story of the Knights Templar, their myths, legends, and the role they play in *The Da Vinci Code,* pick up a copy of our book, *The Templar Code For Dummies* (Wiley).

Mixing in the Illuminati

For much more about the original Bavarian Illuminati, see Chapter 11. But for our discussion here, the second piece of the conspiratorial whammy came when King Karl Theodor outlawed all secret societies in Bavaria in 1784, including both the Illuminati and the Freemasons. Illuminati founder Adam Weishaupt (who really was up to no good) was forced to flee the country, chased by the king's soldiers. He fled in such a hurry that his collection of clearly treasonous papers was discovered and made public, pretty much ruining his plans for a "secret" reformation and the creation of a "New World Order," which was the first time this famous term appeared.

Weishaupt had used his organization to infiltrate Masonic lodges as step one of his plan to get Illuminati members into well-placed positions of power. His next step was really ambitious — to overthrow the kings of Europe. But suddenly, his failed and exposed plans were splashed across the headlines around the world.

How the Masons and Jews wound up controlling the world

The Knights Templar, the Freemasons, the Illuminati, and the Jews were never connected in reality. But in the wake of the French Revolution's bloodbath, the world looked for someone to blame.

Because Weishaupt's Illuminati had planned to overthrow monarchies all over Europe, the first suspect was this now-defunct group. Beginning in 1790, pamphlets were circulated claiming the Illuminati had started the Terror. In America, Illuminati paranoia set in. Freemason George Washington said that he believed Illuminists had infiltrated the fledgling country, and non-Mason

Thomas Jefferson, who had once written with apparent admiration of the Illuminati's stated goals, was accused of being a member and had to defend his own reputation over it.

Beginning in 1792, several conspiracy authors began to combine the Masons, the Illuminati, the Templars, and the Jews in varying combinations to create a worldwide conspiracy of universal control. Following are the main players in creating this story.

Cadet de Gassicourt

In 1792, French author Cadet de Gassicourt published *The Tomb of Jacques Molay*, which described how the supposedly disbanded Order of the Templars plotted for four centuries to exact their revenge against the monarchy of France and the Catholic Church. They survived the years in hiding by morphing into the Freemasons.

John Robison

In 1797, a Scottish Freemason (and inventor of the first siren) named John Robison wrote a pithy book: *Proofs of a Conspiracy Against All the Religions and Governments of Europe Carried on in the Secret Meetings of Freemasons, Illuminati, and Reading Societies.* Essentially, he claimed that the Illuminati had infiltrated French Freemasonry (but *not* English or Scottish Freemasonry), and they had become the French Jacobin clubs where the revolution was cooked up. Masons in Britain were virtuous, but those dirty "continentals" were the real problem.

Abbé de Barruel

Meanwhile, a French expatriate, ex-Jesuit, abbott named Augustin de Barruel met Robison and ran with the Scotsman's ideas. Between 1797 and 1798, he published a massive four-part work called *Memoirs Illustrating the History of Jacobinism.* Abbé de Barruel wove all the theories of the Templars, the Freemasons, and the Illuminati together into one, big, fat, continuous conspiracy theory, along with previous secret societies, dating all the way back to Iran's ancient history. For the first time, the Templars, the Masons, and the Illuminati were all described as having some ancient, mystical knowledge from a distant, pagan past that gave them the incredible power to sway nations.

His multivolume work became one of the most successful publications of the period, and de Barruel got very rich off them. There was just one last player to add to the conspiracy: the Jews.

In 1806, de Barruel claimed to receive a letter from an Italian fan of his Memoirs, who alleged that the secret societies had indeed plotted the French Revolution, but they had done it at the bidding of an evil Jewish sect, who wanted to steal the property of Christians, outlaw or otherwise destroy the Christian faith, enslave them, and create a world government run by Jews.

Because the Jews' lot in life had actually improved during the revolution, they were an easy mark. Abbé de Barruel discovered the devilish doings:

- ✔ The Templars had been headquartered in the Holy Land after the first Crusade in 1119, on top of the Temple Mount, site of King Solomon's Temple, built in 1000 BC.

- ✔ The Freemasons built their ritual around the story of the construction of King Solomon's Temple, so they had to be both Templars as well as Jews.

- ✔ The Illuminati were Freemasons.

- ✔ Therefore, the Templars, the Freemasons, the Illuminati, and the Jews had all conspired to start the French Revolution.

This thinking was truly unique, because French Freemasons had primarily been members of the nobility at that time and among the first to be executed by the "national razor," the guillotine.

Because the stories came from the esteemed Abbé de Barruel, people believed without question. And because he placed the Jews in the position of controlling the secret societies as their willing stooges, he threw them from being a race of people Europe never really thought much about, to the pinnacle of the conspiracy theory pyramid, where *everyone* started to think about them.

Who's in charge? Seeking Masonic authorities

Anti-Masons who accuse Freemasonry of world domination contend there is a supersecret, "high-ranking" group of Masons who really control the world, unknown to the vast herd of unsuspecting men in their neighborhood lodges.

The truth is that Freemasonry has no international governing body. In the U.S., every state has its own Grand Lodge that's sovereign within its jurisdictional borders. In most countries outside of the U.S. there's just one Grand Lodge that's overwhelmingly recognized as the authoritative body in each country.

There are exceptions everywhere, and different Grand Lodges that are largely unrecognized as being legitimate Freemasonry by the larger mainstream groups do exist, such as the Grand Orient of France, female and co-ed Grand Lodges throughout the world, and many others. In the U.S., the most notable exceptions are the predominantly African-American "Prince Hall Affiliated" (PHA) Grand Lodges that co-exist by treaty (in all but a handful of former Confederate states in the South) with their mainstream Grand Lodge counterparts.

What is most important to understand is that there is no such thing as world-wide, universally recognized Freemasonry. Nor is there one, single, authoritative body or person who speaks for Freemasonry. Every Grand Lodge sets the rules for the conduct of their members. And while a Grand Lodge, or the equivalent of its "president," the Grand Master, may make statements about his beliefs, laws, or practices, his authority ends at his own state or national borders.

When you see "high-ranking Masons" or "top Masonic authorities" being quoted, your warning bells need to start ringing, because there are no such things. There are Masonic authors whose opinions are respected, but they're usually expressing their own views, and not any official Grand Lodge position, unless the work so states.

Looking at Masonic plots that were real

There is a very famous incident where a group of Freemasons plotted to overthrow their lawful government. Several Masonic terrorists met secretly in their lodge room and plotted destruction of property. They conspired to take the government into their own hands and drew up detailed plans to place their own candidates in positions of power. Meanwhile, a wealthy Mason began training paramilitary troops, while another conspired with foreign leaders to achieve military and financial backing.

We're, of course, talking about the Founding Fathers and the American Revolution. George Washington, Benjamin Franklin, John Hancock, Paul Revere, the Marquis de Lafayette, and dozens of other famous figures during the revolution were Freemasons, and there are specific Enlightenment philosophies that were part of the Masonic rules and regulations that made their way into the U.S. Constitution. But remember that while these famous men were all Masons, their actions weren't Masonic plots. The U.S. revolution was an attempt to use Enlightenment philosophy to establish a new form of government, just as the lodges were places where Enlightenment thought was put into everyday practice. Still, there have been other very real Masonic conspiracies brewing. Keep reading!

The murder of Captain William Morgan

In 1826, William Morgan and his wife arrived in the upstate New York town of Batavia. Unfortunately, Morgan was the sort referred to in those days as a ne'er do well (sort of a professional bum), claiming he was a former captain during the War of 1812. He also claimed he was a Mason, and on his arrival in Batavia, he attempted to join the local Masonic lodge and put the touch on its members, but was rejected. He had a similar experience when he attempted to join a local York Rite chapter.

So, Morgan decided to get even with the Masons. He made friends with the local printer, who had also been ejected from the local lodge, and they formed a plan to publish a blockbuster — a book that would expose the secret ceremonies of the Freemasons. Unfortunately for Morgan, one of the hallmarks of his character was a very big mouth, and as a result, members of the local lodge found out about his plans in no time flat. After attempting, to no avail, to "convince" him to drop his book plans, they decided to take matters into their own hands. They allegedly abducted Morgan, and hauled him off to Fort Niagara on Lake Ontario, along the Canadian border. And he was never seen again.

In court, the conspirators claimed they paid Morgan $500, put him on a horse, pointed him north to Canada, and told him never to come back again. Morgan's wife Lucinda had a different view of the matter and suggested that the Masons had drowned him in the lake. Twenty-six men were indicted in connection with his disappearance, but only six were ever tried, and none on murder charges. The prosecutor and many of the jurors were Freemasons themselves, and the trial resulted in very lenient sentences.

An explosion of protest quickly spread across New York, then the country. The public believed that the Masons had killed Morgan "according to Masonic ritual," then cheated justice by receiving short sentences from their Masonic friends who controlled the courts and the government, including Governor and Freemason Dewitt Clinton. What began as a small-town crime became a nationwide outrage, and it certainly sold a lot of books and newspapers. Morgan's book, *Illustrations of Masonry,* was published after his death, and it was an instant bestseller. Over the next five years, the anti-Masonic movement grew steadily and went national.

As a direct result of the "Morgan Affair," in 1831 the anti-Masonic Party became the first official third-party political movement in America, running "resigned and reformed" Freemason William Wirt for president (who inexplicably gave a speech defending the fraternity at his own nominating convention). The party was strong enough to carry the state of Vermont, and won 8 percent of the national vote. Anti-Masonic governors were elected in Pennsylvania and Vermont, along with several U.S. Congressmen.

The Anti-Masonic Party lost its momentum quickly, as most one-issue movements generally do. But over the next 20 years, Masonic lodges closed all over the country as men renounced their membership. Nationwide, Masonic membership dropped from 100,000 in 1827 to less than 40,000 ten years later. Masonic membership wouldn't begin to grow again until the 1850s.

Mormons and Masons: Who had the rituals first?

Controversy has raged in both the Mormon Church (Church of Latter Day Saints, or LDS) and Freemasonry concerning the origins of Mormon rituals and ceremonies. Church founders Joseph and Hyrum Smith were both Masons, as was Brigham Young, their successor. Believers in the LDS say that

Prophet Joseph Smith's revelation of Mormon ceremonies derived from the story of Solomon's Temple, and it's merely a coincidence that the church and Freemasonry teach lessons with similar themes and phrases. More skeptical nonbelievers think that Smith simply stole the ceremonies of the Masonic lodge, and counted on the secrecy of both organizations to hide his plagiarism.

Despite her belief that her husband had been murdered by Freemasons (see section above), William Morgan's widow Lucinda went on to marry another Freemason, George Harris, and they became Mormons and moved to Indiana. At some point, while still married to Harris, Lucinda entered into a polygamous marriage with Joseph Smith as the Mormons passed through Indiana on their way to Illinois.

In 1842, Smith received the degrees of Freemasonry, and yet somehow knew the details of the rituals before receiving them. Mormons believe he was divinely inspired. Skeptics point out that his wife Lucinda was the widow of a man who had written the most notorious exposé of Masonic ritual in America, William Morgan's *Illustrations of Masonry*. Shortly after Smith's initiation as a Mason he began to instruct his church leaders "in the principles of and order of the Priesthood" that bore remarkable similarity to Masonic rituals.

In 1844, Joseph Smith was killed in Nauvoo, Illinois, at the hands of an anti-Mormon mob. Wild claims circulated that just as he was shot, he cried out the first words of the Masonic "Grand Hailing Sign of Distress," some say in the hope that a brother Mason might save him.

Popular (And Untrue) Masonic Conspiracy Theories

Hundreds of conspiracies have been attributed to the Freemasons over the years, and the list of conspiracy theories associated with the Freemasons grows every year. In this section, we first list a few for you to chew on, then in later sections we move on to the really popular ones, which we cover in more detail. Here are some conspiracies:

 ✔ **Jack the Ripper was a Freemason.** First propounded by Stephen Knight in his book Jack the Ripper: The Final Solution and popularized by the films Murder By Decree (1978) and From Hell (2001). Knight alleged that the Ripper was Freemason William Gull, court physician to Queen Victoria, and that he killed prostitutes on orders from the Crown to prevent the discovery of an illegal marriage and an illegitimate daughter of Prince Albert Edward. Knight further alleged that the killings were done according to "Masonic ritual," acting out the bloody oaths taken by Masons in their three lodge degrees.

Knight's theory is intriguing, but flawed on too many details of Masonic ritual that he simply invented to suit his story. A key piece of evidence erased by the Metropolitan Police was graffiti that said, *"The Juwes are not the men who will be blamed for nothing."* Knight claimed this reference wasn't to Jews, but to the three fellow craft who attack Hiram Abiff in Masonic ritual: *Jubela, Jubelo,* and *Jubelum.* Unfortunately, the characters have never been referred to as *Juwes* and don't even appear by name in English Masonic ritual! Knight's source for the tale, Joseph Sickert, later confessed that it was all a "whopping fib."

✔ **Most U.S. Presidents, including both George Bushes, were Freemasons.** Not by a long shot. Neither George Bush is a Mason. There have been 14 U.S. Presidents who were Masons: George Washington, James Monroe, Andrew Jackson, James Knox Polk, James Buchanan, Andrew Johnson, James Garfield, William McKinley, Theodore Roosevelt, William Howard Taft, Warren G. Harding, Franklin D. Roosevelt, Harry S. Truman, and Gerald R. Ford.

✔ ***Skull and Bones* is a Masonic group.** *Skull and Bones* is a Yale University fraternity that's a little creepy, but it *isn't* a Masonic group. (See Chapter 13 for more about the Bonesmen.)

✔ **The Ku Klux Klan was created by the Freemasons.** Nope, wrong again. Many Klansmen during its many incarnations may have also belonged to the Masons. But there were also Baptists and Methodists, Lions and Rotarians, NRA and Sierra Club members, as well as subscribers to the Hair Club for Men (except skinheads). The Klan rituals borrowed heavily from the structure of the Masonic lodge in arrangement, officers, and language, but so have a thousand other groups, including college fraternities, ever since the early 1700s.

✔ **Masons worship a Masonic God referred to as the Great Architect of the Universe, which is actually called Jahbulon, which is made up of the words Jehovah, Baal, and Osiris.** Freemasons don't conduct religious worship in their lodges. Their meetings and degrees are opened and closed with prayers, and no one may join a lodge who doesn't have a belief in a supreme being. But the term Grand Architect of the Universe (abbreviated in their ritual books as GAOTU) is used as a generic, all-inclusive term to encompass the faith of all members. The word *Jahbulon* only appears in one degree of the appendant group, the York Rite, and Masons don't "worship" it. Nor is it explained as being comprised of Jehovah, Baal, and Osiris.

✔ **The Masons are a front for their real masters, the Jews.** Freemasonry uses some Old Testament biblical stories and imagery in its degree ceremonies. Masonry was the first social group that openly and freely accepted Jewish members in both England and America. But the major source of this claim stems from the notorious anti-Semitic propaganda document, the *Protocols of the Elders of Zion,* which we discuss in Chapter 6.

✔ **The Masons are a front for their real masters, the Illuminati.** For the lowdown on the Illuminati, real and imagined, see Chapter 11.

✔ **The Masons are a front for their real masters, a race of shape-shifting reptilian aliens.** British conspiracist David Icke believes this rumor is absolutely true. And let's just say we don't and leave it at that.

The satanic map of Washington, D.C.

In 1789, America's new president, Freemason George Washington, hired Pierre Charles L'Enfant to design the new Federal City, the nation's capitol that would eventually bear Washington's name. The area that the city rose from was an almost complete wilderness, giving L'Enfant a bare slate to draw his designs upon.

But according to some conspiracists, the designers of the city were *all* Freemasons, and they purposely designed secret symbols into the map, making it appear satanic. Here are some of the purported Masonic/satanic symbols:

✔ Directly north of the White House is an inverted pentagram (Satan's symbol) made by the intersections of Massachusetts Avenue, Rhode Island Avenue, Connecticut Avenue, Vermont Avenue, and K Street NW — almost. (The Rhode Island Avenue leg isn't finished, but that's a pesky detail when Satan is involved.) The allegations say that the Masons put a Satanic symbol over the White House to show their power. But the inverted pentagram was never considered remotely "evil" until the 1870s, or "Satanic" until the 1970s.

And as Masonic author S. Brent Morris has pointed out, if the Masons were all-powerful, why didn't they build that last leg of Rhode Island Avenue and complete their Unholy Talisman of the Damned?

✔ If you turn the map of Washington sideways, you see a Masonic square and compasses directly west of the U.S. Capitol building. With a stretch, you might make the claim that it sort of looks like a compass. But the so-called "square" up by Capitol Hill isn't a perfect square, is cut off on one side, is in the wrong position, and wasn't a street at all but a decorative canal that was never built.

Of all the men who had anything to do with the original design of Washington, D.C. (George Washington, Charles L'Enfant, Andrew Ellicott, Benjamin Banneker, along with some meddling from Thomas Jefferson), only Washington was a Freemason, and his biggest concern was the placement of the Presidential Mansion on a hill of at least equal height with the Capitol.

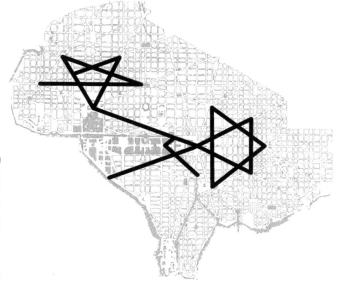

Figure 9-2:
Purported
Masonic
symbolism
in a map of
Washington,
D.C.

The Masonic dollar bill

This theory presupposes that the Freemasons designed the Great Seal of the United States that appears on the U.S. dollar bill. They didn't. The seal was designed by three committees between 1776 and 1782, and the only Mason among all the men involved was Benjamin Franklin. And all his ideas for the seal were rejected.

The symbol on the dollar most commonly associated with the Masons is the unfinished pyramid and the All-Seeing Eye. But this combined image doesn't appear anywhere in the symbolism of Freemasonry. The All-Seeing Eye within a triangle, alone, *does* appear in some Masonic symbolism as a symbol for God, but it predates modern Freemasonry by several hundred years. The All-Seeing Eye is a common symbol in Renaissance Christian art as a representation of the Holy Trinity (symbolized by the three sides of the triangle, with the eye of God in the center). The unfinished pyramid was probably an invention of Charles Thompson, who wasn't a Mason.

Some conspiracy theorists have claimed the symbol is that of the Illuminati (see Chapter 11) and that the appearance of the date 1776 on the seal is commemorating the formation of that group in Bavaria. True, one symbol of the Illuminati was an "All-Seeing Eye." But it was represented by a circle with a darkened dot in the center, not a pyramid shape. And why they don't believe that 1776 is the date of the Declaration of Independence escapes us.

There is a parlor trick that supposedly proves the Masons are involved anyway:

1. **Get out a dollar bill.**

2. **Connect the tip of the All-Seeing Eye to the "N" in Novus, and the "M" in Seclorum, then back to the Eye.**

3. **Connect the second "O" on Ordo with the "A" in Annuit and the "S" in Coeptis, then back to the "O."**

This process not only spells MASON, but also forms a Star of David. Supposedly this "proves" the Jews and the Masons are somehow in cahoots. Of course, you can also make more than 120 different anagrams out of the mottoes *Annuit Coeptis* and *Novus Seclorum,* including *uncircumcised, Micronesian, accordionists, sopranos, despots,* and most importantly, *misconception.*

Scottish Rite 32nd degree rings

There's a hot Internet rumor making the rounds that pawn shops have an inordinate number of Scottish Rite 32nd degree rings for sale. The theory goes that the 32nd degree ceremony includes spells of witchcraft. And the reason pawnshops have so many of them is because inept 32nd degree Masons don't get the spell incantations right and are vaporized in the fiery aftermath of their Luciferian magic gone bad. *Poof!*

Chapter 10

Rosicrucians and the Evolution of Occult Secret Societies

In This Chapter

▷ Deciphering Hermeticism, Rosicrucianism, and Spiritualism

▷ Comprehending Martinism

▷ Discovering occult and esoteric secret societies

▷ Tracking the Aryans from Madame Blavatsky to the Nazi regime

*I*n the late Douglas Adams's book, *The Hitchiker's Guide To The Galaxy,* a group of scientists build the Universe's greatest computer, Deep Thought, with one purpose in mind — to ask it the Answer to the Ultimate Question About Life, the Universe, and Everything. The machine thinks a long time — 7.5 million years — and finally dispenses the answer that Mankind has wanted to know ever since we crawled out of the slime: "42."

> *I checked it very thoroughly," said the computer, "and that quite definitely is the answer. I think the problem, to be quite honest with you, is that you've never actually known what the question is.*

Esoteric and occult studies are a lot like that. Esotericism is the study of "hidden knowledge," mysterious beliefs, or inner enlightenment that can only be understood after years of introspection and study. Like Deep Thought, the problem with esoteric studies is that more than half of the challenge in seeking the Answer to the Ultimate Question about Life, the Universe, and Everything is first figuring out the proper question to ask. Otherwise, you wind up with an answer like 42.

Answering the Ultimate Question About Life, the Universe, and Everything is what esoteric and occult societies try to do, and that's what we discuss in this chapter.

Rosicrucianism introduced the modern notion of the occult secret society. The Rosicrucians were inspired principally by the great movements within Christian mysticism. Many of these movements, from Gnosticism to Manichaeism, along with a whole cartload of other *isms,* have a history stretching back to the first two centuries of the Christian faith. Rosicrucians built for themselves a highly colorful mythology and ritual in the 1700s, then slowly passed from the scene. But, like many other secret societies, they just kept coming back again, particularly in the spiritualism-drenched 19th and 20th centuries.

This chapter goes back to the beginning, explaining the birth of Rosicrucianism, the occult ties between the Rosicrucians and many other esoteric groups, and the influence of Rosicrucianism on dozens of other occult secret societies that came after it. Along the way, you meet a cast of characters that eventually leads to the occult rituals and ceremonies, and the applications of the trappings of secret societies, in the creation of Nazi Germany's symbol-soaked Thousand Year Reich.

Before Rosicrucianism: Hermeticism versus the Enlightenment

The Enlightenment occurred in the period roughly from the end of the English Revolution in the late 1640s up until Napoleon came along after the French Revolution with a sword in one hand and a mop in the other to clean the place up.

What the Enlightenment was really about was the replacement of superstition, magic, and the occult with reason, experimentation, and the scientific method. The philosophers and scientists of the Enlightenment wanted to know why things happened, how things worked, and how humans could interact with them. And they tried to apply this methodology to religion, politics, science, sociology, and everything else. For the Enlightenment thinkers, all the answers to Life, the Universe, and Everything were waiting to be discovered, explained, subjected to the scientific method, and logically catalogued.

Let's just say the Enlightenment thinkers weren't universally hailed as geniuses and heroes. Another category of folks regarded the Enlightenment as flawed, fallacious folly for a different reason. These were believers in the occult, and they had a much different view. They felt that ancient civilizations, Eastern adepts, mystics, wizards, magicians, alchemists, and other practitioners had already discovered the mystical answers to Life, the Universe, and Everything long ago. But they believed this sacred knowledge had been lost to the West — either out of stupidity, blindness, lousy record keeping, or by being branded as heresy and rubbed out by the church.

These folks *knew* that the knowledge was "out there," and it was simply waiting to be rediscovered by just the *right* people. Not the great unwashed rabble, but a very select, special, and sometimes secret society of people. That's where Hermeticism comes in.

The origin of the term *Hermeticism* is a set of religious and philosophical writings attributed to a legendary ancient Egyptian figure known as *Hermes Trismegistus* (meaning "thrice great"). He's sometimes also referred to as the Egyptian god Thoth and the Greek god Hermes, and his writings were said to be extensive. Depending on whose lavish telling of his accomplishments you read, he wrote somewhere between 40 and 40,000 books (even more than Stephen King and Nora Roberts combined) on a huge range of subjects, from Egyptian science — astronomy, math, geometry, and alchemy — to a far-reaching exploration of spirituality, philosophy, and magic.

According to legend, Hermes's writings, known as *Hermetica,* turn up everywhere throughout Greek, Roman, early Christian. and even early Islamic periods, and they obviously influenced the beginnings of these many religions. But the bulk of his writings disappeared with the burning of the Alexandrian Library in 48 BC, and as a result, the scarcity of surviving Hermetic texts just made them more legendary, and the fewer there were for people to actually study, the more mythical and magical the "lost" volumes became.

The problem is that none of this is true. In the 1400s, manuscripts of Hermes's works began to appear across Europe after Gutenberg's printing press began to make books easier and cheaper to mass-produce. Printers needed things to print, and any works purporting to be by Hermes Trismegistus were snapped up as quickly as the ink dried.

There's zero evidence of any of Hermes's writings before the 1400s. The books attributed to him are undoubtedly forgeries or copies of earlier works, with his name slapped on them. But little things like forgeries never kept a good esoteric or occult secret society out of business for very long. At times, it almost seems to be a prerequisite. The Rosicrucians, or the Order of the Rose Cross, was the first organized group to endeavor to wrap what would become a modern secret society around Hermetic works. Naturally, its adherents have claimed it is the oldest secret society in the world, dating back to Ancient Egypt, just like *Hermes Trismegistus.*

The Rosicrucians

In their most utopian form, the Rosicrucians are essentially Christian in beliefs but influenced by Hermeticism, philosophies that predate Christianity by more than a thousand years, and Eastern mysticism. We cover the evolution of Rosicrucianism in the next few sections, starting with Christian Rosenkreutz.

Rosicrucianism has long been associated with a symbol of a cross with a rose in the center. Depending on which source you want to believe, this symbol means different things:

- ✔ The rose is a symbol of "budding" spiritual growth or Christ or secrecy. (This is based on the Roman phrase of *sub-rosa*, when secret societies met under a hanging rose. The idea originated in the Greek legend of Aphrodite passing a rose to her son Eros, who in turn gave it to Harpocrates, the God of silence, to hide his mother's indiscretions.)

- ✔ The cross is a symbol of both life and death; of the quartering of the Universe into the four alchemical elements of earth, air, fire, and water; or simply the cross on which Christ was put to death. To alchemists, mystics, and spiritualists, it's a symbol of the secret of immortality. And to prurient pervs who see Freudian symbols everywhere, the rose/cross is a combined symbol of female and male genitalia.

The tale of Christian Rosenkreutz

The Rosicrucian legend primarily comes from published accounts in Germany about the group's presumed founder, Christian Rosenkreutz. He was supposedly born in Germany in 1378 and was raised in a monastery. As a monk, his travels led him to the mysterious lands of the East in search of spiritual and mystical knowledge, where he studied under masters of the occult arts.

When Rosenkreutz came back to Germany in 1407, he met up with three other monks, with the purpose of amassing the great mystical and scientific knowledge of all time. Over the years, the order increased in size to eight members, who were to travel the world and come back every year to their headquarters, the *Sancti Spiritus,* to share the knowledge with the other members. Their ultimate goal was to assemble the combined knowledge of the world and to unify it into one universal message in preparation of the Final Judgment of God.

Christian Rosenkreutz died in 1484 (supposedly at the age of 106) and was buried in the Sancti Spiritus, where his body's whereabouts were forgotten by the Order. Then, in 1604 during a bit of remodeling, someone was pounding a nail in a wall of the building and whacked a hole in the plaster, revealing the perfectly preserved body of Rosenkreutz, along with all the secret knowledge that had been buried with him. That's the legend, anyway.

Johann Valentin Andrae

Between 1614 and 1616, three pamphlets appeared that had been supposedly written by Christian Rosenkreutz in the mid-1400s and freshly "rediscovered." These writings were *Fama Fraternitatis,* the *Confessio,* and the *Chemical Marriage of Christian Rosenkreutz.* The truth was that most of the legend sprang from the fertile imagination of Johann Valentin Andrae, a Lutheran minister, and was largely a well-intentioned hoax based on his utopian wishful thinking.

Andrae and a small circle of friends set out to invent an organization that would reform social life, through new learning and a new search for the secrets to Life, the Universe, and Everything. The Order's primary precepts were religious piety, charity, anonymity, and secrecy. They were out to improve mankind without society's awareness of this silent, benevolent, and secret group, and their efforts led to the creation of Rosicrucian societies.

The birth of Rosicrucian societies

The emergence of the Rosicrucians has been characterized as a great publicity stunt. Andrae's writings outlined a worldwide organization of practitioners of occult arts, who had supposedly existed and grown in hiding for centuries. Here was the first truly secret society that claimed to be working to change the world from behind the scenes. They possessed strange, hidden, long-lost knowledge from ancient times, and they initiated their new recruits using mysterious rituals. The world quickly divided between those who completely distrusted this unseen group of manipulators and those who couldn't wait to join up.

The problem was that, at first, there wasn't really anything to join. The Rosicrucian stories began to circulate throughout Europe, and Rosicrucian societies began to pop up all over, most popularly in Germany and Holland starting in 1620. Even when Andrae confessed to having invented the whole thing, true believers simply refused to believe him. The Enlightenment was a fertile era of looking for scientific answers to religious questions, and Rosicrucianism was perfect for the period because it straddled the line between superstition and science. It combined science, religion, and the occult — alchemy, magic, Egyptian mysticism, Jewish Kabbalism, as well as Christian teachings — with a special emphasis on reincarnation.

The first Rosicrucians came to America when William Penn invited Johann Jacob Zimmerman's *Chapter of Perfection* to move from Germany and settle in Pennsylvania. Zimmerman's group believed that Christ would return to earth in 1700, and in 1694, they built an observatory in their settlement to predict the precise moment of Christ's Second Coming. Unfortunately for Jacob and his predictions, their calculations were off. No Second Coming was forthcoming, the group quickly disbanded, and several ex-members became known as a wandering group of hermits.

A brief glance at Kabbalah

If you do any looking into esoteric organizations, you stumble into references to the *Kabbalah* (or Cabala, Kabala, Qabalah, or Cabbalah — all spellings are used). It was central to Rosicrucian lore.

Kabbalah is an extraordinarily complex and mystical Jewish course of biblical study. The word Kabbalah is variously translated as "received" or "tradition," meaning the oral tradition of mystical steps received by initiates from the learned Kabbalah adepts. For centuries, it was passed down from mouth to ear by scholars, and a student had to be over 40 to be considered worthy enough to even hear about it. Rabbi Bahya ben Asher, a 13th-century Jew living in Spain, is credited with the first written examination of Kabbalah, although the tradition of Jewish mysticism stretches back much farther, at least to the 6th century before Christ. Over the next 300 years, his writings would cause great excitement concerning the study of secret messages in the Bible — so much so that there would be both Christian and Islamic variations.

The essential purpose of Kabbalah is to seek the hidden faces of God, and by doing so, to understand the origins and operations of the universe. Kabbalah's central image is the *Tree of Life,* which has ten branches emanating from the *sephiroth,* the ten sacred Hebrew numbers, with the whole tree representing a progressive path to enlightenment and knowledge of God. It is usually depicted as a series of ten spheres connected by 22 paths, which are represented by the 22 letters of the Hebrew alphabet. The ten spheres describe the ten attributes by which God can interact with Man and the Universe.

You can't really comprehend Kabbalah without an understanding of the Hebrew language. The belief is that, as God dictated the books of the Torah (specifically, the first five books of what Christians call the Old Testament), he did it in a certain code. For a Kabbalist, the Hebrew language itself is holy. In Hebrew, every letter has a numerical equivalent, and Kabbalists believed that hidden truths and prophecies in the Torah could be discovered by the endless and intricate reweaving of the letters in the holy books, resulting in everything from simple anagrams to complex geometric computations (an *anagram* is a word or phrase formed out of the re-arranged letters of another word or phrase). The numerology aspect of Kabbalah is called "Gematra." But the central belief of Kabbalah is that all the secrets to Life, the Universe, and Everything are in the Torah, if only we can break the code.

If this sounds a lot like the modern book, *The Bible Code* by Michael Drosnin, you'd be right. Drosnin claims that the Torah is written in what is called a "skip-code" — that every fifth letter in every sentence forms a word. Although he successfully used it to predict the assassination of Israeli Prime Minister Yitzhak Rabin in 1995, it seems to have faltered on predictions of meteor strikes and nuclear Armageddon in 2005.

Modern pop spiritualist movements involving Kabbalah, and high-profile followers like Madonna, have sprung up in recent years, which is where you will usually find the different spellings with a Q or a C. For much more about Kabbalah, see *Kabbalah For Dummies* (Wiley) by Arthur Kurzweil.

Modern Rosicrucianism

As scientific experimentation and discovery improved, and as science and the occult diverged from one another, the allure of Rosicrucianism died out, and by the mid-1700s, France was just about the only place Rosicrucians could be found. A French occultist named Eliphas Levi resurrected interest in Rosicrucianism when he wrote a series of books about "transcendental magic" in the mid-1800s.

The largest and best-known modern Rosicrucian group today is the Ancient and Mystical Order Rosae Crucis (AMORC), organized by Harvey Spencer Lewis in 1915. Lewis claimed that King Solomon used Rosicrucian teachings to build his temple, and that's where Freemasonry came from. He claimed that the Egyptian pharaoh Akhenaton, Plato, Socrates, and Jesus were all early Rosicrucians.

Lewis had been an early member of Aleister Crowley's OTO (see the section "The Ordo Templi Orientis (OTO)" later in this chapter) and incorporated some of what he'd experienced there into the AMORC. He was also an inventor, and he developed several peculiar items for use in the AMORC's search for knowledge:

- The Luxatone (a large, triangular screen with flashing lights known in the groovy 1970s as a color organ)
- The Sympathetic Vibration Harp
- The Cosmic Ray Coincidence Counter (that some have claimed to be the precursor of the Geiger Counter)
- The Black Mirror (used to focus thoughts during meditation)

In a famous incident, Lewis "proved" that he could transmute base metals into gold, a secret sought for in vain for centuries by alchemists. But when the experiment was concluded, he proclaimed that the process just wasn't cost effective, and it made much more sense to just go buy the real thing.

In the 1930s, Lewis and the Order built an impressive art deco/Egyptian complex in San Jose, California, that included a planetarium, a library, and what has become a famous Egyptian museum.

Rosicrucianism and "Fringe Freemasonry"

Because of the wild popularity of spiritualism and the occult in the mid- and late-1800s, a small group of British Masons became interested in Rosicrucianism. Many of the men involved in reviving interest in the Rosicrucians joined the Freemasons (see Chapter 9) in search of this secret knowledge. When they didn't find secrets of alchemy, levitation, reincarnation, astral projection, and other such legendary stuff in the Masonic lodge, most of them moved on. Others, however, created their own "side orders," groups that required Masonic membership as a prerequisite but were not otherwise related to the Masons.

Many of these Freemasons, like W. R. Woodmen, Wynn Westcott, Kenneth Mackenzie, S. L. MacGregor Mathers, and W. E. Waite, would eventually be led by their interests to form Rosicrucian groups outside of Masonry, such as the *Hermetic Order of the Golden Dawn*.

There never was and never has been a strong interest in Rosicrucians or the occult by Masonry as an institution, and these same few men represent a tiny radical group that eventually worked outside of regular, recognized Freemasonry. However, two of the Masonic-related Rosicrucian groups are worth mentioning, largely because they still exist today. These groups are covered in the next two sections.

Societas Rosicruciana in Anglia (SRIA)

An English Freemason named Robert Wentworth Little was employed as a clerk by the library at London's Freemason Hall, and in 1865, he claimed to have discovered a cache of Rosicrucian documents there. In 1867, he founded the Rosicrucian Society of England. The name was later Latinized into *Societas Rosicruciana in Anglia* (SRIA). A Scottish group (*Societas Rosicruciana in Scotia*) appeared about the same time.

The group confers a series of degrees (or grades) that are based on the structure of the Kabbalah's "tree of life," but they're essentially a research group with a very limited membership that's extended by invitation only. Local chapters are called *colleges*. They aren't technically a Masonic group, only a group made up of men who are Freemasons.

Societas Rosicruciana in Civitatibus Foederatis (SRICF)

Originally founded in 1880 as the *Societas Rosicruciana Republicae Americae,* the *Societas Rosicruciana in Civitatibus Foederatis* (SRICF) is a very small group made up of 31 colleges in the U.S. and Canada. The SRICF began with a group of Masons who traveled to England in 1878 and were initiated into the SRIA (see the preceding section) at the college at York. They applied for permission to begin an American branch, but the English group refused. The branch in Scotland wasn't nearly so uppity, and they chartered a college in Philadelphia in 1879 and New York in 1880. These two colleges established a High Council in April 1880 and created their own autonomous American organization. Membership is by invitation only. Members must be Freemasons and Christians, and there may be no more than 72 members in a college. It's essentially an honorary research society.

Martinism

A French movement in the late 1700s, called Martinism, borrowed trappings of Rosicrucianism and became a transition between the earlier order and esoteric and occult societies that grew up throughout the 19th century. Martinism combined Christianity with mysticism, and saw Christ as a redeemer who would return man to the state of grace that had not existed since the garden of Eden.

Louis-Claude de Saint-Martin was a poor French nobleman who was born in 1743. As a young believer in mysticism, he traveled throughout Europe, making many converts. He was briefly imprisoned during the French Revolution, but survived because local authorities were in desperate need of schoolteachers. Louis-Claude was only too happy to oblige and become one. Over the years, he became a student of an 18th-century Kabbalist named Joachim Martinez Pasquales, and later translated several obscure 17th-century works by a German mystic, Jacob Böhme, into French. Böhme, known as "The Teutonic Philosopher," had theorized that in order to achieve a state of grace, man had to fall away from God and do battle with the demons and evil angels who caused the sins of the world. Only after spiritual victory over these evils could man again return to God's good graces.

Using both authors as his inspiration, Saint-Martin developed his own philosophy about Life, the Universe, and Everything, called the "Way of the Heart." Saint-Martin's writings were signed by the enigmatic name of the Unknown Philosopher, and they quickly became popular. Study groups began to pop up, called the Society of the Unknown Philosopher.

One of Saint-Martin's biggest objections to the occult, esoteric, and fraternal societies of Europe at the time was their refusal to allow women as members, and his was one of the first to grant women equal membership status. Saint-Martin died in 1803.

Martinism revived

Saint-Martin's writings slipped into obscurity after his death, but an enthusiastic student rediscovered them and changed all that. Gerard Encausse (who went by the name of Papus) resurrected Saint-Martin's concepts. Followers called themselves Martinists. Not surprisingly, there was much crossover between the usual suspects involved in esotericism: Rosicrucians, Freemasons, Gnostics, and these new Martinists. In 1888, Encausse formed a mystery school called the *Ordere Martinist,* and by 1900, there were chapters in a dozen countries with hundreds of members.

Synarchy hijacks Martinism

World War I killed off the principal leaders of the *Ordere Martinist,* and the central organization dissolved. At one point a splinter group attempted to restore the monarchy to France. Others became enamored with a curious movement called *Synarchy,* an attempt to rule European countries by means of secret societies.

World War II all but destroyed Martinist societies in Europe because the Nazis imprisoned or executed most members of so-called "secret societies." But the Traditional Martinist Order made its way to the U.S. through Rosicrucian groups in the 1930s, and it survives today.

The Internet has done much to spread Saint-Martin's philosophies, and new groups have appeared recently along with the traditional ones. They cover a broad range of philosophies and disciplines, with some incorporating Rosicrucian influences, some borrowing from the Memphis-Mizraim branch of Freemasonry that's been deemed irregular by the majority of the mainstream Masonic world, and some simply adhering strictly to Saint-Martin's philosophies.

The 19th Century and Occult Societies

During the Romantic period of the 1800s, society looked back to an earlier age with foggy nostalgia for a simpler time. The Industrial Revolution turned landscapes and cities into a smoke-filled illustration of Dante's *Inferno.* Families were wrenched apart by economic hardship and massive migrations from the rural farms into the factories and slums of the cities.

Scientific discoveries were blasting away at long-held religious beliefs — Darwin's theory of evolution being the most controversial. Additionally, the period had great upheaval for organized religions. Even the largest, most stable denominations were splintering into smaller offshoots, driven by schisms and disagreements over the minutest differences. In the wake of this uncertainty came a new period of charismatic, unaffiliated preachers starting their own independent churches with their own tiny followings. It seemed like everything about society, right down to personal faith, was up for grabs.

Across the U.S. and Europe, almost as a reaction to this wave of uncertainty, an obsession developed for mystical Eastern tales, obscure civilizations, and religions, witchcraft, spiritualism, séances, psychic phenomenon, and almost any variation on occultism that could be dreamed up.

The Hermetic Order of the Golden Dawn

In 1887, a Freemason named A. F. A. Woodford found an "ancient" ciphered manuscript dealing with Kabbalah and tarot in a London bookshop. A note was attached directing anyone who deciphered the manuscript to contact a certain Fraulein Ann Sprengel in Nuremburg, Germany. Woodford supposedly did so, along with fellow occult-minded Masons S. L. MacGregor Mathers and William Wynn Westcott, and they received permission from their mysterious German contact (known in the Order as *Soror Sapiens Dominabitur Astristo*) to start a Rosicrucian society in England. This group formed the original *Hermetic Order of the Golden Dawn.*

A temple was started in London, called Isis Urania, and attracted occultist Arthur Edward Waite (who popularized Tarot cards in the 20th century), poet William Butler Yeats, authors H. Rider Haggard and Bram Stoker, playwright August Strindberg, artist Edward Munch (painter of the famous "The Scream"), writer Aliester Crowley, and many other famous personalities of the period. Crowley would later leave the organization and start a legal war by publishing the rituals of the Golden Dawn in his magazine.

A second, "inner order" also existed, called the *Ordo Rosae Rubeae et Aureae Crucis,* and from the name, it's clear that it derived at least part of its inspiration from Rosicrucian philosophy. This shouldn't be much of a surprise because almost all the founding members of the Isis Urania Temple were also founders of the *Societas Rosicruciana in Anglia* (see "Rosicrucianism and 'Fringe Freemasonry'" earlier in this chapter).

This activity seems to have been driven by the belief of a small clot of men who felt that Freemasonry wasn't secret enough or occult enough, and that the fraternity had somehow forgotten its roots in Rosicrucianism. Most Masonic scholars and researchers challenged the theoretical Rosicrucian origin of Masonry then, and still do today.

The movers and shakers of the major occult movements all seemed to know each other in the later years of the 1800s and into the early 1900s. Sooner or later, fights would break out and one group would accuse the other of not doing rituals properly or of making too many innovations in an "ancient" practice that was made up the previous year, and away they'd stomp in a huff to go start a new group. This is what we like to describe as the "ten guys chanting in their socks in the living room" syndrome. This is why it's so important to keep these circumstances in mind when reading "definitive" books from "high-ranking" sources in these organizations. They seemed to be in a constant state of tantrum, and running off to start a new group.

The traveling Spiritualism circus

When Spiritualism was most influential, traveling performers created very popular theatrical shows of hypnotizing subjects and performing séances to call forth dead spirits. The performances contained all the familiar trappings we know today: floating furniture, crystal balls, communicating by rapping on tables, and of course, the hypnotic trance of the medium who "channeled" the voices of the dead. What first started out in private homes eventually grew into regional and national theater tours, conventions, and even massive summer camps for true believers.

In the early days of the growing Spiritualist movement, women were especially attracted to it. Traditionally, men dominated lecture halls and theater stages, but women "trance lecturers" became quite popular. Not surprisingly, the "spirits" called forth in their performances frequently vocalized support for women's rights and the abolition of slavery. And it was especially effective on audiences when a small, frail, frilly female suddenly spoke in the deep, booming voice of a long-lost loved one. Naturally, widespread accusations of fraud spread over the years, but it never seemed to keep audiences away.

There were many vocal skeptics of Spiritualism, and more than a few investigative groups arose to root out the blatant frauds. The magician and escape artist Harry Houdini was especially passionate about exposing Spiritualist charlatans after the death of his mother brought many out of the woodwork offering to help him communicate with her on the "other side." Others weren't so skeptical. One of the most fervent believers in Spiritualism was the creator of literature's most scientific, pragmatic, and dispassionate practitioners of logic ever to grace the pages of publishing: Sherlock Holmes's author Sir Arthur Conan Doyle.

Golden Dawn splintered into various factions (the *Independent & Rectified Rite of the Golden Dawn* and the *Fellowship of the Rosy Cross,* to name two) when it was revealed in 1914 that the manuscript the Order was based on was a hoax, and the fictitious Fraulein Sprengel was nowhere to be found. There remain at least a half dozen modern groups all claiming to be authentic descendants of the original Order today. Not surprisingly, there have been lawsuits and allegations of trademark violations, which seem to be the fate of so many esoteric organizations the world over.

The influence of Spiritualism

Between about 1840 and 1920, a curious religious mania swept the U.S. and Britain. This mania was called *Spiritualism,* which was a period of time when religious groups like the Seventh Day Adventists and the Mormons arose, espousing the belief that mortal, earthbound humans could directly communicate with God, angels, and the dead. This time coincided with the new technique of Mesmerism (hypnotism), first made use of by Vienna's Franz Mesmer in his practice of healing through "animal magnetism."

One of the principal beliefs of Spiritualism is that that angels and spirits of the dead are closer to God than humans are, and therefore have greater knowledge than we do. So it was common to ask "spirit guides" for their advice. Spiritualists, on the whole, didn't seem to believe in reincarnation, nor was the major Spiritualist movement interested in occult, hermetic, esoteric knowledge or feats of magic.

In the aftermath of the carnage of both the Civil War and World War I, Spiritualism was especially popular, for good reason. In both conflicts, it was almost impossible to find any family who hadn't been touched in some way by death. Spiritualism tapped into the raw emotions of grief, and the comfort of knowing that the departed loved one was doing fine in the afterlife was just too strong for many to resist.

Spiritualism was also popular because it didn't really conflict with Christian beliefs in an afterlife. Just because a parishioner was a Spiritualist wouldn't get them kicked out of most local church pews. In its earliest days, Quakers were drawn to the movement in its original forms, but as it grew in popularity, Spiritualists were especially attracted to Christian Science, Universalist, and Unitarian churches. There have been a few attempts to form organized Spiritualist churches, but there never was one centralized national or international Spiritualist movement.

The Ordo Templi Orientis (OTO)

The *Ordo Templi Orientis* — OTO — (translated as both *Order of the Oriental Templars* and *Order of the Temple of the East*) is an organization with its roots in 19th-century Germany. Its founders were among some of the most influential promoters of esoteric, spiritualistic, and mystical movements beginning in the late 1800s, and the group has gone through several phases. The OTO exists today and is an enthusiastic group, claiming approximately 3,000 members in almost 60 countries (although the bulk of its membership is in the U.S.).

Founding the OTO

While it is usually associated with a notorious character of the 20th century, Aleister Crowley (see "Enter Aleister Crowley," later in this section), the OTO's philosophical founder, was a 19th-century German chemist named Carl Kellner. Kellner was a student of Freemasonry, Theosophy, Rosicrucianism, Hermeticism, mysticism, spiritualism, and every other kind of esoteric *ism*.

Kellner was especially fond of a variety of Freemasonry called the *Rite of Memphis-Mizraim*. This was a series of pseudo-Masonic degrees that had been created in Italy and France, influenced by Napoleon's exploits in Egypt. The majority of the Masonic world didn't recognize the Memphis-Mizraim degrees as legitimate (most Grand Lodges around the world warned their members not to associate with purveyors of these Egyptian rites because they were often promoted by private con artists out to earn a quick chunk of cash by enrolling gullible initiates in their 90+ degrees). Kellner also wanted to initiate women into the degrees, a practice that was absolutely forbidden by the regular Masonic world.

During this same period, Kellner met up with a Bavarian named Theodore Reuss. Like Kellner, Reuss was endlessly fascinated by esoteric groups. In 1880, he'd been involved with a failed movement to revive the infamous *Bavarian Order of Illuminati* (see Chapter 11). In the following 25 years, he joined up with a wide range of groups in the U.K. and Europe.

Kellner's idea was to assemble something like a college or institution to bring all these different philosophies together under one roof because they all touched on each other in some way. He believed that instead of withdrawing into different factions and splinter groups, the various esoteric philosophies needed to band together so that students of them could experience them as a whole.

In 1904, Reuss and Kellner assembled the Memphis-Mizraim Masonic degrees, along with other irregular degrees that mainstream Freemasonry around the world didn't approve of, into what Kellner termed the *Acadamia Masonica,* and the OTO would be its inner circle. Kellner wanted to bring these different degrees from around the world into one consolidated order where only advanced Masons could see them all.

The trouble was that the mainstream Masonic world wasn't really interested in them and continued to refuse to treat them as legitimate degrees of Freemasonry. When Kellner died a year later, Reuss took over and made changes. He was an early proponent of women's rights, so he opened the OTO up to women, and he incorporated a new French Gnostic church service, the *Église Catholique Gnostique,* into the organization, as its official religion.

Enter Aleister Crowley

Aleister Crowley (pronounced *crow,* like the bird) is one of the most enigmatic figures in the world of esoteric studies. The mention of his name in a room full of people who study these subjects usually results in the immediate split into two camps that either admire him as a larger-than-life genius or deride him as a drug-addled pervert. But he was the most influential figure in the occult world of the 20th century.

Crowley was born in England in 1875 and is best remembered in esoteric circles for incorporating "sex magick" into his occult practices. Sex magick involved ceremonies that combined his own sexual appetites. In these days of every imaginable sexual fetish easily accessed and delivered into our living rooms via the Internet, it's easy to overlook just how shocking Crowley's activities were to society at the time.

He was instrumental in the popularizing of Tarot cards and the use of Ouiji boards. He was a mountain climber, a chess master, a prolific author, a mystic, a hedonist, and a heroin addict, and he became popularly known as "the Wickedest Man in the World," a title he enjoyed immensely.

Crowley met Theodore Reuss (see the preceding section) in London in 1910, and it wasn't long before he began to influence his Bavarian friend's OTO. Crowley had claimed in 1904 that he'd been visited by a spiritual messenger of the ancient Egyptian god Horus, who'd passed along the details of a new religion called *Thelema,* which Crowley wrote down as *The Book of the Law* (never mind that it was largely lifted from the earlier satirical work of the French author François Rabelais in the 1500s).

Reuss became an instant convert to the religion and incorporated Crowley's religious services into the OTO's Gnostic Mass. (In 1920, Reuss went so far as to suggest to a Zurich convention of Freemasons that Thelema should be the official religion of all higher degree Masons. The assembled participants were less than impressed.)

Reuss issued charters for OTO chapters around the world, including one to Harvey Spencer Lewis of the Rosicrucians in San Jose (see "The Rosicrucians" earlier in this chapter). When Reuss had a stroke in 1920, Crowley stepped in and proclaimed himself as the new "Frater Superior of the Order of Oriental Templars."

Crowley took the OTO on the road, and went to the United States, but his reception at the hands of the mainstream Masonic Grand Lodges around the U.S. was less than laudatory. Most regular Freemasons were appalled at Crowley's scandalous reputation to begin with and were less than thrilled with his claims that the OTO was an extension of the Masonic degrees.

Lawsuits were threatened, which was something Crowley was getting used to. He had a habit of taking rituals from esoteric groups he'd been thrown out of and publishing their details, which had the effect of shrinking his circle of friends, as well as attracting legal troubles.

Crowley's OTO

Crowley completely rewrote the rituals of the OTO to remove the more overt references to Freemasonry's first three degrees. Crowley frequently associated himself with the name Baphomet, as well as the number "666" and the Beast of the Apocalypse. Both Crowley and his subsequent fans explain away most of his more shocking or sex-filled writings and activities by claiming the rest of the world is just too unenlightened to understand.

Crowley was a lightning rod for trouble. Tales of orgies, mutilation, pederasty (sex between two men, especially when one is a minor), as well as a series of torrid affairs with both sexes swirled around him, along with more pedestrian legal problems. In one notorious episode, a young man died at Crowley's villa in Italy after killing a cat and drinking its blood.

Rumors of sex with children and even human sacrifice at the "Abbey of Thelema" eventually led fascist dictator Benito Mussolini to have Crowley booted from the country in 1923.

The post-Crowley OTO

After World War II, the OTO nearly died out, with the only remaining lodge surviving in California. Shortly before his death, Crowley passed the reigns of the Order to a German named Karl Germer, who kept it alive on paper until his own death in 1962. One alleged member during this slump was L. Ron Hubbard, who was later the alleged creator of the alleged religion Scientology. Allegedly.

In 1969, the OTO was revived almost single-handedly by Grady McMurtry, who had received degrees in 1943 from Crowley himself. McMurtry claimed to have letters that allowed him to invoke emergency powers and revive the Order as its new "Caliph." Naturally more lawsuits and counterclaims erupted from the countryside, with at least three others claiming the right to "own" the OTO. A splinter group largely in the U.K., referred to as the *Typhonian Ordo Templi Orientis,* still survives today, and seems to be directed more to extraterrestrial life and demonology.

These days, most of the schismatic caterwaul has quieted down, and McMurtry's "Caliphate" OTO is considered by most to be the legitimate heir to Crowley's Order. Its current Caliphate is William Breeze, known by his more esoteric name, Hymenaeus Beta.

20th-Century Occultism and the Rise of the Nazis

In the occult secret societies that flourished and grew around the beginning of the 20th century, the occult became wedded to science and reason. The roots in Rosicrucianism from the 1600s became perverted more than any other period in history in peddling this new packaging of an old product. These new societies had their own brand of "scientific" proof, with their own terminology, featuring long-winded explanations for the vital life force that controlled the spirit world, and even new machinery designed to track and measure the forces of that world. They dipped at will into Eastern faiths, pulling out profound-sounding phrases for their New Age occult wisdom.

For these new occultists, Christ was no longer an old-fashioned Messiah, weighted down with all that mouldy old Jewish influence. According to these new thinkers, Christ became just another "avatar," a Hindu word for a deity in human form, only one of many people who influenced world events. The next step was to prove that Christ hadn't been Jewish at all and to prove it "scientifically."

Spiritualism, Theosophy, and Eastern mysticism all congealed after the end of World War I so that, by the 1920s, both Europe and the U.S. were absolutely awash in occult secret societies. In consequence, Germany in 1933 was the setting for a Perfect Storm — all these cultural forces were about to combine with national humiliation and a desire to be superior, like their folk legends of mythological gods told them they once were.

Out of it would come Hitler's Third Reich, which annihilated bourgeois values and Christian faith, replacing them with an entirely new society, built on secrecy, racism, and the occult. The evolution of this Nazi thinking begins with the influence of a 19th-century Ukrainian woman named Helena Petrovna Blavatsky.

Madame Blavatsky's Theosophical Society

It would be hard to invent a more colorful fictional character than Madame Helena Petrovna Blavatsky (known often by her initials HPB), and indeed, it is possible that many of the legends that swirled around her she created herself. She had an incredible influence on esoteric and occult societies that appeared after her death. Her Theosophical Society also had an influence into the 20th century.

A rediscovery of Blavatsky's writings in the 1960s led to the explosion of interest in Buddhism and other eastern religions, as well as the New Age movement of the 1980s and beyond.

Blavatsky the medium

Blavatsky claimed to be many things, and while she was a peculiar little spud in both appearance and personality, she understood showmanship, and during the height of the Spiritualism movement, she became famous for her abilities as a medium. She believed in dressing the part of a mystic, and wore voluminous robes, a babushka (a Russian headscarf), and fistfuls of rings, and carried her cigarettes in a pouch made from an animal's head. Her homes were often decorated in the trappings of the bizarre — one favorite item was a stuffed baboon dressed in a formal morning suit, with a copy of Charles Darwin's *Origin of the Species* tucked under his arm. She regularly engaged in séances and psychic illusions like levitation, astral projection, telepathy, and clairvoyance.

But Blavatsky wasn't calling forth dead relatives to see how they were getting along in the afterlife. Her views differed greatly from the Spiritualist movement of the period, and she was contacting the spirit world to receive Hermetic, esoteric, occult knowledge.

Masters of wisdom and the Great White Brotherhood

One of the coauthors of Johann Valentin Andrae's Rosicrucian pamphlets was Heinrich Neuhaus, and his biggest claim to fame was in publicly identifying where the mythical originators of Rosicrucianism had supposedly disappeared to: Tibet and India. This was back in the 1600s, and Europeans generally didn't go to such exotic and hard to get to places in those days. Thus, Neuhaus had conveniently packed the Order off into the mists of obscurity where it was unlikely anyone would go looking for them.

More than two centuries later, Madame Blavatsky did just that. While she was stomping around Tibet and the Himalayas in the 1850s and '60s, she claimed that she became enlightened enough to be contacted by a spiritual assembly of Masters of Wisdom. These Masters were supposed to have once been very learned mortals who'd discovered the secrets to Life, the Universe, and Everything. Because of their mastery of the occult arts on Earth, they retained the ability, after they died, to communicate with a select few living people who were spiritually enlightened — namely, Madame Blavatsky. At times she would summon them to speak during her séances. Other times they would dictate letters for her to write out, and after the Theosophical Society was formed, the Masters often used this technique to pass along management recommendations and to suggest officer appointments. Amazingly, such letters always seemed to back up M. Blavatsky's recommendations.

After Blavatsky's death, further studies by the Theosophical Society's members added to claims of the Masters' abilities. And of course, they continued to speak to a select few of the Society's leaders, guiding their decisions. A wide range of terms developed over the years, all alluding to the same concept. They were called Hidden Masters, Elder Brothers, Mahatmas, and the Ascended Masters. Later theosophical and Rosicrucian groups have referred to them as the *Great White Brotherhood,* with the term "white" meaning the spiritual aura that surrounds them, and not a racial term. In fact, Blavatsky had described them as Hindu, Indian (dot, not feather), or Tibetan. Others have described the group of Masters as a *Great White Lodge.* Over the years, various claims of membership in the Great White Brotherhood have included Jesus, the Buddha, Confucius, and a raft of others, including Blavatsky's own favorite mysterious spiritual contact, Kuthumi.

In 1873, Blavatsky moved to New York City, and while traveling the American countryside, she met up with Henry Steel Olcott. Olcott was an attorney and an agricultural authority, and had served on the official government commission that investigated the Abraham Lincoln assassination. They became good friends, and six years later, he helped her found the Theosophical Society.

Forming the Theosophical Society

In 1875, Blavatsky, Olcott, and Irish-born mystic and lawyer William Quan Judge, along with 16 others, formed the Theosophical Society in New York. At first, its original purpose was to investigate spiritualists and mediums, and to report on their legitimacy or bogusness. But it soon changed to teach HPB's own religious concepts.

Blavatsky's Theosophy taught that all religions were equally true and meaningful in their core philosophies — it was just their "packaging" that was imperfect. In other words, every religion is correct when you boil them down to their most basic ideas, and where religions fail, or at least stumble and confuse people, is in all the rituals, rules, trappings, costumes, saints, statues, and holy days they attach to themselves over the years. She also believed that esoteric knowledge — Hermeticism, and especially the mind/body/spirit-centered Eastern religions of Asia — contained the simplest, truest, and most important sacred teachings.

Her two-volume book, *Isis Revealed,* published in 1877, put forth the notion that science needed to loosen its corset and accept mystical manifestations like spiritualism and the paranormal as scientific phenomenon, along with castigating religions for losing sight of their cosmic roots.

Blavatsky pulled a world full of inspirations together under one roof for her Theosophical Society. She combined Buddhist philosophy, Rosicrucian mythology, spiritualism, bogus pseudo-science, and packaged it together under an organizational model patterned after the Freemasons. There was an international governing office, but countries had their own regional offices, and local chapters were called "lodges."

The Theosophical Society's logo was a curious symbol that combined an *ouroboros* (a snake wrapped in a circle, eating its own tail), a Star of David, an Ankh (an Egyptian symbol resembling a cross with an oval at the top), and a swastika.

Blavatsky used the swastika because it was a symbol in India for the sun and for positive energy. In its Indian form, the swastika is a cross, with trailing lines that make it look like it is spinning clockwise. Its use in Nazi Germany was the opposite — spinning counterclockwise. Some occult researchers claim this is a symbol of negative energy, but there is no agreement on this point. Pre-Nazi Germans used the symbol as good luck charms during WWI, and it could face either direction. Meanwhile, the swastika is a symbol thousands of years old, and it appears in ancient cultures all over the world as a sign of the sun, power, and luck.

India, Aryans, and the Secret Doctrines

In 1879, Blavatsky and Olcott packed up and moved the international headquarters to Adyar, India, where they could more closely study Eastern religions and philosophy. William Quan Judge stayed home and ran the U.S. side of the Society. While India was an exotic location on the other side of the world, the presence of a motley crew of Western oddballs wasn't unusual — England had colonized India in the 1800s and was in complete control of the country by the mid-1850s.

Blavatsky's Aryans

The term *Aryan* long predated the use of it in Nazi Germany as a description of some master race. The term was used throughout the 1800s to describe an ancient Indian/Iranian language that predates Sanskrit (somewhere around 2500 BC), and became a common term for any of the Indo-European peoples. By the early 1900s, Aryan had become a generic term in some circles used to describe "gentiles." Blavatsky uses the term Aryan in *The Secret Doctrines* to describe the last of what she called five Root Races, dating back millions of years. Blavatsky's view of evolution was that the human race began as a purely spiritual race, and gradually devolved into ape-like creatures. According to her, the Root Races were

- ✔ A perfect, Astral race that all others first originated from.

- ✔ A race that came from the legendary land of *Hyperborea*, above the Arctic Circle, the spiritual center point of the Earth. The Arctic was seen as pure and good, while evil emanated from the South Pole.

- ✔ A race from *Lemuria*, a lost land in the Pacific Ocean that predated Atlantis. These were 7-foot-tall creatures who laid eggs and were considered to be spiritually pure, but they had no intellect. Their downfall was in inter-breeding with animals. They fell out of favor with the gods, who sank Lemuria into the sea.

- ✔ Not wanting to repeat their mistakes, the gods created the fourth race, the Atlanteans,

and provided them with great intelligence. The Atlanteans created the perfect society and incredible cultural achievements before Atlantis was swallowed up by the sea.

- ✔ The fifth race was the Aryans, made up of what are now Hindus, Persians, Egyptians, Greeks, and the Europeans. They appeared just as Atlantis was sinking under the ocean, about 850,000 years ago. Blavatsky creates a hierarchy of the modern races — what some were good at, others weren't. (Interestingly, she felt that "white men" were almost incapable of performing magic.)

Blavatsky's discussion of race doesn't contain much in the way of what people today call "racial characteristics." Blavatsky's terms described a *spiritual* makeup of people from certain regions. She wrote of a Universal Brotherhood of Man and believed that all the peoples of the earth were descended from one common source. She still had a 19th-century personal prejudice of people from certain parts of the world behaving in certain ways. But her writings on the Root Races were not intended as commentary on one ethnic group being "better" than another. Unfortunately, later readers didn't see it that way, and a wave of fascination over this Aryan concept became the bedrock of German movements that led to Nazi theories of a Master Race.

Blavatsky and Olcott remained in India for many years, but HPB eventually moved to England, where she established an Inner Circle of 12 disciples (what good is an occult society without an "inner circle?"). In 1888, she published her magnum opus, *The Secret Doctrines.* Another two-volume work, it was an attempt to combine eastern religions with science. Blavatsky claimed that the text had been "revealed" to her through the Mahatmas, the Hidden Masters. One of the most important items in Blavatsky's *The Secret Doctrines* is the first real concept of the Aryan Race (see the sidebar "Blavatsky's Aryans") — a concept that German occultists and, later, the Nazis took very much to heart.

German occultism, secret societies, and the Nazis

In the years leading up to World War I, there was a fascination in Germany and Austria with Viking paganism, Norse legends, and the study of early Germanic pictograms called *runes* (both the swastika and the dual lightning-bolt symbol adopted by the Nazis are examples of these symbolic runes). Between about 1890 and 1935, two Austrians, Guido von List and Adolf Josef Lanz von Liebenfels, garnered a huge interest in these Nordic legends with their writings.

Guido von List Society

Guido von List was a follower of a Russian-born mystic, magician, and esoteric author, Madame Blavatsky (see earlier in this chapter) and her theories of Theosophy. He salted in his own mix of worship of the legendary Norse god Wotan, along with tales of the magical effects of first-century German and Scandinavian runes. List believed that a secret ancient Aryan priesthood had developed this esoteric knowledge.

List's writings became very popular, and a "Guido von List Society" formed before World War I, with an impressive membership list of prestigious and famous people. One of those fans was Adolf Josef Lanz (who pompously and dishonestly added the noble German title "von Liebenfels" to his name), another Vienna student of the occult. Like List, Lanz had been born a Catholic and had even become a Cistercian monk for a while as a young man. In truth, Lanz remained captivated by the ritual and history of the Catholic Church, especially during its medieval days.

Naturally, it wasn't long before the Society declared the existence of a special, inner circle, called the High Armenan Order, developed to practice secret rites of magic.

Lanz was very interested in List's theories about ancient, secret knowledge of runes, magic, racial purity, and esotericism. The difference was he didn't need List's claptrap about Viking gods. Lanz knew exactly who those secret Aryan priests were: They were Knights Templar.

Ordo Novi Templi

In 1907, Lanz founded the *Ordo Novi Templi* (Order of the New Temple), in the Castle Werfenstein, overlooking the Danube. Lanz developed an occult Aryan philosophy he called *Ariosophy,* which he applied to his new form of chivalric knighthood. His Aryan philosophy espoused Darwin's "survival of the fittest," applied to human beings, he wrote a lengthy paper describing a novel view of mankind. The Aryan Race had descended from a race of extraterrestrials called Theozoa, and the "lesser" races had come from the Theozoa breeding with apes. We're only reporting it.

Germany was not the only place these ideas were being cooked up. There was a worldwide movement growing based on the pseudo-science of *eugenics,* the method of selective human evolution. That's a nice way of saying choosy breeding for "superior" humans, sterilization, and taken to its most horrible extreme, extermination of inferiors. In its mildest form, it was promoted in Europe and the U.S., supposedly to stop hereditary birth defects. But in forms like those advanced by Adolf Josef Lanz and others, it was designed to create a Master Race. Lanz was especially contemptuous of Christian compassion for what he termed the "weak and inferior." He promoted his theories in a magazine called *Ostara* (which is undoubtedly where Hitler first read about it), and it became popular throughout Germany and Austria.

Still, Lanz's Ordo Novi Templi (ONT) seemed to be a secret society that was more directed to political ambitions than engaging in racial purity experiments. It supported the assassination of Archduke Ferdinand in 1914, the action that set off World War I. And the ONT was a key supporter of the Austrian National Socialist Party in the 1930s.

Germanenorden

In 1912, a group of German believers in the occult formed a secret society based on the writings of Guido von List, called the *Germanenorden* (meaning the Teutonic Order). One of the founding members, Hermann Pohl, had something of a cottage industry selling bronze good-luck charms and rings decorated with runes to German soldiers during WWI. One of the most popular was the swastika — a symbol of power, said to be formed by Thor's hammer and the sun. *Germanenorden* was one of the increasing number of Aryan-only groups growing in Germany, and it required new members to promise only to marry Aryan women.

Walvater of the Holy Grail

One thing you can usually count on with fledgling esoteric societies is that sooner or later a power struggle will lead to a schism. Sure enough, the *Germanenorden* quickly suffered from internal squabbles and split off another group called the *German Order Walvater of the Holy Grail,* founded by Hermann Pohl.

Another founding member of *Walvater* was Rudolf Glandeck von Sebottendorff. Sebottendorff was involved in several mystical, occult groups before and after World War I, and in 1909 he claimed he had joined a pseudo-Masonic Memphis-Mizraim lodge in Turkey. From his descriptions of it, this particular lodge combined Rosicrucianism, alchemy, astrology, and even Islamic Sufism.

Pohl believed that Freemasons and Jews were essentially one and the same, and both needed to be run out of the country — a stance that didn't seem to get under the skin of self-described Freemason Sebottendorff, at least not very much. Sebottendorff was charged with increasing the membership, and indeed he did. The rolls of the society went from just 100 in 1917 to more than 1,500 the next year.

Thule Gesellschaft

In short order, Pohl ran out and started yet another occult group, called *Thule Gesellschaft,* in 1918. On the surface, it was a study group for students of Guido Von List's philosophies. But behind the scenes, they were stockpiling guns and ammo to attack the growing Communist Party. So much for esoteric book exchanges.

A year later, Thule Gesellschaft merged with the *Committee of Independent Workers,* and renamed itself the *German Worker's Party,* and it is at this point Adolph Hitler enters the story. He quickly took over the Party and chose the rune of the swastika as the group's identifying symbol. The following year, he changed the name to the slightly more expansive *National Socialist German Worker's Party.* We all know them as the Nazis.

Heinrich Himmler's Nazi Knighthood

If Hitler wasn't especially interested in the occult, some of his pals certainly were. And Heinrich Himmler, Reichsfürer of Hitler's *Schutzstaffel* (better known as the SS, and engineers of the Holocaust), Adolf Hitler's feared internal secret police, was absolutely obsessed by the subject.

Himmler came to the town of Buren in the Westphalia region of western Germany in 1934 and took over the imposing castle of Wewelsburg. The castle was to become the center of a college for new SS officers and Himmler's own elite Knightly Order. The castle became the place of initiation of this new order and the new spiritual center of the Nazi paganism that was based on Germanic legends.

Himmler planned very big. His goal was to make the surrounding village a complete SS colony, only for members of the SS and their families. In 1939, a concentration camp was established to provide 3,900 prisoners to work on the project. More than 1,200 were worked or starved to death building Himmler's dream.

Himmler saw Wewelsburg as his own private Camelot, which, of course, needed a Round Table for its knights. In the north tower, a round chamber was constructed, with a sunken area in the floor and a round, oak table. There were just 12 seats around it, for the top dozen officers of the SS. In the domed ceiling a stylized swastika set in stone can still be seen today, modified with the symbol of the SS at each corner. A different subterranean round chamber immediately below it was to be a crypt for the ashes of all dead SS members, complete with an eternal flame. Another one of Himmler's goals was to find the Holy Grail, and a special room in the castle was set aside for the Grail when it was found.

The *Ahnenerbe Forschungs-und Lehrgemeinschaft* (the Ancestral Heritage Research and Teaching Society) was created to use the methods of science to bend history and archeology enough to back up the Nazis' racial and cultural policies. Ahnenerbe's headquarters were based in Wewelsburg Castle, and Himmler had a lot of projects for them. (In the film *Raiders of the Lost Ark,* the Nazi group looking for the Ark of the Covenant is supposed to be a contingent of Ahnenerbe archeologists.)

The Nazis went to great lengths to engineer an elaborate explanation that Jesus was descended from Jacob, who, they said, wasn't Jewish at all, but an Aryan. Another part of Ahnenerbe's mission was to prove the origin of the Aryans, and they sent archeological expeditions to India and Tibet to seek evidence of the earliest appearance of their "Master Race" — coming full circle to Madame Blavatsky's writings.

Chapter 11

The Illuminati: The Bavarian Boogeymen

In This Chapter

▷ Bring on the "Illuminated Ones"

▷ Introducing Adam Weishaupt's Illuminati and his world takeover plans

▷ Reinventing the Illuminati

*T*he supersecret society called the Illuminati seems to be everywhere you look in the world of conspiracy theories. This group supposedly consists of the ultimate world-dominating evil geniuses. Their universal logo, the All-Seeing Eye and the unfinished pyramid, is on the back of the U.S. dollar bill, along with their motto, "A New World Order." One of their earliest members, Thomas Jefferson, wrote their criminal influence into the Declaration of Independence. They created all that is evil, including the European Union, barcodes, injected microchips, Paris Hilton's career, and ATM fees.

The Illuminati are somewhat unique in the catalog of secret societies in this book, because in all probability, *they don't exist.* Sorry to let you down like that.

There *was* one famous group called the "Illuminati" in the 18th century. It lasted less than eight years, and its membership was very, very small. Many other groups followed, even to the present day, claiming the mantle of the original Illuminati, or having that moniker stuck on them without their having asked for it. In fact, in the alternate universe of the Internet, accusations about the "vast influence" of this little-known secret society get thrown around constantly.

If you first heard of the Illuminati in Dan Brown's novel, *Angels & Demons* (Pocket), the truth is a lot more interesting than the fiction. This chapter explains who the real Illuminati were, where they came from, and just why their legacy continues to capture the public imagination.

The Original "Illuminated Ones"

The Enlightenment, a period that lasted roughly throughout the hundred years of the 1700s in Europe and America, was an intellectual, scientific, and philosophical movement all rolled into one. It was a time when the scientific method of experimentation and reason replaced the more superstitious attitudes of the Middle Ages — a time of revolution, scientific discovery, and invention.

The very term *enlightenment* was chosen as a contrast to the Dark Ages, and light and illumination became a metaphor for knowledge and republicanism (meaning governments free of kings, popes, and their "divine rights"). In fact, late medieval adepts at alchemy or the sciences were sometimes called "the Illuminated Ones."

The first group to be associated with the term *Illuminati* was known in Spain as the *Alumbrados.* Appearing in the late 1400s, not much is known about this sect of Christian mystics. They apparently believed in trancelike meditation to the exclusion of all other thoughts in order to commune with God, and they developed decidedly un-Catholic beliefs, such as the notion that female adepts copulating with priests released souls from Purgatory. Not surprisingly, the Spanish Inquisition came crashing down on the Alumbrados like a ton of evangelical bricks.

What really brought down the wrath of the church on the Alumbrados was their belief that man could achieve enough perfection through meditation and prayer to become sinless. Where they got into hot water was the belief that if you achieved sinless perfection, you would no longer have to fast or even pray, and you wouldn't have to deny your physical body anything anymore. Your mind would become divine, so whatever you did with your body was of no consequence. See if your partner buys that story.

A French group appeared in the early 1600s known as the *Illuminés,* and they seem to have been an offshoot of the Spanish Alumbrados. But these groups have no real connection to the Illuminati that's at the center of so many conspiracy theories today, apart from the same name.

The Bavarian Illuminati: Short Life, Long Legacy

In 1776, just before the Continental Congress declared American independence from England, on the other side of the world a new "secret society" that was to become the Illuminati — the *real* Illuminati — was born in Ingolstadt, Bavaria. First called *The Perfectabilists,* the group was the brainchild of a young university professor named Adam Weishaupt.

Adam Weishaupt

The man who founded the Illuminati had an unlikely background for the leader of such a radical organization. Adam Weishaupt was born in Ingolstadt in 1748. When his father died seven years later, Adam was placed in the care of his grandfather, Baron Johann Adam Ickstatt, who was curator of the University of Ingstadt. The University of Ingstadt was a Catholic school, and the majority of the administration and teaching staff were Jesuit priests. Weishaupt graduated from the university in 1768. He spent another four years there as a tutor, and in 1772 he became a full professor of civil law.

What makes all this important in his development is that, a year later, Pope Clement XIV had an explosive disagreement with the Jesuits and completely dissolved the Order. As a result, the young Weishaupt was appointed to the chair of canon (Catholic) law, the first non-Jesuit and layman to have the position in almost 100 years.

What made this appointment ironic is that Weishaupt was privately very anti-Catholic. He spent years studying the philosophies and beliefs of the freethinking Enlightenment writers and had no patience with superstition, miracles, or sacraments. Unfortunately, he was in the sticky situation of earning his livelihood at a Catholic university, teaching canon law as proscribed by the Vatican!

Spartacus and the Areopagites

On May 1, 1776, Weishaupt formed his secret society, with just five original members, who were referred to as the *Areopagites* (named after the hill in Greek mythology where Ares, the God of War, was tried and acquitted of murder). Weishaupt had a big goal in mind for such a small bunch. He believed that a group dedicated to mutual aid, intellectualism, and philosophical free thought could help change the world by influencing the movers and shakers of society.

In addition (at first, anyway), they had no interest in recruiting anyone much over the age of 35 or so, because such "old" men were too creaky and set in their ways. This attitude would change over time, as they discovered they needed important, well-placed men who were already in positions of some influence to infiltrate the military and halls of government.

Because of his position at a Catholic university, which would undoubtedly be less than ecstatic over one of its professors writing anti-Catholic essays, Weishaupt and his organizers communicated using code names. At least two of the other four members were students at the university, known by their secret names Ajax and Tiberius. Writing as Spartacus (the name of a slave who led a massive revolt against Rome in 73 BC), Weishaupt outlined a secret plan to infiltrate the Freemasons' lodges, and then overthrow governments of nations and churches, take over the world, and create a new world order of tolerance and equality. It was as simple as that.

But a peaceful social change wasn't really what Weishaupt had in mind. In order to alter society, kings and princes, as well as church leaders, all had to be, well, gotten rid of first. These folks were the foes of his brand of enlightenment and republican thinking. And, of course, because he and his four young friends saw themselves as being superior to most of the common herd, they would remain in control of this new, improved society.

The name of the organization itself changed over time from *Perfectabilists* to the *Bees* and finally the *Illuminati*. In code, the organization was represented by a dot within a circle. The symbol was meant to represent the Sun illuminating all bodies in its orbit.

The Masonic connection

In 1777, Weishaupt joined a Masonic lodge (see Chapter 9) — Munich's *Lodge Theodore of Good Council* — and began looking for like-minded brethren to recruit into his circle of the Illuminati. Unlike the overwhelming majority of so-called secret societies that sprung up all over Europe in the 1700s, Weishaupt's Illuminati was definitely not preoccupied with occultism, mysticism, esotericism, or hidden knowledge. At least, not the medieval, alchemical kind of stuff that groups like the Rosicrucians were hunting. In fact, anything that seemed to have been influenced by Judaism, Kabbalah, and Catholicism in particular, wasn't allowed to seep into the Illuminati rituals.

What there *was* plenty of was secrecy. Major concentration centered around the memorization of ciphers — secret writing codes. As the years progressed, Illuminati members were instructed in how to mix poisons, prepare for suicide in case of discovery, and even construct "infernal machines" in which to hide their secret papers (*infernal machines* are explosive boxes that self-destruct if tampered with). The Illuminati created groups of members who were supposed to infiltrate Masonic lodges and take control of them. Code-named the *Insinuators,* they quickly invaded the membership of Munich's *Lodge Theodore of Good Council* and totally controlled it by 1779.

A friend of Weishaupt's, Baron Adolf Franz Friederich Knigge, was a well-known diplomat and Freemason in Bavaria and assisted Weishaupt with developing ceremonial rituals for the new Illuminati, roughly based on the Masonic model. He became a member of the Illuminati in 1780. Eventually, Knigge crafted 12 degrees in all for the group, divided into several groups:

> ✔ **Nursery:** These initiatory degrees were designed to determine whether new members shared the group's philosophical beliefs and to impress upon the candidate the importance of secrecy.

- **Masonry:** Patterned after the degrees found in Freemasonry, the initial "Masonry" degrees weren't very different from what occurred in regular lodges. Again, as candidates climbed the ladder of degrees, the goal was to find out whether they would go along with the more revolutionary aims of the Illuminati.

- **Lower Mysteries:** Later degrees slowly exposed the candidate to more of the Illuminati's anti-monarchial, anti-Catholic goals.

- **Greater Mysteries:** The highest degrees were designed to teach new leaders how to bring in new members.

With the new degree structure finally in place, and Knigge's help in recruiting prominent and influential members, the Illuminati started to catch on in intellectual, Masonic circles. The German poet Johann Goethe became a member, and in a relatively short period of time, the group attracted at least 2,000 members in Germany, Austria, Belgium, Holland, Denmark, Sweden, Poland, Hungary, Italy, and France.

The Illuminati was designed to be a society of Enlightenment-era thinkers, first and foremost. In spite of the usual accusations that appeared after the group's demise, Weishaupt conceived of the Illuminati to make society happier by enlightening the mind. It's philosophy encouraged the end of superstition in both science and faith, and sought intellectual equality between the sexes. While Weishaupt was anti-Catholic, Knigge was a practicing Christian, and neither man intended the group to be anti-Christian.

The Congress of Wilhelmsbad

In 1782, a curious event occurred in the town of Wilhelmsbad, billed as a Congress of Masonry. Freemasonry (see Chapter 9) was developed to enhance society by taking good men and improving their character, making them better citizens. Masonic secrecy was simply a demonstration of honor among its members.

But Freemasonry developed very differently on the European continent than in Britain and the Americas. It took some strange and sinister turns, especially in the German states, with the Illuminati's growing influence in Masonic lodges on the one side, and another German group called the *Rite Of Strict Observance* (see Chapter 9 for more about Baron Von Hund's *Rite of Strict Observance*) on the other. These new groups were something different, with a militant obsession over secrecy, and almost no interest in any of that character-building malarkey.

Mainstream Freemasons were alarmed about the directions these new groups were taking them. Delegates came to the Congress of Wilhelmsbad from Austria, France, Italy, Holland, and Russia to discuss the matter. More than a few disgruntled Masons went home convinced that they had to do something to stop this new movement.

Illuminati and the French Revolution

We talk about the influence John Robison's book, *Proofs of a Conspiracy,* and the Abbé Barruel's *Memoirs* had on the world of conspiracists in Chapters 2 and 6. Their books are still cited today as source material for conspiracy theorists, even though so much of their information was simply conjecture or invention.

Not to bore you with line-by-line refutations, but both authors claimed Illuminati *Insinuators* were in Paris infiltrating specific lodges. They go on to name the men, lodges, and dates, but time and time again, they get them wrong.

Figures of the revolution like Charles Maurice de Talleyrand-Périgord and Honoré Gabriel Riqueti, Comte de Mirabeau have never been proved to be either Freemasons or Illuminati, in spite of Robison and Barruel's accusations. Both claim these men, and more, made speeches in lodges that didn't exist when they say they did. They both repeatedly put men who couldn't have been there in lodges that weren't open, or even chartered yet. They put words in the mouths of men who never said them.

The Illuminati cracks up

While the Congress of Wilhelmsbad sowed discontent over the Illuminati's influence among Freemasons, the Illuminati itself was also starting to crack from within. Weishaupt became bolder in his professional life, and he increasingly subjected his Catholic students at the University of Ingoldstadt to his anti-Catholic tirades.

Meanwhile, Knigge became convinced that Weishaupt was really a closet Jesuit spy, and he came to completely distrust him. Knigge handed over all his Illuminati material in 1784 and walked out of the Order. Other defections soon followed for different reasons.

Several ex-members went to the duchess of Bavaria, Maria Anna, with Illuminati documents and a membership list. Confronted with clear evidence of a group that was actively gunning for their regal positions, she took it to her husband, the duke of Bavaria, Carl Theodore. As monarch of Bavaria, he quickly enacted a law forbidding any and all groups, clubs, or societies that hadn't been authorized by the state, and a year later clarified his position by naming the Illuminati specifically as the group he was really after.

Weishaupt soldiered on, creating a flurry of anti-Catholic and anti-monarchial pamphlets. The duke at last issued arrest warrants against him and the Areopagites in 1785. Weishaupt fled the country to Saxe-Gotha-Altenburg in central Germany, but left behind his incriminating papers, outlining the Illuminati's ambitious, if not bizarre and downright silly, plans for world domination. They were widely published throughout Europe to expose the Illuminati and to flush out other members, many of whom were in government, military, and university positions. A large number of them wound up in prison, and more were banished from Bavaria altogether.

The Bavarian Order of the Illuminati died officially in 1785, and its secrets and Evil Plans For World Dominatio were discovered, published, and ridiculed, eventually worldwide. The movement was never popular and died out completely by the end of the century. But the phantom of the Illuminati survived in the public's memory. Because of its ties to many European Freemasons of the period, the two groups became intertwined in the public imagination.

As for the Illuminati's founder, Weishaupt became a professor at the University of Gottingen. He wrote several apologetic treatises about the Order over the years. And he promised to never, ever, ever try to take over the world again. Cross his heart.

Illuminati in America?

The life and death of the Illuminati in Europe has been well documented, and many of the organization's papers were greatly publicized after Adam Weishaupt (see the previous sections) fled Bavaria. But the Illuminati's time span coincided with the early days of the fledgling United States, during and immediately after the American Revolution. Trustworthy records of the group's activities in America — if indeed there were any — are nonexistent.

George Washington was sent a copy of John Robison's book, *Proofs of a Conspiracy* (see Chapter 9 for more about this important book), warning him of the spread of Illuminism, and the possible infiltration of Freemason lodges (of which Washington was a member). He believed that none of the Lodges were contaminated with Illuminati principles, but in a follow-up letter, he explained that he didn't

> . . . doubt that, the Doctrines of the Illuminati, and principles of Jacobinism had not spread in the United States. On the contrary, no one is more truly satisfied of this fact than I am. The idea that I meant to convey, was, that I did not believe that the Lodges of Free Masons in this Country had, as Societies, endeavoured to propagate the diabolical tenets of the first, or pernicious principles of the latter (if they are susceptible of separation).

Some researchers have alleged that a Columbia Lodge of the Illuminati was started in New York City in 1785. Over the next four years, as many as 14 more Illuminati lodges sprung up in the 13 states, including one in Virginia that supposedly counted Thomas Jefferson as a member (see the sidebar "Thomas Jefferson and the Illuminati" later in this chapter). But there is no proof whatsoever that these lodges ever existed.

The supposed Columbia Lodge of the Illuminati was claimed to have been the fraternal refuge of New York governor Dewitt Clinton, newspaper editor and future politician Horace Greeley, and New York politician Clinton Roosevelt. Roosevelt himself, it has been claimed over the years, used the philosophy of the Illuminati in his 1841 book, *Science Of Government Founded On Natural*

Law. He was a distant cousin of President Franklin Delano Roosevelt (FDR), and some people claim that the book is a blueprint for both Karl Marx's 1848 *Communist Manifesto* and FDR's socialistic New Deal programs of the 1930s. Those folks looking under the rug for a conspiracy claim that the Illuminati, through Clinton Roosevelt, created Communism along with FDR's New Deal programs. And as icing on the cake, FDR (who was also a Freemason, by the way) put the All-Seeing Eye and the unfinished pyramid, which are, as any good conspiracist knows, symbols of the Illuminati (or the Masons; or both), on the back of the U.S. one dollar bill. (The All-Seeing Eye in a triangle that appears in the U.S. Great Seal really started out in the Renaissance as a Christian symbol for God, with the triangle representing the Holy Trinity. See Chapter 9 for more about the supposed Masonic symbols on the dollar.)

Building a Boogeyman: The Illuminati as All-purpose Evil

After the death of the Bavarian Illuminati, a bewildering amount of literature poured out of Europe purporting to tell as many lurid details of the organization as authors could discover (or make up). Much like today, tales of a supersecret group engaged in conspiracies to overthrow the kings of Europe, especially during the aftermath of the bloody French Revolution, sold lots of newspapers and books all over the world. In spite of its small size, short life span, and publicly ousted officials and founders, the Illuminati captured the minds of the public in the early 1800s. After that, tales of the Illuminati slipped into obscurity.

The Illuminati and the occult

In the 1860s, a French magician and author named Eliphas Lévi wrote a series of books and pamphlets that became the centerpiece of modern occult lore. In his book, *A History of Magic,* Lévi mistakenly claims that the Bavarian Illuminati was occult and its members had "habitual communications with the dead." The last thing Weishaupt's Illuminati involved was the occult. Nevertheless, Lévi claimed that the Rosicrucians, the Knights Templar, the Freemasons, and the Illuminati were all secret magicians dabbling in occult practices.

In the 1870s, a German named Theodor Reuss was busy dabbling in obscure, irregular Masonic organizations, and in 1880, he started his own Order of the Illuminati in Berlin and Munich. The group never managed to attract many members, so in 1895, Reuss decided to invent his own Masonic lodge that claimed to be a lodge of the Illuminati. Reuss would go on to create the *Ordo Templi Orientis* in 1906, and his successor Aleister Crowley took the claims of the Illuminati and the occult and embellished them (see Chapter 10).

Thomas Jefferson and the Illuminati

The evidence usually cited to peg Jefferson as a member of the Illuminati is based on one letter he wrote to Bishop James Madison in January 1800. The letter is frequently quoted out of context, leaving out the part in which he makes it clear that he knows nothing about the Order, apart from what he'd just read in Abbé Barruél's book, published after the French Revolution (see Chapters 2 and 6 for more about Barruél's important book). The spellings are Jefferson's:

I have lately by accident got a sight of a single volume (the 3d) of the Abbé Barruel's Antisocial Conspiracy, which gives me the first idea I have ever had of what is meant by the Illuminatism. . . . Barruel's own parts of the book are perfectly the ravings of a Bedlamite. But he quotes largely from Wishaupt whom he considers as the founder of what he calls the order. . . . I will give you the idea I have formed from only an hour's reading of Barruel's quotations from him, which, you may be sure, are not the most favorable. Wishaupt seems to be an enthusiastic philanthropist. He is among those . . . who believe in the infinite perfectability of man. He thinks he may in time be rendered so perfect that he will be able to govern himself in every circumstance, so as to injure none, to do all the good he can, to leave government no occasion to exercise their powers over him, and, of course, to render political government useless. . . . Wishaupt believes that to promote this perfection of the human character was the object of Jesus Christ. . . . I believe you will think with me that if Wishaupt had written here, where no secrecy is necessary in our endeavours to render men wise and virtuous, he would not have thought of any secret machinery for that purpose.

It should be pointed out, as an aside, that the Bishop James Madison to whom the letter was written wasn't President James Madison (they were cousins). But for a dose of extra irony, there is actually a secret society called the *Bishop James Madison Society* at William and Mary College in Virginia. Started in 1812, it's the second oldest secret society on campus. The only older one is the Flat Hat Club, to which Thomas Jefferson belonged.

Nesta Webster and the Illuminati's conspiracy against civilization

In 1920, an English conspiracy theorist named Nesta Webster published a series of articles in the *London Morning Post* based on the *Protocols of the Elders of Zion,* a notorious piece of Russian anti-Jewish propaganda (see Chapter 6). The next year, she extended her articles and published them as *The Cause of World Unrest.* This influential work resurrected Barruel and Robison's claims that secret society caused the French Revolution, making the strong charge that it and all the unrest in the world since the revolution were caused by a Jewish/Freemason/Illuminati conspiracy, using powers of the occult. Webster believed this was a conspiracy against civilization, and her theories became incredibly popular. Winston Churchill and Lord Kitchener (England's Field Marshal in India) were fans of her theories.

While her theory that the Illuminati (largely Jewish) world conspiracy was the source of Bolshevism (Communism) in Russia was quickly accepted by prominent politicians, her viral anti-Semitism was less than admired after World War II ended. She strongly supported fascism and the Nazi persecution of Jews and said Hitler successfully managed to stop the Jewish plan to rule the world. Webster's writings have influenced many conspiracists since the 1920s. She is frequently quoted by modern conspiracists who believe her every word.

The Illuminati today: All things to all people

Conspiracists say the Illuminati, or something like it, still exists today, acting as the puppet masters behind presidents, kings, banking, business, and the United Nations. As Benjamin Franklin once said, "Three may keep a secret when two of them are dead." Such a conspiracy that involves hundreds of evil geniuses is unlikely to have remained secret for all this time, yet there's never been a snitch.

The Illuminati has become a catchall name, a ghostly stand-in for business-men who own too much, giant bureaucracies, and government secrecy. Over the years, the Illuminati name badge has been pinned by conspiracists on left-wing socialists and communists, multinational capitalists, and right-wing political pundits. Even politicians diametrically opposed to each other on virtually every socio-economic level are frequently lumped together as being "elites" who secretly think alike and are supposedly part of the Illuminati. The Internet has only fueled the growth of this theory.

What makes the allegation of an Illuminati conspiracy for world control so comical is that the original aim of the Illuminati wasn't totalitarian control of the world, but anti-Establishment revolution.

The John Birch Society's Illuminati

The ultra-right-wing John Birch Society did much to resurrect the specter of the Illuminati in the 1960s and pin its tail to the backside of Communism. The society's founder, Indianapolis candy manufacturer Robert F. Welch, believed everything he read in John Robison's and Barruél's books about the Illuminati, the European Freemasons, and the French Revolution and con-cluded that Adam Weishaupt's Illuminati was the model for Marxism, Soviet-style Communism, the Council on Foreign Relations, and the United Nations.

Welch referred to the modern Illuminati as the "Insiders" and even alleged in his book, *The Politician,* that World War II general and republican president Dwight D. Eisenhower was an insider working for the Communists. Gary

Allen's 1964 book, *None Dare Call It Conspiracy*, was widely promoted by the Society, and it laid out a supposed roadmap of the modern Illuminati, combined with the financing of the Rockefellers and the Rothschild banking family. The book certainly struck a chord in America by selling 7 million copies.

Dan Brown's Illuminati

Dan Brown, like many authors, resurrected the Illuminati as little more than boogeymen for his first Robert Langdon novel, *Angels & Demons*. Using the Illuminati allowed Brown to engage his characters in Enlightenment-style dialogues about the supremacy of science over religion. In the end (stop here if you haven't read the novel), it turns out that the mysterious head of the Illuminati, Janus, has perpetrated a hoax and resurrected the name of the Order as a diversionary tactic to hide his own individual treachery. It's a favorite Brown tactic — use the bad guy to spout your most controversial ideas, so you have a back-door escape hatch.

"The brotherhood of the Illuminati is also factual," says Dan Brown in his "Author's Note" in *Angels & Demons*. Not the way he wrote it, it isn't.

Brown's fictional Illuminati was supposed to have been a group of scientists who rebelled secretly against church dogma in the 1500s. According to his story, scientists who failed to knuckle under to church teachings and demands were arrested, tortured, and branded on the chest with a superspecial branding iron identifying them as members of the subversive group, and their bodies pitched into the streets of Rome as a warning. According to Brown, astronomer Galileo Galilee was a member, and they met secretly in an underground *Church of the Illumination*. Eventually, in the 1600s, this Illuminati became dedicated to the toppling of the church and Christianity itself. They became Satanists and were referred to as *Shaitan* — the Islamic word for Satan — by the Catholic Church. Breathlessly, Langdon describes them as the "world's oldest and most powerful satanic cult."

Brown even gave this Illuminati a spiffy logo, a clever bit of calligraphy that spells out their name, which looks identical upside down or right side up. Far from being an artifact from history, this "ambigram" as Brown calls it, is an invention of his friend, artist John Langdon, whose name he attached to his fictional hero Robert Langdon in gratitude.

Brown uses a clever device in his books, dressing up old, secret, and often fictional societies to get in his licks against the church. The history of the Catholic Church's activities is long, exciting, and sad enough without Brown exaggerating it to an absurd degree. And one thing is for certain: The one thing the real Illuminati was *not* was satanic.

Texe Marrs, ZOG, and the Illuminati

Former U.S. Air Force officer turned evangelical minister, Texe Marrs (no relation to conspiracy author and fellow Texan Jim Marrs) preaches a message of end-times prophecy, combined with anti-Semitic, ZOG (Zionist Occupied Government), and Illuminati obsession. He is one of the most prolific anti-Semitic conspiracists in America, and believes that the U.S. government is little more than a willing puppet of Israel. His bewildering pile of books, DVDs, CDs, tapes, newsletters, and other merchandise, along with a weekly radio show broadcast via shortwave, covers everything from American "gulags" (secret concentration camps for rounding up dissidents) and a supposed Jewish domination of American, European, and Soviet governments, to a crypto-Jewish/Masonic/Illuminati plan to destroy the world. Or Christianity. Or world banking. It gets confusing after a while.

For those interested in kitsch, his for-profit *Power of Prophecy* "ministry" has a 192-page catalog available for a paltry $6, so you too can keep your ear to the ground to hear the onrushing train of worldwide destruction. He also sells water filters.

David Icke's version of the Illuminati

Former British soccer player, self-proclaimed Messiah, and professional conspiracist David Icke has concocted his own theory of the Illuminati, and they aren't of this earth. It's probably true that Ickes has done more than any other conspiracy author to promote the concept of an all-controlling cabal of elites who are working secretly behind the scenes to dominate the world.

Icke believes the Illuminati are actually several races of alien reptiles who live underground, and who can change their outward shape to resemble humans. Icke claims these alien Illuminati make up the British royal family, the Rothschild banking family, the family of both Bush presidents, the Freemasons, the Jews, and country singer Boxcar Willie, among many others. For more about Icke's unusual theory, see Chapter 16.

Chapter 12

Secret Societies of Terror and Death

In This Chapter

▷ Founding the world's second-oldest profession

▷ Checking out flying ninjas and low-life thugs

▷ Peeking under the sheets of the Ku Klux Klan and other hate groups

*T*his chapter opens with the facts on the most sinister of secret societies, the ones that specialize in assassination. The very word *assassin* comes from one of the oldest of these dark brotherhoods, the "Assassins," a brutal and bizarre cult that existed a thousand years ago in the Near East. It's not quite so distant as it sounds; the Crusader knights of Europe ended up on a collision course with them, which fixed the Assassins in the mythology of Western civilization. They were called assassins, or originally the *hashasshim,* because they liked to smoke enough hashish beforehand to get themselves in just the right mood to go out and kill the targets they'd been given by their overlord, the Old Man of the Mountain.

From the Middle Ages, the chapter explores the world's other murderous secret societies, as they changed in response to the world around them. By the 19th century, secret societies with a murderous purpose were generally less inclined to be religious cults, and more likely to be politically or idealisti-cally motivated, although their victims were just as dead as those of ten centuries before.

The 20th century added more elements to the mix, but the effectiveness of inspiring fear in the enemy by the use of ruthless bloodshed, without pausing to spare the innocent, remained the same. Greed combined with the rivalry between gangs to give birth to the infamous secret society of the 1940s called Murder, Incorporated. Other 20th-century fraternities of terror, like the Ku Klux Klan, were based on the most deadly scourge of that century — race hatred. And with the dawn of the 21st century, religious terrorism has taken center stage again, featuring secret societies like Al-Qaeda, that resemble nothing so much as the Assassins of ten centuries ago.

The Ancient Brotherhoods of Death

The idea of a secret society whose members are "killers for the cause" is a very old one, with a variety of types. Yet even in ancient times such a thing was unusual, and unnerving, because it involved such intense fanaticism. Most developed ancient societies were more ruthlessly sophisticated and shrewd than that.

In ancient Rome, for example, the streets were ruled by the mob, and the mob was ruled by the gangs. The most violent and enterprising of the gang leaders were usually in the pocket of a particular senator. Generally, the gangs were used to get out the vote, by intimidation, if necessary. And if the senator wished to be rid of someone of the opposition, he used gang leaders as hired assassins. But this wasn't strictly their purpose.

Still, the idea of a secret society devoted to assassination is even older than the Assassins, and more common than it's comfortable to think. Following is simply a selection, an enlightening list of the most famous, or infamous, assassins.

The Sicarii

The Sicarii were a secret society of Jewish assassins in the time of Christ. As with so many other bands of assassins, the Sicarii achieved the blind devotion of their membership with a toxic blend of religious fanaticism and political mania.

The Latin for a dagger is *sicarius,* and *Sicarii* literally means "men who wield a dagger." The term is also used for a kind of gladiator in the arena of Rome, because gladiators were named by the type of weapon they carried.

Julius Caesar had been a great friend and admirer of the Jews, giving them a cozy period as a client state to the Roman Empire, in Judea. It was ruled by the puppet Hasmonean dynasty of Jewish kings and queens, who had more privileges than most of Rome's conquered provinces. But the relationship between the Jews and their conquerors (the Romans were at the end of a long line of them, including the Babylonians, the Assyrians, and the Seleucid Greeks) began to sour rather badly in the next century.

This new bitterness grew out of two forces: the Zealots and the Sicarii:

- The Zealots were the Far Right political party in Judea. The modern-day word *zealot,* for someone who is blinded by their ideology, comes from here.
- The Sicarii were a secret society made up of Zealots, no longer content with just starting riots against the Roman occupation.

The Sicarii were determined to start a bloody rebellion, and did so in part by assassinating anyone of the other parties that they labeled as "Hellenized," meaning they'd been influenced by or were somewhat sympathetic to the Roman overlords. The Sicarii finally got their doomsday scenario in 68 AD, when the Roman legions, sick of all the violence, invaded the difficult province — the first of three long wars that annihilated the nation and dispersed the Jews across the face of the earth.

Devoted Jews were horrified at how willing the Sicarii were to spill blood even on the Temple Mount, the site of the holiest shrine in Jerusalem, Solomon's Temple. But it was too tempting, in the crowds that mobbed the place during a religious festival, to be able to get in, kill the target, then disappear into the crowd, for the Sicarii to pass it by simply out of reverence. As long as the blood that was spilled was that of a Roman or a Roman sympathizer, real or perceived, the Sicarii were just fine with it.

A band of Sicarii most likely arranged the final dramatic stage of revolt from the cliff-top city of Masada, leading the rebels in mass suicide rather than surrender. They didn't call them Zealots for nothing. When the Romans caught one of them and tortured him, the historian Josephus said that their "courage, or whether we ought to call it madness, or hardiness in their opinions, everybody was amazed at." He goes on chillingly to say that even Sicarii children, when tortured, wouldn't recognize Caesar as their sovereign.

Judas Iscariot, the disciple who betrayed Jesus Christ, was probably a Sicarii —*Iscariot* is easily translated as a Latinized version of *sicarius,* meaning "one of the Sicarii." So much for following Jesus' advice of "rendering unto Caesar what is Caesar's, and unto God what is God's."

After Judea was in ashes, the Sicarii hotfooted it to Alexandria in Egypt, where there was a very large Jewish population, and attempted to get them to revolt, too. The Jews of the city replied by putting all the Sicarii they could lay hands on to death. The rest were captured by the authorities one by one, and soon disappeared from the stage of history.

The Assassins

The Crusades, which began in the late 11th century, established four small nations in the Holy Land, called the "Latin" or the "Crusader" states, or even by their own French name for it — *Outremer.* They lasted two centuries, from about 1098 until the fall of the city of Acre, the last Crusader stronghold, in 1291. Meanwhile, the founder of the Assassins in Persia established a separate colony of Assassins, with their own "Old Man of the Mountain," in Syria. It was here, on the border between the Latin State of Antioch and Syria, that the explosive contact between the two was made, and the legend of the Assassins was born in the West.

Hassan as Sabbah

The Assassins were founded around 1090 AD by an Ismaili imam and holy man named Hassan as Sabbah, a name with many and various spellings, but a singular ability to strike fear into the heart of both East and West. (An *imam* is a holy leader, to Shiites, one chosen by God.) By the time Hassan was through, powerful kings as far away as Britain and France and the Holy Roman Empire quivered in their shoes at the thought of ending up a target of the Assassin leader who was called "the Old Man of the Mountain" by the Christians, derived from his Arabic title *Shaykh al Jabal,* the Prince of the Mountain.

The first of these princes, Hassan, was born in Persia (Iran) in 1056 to a family of "Twelver" Shiites, the dominant sect of Shiite Islam, but he later converted to Ismailism, a smaller and more mystical, esoteric form of Shiite Islam that was just about to have its greatest flowering in history; the Fatamid Dynasty that ruled Egypt at this time was Ismaili.

Hassan left his homeland to be educated at the university in the new capital of Cairo. The city, and its famous college, had been founded by the Fatamids, who ruled Egypt, North Africa, and parts of Saudi Arabia from the 10th to the 12th century. Soon Cairo rivaled Baghdad as the intellectual center of Islam. It was there, at the Al-Azhar University (which still exists and is one of the oldest universities in the world), that Hassan learned the secret rituals of the nine levels to the attainment of enlightenment, as well as mystical and occult secrets of other beliefs, from Kabbalism to Neoplatonism.

At the time of Hassan, the majority of the world's Muslims were Sunnis, as they are today. The split between Sunni and Shiite began as a dynastic argument over who would follow the Prophet Mohammed. Later it degenerated into other arguments, one of them being that Shiite sects are often more oriented to mysticism, ecstatic faith, and divine revelation than are Sunni Muslims.

Eventually Hassan left the university and set out to form his own Ismaili sect, actively seeking followers, which he found on his journey back to Persia. He made his sect's new home in a magnificent mountain fortress called Alamut, famous for its gardens, its libraries, and its inaccessibility to an invading army. Hassan liked the mystical number of seven, and so instituted seven ritual levels to admission, similar to those he learned in Cairo. In an amazingly brief time he became a real power in Iran. Hassan's sect would one day be called "Nizari Islam." Like the parent Ismaili sect itself, Nizari arose out of a disagreement over the line of the caliphate.

The Fatimid Dynasty ended and the Nizari sect was born in the same event — the death of the eighth Fatamid caliph, al-Mustansir, in 1094. His elder son, named Nizar, was to follow him. But he was in Alexandria when his father died, and a powerful clique in the military double-crossed him. Their leader, General Al-Afdar, decided that Nizar's younger brother, Mustali, would be a lot easier to handle. So he married off his daughter to Mustali, and then hustled him onto the throne.

This raised a clamor all over the Muslim world, and many important men refused to accept Mustali as caliph. Of these, the most important was Hassan as Sabbah. Thus he became the spiritual father of "Nizari" Islam. Hassan would have his vengeance fairly soon and in the fashion that made him famous. In 1130, as the Fatamids grew ever weaker, an Assassin sent out from Alamut killed the son of Mustali, al-Amir, in the name of al-Nizar.

Ismailism

Of course, the Nizaris were only the latest sect at the end of a very, very long line. At the time Hassan founded the Assassins, the Near East was an over-heated stewpot, with wars large and small, religious and political, boiling over everyplace. You had the major and minor Islamic sects, the Christians, the mighty Seljuq Empire of newly-converted Sunni Turks, the Jews, the pagan Mongols, the Druze, important sects of Gnostic Christians, and all the various military orders, kings, and warlords of both Islam and Christianity.

Still, Hassan managed to come up with something fresh. In his new sect of Ismailism, Hassan became an imam with the unquestioned loyalty of his fol-lowers, who believed him to be holy and infallible. He would live into his 90s, never again leaving the mountain fastness of Alamut, and in that time he fash-ioned this secret society in his own image.

Playing mind games

For Hassan, one of the most important aspects of the faith was the willing-ness to both kill and die in Allah's service, without question. He invented tac-tics that gave to him the absolute, blind devotion of his followers. Hassan had an entire bagful of tricks he used for this, many of which are used in the reli-gious cults of today. He liked to get recruits young to make a bigger impact. He moved the best recruits into Alamut, cutting them off from any friends or family who might contaminate them with the teeming outside world of other beliefs. And he liked to play mind games on them; this became an Assassin trademark.

According to legends, when the Old Man felt that a candidate was just about ready to be sent out on a mission, he had the man drugged into unconscious-ness. The candidate awoke to find himself in the private gardens of Alamut. Milk, spring water, and even wine, which was forbidden in their daily life, flowed from various fountains, surrounded by every sort of greenery and flower imaginable. The garden was also filled with beautiful and *really* friendly women, who would spend the next three days introducing this young man, born in poverty and accustomed to an incredibly grim life, to every sort of sensual pleasure imaginable. These accommodating ladies would feed the young man honey cakes, pouring him as much wine as he could hold, and basically drop grapes into his mouth like something out of an old Warner Brothers' cartoon.

When he awoke once more, the candidate found himself in the receiving hall, on the floor before the Old Man of the Mountain. When he was asked where he'd been, he replied that he'd been in Paradise. Small wonder. Then Hassan promised him that, if he fulfilled his mission, and if he were killed, he would spend eternity in that pleasure garden. Especially considering the harshness of everyday life in the desert, its little wonder they agreed to give up their lives in the cause without question.

Hassan played a lot of other tricks, as well, to prove to his followers that he had a personal pipeline to Allah, like the Jim Jones of medieval Persia. One favorite was to place a follower into a hole in the floor of the receiving chamber. Then, with only his head exposed above the floor, Hassan placed a large platter that had been cut in two on either side of his neck. They splashed some animal blood all over it, and then called in the troops. When the head spoke, answering Hassan's questions about what life was like in Paradise, the whole room was awestruck. Of course, after the room was cleared, Hassan was left with one small annoyance. So the man was then pulled out of the hole in the floor and beheaded, his head hung on a spike outside the entrance to the hall, as a reminder that Hassan had the divine power to call back the dead to speak.

The position of the Old Man of the Mountain passed from father to son. Of course, Hassan couldn't pass the office on to a son, because he'd had them both murdered, but never mind that. The rule held after his death.

Assassin methods and targets

The terrifying part about the Assassins was that they'd put out a hit on anybody who crossed them, of any kingdom or faith. The even scarier part was that they weren't striking goatherds and milkmaids, or even the petty nobility — they were killing imams and kings, princes and potentates, anyone perceived as an enemy of their faith who was high enough to be worth the bother. That was Hassan's motto — whenever possible, don't fight the whole army, just kill the king or general leading it. Sometimes, just the threat was enough.

One Seljuk sultan who put Alamut under siege awoke to find a dagger stuck in the ground beside his bed. A messenger arrived and said that had the Old Man of the Mountain wanted him dead, the dagger wouldn't be in the hard ground, but rather buried in his soft breast. The Turks all went home.

The Assassins didn't like the Christians any better. Their first Christian victim was a powerful and respected figure, Raymond II, count of Tripoli. Soon after came Conrad of Montferrat, king of Jerusalem. Though some said the Assassins were paid by King Richard the Lion-Heart, it was more likely revenge for Conrad's attack on Assassin shipping. But this sort of thing was still shocking to royal sensibilities, particularly in the way it was done.

Prince Aly Khan: Holy man, ladies' man

Back in the 1940s and 1950s, it was still possible to put "International Playboy" down as a legitimate job description, even though they were already something of a dying breed. One of the last and most famous was Prince Aly Khan, husband to movie star Rita Hayworth, premier sportsman and horseracing fanatic, lady-killer extraordinaire. He married twice and had affairs with just about every big-name actress and socialite of the day, becoming one of the hottest sex symbols in the world. Unfortunately, he wasn't Euro-trash joke royalty — he was a direct descendant of the Prophet Mohammed, spiritual leader to the world's 20 million or so Nizari Muslims, who count the Old Man of the Mountain as their founder. His father was the "Agha Khan," titled in both Britain and India, the imam of the Nizaris.

The prince's conservative father was rather put out with Aly's dissolute life (though Aly Khan was a war hero and later a permanent delegate to the UN), and so passed him over for the succession, naming Aly's young son Karim, who's the present Aga Khan. What's really weird about all this is that Rita Hayworth and Aly Khan had a daughter, the lovely American Princess Yasmin Aga Khan. Thank God she never decided to go into the movies like her mother. In a faith that considers any representation of the Prophet or his immediate family to be heresy and apostasy, one can only imagine the Islamic reaction to Yasmin tap-dancing her way through *My Gal Sal,* or *Tonight and Every Night.* Or worse, stripteasing her way through *Gilda* or *Salome.*

Aly Khan loved fast cars, fast horses, and fast women; the fast cars killed him in an auto accident in Paris in 1959. Karim Aga Khan is still the Nizari imam. It's a shame he doesn't have more power in the Muslim world, due to his commitment to modernization, peace, equality, and an end to poverty. His faith, grace, intelligence, and commitment are something that the new nutcase president of Iran, Mahmoud Ahmadinejad, could really learn from. The Imam has spent his life as a very effective ambassador for Islamic architecture and culture.

The Assassins always wore white, and struck with their sacred golden (and sometimes poisoned) dagger. They liked to hit their target in a very public place; they especially liked the emotional shock of killing a victim in a church or mosque. No one was above an Assassin blade — the young Prince Edward, later the mighty King Edward I of England, was nearly killed by a poisoned Assassin's dagger in 1271 when he was on crusade, simply because he made overtures of peace to the Assassins' deadliest enemy, the Mongols. This is why the Assassins struck fear into royal hearts as far away as Europe.

It wasn't just the Crusaders and their fiercest warriors, the Knights Templar, who ended up by calling the game a draw where the Assassins were concerned. The other figure of Crusader myth, Saladin, the greatest general the Islamic world has ever known, was also checkmated by the Assassins. Saladin was a Kurd and a devout Sunni who defeated both the Christians *and* Fatamid Egypt. But when he attempted to conquer the Assassins of Syria, he was undone. After three nearly successful attempts on his life, Saladin came to an agreement with the Assassins and just went around them, like everyone else in the East at that time.

Yet, the Assassins finally endured two fatal blows in the 13th century — the Mongols overran and destroyed most of the fortress of Alamut, and in 1273 the Mamluks, who also defeated the Crusaders, did the same to the Syrian Assassins in Masyaf. Surviving Assassins wandered for a time, trying to hold their identity together. Some even hired out their skills to their Mamluk conquerors. But their real survival came with carrying Nizari Islam underground, hiding in Iran disguised as everything from tailors to Sufi Muslim mystics.

It's probable that the success of their underground network can be seen today, in the fact that Iran is the only nation of the East to be overwhelmingly Shiite. They finally reappeared openly in the 19th century to claim their right to a spiritual identity (see the nearby sidebar "Prince Aly Khan: Holy man, ladies' man").

The Thugs

The Thugs, or the more proper Indian plural, *Thugee,* were a secret sect of criminal assassins in India, going back at least to the 14th century.

The word *thag* means "thief" in Hindi. The modern-day word *thug,* for your basic, low-life, violent criminal, comes from here.

The Thugs were extremely organized, with bands scattered all over India, but bound together by their fraternity. The leader of each band was called the *jamaadaar.* They all worshipped the goddess Kali, and had their own terminology and signs of recognition. But beyond that, don't confuse the Thugs with anyone like the Assassins or the Sicarii (covered earlier in this chapter), who at least had some sort of idealistic purpose for their ritual killings. The Thugs fully earned their name because they were killers for one thing only, and that was money. They haunted the roads of India for centuries, cozying up to travelers, making them feel at ease, before they murdered them and stole all their belongings. The bodies were then buried, or, if there was a reason to hurry, dumped into a well or pit.

Yet, it was all done according to their own bizarre ritual; even the pickaxe, or *kussee,* a tool for digging graves, was sacred to them. The group was extremely superstitious, and used all sorts of signs and omens to determine which fork to take in the road, which person to attack, and so on. The Thugs who picked up victims on the rivers, claiming to be on pilgrimage, were called *Bungoos.* Prayers, incantations, and the burning of Indian brown sugar, called *jaggery,* were all a part of the post-assassination ritual.

Thug rituals and weapons

The initiation of a new candidate was tedious and time consuming on two counts: first, because it usually took years of tagalong status to become a full-fledged Thug, and second, because the ceremony made a college commencement look hurried.

Dressed in white, wearing a crown of flowers, the initiate was presented to all the various jamaadaars, with long ritual prayers by the guru. Then they went outside, and the jamaadaars sat down in a circle with the initiate in the middle, and waited for some sort of omen. And waited. And waited. It could be anything, a rising wind, a falling bird, a clap of thunder or a passing animal, to show Kali's blessing on the ceremony. Then they headed back inside for a feast.

Their weapon of choice was called a *rumaal,* from the Sikh word for a turban or headdress, often yellow, a sacred color to Kali. But the Thugee had a more practical use for it. A coin, or more than one coin, was placed in its folds, lending the cloth the necessary weight to be whipped quickly around the target's neck, where it was used with practiced skill to strangle the victim. This is sometimes called a *garrote.*

English royalty was honorably beheaded in the old days. But in the Muslim East, those of the royal blood were usually garroted. Beheading was deemed a demeaning death for the worst sort of low-born scum. Later on, in the 18th century, Western seamen imprisoned and enslaved by the Islamic Barbary states of North Africa were usually beheaded when executed, as a sign of their lowly status, although they were occasionally burned or crucified.

The goddess Kali

Thugs were drawn from both the Muslim and the Hindu communities, but ultimately the original faith of a Thug didn't matter, because induction into the society entailed the worship of the Thugee goddess, Kali, also called Bhowanee.

Many peaceful Hindus worshipped Kali, even though she was a goddess that symbolized annihilation in the original Hindu pantheon. Kali has worn many faces over the centuries in the complex Hindu religion, including that of a typical earth-mother goddess. But the Thugs formed their own sort of breakaway sect, in which the goddess not only forgave their murderous thievery, but blessed them for it. Very convenient. After the Thugee became an institution, membership often passed from father to son. They also got new recruits, as in the mythology about the Romany "gypsies" of Europe, by kidnapping and raising the children of their victims.

Destruction of the Thugs

Estimates of how many deaths were on the hands of the Thugee range far and wide, anywhere from 100,000 to 2 million over the course of their existence. But the fact is that they got out of hand, and the British Raj in India finally decided that something had to be done about it.

The term *raj* means "rule" in Hindi, and the British Raj is the name commonly given to the British Empire in India.

When one Lord William Cavendish-Bentinck became Governor General of India in 1828, he declared war on the Thugee. He used all the modern methods, including a sort of witness protection program, offering immunity to Thugs who testified in court against their former brethren. Soon a whole police bureau popped up called the Thuggee and Dacoity (bandit) Department. It was incredibly efficient, and the destruction of the Thugee was reputed to be complete by the 1870s. The end of their reign of terror helped secure for Britain a great deal of Indian loyalty.

Yet, the legend of the Thugee lives on, in everything from *Indiana Jones* movies to computer games. British and Anglo-Indian authors like Kipling and Conan Doyle incorporated the strange sect into some of their stories, and the legend was born. Although aspects of the cult, like their glassy-eyed devotion to the "bloodthirsty" goddess Kali would be overplayed in the West, the Thug image as the most murderous secret society of all time is really a fair statement.

The ninjas

Ninjas were Japan's original "Men in Black." Of course, it's only myth and supposition that always dresses them in black — the main thing a ninja assassin was trained to do was to blend in with his surroundings until he found the moment to strike. But because the favorite time for a ninja raid was the middle of the night, it's not unlikely that they were often dressed in the famous black karate-style jacket and pants, with a long black cloth belt, and a black cowl covering their faces up to the eyes. They even wore black *tabi,* the classic Japanese socks with a special purse for the big toe, to fit into their straw sandals.

But in their day, ninja were famous for wearing disguises, dressed as anything from a monk to a beggar to an enemy guard, so long as they blended in, unseen.

Origin of historical ninjas

The height of the period of the historical ninjas was from the mid-1400s to the mid-1600s. Most were trained in two particular areas of Japan, Iga and Koga, in which whole villages were devoted, apart from the usual fishing and agriculture, to the training and hiring out of ninjas.

Schools were there that trained promising young men from childhood. Very often these skills were passed from father to son, until whole families became famous *ninjutsu,* which means practitioners of the art of stealth. These highly skilled specialists were also called *shinobi* in Japanese. By the late 15th century, they weren't only master assassins, but also spies, or *sekko,* adept at all forms of espionage.

As it was in Europe, this was a period in Japan when powerful Japanese warlords, called *daimyos,* were battling it out for supremacy with one another in order to achieve the title of "shogun," a warrior dictator. Ninjas would've been an essential tool. That's what makes it so surprising that, as far as social status is concerned, the ninja was near the bottom.

Again, this would've been a bias recognizable to Europeans of the same period. Like a chivalrous knight, the samurai warrior lived by a code, called *bushido,* "the way of the warrior." The samurai, or "servants to the lord," were of the nobility, far above the common Japanese foot soldier in status. Spying, assassinating, and lurking around dark corners were absolutely beneath them. So, with the same easily compartmentalized ethics of a knight, they hired somebody else to do it for them. Consequently, no matter how skilled, the ninja was still a paid mercenary. (We don't even know how much he was paid, because the whole subject was so distasteful to the samurai.)

Ninja tactics and weapons

Ninjas are now a great favorite of teenage boys, and these kids are right about one thing — ninjas rock. They created staggeringly clever devices to aid them in intelligence gathering and sneak attacks. For example, they used a miniature ear horn, called a *saoto hikigane,* which could be placed against a wall in order to hear conversations on the other side, including of guards, to determine their movements before attempting to get inside. Everything a ninja carried had to be portable, and the great ninja masters developed advanced tools of their trade. More than any other early sect of assassins, these guys were the 16th-century James Bonds.

This business of climbing over and through castle walls like invading ants was something for which the ninjas were famous. Some of the items that could be found in the black kit bag hanging from a ninja's belt, or wrapped around his shoulders on a holster, are as follows:

- A climbing rope with a grappling hook, or even a portable climbing ladder of rope with an iron hook, to be tossed up a castle wall

- A clever, hinged saw, as well as other cutting tools, that could be quietly used to cut their way through wood or plaster walls

- A small lacquered box with several compartments called an *inro,* a medicine box, containing first-aid potions for the wounded, or poisons for intended victims

Many weapons could also be found there, including:

- **Ninja "stars":** Hand-sized pointed metal projectiles to be thrown like murderous Frisbees.

- **Tetsu bishi:** Could be tossed on the floor in front of an enemy in pursuit. They always landed with a sharp point up — samurai wore thin-soled shoes, and this was a great way to slow down a pursuer.

- **Katana:** A ninja's most important weapon — his sword. A katana was razor-sharp but slightly flexible, to help parry the blows of an opponent. Even this was also used as a tool; a ninja finding his way in the dark could extend the scabbard of his sword outward, and then hold the entire thing in his teeth to help him feel his way along. Should he encounter an enemy, it was an easy matter to knock the scabbard off and lunge with the sword in the dark.

- **Kusarigama:** A devilish device, miniaturized from common farming tools. It was a chain with a heavy ball on one end and a sharp sickle on the other. They practiced with it endlessly, like a gaucho with a whip, until they could fling the ball to strike a pursuer, preferably wrapping around his leg. Then they could pull an enemy off his feet, retrieve the sickle end in a flash, and make the kill. They also carried a smaller auxiliary knife in a scabbard.

- **Explosives:** Come in many shapes and sizes. The matchlock guns of the period were rarely used by them, but ninjas were masters at using black powder.

Sometimes during a battle, a ninja's chief task was to set fire to the enemy warlord's compound. Small explosives could come in handy for this. A larger bomb might contain black powder packed tightly into a clay pot or metal cylinder, the powder salted with shards of metal and glass to do the utmost shrapnel damage. They also used small, paper-wrapped bombs, almost like grenades, particularly to frighten or scatter people rather than to kill. And how did they light these things? In those days, before the invention of the sulfur match, small tinderboxes were used, striking metal on flint with pieces of an oil-soaked rag at the box bottom, which could take a whole lot of tedious tries in order to get a spark. Ninjas carried with them pieces of smoldering cord in a clever lacquered and weatherproof box.

Yes, they looked a little like members of a SWAT team when they headed out for a job. But part of their deadly skill came in dexterity and familiarity with their tools and weapons, as well as intelligence about their target. For example, when they had to get across a castle moat, they invented collapsible, portable boats or rafts. Another incredibly clever device was a pair of "water spiders," round rings of wood that would float, like balsa, with thick pieces of rope to attach a footpad at the center. The ninja then used it to virtually walk across the water of the moat, smoothly and silently.

Separating myth from fact

With such an incredible array of skills, it's not surprising that myths of the ninja arose ascribing to them all sorts of magical powers, like being able to fly across rooms or turn themselves into a flying weapon. They must have almost seemed to be flying to anyone who watched a ninja raid and survived to tell the tale. Among the many skills they practiced was the art of gymnastics and acrobatics, and they often quickly and silently launched themselves up into human pyramids to get over walls. They even used spears to pole-vault over ravines or obstacles. They tossed ropes between buildings, and then shimmied across with their hands and feet like bats hanging upside down.

It's easy to see why ninjas required so much training. They learned everything, from the proper way to don disguises and blend in, to how to stay underwater for hours at a stretch and breathe through a reed. Of course, warlords did try to guard themselves. They built ninjaproof homes, with things like stairwells that could be collapsed, or hiding holes, or even "nightingale floors," where the wood was fashioned with air pockets that made it sing whenever anyone walked across it, warning the intended victim.

The ninjas died out in Japan after the late 1600s. Several forces contributed to this, the most important being the rise in 1638 of the Tokugawa Shogunate. Japan experienced two and a half centuries of peace, during which the skills of the ninjas weren't required. They eventually were blended into the shogun's army. And so they fell into the obscurity of a Japanese legend virtually unknown here until the last few decades. Of course, nowadays the once obscure ninja are a staple of computer games and Japanese anime, as well as *manga,* popular graphic novels named after the Japanese word for comic strips. (See *Manga For Dummies* by Kensuke Okabayashi.)

Murder, Incorporated

Secret societies of murderers aren't only the stuff of ancient times. In fact, with Murder, Incorporated, they became as modern and streamlined and capitalistic as any business on Wall Street.

Lepke Buchalter was the only major mob boss to ever go to the electric chair, and it was Murder, Incorporated that put him there. This very secret society existed all through the 1930s and '40s, acting as a firm of murder-for-hire hit men for the mob as well as other clients. The colorful name was hung on this guild by the newspapers; within the Mafia, it was referred to as "the Combination."

Its founding is shrouded in mystery, though it was probably set up by Bugsy Siegel and Meyer Lansky, the two Jewish mobsters who were close friends of Mafioso Lucky Luciano, whose enforcers ran the show. Later both men drifted into other work, principally setting up gambling for the mob, and the underboss in charge of the Combination became Louis "Lepke" Buchalter, who was a chief liaison for assignments from "the Commission," which was the name Lucky Luciano had given to the governing board of the Five Mafia Families of New York (see Chapter 14 for more info).

Have you seen Judge Crater?

In 1930, there was a very famous disappearance of a member of the NY State Supreme Court named Judge Crater, "the Missingest Man in New York." You may have heard of him before. Somehow, his name became a national joke for five decades whenever someone was missing, a staple of stand-up comics from the Catskills to *The Tonight Show*. Conspiracy theorists have even speculated he was a victim of alien abduction — in the film *Close Encounters of the Third Kind*, during the scene near the end when missing people are pouring off the alien ship, some guy is standing there by a board full of pictures, crossing them off one by one as each appears.

One of the pictures is of Judge Crater. However, his disappearance is far more likely to have been the work of Abe Reles. After all, Crater's mistress went missing later that same year. It seems doubtful that the aliens came back to get her because the judge was pining.

In 2005, a letter turned up written 50 years before by the wife of Robert Good, one of Reles's paid killers, disclosing that Judge Crater had been killed and buried under the boardwalk at Coney Island. Bones had indeed been found at that location in the 1950s, but were never identified. They were quickly reburied in Potters Field, a mass grave for the poor.

Lepke is a diminutive of *Lepkeleh,* which means "little Louis" in Yiddish, and it was the nickname Lepke's beloved mother had given him. Ah, a boy who loves his mother!

Buchalter was the most ruthless of the short-lived but powerful "Jewish Mafia" of 1940's New York that often worked hand-in-glove with the real Italian Mafia. Lepke's biggest going concern was labor racketeering — he practically invented it. While others were making the usual mob bucks on booze, gambling, and prostitution, Lepke was muscling in on labor unions, forming his own army of scabs who could be hired by either side in a labor dispute. The number of murders he committed or ordered is staggering; Lepke had everything but a conscience.

Murder, Incorporated was a going concern, with many a mobster picking up extra money freelancing for Lepke; he liked to send men far from their home city to do the job, where they weren't known.

As well as the Combination, this secret society was often called "the Brownsville Boys" by insiders, because its two most trusted and efficient hit-men were from Brownsville in Brooklyn — Martin "Bugsy" Goldstein and Abe "Kid Twist" Reles. High or low, famous or infamous, it didn't matter to these two natural-born killers. If the blood was bought and paid for, you were a dead man.

Unfortunately for Lepke, he ended up in the determined gun sites of the most successful and ambitious of all "mob-busting" federal attorneys, Thomas Dewey, who would one day be governor of New York. Despite so much blood on his hands, Lepke went down for only one murder — that of a man named Joe Rosen, a candy store owner who'd once been a trucker, driven out of business by Lepke's takeover of the N.Y. Teamsters. Rosen had sworn his revenge on Lepke. Despite the mobster's warnings, Rosen decided to rat him out to Dewey. Lepke ordered his Brownsville Boys to kill Rosen, one of dozens of such crimes. But this order was heard by two people that Dewey talked into turning state's evidence: Albert Tannenbaum and Abe Reles. Both were hit men. But the jury believed them, sentencing Lepke to the chair, as well as his two closest Murder, Inc., associates, Mendy Weiss and Louis Capone (no relation to Al Capone).

There was a little justice for the two rat/hit men. Alfred Tannenbaum ended up testifying at several mob trials, after which he was banned from U.S. soil as part of his deal. He died in 1976. As for his fellow stool pigeon, when the really creepy Abe Reles decided to sing, prosecutors couldn't quite believe what they were hearing. They had in their hands the most feared, ruthless, and conscience-free hit man in the business.

A gun was far too impersonal for Reles; his favorite weapon was an ice pick driven through the victim's ear into his brain. He got so good at it that the coroner mistakenly labeled several of these hits a cerebral hemorrhage. Reles liked to kill for the sheer joy of it — he once murdered a car wash employee for leaving a smudge on his fender. Prosecutors, though repelled by him, were forced to protect him for the prospect of breaking up Murder, Inc., forever. But this was long before the witness protection program, and despite being under heavy guard, Abe Reles "fell" from a hotel window on Coney Island in 1941. It wasn't exactly a shock when it was uncovered many years later that the cops guarding him had been paid a hefty bribe to look the other way, probably by Frank Costello, head of the Genovese family. Reles became known in history as "the canary who could sing but couldn't fly." Yet, there was one victory, because when the supposedly "untouchable" boss Lepke ended up sitting on "Old Sparky," Murder, Inc. was history.

Hate Group Assassins

Anyone who kills is someone who hates, right? Well, not exactly. As the stories above about thugs and ninjas relate, some secret societies kill with very little in the way of emotion. But other secret societies kill with more than a surplus of emotion, driven by a blinding and fanatical hatred for those of another race or another faith.

The Knights of the Ku Klux Klan

The Klan isn't precisely a secret society of assassins. Or so the Klan says. If you ask the remnants of the Ku Klux Klan what they do today, they'll reply that they simply defend the white race. But the truth is that the Klan has been behind far too many shootings, bombings, and church burnings not to deserve a place on the list beside the Assassins and the Thugs.

The Ku Klux Klan is a peculiarly American institution. Does that mean that other nations don't have secret societies based on hatred of other races? Not at all. In fact, throughout history, whole nations have been founded on race hatred. As for the KKK-type organizations of other countries, you'll find a list of some famous ones at the close of this section. Unfortunately, there are lots to choose from.

Yet, the fact remains that the Klan is unique to America, for several reasons. The KKK was an outgrowth of the American Civil War, and in its opening years, it concentrated strictly on a hatred of the newest group of American citizens, the "Free Blacks," or former slaves freed by the war. Like some multiheaded monster out of a Greek myth, the Klan would be decapitated three times, but each time it would return, different from before, but always with the same core message of hate.

Birth of the first Klan

When the Confederacy, the union of breakaway states in the Civil War, was defeated in April of 1865, there were a lot of Northerners who wanted to make the South pay for starting the whole bloody mess. The defeated South was occupied by victorious Northern troops, and many Northerners thought the only way to treat the former enemy was to grind them under the conqueror's boot heel. And apart from that, one of the favorite ploys of Northerners to humiliate the still proud Southern aristocracy was to place their former slaves in positions of authority over them. Soon the South struck back, mainly in the form of the underground guerrilla force called the Ku Klux Klan.

There's some debate about how this really weird name was chosen. Most historians think that the name came from the Greek word *kuklos,* meaning "circle," as in a circle of brothers. The "Klan" was added later for the alliterative sound of it, and also because so many of these men were of Scots-Irish heritage and the word harked back to the Scottish clans.

According to the Klan's version of history, their founder and first "Grand Wizard" was the famous Confederate general Nathan Bedford Forrest. In reality, Forrest was offered this job as an honorary position, and accepted it, from the mysterious "six Southern gentlemen" who founded the Klan in his home state of Tennessee. Historians aren't certain of the identities of any of these six men; this was a dangerous time, and making war on the Northern occupation was a hanging offense.

The worst of all Klan punishments were reserved for anyone who ratted them out to the authorities. That's why they wore the hoods to begin with. Plenty of people knew who the Klansmen really were, but maintained either an admiring or a frightened silence. As for the ex-General Forrest, he'd taken a stand for racial equality by 1870, and long before that had disowned the Klan because of their use of violence and terror.

Soon the president, the former Union general Ulysses S. Grant, was forced to declare war on the Klan. In 1871, he put through the Republican Congress The Force Acts of 1870 and The Civil Rights Act of 1871, often called The Ku Klux Klan Act. They gave federal troops the right to intervene when the Klan did things like attempting to frighten newly enfranchised blacks away from voting. They could declare martial law, if necessary, to get the job done. It would break the back of the Reconstruction Klan.

"Birth of a Nation" and the rebirth of the Klan

Anyone who denies the ability of movies to affect society needs to bone up on director D. W. Griffith and his greatest work, the 1914 film *Birth of a Nation*. Unfortunately, it can be a painful film to watch, in terms of its primitive racial stereotypes. In *Birth of a Nation,* members of the Ku Klux Klan of the post–Civil War era are portrayed as the good guys, not the bad guys. They're the ones who ride in at the end to save the day.

Griffith was Southern born and bred; his father had been a colonel in the Confederate army. Like many Southerners, he was raised on stories of the brutality of the Northern occupiers after the war. His previous films had been everything from westerns to Biblical epics, but it all jelled for Griffith when he read a novel almost as influential as his film would be, called *The Clansman*. It was written by Thomas Dixon as part of a trilogy of novels set in the South, nowadays sold as a historical document under the title *The Reconstruction Trilogy*. The three novels separately are *The Leopard's Spots, The Clansman,* and *The Traitor*.

Dixon wasn't a sinister character; he was a Baptist minister, a lawyer and legislator, and a supporter of abolition before he turned to writing. But like Griffith, he'd inherited his ideas on race from his Southern childhood, and, like Griffith, he'd been raised on stories of the Klan as the protectors of defeated white Southerners. Griffith decided to film the novel *The Clansman* as *Birth of a Nation,* and both the feature-length film and the American race riot were born.

This wasn't just because the film portrayed African Americans negatively — it was because it was so good at doing it. *Birth of a Nation* was the first feature-length film, with a ticket price, and even an intermission, that put it on a par with respectable stage shows. It would leave the contemptuous term "flickers" in the dust. D. W. pulled out all the stops and used all the new techniques, things people had never seen before, like close-ups, two-shots (films previously were shot from one distant angle on one camera, just like a stage show), cross-cutting and other editing effects to play with time, flashbacks, and numerous other devices that we don't even notice today; they're simply understood as part of the language of film. It's a language that was, to a great degree, invented by D. W. Griffith. This is why modern film lovers have such conflicted feelings about *Birth of a Nation* — it was a giant leap forward for film, and a giant leap backwards for race relations in America.

It's difficult to overstate the popularity of the film when it hit. Really, only *Gone with the Wind* or *Star Wars* can compare in terms of the number of people who saw the film. Until long into the period of the "talkies," the arrival of sound in 1929, it was the highest-grossing picture of all time. But when black Americans saw the way they were portrayed in it, as evil schemers and rapists of White Womanhood, they began rioting from L.A. to New York, and from Philadelphia to Minneapolis. Many cities refused to play it at first, fearful of what would happen.

The politics of change

Beginning around 1900, over a million African Americans left the economically depressed South and moved North (in what was known as The Great Migration) to find more freedom and opportunity. What they got, of course, was lousy factory or service jobs, oppressive bigotry, and *Birth of a Nation*.

In the period of World War I early in the 20th century, white Americans had the jitters, not only over black Americans, but red ones, as well. No, we don't mean the Apache or the Sioux. These "Reds" were Bolsheviks, the communists that had brought down the Russian government, and were now, it was said, trying to do the same in America. The street-corner politicians said that a pack of Jewish anarchists were using African Americans as a pawn in their sinister game.

And so white Southerners, still licking their wounds from the Civil War, watched with undisguised glee as bloody race riots began to break out all over the sanctimonious North, and the West, as well. The arrival of race hatred in the North was soon to combine with one more factor to breathe new life into the Klan.

A nation of joiners

The 1920s was the Golden Age of American fraternalism, spawning a nation of joiners. Every man had a lapel pin, every woman an auxiliary. Most men belonged to a fraternal group like the *Freemasons,* the *Elks,* the *Buffalo,* and the *Moose.* These were overwhelmingly white and Protestant, but the Catholics had the *Knights of Columbus,* the Jews had the *Sons of Israel,* and the African Americans had the *Prince Hall Masonic Lodges* and the *Knights of the Flaming Circle.*

These and literally hundreds of other groups offered not just fun and friend-ship, but the serious perk of insurance and a safety net for a man's family should he be killed or disabled, in those days long before Social Security. Because we're talking millions of members here (and millions of dollars in dues), most of these fraternities employed professionals for the purpose of organization and membership drives.

One of these professionals was an un-Reconstructed Dixiecrat from Atlanta named Colonel William J. Simmons, a member of at least 12 fraternities and a professional recruiter for the *Woodmen of America.* He was "inspired" to create a new Ku Klux Klan by three separate incidents:

✔ The release in February 1915 in Atlanta of *Birth of a Nation.* Colonel Simmons was an absolutely rabid fan of the film.

✔ The rise of social disorder all over America, from race riots to draft riots to "Red scare" riots, as well as the freewheeling lack of morals in the "flappers" and "sheiks," the flaming youth of the Prohibition-era 1920s.

✔ The formation of a sinister gang of thugs made up of a couple of dozen prominent men in Atlanta politics, called *The Knights of Mary Phagan.* Mary Phagan was a 13-year-old employee of an Atlanta pencil factory, who was found raped and murdered in April of 1913. On incredibly flimsy evidence, the factory manager, a Jew named Leo Frank, was tried and convicted for the crime. The governor of Georgia commuted his death sentence in preparation for a new trial, when evidence of his inno-cence was uncovered. But in August, the Knights of Mary Phagan roared into the work farm where Frank was being held and lynched him.

Two months later, these "knights" met atop Atlanta's famous landmark, Stone Mountain, the proposed site for a monument to the fallen warriors of the South. They built an enormous cross and set it on fire against the night sky. It was so bright it could be seen all over Atlanta, a deadly warning that was really unnecessary; half the Jews of Georgia had already fled the state. They claimed that the inspiration for this desecra-tion of the cross was the mountain-top signal fires of the Scottish clans. Colonel Simmons co-opted (stole) it as a dramatic centerpiece for his new Klan ritual.

Klan wardrobe

Many theories exist on the meaning of the Klan's signature white robes and goofy pointed hats. The robes are pretty simple — they supposedly stand for both purity and the white race. It should be noted that the first Klan, during the Reconstruction, didn't really have a strict dress code. Often these night riders simply wore dark clothes and a burlap sack over their heads. Later Klan uniforms were out of the imagination of D. W. Griffith and Hollywood rather than Nathan Bedford Forrest.

As for the pointed hats, it makes people think of old-fashioned dunce caps that bad children had to wear in the last century, but this only dates from the 1840s. The pointy cap is much older, and has had many meanings. For example, in the 13th century, the Catholic Church forced Jews to wear pointed hats, or *Judenhuts,* in the same way Hitler made them wear yellow stars. But holy men from ancient Hindus, Celts, and even Iranian Scythians wore pointed hats. (The image of witches and wizards in pointed hats probably comes from this Celtic/Druidic root.) In the

Christian world, the most common meaning behind the high pointed hat is the same meaning as the towering spire on top of a cathedral; it signifies the person reaching for the grace of heaven. This meaning has survived in Europe to the present day. American tourists get really nervous when they come across ritual festivals like those of the *Nazarenos,* the *Brotherhood of the Passion,* a fraternal order of Catholics in Spain who wear robes and pointed hats with hoods of scarlet and black when they march in solemn procession during Easter.

It's doubtful, however, that the Klan in 1870 knew anything about the Nazarenos. It's far more probable that the inspiration for the pointed hat came from the fact that the dreaded executioners of the Spanish Inquisition wore them, in drawings from books that were common currency in the South. These night riders wanted to inspire terror, so they unwittingly borrowed a symbol from Catholicism, a religion that they despised. Go figure.

All these forces prompted Simmons to create a new fraternity, dedicated to "100-percent Americanism," and patterned after the long-dead Ku Klux Klan. But so little was known of the rituals of the Reconstruction Klan that the Colonel had to invent most of it out of whole cloth. He clearly had a swell time, using his knowledge of fraternal organizations to create a modern Klan ritual.

The secrets of this new ritual were never that secret. New initiates were referred to as being "naturalized," a reference to their new "citizenship" in the "Invisible Empire," another name for the Klan. As with Freemasons, new recruits had to memorize some ritual, but for many the hardest part was picking up on Simmons's absurd new Klan lingo, all of it starting with a *k.* As if grown men in those outfits needed to prove they had a sense of humor, the Colonel's nomenclature had a stunningly stupid ring to it.

✔ The Klan lodge was called a "klavern," and officers included the Titan, Cyclops, Kligrapp, Kludd, Nighthawk, Klabee, Kloreore, King Kleagle, and Grand Goblin.

- ✔ Their book of ritual was the Kloran.
- ✔ Conventions were referred to as klonvocations.
- ✔ Fundraisers were kleagles.
- ✔ Dues were called klecktoken.

In pretty short order, officers, rituals, and manic rhetoric all revolved around one thing — the dues, because in order to perfect yourself in your "klannish-ness," you had to cough up at least a ten-buck klecktoken every year. And, as the Most Worshipful Grand Goblin probably never admitted, with 4 million members, that made for a slush fund that was a konsiderable kernal of kash in 1925.

A recruit swore to hold his secrets and keep his oaths until "death and the call of your Eternal Maker." He (or she — there was also a popular ladies' auxiliary) was then solemnly asked a series of nine sacred questions, to which he was expected to give an equally solemn "yes." They included krap-ola such as, "Do you believe in Klannishness and will you faithfully practice same toward your fellow Klansmen?" "Is the motive prompting your ambition to be a Klansman serious and unselfish?" "Are you a native-born, *WHITE!!!,* Gentile American citizen?" And our personal favorite, "Do you swear to preserve and protect the sacredness of White Womanhood?"

There were also recognition signs for one another, just like the Masons. For example, a Klansman might say the word "Ayak," meaning "Are you a Klansman?" If he found one, he might get the answer, "Akia," which means "A Klansman I am."

There's one thing that's essential to understand about this new Klan. The Klan of the Civil War South was principally about hatred of the new class of "Free Blacks" and their supporters. But this reborn Klan was far more about a deep hatred of Jews, Catholics, and most foreigners in general. Yes, they hated black Americans, but the lives of African Americans in that period were so marginalized, so beaten down, that they didn't seem to present the sort of threat in the 1920s that Jews and Catholics did. After all, a lot of Jews and Catholics looked just like normal people! They could be out there, infiltrating our businesses and fraternities and neighborhoods, and we wouldn't even know it! This, for the Klansman of 1920, was an intolerable situation.

Hijacking the Klan

For a little man, Colonel Simmons had a big dream. He wanted to send the Klan north of the Mason/Dixon line, for the first time in history. The whole country, including Simmons, had gone secret-society crazy. So why not add the Klan to the list? Simmons hired a public relations firm to help him, but they wouldn't do the job nearly as well as a fast-talking, hard-drinking traveling salesman named D. C. Stephenson.

David Curtiss (Steve) Stephenson was born in Oklahoma, migrated to the Midwest, and arrived in Evansville, Indiana, in 1920 as a typesetting salesman, the same year the Klan arrived. He was a powerful public speaker, and also very politically minded. But more than anything else, he was a savvy businessman and opportunist. Within a year of joining the struggling Simmons's Klan, Stephenson had become a professional recruiter for the organization.

Stephenson's rise in the Klan

Stephenson clearly saw the money and power to be had; money from the avalanche of membership dues, and power in the form of calling the shots for a huge voting block. Soon his Klan career soared like a comet, with Stephenson, nicknamed "the Old Man," becoming the Grand Dragon of 22 states, ruling over 4 million Klansmen from his palatial home in Indianapolis. Under his leadership, membership went through the roof; in Indiana alone, it rose to over 300,000 — an astonishing one-third of the men in the state. For the next four years, Stephenson was the most powerful single force in Midwestern politics, ordering mayors and governors around as if they were waiters.

Most of the down-to-earth farmers and businessmen of the Midwest who flocked to join the Klan knew nothing at all about the Ku Klux Klan of the Old South — many just thought it was a neat Greek name for a fraternity with some cool rituals and fancy uniforms. They didn't make the connection to violence in the name that we do today. They'd have to see that violence in action before they walked away from the Klan.

At the top of his game, Stephenson enjoyed an opulent lifestyle, hosting grand parties, flying back and forth to address huge Klan rallies, indulging without restraint his taste for the finest food, bootleg booze, expensive cigars, and good-looking women. He lived like a gangster, with two armed bodyguards at all times. In other words, being catapulted out of poverty and obscurity had definitely turned his head. It seems unbelievable today, but Stephenson had set his sights on becoming president of the United States. And he nearly made it, too.

The Old Man had been a Democrat before turning Republican, and he had stooges in both parties, but especially the Republican Party. One of Indiana's senators was on his deathbed, and the governor, who had the responsibility of appointing someone to fill out the term, was in Stephenson's pocket. If he became a senator and moved to Washington, Stephenson believed his lightning political career would carry him to the White House on the shoulders of millions of Klansmen.

But pride, as they say, goeth before the fall, and although Stephenson was high, he was standing on a cliff with his foot on a banana peel. The Old Man once said, "Everything is fine in politics as long as you don't get caught in bed with a live man or a dead woman." His joke would come back to bite him in the backside. No, it wasn't a live man. It was a dead woman.

Stephenson the lady-killer

Stephenson was a portly, short sort of a guy, with thinning blonde hair and a pasty complexion, but when he looked in the mirror, he saw God's gift to women. Wherever he went, no waitress or hotel maid was safe, particularly if he was drunk, which was fairly often. The fact that he would marry four times serves to highlight his ability to get along with women. By 1925, he'd already bought or bullied his way out of a couple of rape charges, and this had made him even bolder. He clearly thought that any woman who caught his eye was fair game.

Unfortunately for her, the next woman to catch his eye was a pretty secretary in the Indiana Statehouse named Madge Oberholtzer. Stephenson sat next to her at the governor's inaugural dinner, the symbolic peak of his political power, because the governor was his hand-picked man. He was ripe and randy that night and began maneuvering Madge at once. When she admitted her dreams of being a writer, he convinced her he was writing a textbook, on nutrition of all things, and that because she was in the Department of Education for the state, he proposed that they write the book together.

Closing the trap

But on the night of March 15, 1925, when Stephenson lured Madge to his house on the pretext of beginning work, he had something else entirely in mind. By the time Madge arrived, he was already blasted, and before she knew what hit her he'd drugged her, assaulted her, and hauled her, half-conscious, into his private stateroom on the night train to Chicago. Over the course of the next three days he held her prisoner, raping and brutalizing her repeatedly, while her family desperately searched for her. At last, after three hellish days, Madge was able to slip away for a moment from one of Stephenson's bodyguards. She then calmly walked into a drug store, purchased a bottle of mercury bichloride, and swallowed it.

Mercury bichloride is a highly toxic form of mercury, sold in those days in a concentrated form to be mixed with water for use as, among other things, an antiseptic. Mercury poisoning is a dreadful and painful death.

Madge had clearly hoped the poison would be fatal, but instead it made her desperately ill. Stephenson, ever the gallant gentleman, threw her in the back of a car and drove through the night with her and his two bodyguards, then dumped her at her home while her parents were out looking for her.

The pope of Kokomo

One of the few comic moments in this whole Klan business came about because of the fear of "popery," or Catholicism, that was pumped up by 1920's Klan organizers. Somehow, the rumor started amongst the Klansmen of the state of Indiana that the pope was building a multi-million-dollar "palace" in the city of Washington, and that he was planning to move the Vatican to the United States. No, we're not kidding. Several Protestant ministers had even commented on the danger during their sermons. Then the rumor got started that His Holiness had been tossed out of Washington, and was shopping for property in Chicago. And Chicago was uncomfortably close to Indiana. Once this rumor spread, the Klan went into high gear. Literally.

According to the *Indianapolis Times,* after a particularly heated rally in Kokomo, a bunch of Klansmen drove out onto Highway 31, armed and ready to face the Catholic hordes. Word had come down that Chicago didn't want the pontiff, any more than those folks in England or France did. The pope was living in disguise in the Windy City, and he was coming with his minions to Indiana to scope it out for a new Vatican. Well, by God, Hoosiers would give him the welcome he deserved if he tried it! This nonsense went on for weeks. For sheer, baggy-pants burlesque, it's hard to beat the image of a bunch of farmers with shotguns waiting out in the middle of nowhere for the pope's army to invade the nation of Indiana.

Madge's death was agonizing; it took nearly a month. She'd not only been beaten, raped, and poisoned, but she was also covered with vicious bites inflicted on her by Stephenson. Her doctor said it looked as if she'd been attacked by cannibals. All he could do was give her morphine for the pain. Pathologists later said a secondary cause of her death was septicemia, an infection from the horrific bites.

Death of the Klan in the Midwest

Stephenson was fond of telling people that he was the most powerful man in America, and that he outright owned the state of Indiana. He would find himself wrong on both counts. Will Remy of the District Attorney's office was sometimes called the "boy prosecutor," but he couldn't wait to try Stephenson, with Madge's deathbed statement as evidence, despite the death threats aimed at him. The men in the jury were equally unimpressed by Stephenson's position, and sentenced him to life imprisonment. The *Indianapolis Times* would win the Pulitzer Prize for its exposure of Klan corruption in the Midwest.

The Klan was dead in Indiana, and would soon die across the Midwest. Although the hard times of the Depression just around the corner were a factor, the fact is that once people discovered what sort of man Stephenson really was, they couldn't tear up their membership cards fast enough. The numbers of the faithful plummeted, and the Klan would never again be a force of any legitimate political power in the United States.

The Klan goes underground

In the mid-1920s, Klan membership in the United States was estimated at roughly 4 to 5 million. By 1930, after the one-two punch of the Great Klan Scandals and the Great Depression, membership hit 30,000. That's not a drop, or even a plummet — that's the Wrath of God. By 1970, the figures were estimated at just 2,000 to 3,000. Unfortunately, there has been a rise to 5,000 in 2007, as high as 10,000 in some estimates. Yet, the Klan of old was deader than a dead hog by 1950. So, what do you do when you can't sway elections anymore? You go underground and start blowing things up.

Mississippi burning

The Klan in its death throes would kill more people than it had in its heyday. Klan diehards were unfazed by their small numbers; when a mayor or governor passed laws against cross burning, they bought neon crosses to go with their permanent press sheets. This diehard group of violent men still believed, mistakenly, that the Ku Klux Klan was forever. As the society around them began to change and to integrate, they used violence as their last remaining weapon.

During the Civil Rights Movement of the 1960s, the Klan was behind one act of terror after another: the assassination of NAACP leader Medgar Evers in June of 1963; the bombing of the 16th Street Baptist Church in Birmingham, Alabama, in September of 1963, one of dozens of such bombings, in which four little girls were killed; the drive-by shooting of Detroit housewife and volunteer Viola Gregg Liuzzo, who was driving demonstrators back and forth to Montgomery, Alabama; and the senseless murder of Lt. Colonel Lemuel Penn, an African American who'd fought in World War II in the Pacific, and who was simply driving home to Washington, D.C., from a training session at Fort Benning, Georgia. His Washington license plate was spotted by a carload of Klan goons, who followed his car and killed him, thinking he was another Civil Rights worker.

There were other deaths as well, and many more innocent people hurt during street rioting, from a Boston nun to a black newspaperman. But of all the deaths, the ones that captured the public imagination with the greatest intensity were those of three young and idealistic Civil Rights workers who'd gone into the heart of Klan country in Mississippi to register African Americans to vote — James Chaney, Andrew Goodman, and Michael Schwerner. On the night of June 21, 1964, they drove out to investigate a burning of a black church, and on the way back to Meridian they were pulled over for a traffic violation. Briefly jailed, they got back into their car, and two carloads of Klansmen ran them off the road. The young men were beaten, shot, and then buried on a farm six miles from Philadelphia, Mississippi.

The secret codes of white supremacists

The white supremacist movement has its own secret language, symbols, and slogans. Swastikas, lightening bolts, spider webs, and Nazi symbology all commonly appear as tattoos, graffiti, or logos. Likewise, many acronyms are used to disguise white supremacist and neo-Nazi slogans from outsiders. Some of the most common include

- **RAHOWA:** Racial Holy War

- **ORION:** Our Race Is Our Nation

- **WPWW:** White Pride World Wide, commonly used as a greeting between white supremacists.

- **KIGY:** "Klansman, I Greet You." This acronym pops up on Web sites, in e-mail addresses, or as a salutation in messages to indicate membership in the KKK. The phrase dates back to the Klan of the early 1900s, along

with similar expressions: AYAK (Are You A Klansman), and AKIA (A Klansman I Am).

- **311:** K is the 11th letter of the alphabet, so 311 means three 11s, and stands for KKK.

- **14** or the term **14 Words:** Shorthand for the phrase, "We must secure the existence of white people and a future for white children." It was coined by leader David Lane of the 1980s hate group *The Order* (now defunct), which engaged in bombings, robberies, and murder. Lane died in prison in 2007.

- **88:** H is the 8th letter of the alphabet, so 88 stands for *Heil Hitler.* It often appears in e-mails. Sometimes combined as 14/88. Using similar logic, 18 stands for AH, Adolf Hitler.

- **ROA:** "Race Over All." A greeting used by groups like *Volksfront* (see "The wide world of hate groups" later in this chapter).

The FBI, under the leadership of J. Edgar Hoover, swarmed into the South, particularly Mississippi, to take on the Klan. Some Southerners viewed it as another Yankee invasion. The Klan continued in Stephenson's footsteps to rain hate down on Catholics and Jews as well as African Americans, but in the highly charged atmosphere of the 1960s South, tension between blacks and whites brought the Klan some support even in heavily Catholic cities like St. Augustine, Florida.

Yet the Klan, not known for its intellectualism, had badly miscalculated in their bloody efforts to fight integration in the South. They were losing their base of supporters. High-profile politicians who once could've been counted as friendly to the Klan were now denouncing them; even the most right-wing major political figure of the day, Alabama governor George Wallace, was taking them to task for the shootings and bombings. By the end of the decade, people of all stripes were just plain sick to death of all the bloodshed. And by the middle of the 1970s, the joke in Mississippi was that the best place to meet an FBI agent was a Klan meeting.

The Klan today

The Klan has little brand-name power anymore. There's no one single Klan — it splintered apart long ago. Today, there are somewhere between 100 and 150 small groups out there calling themselves the Klan; two thirds are in the South. Several in the country could be said to be prominent, if any of them could be called that — the *Imperial Klans of America,* the *American Knights of the KKK,* the *Bayou Knights of the KKK* in Texas, Louisiana, and the Southeast, and the Texas-based *Knights of the White Kamelia.*

Membership numbers can't be trusted. For example, the one *claiming* to be the biggest is the *Knights of the Ku Klux Klan* in Zinc, Arkansas. Its national director, the Reverend Thom Robb, refers to this as the Klan's "fourth era," a kinder, gentler Klan, preaching love and not hate. God is invoked a great deal, and he claims that race-mixing is a product of Satan. Yet, he also claims a massive membership, while the Southern Poverty Law Center estimates his membership at 50.

The spawn of the KKK

Aggressive young racists today tend to perceive the Klan as being creaky and out of date. Yet there's little question that the ugliest legacy of the Klan has been the number of smaller, and even more virulent, hate groups that have been spawned in its wake.

The racist skinhead movement began in the late 1970s in England, coinciding with the punk rock music culture. What originally started as a fashion statement, quickly morphed into a white nationalist political movement, and they have been historically known by their shaved heads, high-top military-style boots, and openly racist tattoos. Skinheads have a far right-wing, neo-Nazi ideology, and are especially violent — Jews, Muslims, gays, and left-wing political groups are their frequent targets. The skinhead movement spread to Europe and North America, and most recently, Russia. Estimates vary wildly, but some sources claim there are 120,000 skinheads worldwide.

The second generation of skinheads has become more media-savvy. Many have grown out their hair, and traded the Doc Martin stompers for wing-tips. They've become the entrepreneurs of hatred, making money off everything from white supremacist rock music to hatemongering documentaries. Likewise, "hate radio" podcasts are bringing their messages of racism to a worldwide listenership.

Here are a few of the more common modern race-hatred groups around the U.S.:

- **White Aryan Resistance (WAR):** A group founded in 1983 by Tom Metzger. An ex-Klansman, he reaches out to young skinheads with heavy-metal rock music that carries a racist message. Metzger has begun to advocate what he calls the "lone wolf" method of organizing white supremacist groups, meaning that no group member should wear anything or discuss anything that gives him away — hide behind the golf shirt or the old suit and tie, until the time to strike. There are now two prominent companies out there doing white supremacist rock: Resistance Records and Panzerfaust Records.

- **Aryan Brotherhood:** This is largely a prison-based hate group, started in 1967 in California's San Quentin prison. On the outside, they function as a street gang, combining white supremacism with violence and a lucrative trade in methamphetamine.

- **Aryan Nation:** This is the so-called "political wing" of the white supremacist Church of Jesus Christ-Christian — and splinter groups like *Ayran Nations of South Carolina,* whose motto is "Violence Solves Everything," and *The Order,* all of whom have conspired to commit various acts of racial violence.

- **World Church of the Creator:** Holocaust deniers all, this violent fascist organization is still up and running, despite the fact that their leader Matthew Hale went to the slammer in 2003 for plotting to kill a federal judge. In an unintentionally hilarious attempt at public relations, it has recently changed its name to *The Creativity Movement.*

- **Nazi Low Riders (NLR):** Affiliated with the Aryan Brotherhood, the NLR is a prison and street gang that became popular in the 1990s. They combine the usual violence and white supremacism with drug dealing.

Black Supremacism

White supremacist groups don't have the corner on hate. Black separatist groups appeared as early as the 1930s, but the 1960s saw the emergence of the "Black Power" movement and the growth of both black separatist and black supremacist groups:

- **The Nation of Islam,** currently led by Minister Louis Farrakhan, is the most famous of the U.S. black supremacist/separatist groups.

- **The Neuwabians,** a lesser-known group, founded by Malachi Z. York in the 1970s, combines black supremacy with Egyptian symbols, ancient alien astronauts, hollow Earth theories, Freemasons, Islam, Christianity, Rastafarianism, and, unbelievably, Dr. Seuss into a bizarre black separatist movement. In 1993, the group built *Tama-Re,* a massive Egyptian-themed African-American colony outside of Eatonton, Georgia. York was imprisoned in 2002 on over 100 charges of child molestation, and Tama-Re was sold and demolished.

Some violent black supremacist groups have crossed the line from simply preaching hatred to racially motivated killings. The more famous ones are

- **The Black Panther Party:** The most famous group from the 1960s. While it started as a violent black separatist organization, it changed direction in the 1970s and became a proponent for socialism for all races.

- **The New Black Panther Party:** Formed in 1989 in Dallas, Texas, by former *Nation of Islam* minister Khalid Abdul Muhammad. Their message is virulently racist, anti-Semitic, and violent.

- **Death Angels:** A violent offshoot of the *Nation of Islam,* believed responsible for at least 14 murders in San Francisco between 1973 and 1974 (they came to be known as the "Zebra murders," named after a radio channel used by police working on the case). As many as 70 killings across California may have been committed by the Death Angels.

- **Nation of Yahweh:** A black supremacist religious cult founded by Yahweh ben Yahweh (aka Hulon Mitchell, Jr.), who taught that blacks are the true Jews, and that white Jews are Satan's spawn. An inner circle called *The Brotherhood* went on a killing spree in 1986, murdering random white "devils" around Miami, Florida, and cutting off their victims' ears as trophies. Former Oakland Raiders player Robert Rozier was a member who admitted to murdering seven whites to gain favor with Mitchell. Cult defectors were beheaded.

In what has to be the strangest ideological dance among race-baiters, amazingly some white and black separatist groups *do* get along with each other. Some separatists on both sides of the color bar are in favor of peacefully keeping the races apart, and have no problem working together for that goal. White supremacist Tom Metzger has addressed gatherings of the Nation of Islam, at the invitation of NOI's Louis Farrakhan. Likewise, black separatist, Holocaust denier, and anti-Semite Robert L. Brock spoke to a 1994 Aryan Nation conference dressed in a KKK robe.

The wide world of hate groups

While the KKK and its kindred imitators are known across the U.S., there are groups on the march across the world that have racism, bigotry, and violence as their motivating creed. The Internet has made both the growth and the tracking of hate groups around the world grow at an exponential rate. Online sites that recruit for these groups can now look every bit as slick, professional, and appealing as a Fortune 500 corporation or a church Web site. And their targeted enemies are as varied as the countries in which they reside.

There are hundreds of international violent hate groups around the globe, but here is a smattering of them:

- **Blood & Honour:** A British neo-Nazi group formed in 1987 as a white supremacist recording company. Their armed wing, *Combat 18* (or C18) was formed in the early 1990s, and conducted attacks on left-wing political groups and immigrants. Several C18 members within the British Army were arrested in a crackdown between 1998 and 2000. Foreign divisions of Blood & Honour have been hunted down and outlawed in Germany and Spain, but C18 cells remain elusive because of their leaderless structure.

- **Volksfront:** One of the fastest growing neo-Nazi, skinhead groups in the world. Originally started in 1994 by Randall Krager in the Oregon State Penitentiary, Volksfront (German for *popular front*) has spread to at least seven countries.

- **Génération Kémi Séba (KGS):** A violent French black Muslim separatist group. Based on *Nation of Islam* teachings, KGS is fiercely anti-Semitic and anti-white. Formerly known as *Tribu Ka,* the group was outlawed in France, but has reappeared since 2006 with its new name. Central to their beliefs is the idea that France's 6 million Muslims are being held in poverty and ignorance by the country's 600,000 Jews. You do the math.

- **Watchmen On The Walls:** An evangelical "ministry" group, based in Latvia, that stages fierce protests against gays and lesbians in Europe and the U.S. The group has spread into the U.S. Pacific coast via waves of Slavic immigrants, and it has stepped up the intensity of its protests to include violent attacks. A group of Watchmen murdered a gay man at a picnic in Sacramento, California, in 2007, and the organization remains unrepentant. Instead, it has stepped up its violent rhetoric.

- **Jewish Defense League (JDL):** With a world full of violent anti-Semitic groups dedicated to killing Jews, it's only natural that a group arose to fight fire with fire. The JDL was formed in 1968 by radical Rabbi Meir Kahane in New York City and immediately attracted hundreds of Orthodox Jews to sign up as a vigilante force to protect themselves from frequent attacks. In the 1970s it grew into a worldwide terrorist organization, engaging in assassinations, bombings, and especially anti-Soviet activity. In the 1980s, the JDL committed at least 18 known violent attacks in the U.S., but after arrests and schisms within the leadership, today they seem to be more of a protest group.

In 2007, the European Union made "incitement to racism" a crime in all 27 member nations. Meanwhile, Germany has had a long-standing law that forbids the use of symbols connected with Hitler's Nazi Party or the public declaration of Holocaust denial. Nevertheless, anti-Semitism is on the rise worldwide. Between 2005 and 2007, Israel's Tel Aviv University reports that attacks on Jews worldwide have doubled.

Chapter 13

Frolicsome Fraternalism and Nefarious Foes of Freedom

In This Chapter

▷ Exploring the Victorian fascination with fraternal groups

▷ Explaining the connection between secret societies and college fraternities

▷ Unmasking secret societies with a sinister bend

*T*here was a time in America when every red blooded adult man, armed with a fraternal ring or a club pin in his lapel, trotted off to his lodge each week, armed with a secret handshake and a password.

This chapter discusses the phenomenal growth of fraternal "secretive societies" in the 1800s. It explores some of the positives of secret societies, including the social safety net of the fraternal organizations. And we talk about the formation of similarly styled college fraternities and university secret societies like Yale's infamous *Skull and Bones.*

Then we jump to an examination of a few of the many secret societies that really did have the destruction of the social order as their aim (and still do today, in some cases). Some are historical and had revolution on their collective minds. But such nefarious foes of freedom aren't just confined to the past, as the formation and activities of the Islamic terrorist organization Al-Qaeda has shown.

The Golden Age of Fraternalism

The 19th century in America was a period of tremendous upheaval for society. The Industrial Revolution brought millions of people into the cities off the farms, and extended families that had stayed together for generations were left behind. The cities became places where everyone was a stranger. This, combined with a strong period of anti-Masonic sentiment throughout the 1830s, resulted in an increase of new fraternal organizations, basing much of their organization and ritual on the pattern of the Masons.

Throughout the 1800s, fraternalism exploded across the U.S. Literally hundreds of these secret societies were created, all with passwords, secret handshakes, flamboyant names for officers, and elaborate, fictitious tales of their origins. All of them had initiation ceremonies and levels of membership based on rites of passage. Most were created for men only, but as the century progressed, women's groups began to develop too, either as their own independent organizations, or as "women's auxiliary" groups to the larger fraternities.

In the 1870s, the *Independent Order of Odd Fellows* eclipsed the Masons for a while in terms of membership numbers. The other large group was the *Knights of Pythias,* actually formed during the Civil War with the blessing of the U.S. Congress and Abraham Lincoln, with the hope that a new fraternity, with no past history, may draw members from the North and South to help unite the war-torn nation.

The birth of the fraternalism movement

In the late 1820s, nationwide suspicion fell on the Freemasons in the United States, especially after the Morgan Affair (the disappearance of Captain William Morgan and the subsequent trial of Masons, discussed in Chapter 9). Masonic lodges closed all across the country and state grand lodges fell on hard times until the 1840s.

But the Masons' losses benefited a steadily growing gaggle of other fraternal groups who blatantly patterned themselves after the Masonic model of a series of levels or degrees, based on elaborate ritual ceremonies, with exalted officer names and increasingly bilious titles. All of them made their own attempt to imitate Freemasonry's initiation experience for their new members, in a wildly varying range of legendary origins and seriousness.

Inspiration: Myths, legends, and other interesting things

While the principal role of the fraternal groups was for fellowship (and perhaps business contacts), virtually all groups stressed the life-changing experiences of progressing through their degree rituals. And these rituals could literally be inspired by anything:

- Biblical allegories (like the *Knights of the Maccabees*)
- Greek and Roman myths (like the *Knights of Pythias*)
- Native American legends (like the *Improved Order of Redmen,* who also claimed to be descended from the American colonists who dressed as Indians and threw English tea into Boston Harbor)
- Popular novels (like the *Supreme Tribe of Ben Hur,* based on the book *Ben Hur* by General Lew Wallace; or the *Independent Order of Foresters,* based on *Robin Hood*)

✔ Professions inspired many groups that developed for specific types of workers (like the *Brotherhood of Railroad Trainmen*), and many of these would eventually morph into labor unions in the 1900s.

Other fraternal groups organized themselves by nationality or racial or religious lines, each with their own rituals, passwords, handshakes, and "secrets":

✔ *Ancient Order of Hiberneans* formed in the U.S. in the mid-1800s and primarily for Irish Catholics. Regarded as "unwanted" immigrants, Irish and Italians formed dozens of fraternal groups across the U.S. German, Polish, Russian, and many other groups of immigrants created their own clubs to associate with people from back home.

✔ *B'Nai Brith* started in New York in the 1840s because so many other fraternal groups refused to allow Jews to join. The opposite was true of the Catholic order, the *Knights of Columbus,* who formed because of Vatican threats of excommunication for parishioners who joined the Masons.

✔ African-American fraternal groups were hugely popular in the black community and played as important a role as black churches in spreading messages of morality, brotherly love, charity, and mutual aid. Like so much else in American society, an unspoken "separate but equal" convention became commonplace until the 1970s — a social situation that still exists to an extent today, with notable exceptions. While the Masons, the Odd Fellows, the Knights of Pythias, and hundreds of others were supposed to be colorblind according to their own rules, in practice that wasn't so, and unwritten rules kept blacks out. The result was the growth of "colored" versions of the same fraternal groups, with no connection to their white counterparts, apart from the similarities in name and rituals:

   • *Prince Hall Freemasonry* (named after founder Prince Hall in Boston)

   • *The Colored Knights of Pythias*

   • *Grand United Order of Odd Fellows*

Additionally, dozens of independent black fraternal groups formed over the years. The same is true of historically black college fraternities and sororities, which were formed because white students wouldn't vote blacks into their frats. These include

   • Omega Psi Psi

   • Alpha Phi Alpha

   • Kappa Alpha Psi

   • Phi Beta Sigma

And sororities like

- Alpha Kappa Alpha
- Deta Sigma Theta
- Sigma Gamma Rho
- Zeta Phi Beta

✔ Whites-only groups also formed, and the Ku Klux Klan (see Chapter 12) is the best known and the most notorious. The U.S. has been through several periods of nativism in its history, promoting the notion that America was for White Anglo-Saxon Protestants only. Organizations like the *Know Nothings* (named for the answer members were to give if questioned about the group) wielded much political power for a while in the mid-1800s.

Secrets of initiation

The neophytes who joined these groups, along with outsiders who didn't join, generally believed that the secrets of these secret societies were their passwords, identifying handshakes, and other hand signals, along with the ceremonials themselves. But overwhelmingly, men who joined one, or as many as they could afford, knew better. The true "secrets" of these orders were considered by their members to be the life-altering truths and lessons experienced by participating in the ceremonies. Even today, men and women who join similar secretive societies vividly recall their initiation night with great clarity.

Reading through the rituals for dozens of these organizations reveals remarkable similarities between them. The initiation of a new member was designed to lead him from the outside world into the very different, solemn, and even sacred space of the lodge room:

✔ He was almost always blindfolded and underwent several trials or questions put to him, as he was led through the room by a brother whom he came to trust.

✔ He was required to take an *oath* or *obligation* in which he promised to keep the secrets of the lodge, to support his lodge brothers, and to protect their families. These pledges were almost always accompanied by the threat of a grisly penalty that threatened to lop off limbs, gouge out eyes, apply hot pokers, or other suitably terrifying punishments.

✔ Members were encouraged to contemplate their own mortality as a lesson to improve their lives and to live as though they could be gone tomorrow. Death was a constant theme in the hundreds of secret societies that formed. Images of coffins, skulls, and skeletons were common, and the secret societies were in the side business of selling insurance policies (and there were loads of them).

✔ *Enlightenment* occurred when the new member's blindfold was removed. Depending on the order, this event was commonly accompanied by a startling event: bright lights, loud noises, and in more than one case, a burst of real flame. Special effects became more and more common, and fraternal supply manufacturers invented new and exciting ways to stage degrees.

✔ Religious faith (usually liberal forms of Protestantism, although there were notable exceptions like the Catholic *Knights of Columbus* and the Jewish *B'nai Brith*) was almost always folded into the rituals. The majority of these societies tried to espouse the Masonic model of being open to all faiths (why limit your potential membership base?), and many used generic terms for God to keep things ecumenical (Great Chief, Great Captain of Salvation, Great Spirit, and so on). The overwhelming majority of them encouraged their members to be religious and to go to church on Sundays, but there's no question that a large number of men felt that they got their weekly dose of religion in their lodges — something their wives and ministers didn't agree with.

Bear in mind that the Victorian period when all this was going on was also the period of explosive growth in belief in paranormal, psychic, and occult subjects, combined with new discoveries of ancient Egyptian temples and artifacts after Napoleon's exploits there. The period also consisted of tent revivals and traveling evangelical preachers not affiliated with mainstream churches, who were creating their own take on traditional Christian teachings. The result was a century of new religious and philosophical ideas flying across the countryside and being expressed in a wide variety of new and innovative (and often unexpected) settings.

Parody and fun orders

Not all groups were about death, doom, and gloom. With the huge growth in fraternal societies in the 1800s came more than a few parody groups. Many existed for the sole purpose of hazing new candidates and then allowing the new guy to participate in exacting revenge on the next generation of candidates.

Other groups, like the *Masonic Ancient Arabic Order of the Nobles of the Mystic Shrine* (Shriners), grew up within the existing orders as a side group, often for the sole purpose of dressing in costumes, putting on a brief ceremony, then getting down to some serious drinking. Like the Shriners, an incredible number of these fun groups used Oriental, Arabic, and Egyptian sources for their inspiration:

✔ The Odd Fellows' Oriental Order of Humility

✔ The Veiled Prophets of Baghdad

✔ The Knights of Oriental Splendor

✔ The Knights of Columbus' International Order of the Alhambra

✔ The Knights of Pythias' Dramatic Order of the Knights of Khorassan

As a side consideration amidst all the drinking, paddling, practical joking, and projectile puking, these groups quite often created charities (the *Shriner's Hospitals for Children,* being the largest and most successful of its kind).

Benevolent benefits

Masonry had become the club for movers and shakers in the early 1800s, which led to suspicion by the general public. Many of the new groups that formed in the wake of the Masons were promoted as being more egalitarian than the Masons had become and concentrated more on the needs of the growing working class. As literally hundreds of new fraternal groups formed around the U.S., they added new benefits for members like insurance programs, death benefits paid to the members' widows, retirement homes, and orphanages to care for members' children — in short, the sort of safety-net programs taken over by the government in the 20th century.

By the end of World War I, many fraternal groups died out. And by the Great Depression in 1929, many more were wiped out because of economic reasons, but also because their mission had been taken over by Social Security, relief programs, county and state homes for the aged, public orphanages, and many other things the fraternal groups had originally been formed to provide.

What about women?

The overwhelming growth of fraternalism in the 1800s wasn't confined to men only, although secretive societies for women weren't nearly as common or popular. Women, as a broad generality, seemed to gravitate more to church and the social aspects of the congregation. Nevertheless, stand-alone and auxiliary orders for women did exist. Some of the most notable were attached to the men's fraternal groups:

- *Order of the Eastern Star* (Freemasons)
- *Rebekahs* (Odd Fellows)
- *The Pythian Sisters* (Knights of Pythias)

These groups were mostly designed by men within the larger parent organization to provide experiences similar to the men's rituals, without actually conferring Masonic, Odd Fellows, or Pythian degrees on the ladies. While they had elaborate initiation ceremonies and involved rituals, passwords, handshakes, and other trappings of the men's groups, they were totally separate.

Female and co-ed Masonic orders were formed in France, Belgium, and England in the 1800s, and a few such lodges still exist in the U.S., but are regarded as unrecognized and clandestine (secret) by mainstream Freemasons.

The fraternal military orders

The veterans of the Civil War influenced fraternalism in a major way in the decade after the conflict ended. The *Grand Army of the Republic* (GAR) was formed in 1866 as a group for veterans of the Union Army, primarily to dress in uniforms, wield ceremonial swords, and march in parades (along with becoming a huge lobbying organization that influenced the Republican Party for decades).

The result was that every major fraternal organization in the country bought the same uniforms and swords, marched in the same parades, and competed with the GAR with their own military drill teams: *The Knights Templar* (Freemasons), the *Patriarchs Militant* (Odd Fellows), along with uniform drill teams of the *Knights of Columbus,* the *Knights of Pythias,* and many other orders. The *Soldiers of Woodcraft* (Modern Woodmen of the World) were a little different. They marched with large axes and performed firemen's drills.

College Fraternities and Secret Societies

The first college fraternity in the U.S. was called FHC (probably standing for the Latin phrase, *Fraternitas, Humanitas, et Cognitio* meaning *Brotherhood, Humanity, and Knowledge*), and was founded at the College of William and Mary in Williamsburg, Virginia, in 1750. Because of its initials, it quickly became nicknamed the Flat Hat Club, as a reference to mortarboard caps regularly worn by students in those days (not just on graduation day). Perhaps its best-known member was Thomas Jefferson, who entered William and Mary (W&M) in 1760. Patterned in some ways after Masonic lodges, FHC had secret handshakes, passwords, special medals, and membership certificates.

Phi Beta Kappa was started as a secret debating society at William and Mary in 1776 by student John Heath — some say out of revenge for being denied membership in FHC. Many of its founders were Freemasons.

Fraternities with a Masonic connection

Most college fraternities share some characteristics of the Masonic fraternity: a ritual ceremony, an oath of fidelity, an air of mystery or secrecy, a philosophy of high idealism, or the strong tie of friendship. But several college fraternities were started in the last century specifically for Freemasons, or with a blatant Masonic connection:

- ✔ **Acacia** was originally started in 1904 at the University of Michigan as a fraternity for Masons only, and the organization was to be built on the ideals and principles of Freemasonry. Members were supposed to be driven by a desire for high scholarship and character, keeping the group free from "unbecoming activities" that for years had been a blot on the fraternity lifestyle. That was the theory, anyway. In 1934, the Masonic membership requirement was dropped, largely due to reduced membership during the Great Depression. However, because Acacia was founded by Master Masons, it still enjoys an informal spiritual tie to Masonry.

- ✔ **Sigma Mu Sigma** started in 1921 at Tri-State College in Angola, Indiana, by three Knights Templar and nine Master Masons. It too dropped the Masonic affiliation during the Depression.

- ✔ **Square and Compass** fraternity began as a Masonic club in 1897 at Washington and Lee University in Lexington, Virginia. It officially became a college fraternity for Masons in 1917 and enjoyed tremendous growth over the next 11 years. Fifty-seven chapters formed with 5,000 members, including 15 college and university presidents, as well as professional and government leaders. In 1952, it merged with Sigma Mu Sigma. Today, there are ten active chapters of Sigma Mu Sigma–Square and Compass.

Other fraternities were influenced by different popular fraternal groups. Pi Kappa Alpha, for instance, based its ritual on the Independent Order of Odd Fellows.

Skull and Bones

During the presidential election of 2004, both Republican candidate George W. Bush and Democrat candidate John Kerry were asked about their membership in a Yale fraternity known by the decidedly creepy name of Skull and Bones. John Kerry said, "It's a secret," and changed the subject. Bush's answer was similar: "It's so secret we can't talk about it."

Skull and Bones is the oldest fraternity on the Yale University campus. Its original name was the Eulogian Club, and was a U.S. chapter of a German student organization. According to Skull and Bones lore, the club's name came from Eulogia, a supposed Greek goddess and patron of eloquence and debate, who ascended into the heavens in 322 BC. "Bonesmen" refer to themselves as the Knights of Eulogia, and the number 322 appears on their letterhead.

Originally founded in 1832 by William Huntington Russell (another disgruntled student who couldn't get into Phi Beta Kappa), the Eulogian Club originally met in a chapel on campus, and the members posted their symbol, a skull and crossbones, on the door. In 1856, the fraternity moved into its permanent and distinctly spooky headquarters — a windowless, austere pile of a building on the Yale campus, called The Tomb.

Creepy décor and ceremonies

Break-ins and leaked videos of the Tomb's interior reveal it to be a typical college frat house with décor reminiscent of the *Addams Family*. Skulls are a big motif, and supposedly the skull of famed Indian chief Geronimo is housed there too. Skull and Bones' ritual ceremonies are closely guarded. Bonesmen undoubtedly love the infamy and wild speculation, as most college students would.

The 2000 movie *The Skulls* presents an over-the-top tale of the club that has little to do with reality, but it's claimed that real initiates must lay in coffins and confess their most lurid sexual secrets to the other members.

Famous Bonesmen and the CIA

Bonesmen are accused of appointing each other to powerful business and political positions. Because Skull and Bones has an impressive list of famous and powerful members, past and present, conspiracy theories have naturally grown up around the fraternity.

The most common belief is that the CIA was created largely by Bonesmen — dramatically portrayed in the 2007 film *The Good Shepherd.* Interestingly, the CIA actually developed a Web page to debunk or correct errors in the film — strange behavior for a government agency devoted to secrecy. But it is true that many of the founding members of the CIA, like Sherman Kant, James Angleton, Norman Holmes, and "Bay of Pigs" planner Richard Bissell, Jr., were Bonesmen. And of course, before he was Ronald Reagan's vice-president, and then president himself, Bonesman George H. W. Bush was director of the CIA.

In addition to the two Bush presidents, other members of Skull and Bones included

- President William Howard Taft
- Henry Luce, founder of *Time* magazine
- William F. Buckley, Jr., founder of *National Review* (and himself a former CIA operative)

Skull and Bones started to admit "Boneswomen" in 1991, resulting in a failed legal protest by the society's older "patriarchs," led by Buckley himself.

Just for the record, Yale's *Scroll and Key, Berzelius,* and *Wolf's Head* secret societies also meet in imposing, windowless buildings, very similar to, and just as creepy as, The Tomb. High-profile, financially well endowed, exclusive secret societies for seniors have been a hallmark at Yale for 170 years, and Skull and Bones is far from the only one.

Revolutionary Brotherhoods

There are hundreds of cases of militaristic secret societies throughout history that have tried, and at times succeeded, in staging coups, rebellions, and takeovers of governments. Some, like Boston's *Sons of Liberty* (of Boston Tea Party fame), between about 1766 and the start of the American Revolution, are revered as patriots by one side and traitors by the other. Such is the role of the winning team when writing history.

In the following sections, we cover a few notable revolutionary societies.

Copperheads and the Knights of the Golden Circle

In the years leading up to the Civil War, several organizations started in the North that sympathized with the rights of southern states, proclaiming that there wasn't anything in the Constitution that said a state *couldn't* secede from the Union, if it so desired. Some of these Northern sympathizers formed into clubs, some more secret than others. The *Copperheads* was one such club.

The Copperheads were named for their use of a large copper penny depicting lady Liberty, used as identifying lapel badges, and were set up much like other fraternal groups, with initiations and symbolism. They eventually became known as a front organization for a variety of subversive and deadly activities in the North.

George Bickley's knightly order

The most notorious group connected with the Copperheads was the order of the *Knights of the Golden Circle.* Founded in 1854 by an eccentric character named George W. L. Bickley, the group was first headquartered in Cincinnati. Bickley had an impressive-looking pedigree, with a wall full of medical degrees — all of which were forgeries. Like so many other fraternal groups, his elaborate degree rituals were very appealing, but his had a darker purpose. The first degree was the *Knight of the Iron Fist,* and it was a probationary position. After a candidate reached the two "inner" levels of the degrees (*Knight of the True Faith* and *Knight of the Columbian Star*), he was told the true purpose of the Order.

The Order's secret goal was for the Knights to eventually invade and overthrow the government of Mexico to make it a new Southern slave state. Ultimately, they wanted to take over the island of Cuba and control access to the Gulf of Mexico's shipping. Using Havana as its center, a great "golden" circle was drawn that included Maryland, Kentucky, Missouri, all the Southern states, plus part of Kansas, most of Texas, Mexico, Central America, part of South America, and all the West Indies.

Their dream was a new Southern Empire that produced most of the world's cotton, sugar, and tobacco, along with a substantial part of its best coffee and rice. Pretty exciting, as dreams go, especially if you were a plantation owner who was in danger of losing his "peculiar institution" (their precious euphemism for slavery) and "cherished way of life."

The Order's local chapters, called "Castles," became recruiting stations, and the ritual was a way of sounding out men's political sympathies. Only the most trusted and dedicated secessionists made it past the mumbo jumbo lower degrees to discover the real purpose. Castles formed in both the North and the South, and if the rumors were to be believed, the order had something like 60,000 men in the non-slave state of Missouri alone. The Knights were strongly represented in Ohio, Indiana, Illinois, Iowa, and Missouri, as well as all across the South.

The Mexican invasion plan

Twice in 1860, large groups of Knights assembled in Texas and Louisiana to begin the invasion of Mexico. As many as 16,000 are believed to have shown up along the banks of the Rio Grande in April, but Bickley never arrived with his mass of men from the North that he'd promised. At last, he showed up in October, claiming the troops were right behind him, but that his shipment of weapons had gone missing.

When the Civil War started, the Knights drifted apart. The real Confederate Army needed them as soldiers, and the Order was swallowed up in the carnage that followed. They briefly tried to reorganize without Bickley under the name *Order of the American Knights* in 1863, and again the next year as the *Order of the Sons of Liberty,* but they quickly passed into obscurity. Meanwhile, Bickley was arrested in Indiana for spying in 1863. He died in 1867. But the story doesn't necessarily end there.

The lost Confederate treasure

Canada became the refuge of choice for Confederate officers and politicians fleeing war-crime trials after the end of the Civil War. Warren Getler and Bob Brewer, co-authors of *Shadow of the Sentinel,* believe the Knights of the Golden Circle spirited off the treasury of the Confederacy to Canada, then when the war ended, brought back the gold and silver coins and buried them throughout the South to prepare for a new Southern uprising. One version says that Jacob Thompson, Clement Clay, and Thomas Hines, all associated with the Knights of the Golden Circle, managed to amass $2 to $5 million in gold and silver and smuggle it into Canada before the war ended.

Of course, ever since the end of the Civil War, there have been dozens, if not hundreds, of claims of secret buried treasure belonging to the Confederacy, often involving gold bars stamped "CSA" (Confederate States of America). Allegedly, they've been buried in forgotten mineshafts, sunken in shipwrecks, hidden in false graves in Southern cemeteries, and submerged into bogs and even the Everglades.

One version even identifies outlaw Jesse James as a Confederate spy and a Knight of the Golden Circle, hauling some $90,000 off to a secret location in New Mexico. (Of course, the wacked-out claims made about Jesse James over the years could fill a book by themselves, including that he killed the "real" John Wilkes Booth in a hotel room in 1890, and that he faked his own death and lived until 1947.)

With all that stolen and hidden gold being spirited off into the night, it wouldn't be surprising if the other, more accepted, theory really is true — the Old South just went broke.

The Fenian Brotherhood

When they clash, Irish and English politics are challenging to navigate through just on their own. But when the ongoing disputes bubbled over into the U.S., very peculiar developments took place. Such a case involved the *Fenian Brotherhood* and their grandiose plans to invade Canada.

The *Irish Republican Brotherhood* (IRB) formed in Ireland in the 1850s and led a failed revolt against English rule in 1867. Members of the group often referred to themselves as the *Fenians,* a word derived from mythological Celtic warriors, the *Na Fianna,* who were legendary protectors of Ireland. The IRB's Fenians became the most influential group in Ireland who campaigned for violent overthrow of the English government in the fight for Irish independence.

The Irish invasion of Canada

In 1858, the *Fenian Brotherhood* was formed as a secret society in the U.S. by immigrants who carried the conflict between the Irish and the English to North America. The Fenians hatched a daring plot: They'd invade Canada (which was an English province), hold it hostage, and force the British to declare Ireland independent if they ever wanted to see Canada alive again. Think big, we always say.

The Fenians raised money by selling bonds to hundreds of thousands of gullible Irish immigrants; the bonds would be redeemable six months after Ireland was declared a republic. Weapons were purchased, and plans were made. Curiously, the U.S. government, involved in its own Civil War, did nothing to prevent the planning of the Canadian invasion — mostly because the British had failed to back the North's Union cause. So, on May 31, 1866, some 800 Fenian troops crossed the Niagara River into Canada at Buffalo, New York. (The Canadians claim 1,500, mostly to make it sound like a bigger deal than it turned out.)

The U.S. Army finally decided an international incident was a lousy idea and cut off the supply lines and reinforcements to the Fenians. While the little group briefly managed to capture Fort Erie and make a few more raids along the St. Lawrence Valley, the whole adventure was doomed from the start.

After a week or so, the Irish were convinced to return to their homes when the U.S. Army bought them all railroad tickets home, in exchange for their solemn promise that they wouldn't invade any more foreign countries. Still, fear of Fenian mischief was one factor that drove the Canadian provinces to form a confederation the next year for mutual protection.

Irish invasion redux

In 1867, the Fenians caught Canadian invasion fever again, and 6,000 uniformed Fenian soldiers marched through the streets of Philadelphia at a national convention (one wonders how the government would react today if 6,000 armed, white militiamen were to do the same thing through the City of Brotherly Love).

In 1870, an estimated 15,000 Fenians crossed into Canada from New York and Vermont to try again. Reportedly, one volley fired by Canadian troops sent them packing back across the border. Another attempt was made in 1871, and rumors of another invasion flew across western Canada in the 1880s. They were taken seriously enough that British warships were anchored offshore during the celebrations opening the Canadian pacific railway in 1885, just in case the Fenians attempted any terrorist activities.

Officially, the IRB withdrew its support for its American brethren in 1867, mostly over internal feuds and a major split between factions. The IRB was finally dissolved in 1924 after a lengthy political battle and the signing of the Anglo-Irish Treaty that created the Irish Republic.

The Shield Society

Yukio Mishima had a dream. Throughout the 1950s and '60s he was one of Japan's hottest young authors and playwrights. But that wasn't enough.

Mishima (born Kimitake Hiraoka in 1925), was the product of an odd family background. His father was a brutal man who disciplined him ruthlessly, but Mishima was actually raised by his peculiar grandmother, Natsu. She had her own personality quirks and refused to let the young boy go outside in sunlight or play with other children. It's not surprising that the adult Mishima became fascinated with images and philosophies about death.

Mishima had a succession of gay partners and became fascinated with body building. Even though he was just 5-feet 2-inches tall, he developed a tough-guy look and many people mistook him for a westernized gangster — something that delighted him to no end (in fact, he appeared in a Japanese movie as the title character, a gangster called *Tough Guy*).

While Mishima became very famous, a poll in the 1950s revealed that 50 percent of the female population of Japan would rather kill themselves than marry him. Nevertheless, he married his wife Yoko in 1958, and they had two children. Still, his three favorite fetishes were armpit hair, sweat, and white gloves. And death — preferably suicide.

In 1967, Mishima joined Japan's Ground Self-Defense Force (their version of the Army, formed by treaty with the U.S. after World War II). Then, in 1968, he formed a private military organization called *Tatenokai,* or the *Shield Society.* It was made up of young men, mostly students, who'd studied martial arts and who proclaimed allegiance to Japan's Emperor.

At the end of World War II, Japan's Emperor Showa (known in the U.S. by his more familiar given name, Hirohito) renounced his claim of divinity, something no emperor before him had ever done. Men like Mishima were ashamed of the emperor's actions, and the members of Tatenokai wanted to return Japan to what they saw as a proper veneration of their emperor as a god — whether the emperor liked it or not. They were great followers of the Bushido code of Samurai conduct, and Mishima and his private army hatched a plot to stage a coup and influence the Japanese military to join with them.

On November 25, 1970, Mishima and four members of Tatenokai raided the office of the Tokyo commander of the Eastern Command of Japan's Self-Defense Force. They tied the commander to his chair and then unfurled a banner detailing their manifesto from the office balcony. Mishima stepped triumphantly onto the balcony, dressed in his very spiffy Tatenokai uniform, and addressed the SDF troops who gathered below.

Unfortunately, his attempts to rouse them to his cause of re-deifying the emperor didn't exactly meet with wild cheers and applause. Laughs, catcalls, and loud farting noises, accompanied by hurled vegetables, greeted his remarks (we're big believers in bringing rotting vegetables to public speeches and live theatre performances).

It didn't look like the coup could be pulled off with just his four loyal Tatenokai members, so Mishima went back into the office and committed *seppuku* (ritual suicide), along with his second in command, Masakatsu Morita. Of course, Mishima had long planned for this possibility, and had carefully written out his *jisei* (death poems) ahead of time. The remaining members of the order — between 90 and 100 — quickly disbanded.

Operation Werwolf

In the closing days of World War II, the Nazis set up a secret guerilla warfare unit called *Werwolf* to wreak havoc on the Allies, just in case Germany lost the war. SS Lt. General Hans-Adolf Prutzman was made General Inspector of Special Defense and placed in charge of the unit. Prutzman arranged for his

Werwolf troops to be instructed in the latest methods of insurgency that sound remarkably similar to activities in modern-day Iraq: arson, sniper attacks, sabotage, and the building and use of improvised explosive devices.

Werwolf was comprised of approximately 5,000 troops drawn from the SS, as well as Hitler Youth groups. On March 25, 1945, German propaganda minister Joseph Goebbels gave a speech known as the "Werwolf Speech," in which he urged all Germans to fight to the death, and postwar insurgency lasted several years after the end of the war — as late as 1950, by some estimates. Allied troops, especially French and Soviet forces, reacted against insurgency strikes after the end of the war with strong retaliation — summary executions of uncooperative civilians, and destruction of entire villages when suspected guerillas weren't turned over.

While the degree to which Operation Werwolf troops were effective is disputed by some historians, there's no question that Nazi insurgency throughout France, Poland, Germany, and the Ukraine continued at least four years after the war ended. If they'd been as organized and well equipped as General Prutzman had wanted, postwar Europe may very well have been far bloodier than it ultimately was. Meanwhile, some believe that the influence of Werwolf activities — real and legendary — influenced former Hitler Youth to keep the concepts of neo-Nazism alive, right up through today.

Al-Qaeda

A young, idealistic millionaire from Saudi Arabia named Osama bin Laden saw the Soviet invasion in the mid-1980s as the beginnings of a holy war against Islam *(jihad)*. Bin Laden spent a not-insignificant part of his inherited fortunes on importing Muslims into Afghanistan from dozens of countries throughout the Middle East. Bin Laden paid to transport, train, and arm thousands of these *mujahedeen,* who were in turn supported by the U.S. By 1988, the Soviets gave up and went home. But bin Laden and his fellow *jihadists* did not.

With the Russian troops gone, Afghanistan fell into a civil war, fought between mujahedeen warlords, and the government fell to pieces. By 1994, the fundamentalist Taliban began to take over the government of the country, and enforced the most brutal application of Islamic Shar'ia law the world had seen in centuries.

The 1990 Gulf War

In 1990, Saddam Hussein invaded Kuwait, which put Iraqi forces within striking distance of the oil fields of Saudi Arabia. Bin Laden went home to Saudi Arabia and offered the services of his mujahedeen to the Saudi King Fahd. Instead, the king gave U.S. and other Western troops the unheard of opportunity to base military forces in the sacred home to the holy sites of Mecca and Medina.

Having the infidels so close to such sacred Islamic sites was too much for bin Laden and his fundamentalist group's prickly religious sensibilities, and he turned his anger on Saudi Arabia's ruling family. After making public statements denouncing the Saudis, he was exiled to the Sudan and his Saudi citizenship was revoked. In 1996, Sudan expelled him, but the Taliban government of Afghanistan welcomed him with open arms.

The Taliban made Afghanistan an isolated country in the world — only Pakistan, Saudi Arabia, and the United Arab Emirates recognized them as the legitimate government of the country. Such universal scorn made Afghanistan the perfect place for his private army of terrorists to grow and recruit new members without government interference.

Organization of Al-Qaeda

In 1998, bin Laden formed a new group called *Al-Qaeda* ("the base"), with the avowed purpose of expanding the holy war far outside of Afghanistan's borders. Bin Laden was especially admiring of the tactics used by Muslim terrorist organizations like Hezbollah.

Al-Qaeda was patterned along the classic lines of a secret society, and it remains so today. Secrecy and strict obedience to superiors are hallmarks of the organization, and the name Al-Qaeda itself was considered secret information. They never used the name in public until after the 9/11 attacks made them front-page news.

According to captured internal Al-Qaeda documents, the goals of the organization are to

- Establish the rule of Allah on Earth
- Attain martyrdom in the cause for Allah
- Purify the ranks of Islam from the elements of depravity

Seized documents and testimony of captured members have revealed some details of the inner workings of the group:

- Bin Laden is the *emir* (religious leader) of the organization, as well as its chief of operations. A *shura council* of between 20 and 30 advise him on activities.

- A *law committee* decides whether knocking down skyscrapers and killing more than 3,000 civilians conforms to Islamic law or not.

- A *fatwah committee* issues religious pronouncements, like a 1998 order for Muslims to kill all Americans.

- A *business committee* handles the extensive finances of Al-Qaeda, paying members, authorizing expenses like training suicide pilots, along with managing their many for-profit businesses.

✔ In 1995, Al-Qaeda formed *As-Sahab Foundation for Islamic Media Publication,* for the production of propaganda videos and publication, run by Adam Gadahn, an American convert to Islam.

Al-Qaeda's activities

In February 1998, leaders of Al-Qaeda issued a fatwa under banner of "The World Islamic Front for Jihad Against the Jews and Crusaders" stating that it was the duty of all Muslims to kill U.S. civilians and military personnel and their allies, everywhere. Since then, activities known to have been carried out by Al-Qaeda include the following:

✔ Two hotels bombed in Aden, Yemen, in December 2002, designed to scare off U.S. involvement in famine relief efforts in Somalia

  They were the wrong hotels, with no Americans in them, but it was the first attack on civilian targets by Al-Qaeda.

✔ A failed plot to kill Pope John Paul II in 1994 during a visit to the Philippines, and a similar failed plan in 1995 to kill President Bill Clinton

✔ Bombings of U.S. embassies in Dar es Salaam, Tanzania, and Nairobi, Kenya, on August 7, 1998, resulting in 300 deaths, mostly civilians

✔ A plan to blow up 12 U.S.–Pacific flights in 1995, and a failed bombing at Los Angeles International Airport in 1999

✔ USS *Cole* bombing in Aden, Yemen, on October 12, 2000, killing 17 crew members and wounding 39

✔ The attacks on the World Trade Center and the Pentagon on September 11, 2001

✔ A failed attempt by Richard Reid to explode a shoe bomb on American Airlines Flight 63 from Paris to Miami in December 2001

✔ A fuel tanker explosion outside a Tunisian synagogue in April 2002

✔ Attack on a French tanker off the coast of Yemen in October 2002

✔ A car bomb attack and a failed attempt to shoot down an Israeli jetliner in Mombasa, Kenya, in November 2002

✔ Car bomb attacks on residential compounds in Riyadh, Saudi Arabia, in May 2003

Al-Qaeda has also been implicated in the 1993 World Trade Center bombing; a series of incidents in Saudi Arabia against U.S. targets between 1995 and 1996; the October 12, 2002, nightclub bombing in Bali, Indonesia; and the May 2003 suicide bombing attacks in Casablanca, Morocco.

By the end of 2004, the U.S. government claimed to have two-thirds of Al-Qaeda's leadership from 2001 under arrest or killed, but attacks attributed to the group have both continued and increased. Because of the high-visibility 9/11 attacks, Al-Qaeda has become much like a popular and successful franchise, and terrorists no more organized than three high school friends with a post office box have started to claim "links to Al-Qaeda."

The Internet has been used as a way to broadcast propaganda, recruit new members, and communicate with worldwide operatives. The result has been self-spawning Al-Qaeda–styled groups. Both authentic Al-Qaeda cells and copycat organizations fully understand the use of public relations and the effects on the public if it's believed that Al-Qaeda is everywhere and can strike anytime.

Chapter 14

Thugs, Mugs, and Lugs: The Mafia and Other Underworld Societies

In This Chapter

▷ Conquering Sicily: The oldest game in power politics

▷ The Black Hand: Shaking down the Five Points gangs

▷ Nation building in the Mafia: The Five Families

▷ Playing the mob's pinup boy, Don Vito Corleone

*W*hen you hear the word *Mafia,* a definite set of images probably comes to mind. One may be of Marlon Brando as Don Vito Corleone from *The Godfather.* But there are others, too: John Gotti in an expensive suit, grinning as he breezes out of the courtroom; or one of his victims, like Paul Castellano, and his bullet-ridden body lying on the pavement in front of his favorite restaurant. (Restaurants seem to be a great place to nail a Mafia don; it was Gay Talese, in his 1971 book on the Mafia, *Honor Thy Father,* who joked, "They always die with spaghetti in their mouths." You'd think they'd start buying TV dinners.)

This chapter covers the major secret societies of the criminal underworld. But a substantial portion of this chapter examines just how much truth there is in any of the myths of the secret society called the Mafia, or Cosa Nostra. Exposing secrets and rituals is hard enough; but myths can be even harder to tackle, because they're so pervasive and so elusive.

Some people believe in the myth, particularly in America, of the don as a man of honor, with a code of ethics that forbids drug dealing or violence against innocents. According to John Dickie, author of *Cosa Nostra,* this belief is common but misleading. Where old-style American Mafiosos are concerned, we're not certain we agree, but Dickie emphatically states:

There was never a good mafia that at some point became corrupt and violent. There never was a traditional mafia that then became modern, organized, and business-minded. The world has changed, but the Sicilian mafia has merely adapted; it is today what it has been since it was born: a sworn secret society that pursues power and money by cultivating the art of killing people and getting away with it.

This chapter explores not just the organization of the Mafia, but some of the characters who built it. We'll leave it to the reader to decide if there is any truth in the legends of Mafia honor. But you can't understand the typical Mafia don without a nodding acquaintance with the source of Mafia culture.

Birth of the Mafia — Queen Mother of Criminal Secret Societies

Most underworld secret societies owe at least part of their structure and ritual to the most infamous of them all — the Cosa Nostra, or the Mafia. The Mafia was born on the sun-drenched, rocky island of Sicily, just off the boot of Italy across the Strait of Messina. Because of its history and geographic location, Sicily has always had a dialect and culture of its own, distinct from mainland Italy.

In order to understand the psychology of the Mafia, it's necessary to understand the psychology of the typical Sicilian, a mind-set that was created by the political and social realities of the region.

Sicily: Mafia's motherland

Sicily sits in an extremely strategic position, smack in the middle of the Mediterranean trade routes. Consequently, just about everyone had a shot at owning the place, for to take and hold Sicily was a necessity for every general from Scipio Africanus to George S. Patton. Phoenicians and Greeks, Byzantines and Arabs, and then in the 11th century the Norman French, of all people, all had their turn on the Sicilian throne.

It serves to highlight the foreign rule of the island that one of Sicily's greatest kings was a German, Frederick II, who protected and encouraged Sicilian art and poetry in the time of the Crusades. He's probably the main reason why the Sicilians don't all speak French. Apart from being strategic, Frederick's Sicily was rich in culture and in cash, the result of two things that it retains today — its busy ports and its grain production. That's what makes it so unforgivable that for the next 800 years, feuding landlords would run this first-rate property into the ground.

By the 13th century, kings of Spain and France both claimed the title of king of Sicily. Not that either one was actually going to live there. The Spanish Borbón kings most often held Sicily. But by the late 18th century, as the revolution broke out in France, revolution-fever swept all of Italy, as well. A huge number of Italians were on the side of Napoleon when he invaded Italy, because Napoleon was going to bring down the feudal system. In Italy, sending the kings, dukes, barons, and dons to the guillotine seemed like a swell idea.

From the fall of Napoleon to the rise of Mussolini a full century later, a series of revolutions and lousy kings kept Sicily in a constant state of turmoil. Most of these kings cared far more about what was happening on the mainland. So, in effect, Sicily was ignored into poverty and anarchy. The land was abandoned, cursed with absentee landlords and uncaring monarchs.

The Sicilians were a tribal people, with a culture built on an ancient bottom-to-top pyramid: the family, the clan, the tribe. The clan was perhaps the most important. It was that unit of the extended family, often numbering into the hundreds, that expressed the tie of blood so important to the Sicilian people. Every clan had its leader, and that leader was called a *don,* a word of Spanish origin that simply meant "sir," the title of a gentleman or a person of noble blood and rank.

During this period between Napoleon and Mussolini, the dons, the men of honor, took hold of the island, becoming the only force for social order that existed on a local level. And, although many of the dons were respected as well as feared, the fact is that the Sicilian peasants would just as soon have cut their heads off, too, given the chance. That's because the dons had their hands in every business dealing on the island, and they always got their cut. Every Sicilian peasant at harvest time ended up with granaries that were bulging. And by the time the government and the dons had gotten done stealing their share, the peasant was left with a tiny pile of grain to feed his family. Hunger was a constant and haunting specter over their lives, and most peasant families never saw a plate of meat. They couldn't afford it.

The dons of the various powerful Mafia clans ruled Sicily with small armies of "soldiers" called *soldati* that were rarely seen without their favored weapon, the shotgun. They had no qualms about using it on anyone who got in their way.

The Code of Silence, the sacred *Omertà,* governed the lives not just of the Mafiosos, but of the entire population. This code would follow the Mafia to America. Its definition was simple: If you found yourself in the unfortunate position of being questioned by a civil official about one of the dons or his men, you didn't *see* anything, you didn't *hear* anything, and you didn't *know* anything. Otherwise, there was a shotgun in your future.

Morphing into "Mafia"

So, just how many different explanations are there for where the word "Mafia" comes from? A lot — all with different levels of believability:

✔ The linguists contend that the word grew out of an adjective in Sicily, *mafiusu,* which had its roots in the Arabic word *mahyas,* which means "boasting" or "bragging." The adjective mafiusu is usually translated as meaning "to swagger," implying someone proud or arrogant.

✔ Others say the word arrived on the scene after a play called *I mafiusi di la Vicana,* which means "The Beautiful People of Vicaria," a story which takes place in the 1850s among the gangs in a Palermo prison, although the word is only used in the title, to give it local flavor.

✔ Though it may or may not have come from there, the most widespread early usage of the term came out of a wildly popular 1890 opera by Mascagni called *Cavalleria rusticana,* which means "rustic chivalry." All the men in the play are called "Mafiosi," and all are the victims of swaggering pride and blind honor, the result of the wild, romantic Saracen blood in Sicilians. In fact, the music of this opera is playing all through the last half-hour of *The Godfather Part III.* But in reference to the swagger of *gangsters* calling themselves "men of honor," the word first appeared in a police report of the prefect of Palermo in 1865.

✔ The most romantic version of all came out of the occupation of the island by the Borbón king during the revolution of 1848. Two Spanish soldiers rape and murder an innocent Sicilian peasant girl, dumping her body in a church. When her mother discovers the body, she runs into the street, crying, "Ma fia! Ma fia!" which means, "My daughter!" She will get justice only from the dons of the island, who arrange for the assassination of the murderers as part of their battle to take back their homeland, taking "Ma fia!" as their battle cry. Okay, maybe not, but it's a great story.

The birth of the Cosa Nostra

By the 19th century, all the years of living as a conquered people had left their mark on the Sicilian mentality. Whoever ruled from the capital, the port city of Palermo, didn't much matter to the common folk. If you get conquered enough, a certain level of indifference, if not contempt, to the civil authority is a natural by-product. The attitude is simple enough to understand — pay lip service to whoever's in power, and pay your taxes as well; but we all know who's really in charge.

While the lip service was being paid to the government, it was the dons of the clans that had the real power. Generally speaking, the foreign government of Palermo couldn't have cared less who stole a farmer's cow, or who'd gotten the farmer's daughter pregnant. These matters of great importance to a peasant were of little or no importance to the Borbón king. The don settled these issues, and his word was law. He was paid a tithe, like a tribute tax, by the peasants who owed him fealty, and they gave it over sometimes out of fear, but more often than not out of intense loyalty and respect, in the beginning.

But as the dons became more powerful, they also grew more ruthless and were usually involved in many crimes, such as stealing cattle or sheep, extortion, and muscling in on just about any sort of business deal that took place on the island. The respect of old turned to fear and then terror.

Vendetta!

The system of local power and control under the dons didn't necessarily bring the plus of stability along with it. The problem was that, along with the freight of the don's authority in each village and town, came the heavy baggage of the *vendetta,* which comes from the Italian word for revenge. The vendetta was a fierce, violent, and sometimes interminable war between two Sicilian families.

All through the Middle Ages, Europe *had* kings, but in most places, it was the power of the local warlord or feudal baron that was the real authority over daily life, just as in Sicily. Of course, these petty feudal lords were constantly making war on each other, all over Europe. Yet, as Europe progressed into the Renaissance of the 15th century, the power of kings became greater, with the power of feudal lords lessening, until the nation was bound together into a tighter, unified whole.

This process didn't occur in Sicily. There, the dons, similar to feudal warlords in their position of clan patriarch, often made war on one another in the same fashion as the days of old. But since the clan was the central structure of these warring factions, it wasn't just an impersonal war over territory. It was a blood feud. When you attacked an enemy, you didn't just kill his sergeant-at-arms or his knight; you killed his uncle or his cousin or his brother. This is why vendettas could go on for years between two families, sometimes until all the men of both clans had been killed. This incessant vendetta violence, along with the extortionate demands of the dons, is what drove over a million Sicilians to leave the land of their birth in the early 20th century.

For those remaining in Sicily, the grip of the dons would only tighten. They organized themselves into the "Cupola," a governing body of the Mafia families. Because of the number of families represented, the Cupola had a complex organizational pyramid. It met in Palermo, and there's no question that the Palermo-area families had the greatest power. But theoretically, all the families on the island were represented in a system of "mandamentos," or provincial areas. (For more on Mafia families, please see "The Big Five of the Commission," later in the chapter.)

A *mandamento* is an old term for the district of a Sicilian magistrate. The dons hijacked the word and used it to describe a connected area controlled by three mafia families. One don was chosen to represent all three in the Cupola; he was called a *capomandamento*. At the dawn of the 20th century, over a million Sicilians left the economically depressed island; this was roughly a quarter of the entire population. About 800,000 of them came to America. By 1903, newspapers across America decried the fact that Italy was "dumping its criminals" at our doorstep. By 1910, there were more Italians in Little Italy on the Lower East Side of Manhattan than there were in the city of Rome. This was the beginning of the prejudice all Italian-Americans would have to fight, the myth that Italians were inclined to criminality.

The Mafia and Organized Crime in America

When Sicilians first started arriving in America, there were lots of "made men," or members of the Mafia, on those boats. Many of them were on the run from either the law or the vendetta of another family. And the fact is that, when they got here, they discovered that things weren't very different in New York than they'd been in Palermo, especially where politics and influence peddling were concerned. The Mafiosos who'd done well in Sicily were starting all over again, but they would do well here, too.

Many of the Mafiosos who came to the U.S. hadn't really thought of staying; they were on the lam, for one reason or another, and they were going to bide their time in America before returning. Yet, most never went home again, unless the federal government deported them.

Tales of the Five Points gangs

It was rough going in the beginning, for all these Sicilian immigrants. Life in America was better than what they'd left behind; there was more promise for a brighter future. But it was incredibly rough going in the beginning. The newly arrived Italian immigrants ended up in Little Italy, some in Brooklyn or Greenwich Village; but the bulk of them were dumped in Five Points, a grim slum on the Lower East Side of Manhattan. There was a very definite pecking order in the Five Points, based on who'd already gotten there and assimilated into the culture, and who was just getting off the boat.

This area was called "the Five Points" because it sat on five corners created by the convergence of three streets; Anthony, Baxter, and Park. It was near a 48-acre lake called the Collect Pond that had once been a source of fresh water, but became horribly polluted by sewage and industrial runoff from the tanneries and slaughterhouses of the area. The pollution caused more than a god-awful smell throughout the neighborhood — it caused continuing outbreaks of typhus and cholera, as well. Disease spread like a wildfire, because the density of immigrants on the Lower East Side was roughly 700 people per square acre, the highest in the world. (None of these streets of Five Points have the same name today — in fact, the pond was filled in and the whole area turned into Columbus Park in the late 19th century.)

Many of the newly arrived Sicilian Mafiosi got right into bed with the most corrupt gang of all in New York — Tammany Hall and the Democratic Party machine. These folks slowly transformed into the Black Hand, the ruthless gang that was the seed of the American Mafia. The Black Hand hustled votes (called "ward heeling") just as they'd done at home, muscling in on business, often construction, giving out jobs for votes, and so on. This aspect of the Black Hand, in fact, led to one of the Mafia's most lucrative ties in America — control of organized labor.

Paddywhacked — The Irish Mafia

The street gangs who ruled the Five Points neighborhood of Manhattan were eager to greet Sicilians — with a club. Most of the toughest gangs at the time were Irish, who'd arrived in a mass during the mid-1800s because of the Irish Potato Famine. Their gang names, chosen to instill fear, seem a little silly to our ears — not just the Bowery Boys or the Five Pointers, but the Plug-Uglies and the Dead Rabbits.

However, despite the names, much of gang life and lingo is startlingly similar to today. These gangs wore colors, they called their headquarters their "cribs," and their area of strength was called their "turf." The biggest turf wars began when the Little Italy neighborhood was born, and Five Points was inundated with Sicilians.

The irony is that the Irish, first off the boat in the immigrant age, were also the first to begin assimilating, and a popular place to assimilate into was the police force, which was populated by more Irishmen than any other ethnic group.

This is where the classic gangster story was born, out of the reality of the Lower East Side. It was the plot for dozens of gangster films. Either two brothers, or two close friends who grow up together in the New York slums, take different paths, one into gangsterism, the other into politics or law or the District Attorney's office. Sooner or later, their worlds collide, with painful choices all around, dead sons, and weeping Irish mothers that didn't leave a dry eye in the house. In 1938, it was a Jimmy Cagney movie. In 1928, it was a common story of the rackets on the Lower East Side.

Hey! Watch who you're calling a bohunk!

You might not know what the word "Paddy" means, a sign that American society is going in the right direction. In fact, this aspect of New York in the 19th century was an ethnic reflex that spread to the rest of the nation along with the Mafia. In the melting pot of America, everybody, and we mean *everybody,* had an ethnic nickname that was, to at least some degree, pejorative as well as jocular. Meaning simply that, some guys used it to start a fight, while other guys used it in a friendly way to their buddies. As to determining whether the name was an insult, the source and the tone told you all you needed to know. The Irish were "Paddies" and "Micks." Hungarians were "Hunkies," the Dutch were "Clog Wogs," the Ukrainians were "Bohunks," the Germans were "Huns" or "Fritz," the Jews were "Yids" or "Kikes," and the Scotch-Irish were "Cohees." It was just that kind of world. Little wonder that the gangs formed up along ethnic lines.

And the Sicilians of the newest gang, the "Black Hand," were the "Guineas," the "Wops," and the "Mustache Petes," based on a common newspaper cartoon image that had been taken from a photo of an arrested member — high stiff collar, bowler hat, cropped hair, and an enormous mustache. By 1910, they were outmaneuvering the Irish gangs all over the Lower East Side.

The Kosher mob

A *Jewish* Mafia? In the late 19th century, the reaction to this piece of Americana was a bit comic, from Jew and Gentile alike. Most of the major newspapers of the day took an anti-immigrant stance, and the wafting aroma of race prejudice was usually there, in all their coverage. But a Jewish Mafia? Even the newspapers were surprised. Many essays of the day took an attitude indicative of one quote: "The Jew, whatever his faults, has never before been a threat to public order." As for the Jewish community's reaction, it was nothing less than appalled.

The Jews of Europe were used to living in ghettos — the very word has its roots in the Austrian language for "Jewish Quarter." Aryans without business there were discouraged from going, and relations between Aryans and Jews were looked on with distaste. But when the Jews arrived in free-wheeling America, they discovered that it wasn't so easy to control their children. Yes, Jews lived in neighborhoods together, but no one was locking you in at night; no one was saying that you had to stay south of Delancy Street.

There was bound to be inter-mixing, and different races came into contact with one another with much greater ease and social acceptance. It was nearly impossible to keep your son from mixing with the young Irish and Italian gangs. For a race born and bred in respect for the law, it was a painful scandal for old-world Jewish parents when their 14-year-old son was out running the numbers.

Although the Kosher mob was pretty short-lived, it would leave an indelible mark on the Italian Mafia, as will be seen in the stories of infamous Jewish hoods like Bugsy Siegel and Meyer Lansky.

Shadow of the Black Hand

The Black Hand, borne of the Sicilian immigrants, soon became the most feared gang on the Lower East Side, putting the ruthless Irish mob in the shade. Their favored method of punishment was called "barrel murder" — shooting a victim or cutting his throat, then folding the body over into a barrel and leaving it on a public street to be found by some innocent with a blood-curdling scream that would create terror of the Black Hand in the whole neighborhood.

The first two law-enforcement officers to start investigating these barrel murders were Joe Petrosino of the New York Police Department, one of the first Sicilian-Americans on the force, and David Hennessey, the Police Chief of New Orleans. They were both later assassinated by the Mafia (see "The Ongoing Struggle to Crush the Mafia," later in this chapter). Both men understood the fact that the Black Hand was a sort of seafaring mob, very strong in the dock neighborhoods of both cities, because there was a tie between the Black Hand and the Mafia back home in Sicily that was growing stronger as time passed. It's interesting to note that during this period, in newspaper reports, the word "Mafia" was used, perhaps for the first time in America, rather than the more popular term "Black Hand."

All the gangs of the Lower East Side made money the same way, from extortion, gambling, theft, and prostitution. But the forces of Puritanism in American were about to unleash a constitutional amendment that would make millionaires out of these young Italian toughs (called *picciotti*), literally overnight.

Prohibition and the birth of the Rackets

Prohibition was the common name for the Eighteenth Amendment to the Constitution, which went into effect in America in 1920, and made it illegal to transport or manufacture liquor. It was the first time an amendment took away a freedom rather than protecting one, the result of an incessant 20-year din on the part of the Anti-Saloon League, the Women's Temperance Movement, and a lot of other loud killjoys.

Making a racket

Did you ever wonder where the term "the rackets" came from? Well, even if you didn't we're going to tell you. In the grand old days of the Five Points gangs, the gangsters used to hold dances to raise money and to have a good time. They sold tickets to these dances, and being gangsters, would often use a bit of a strong arm to get people to buy them. In those wild pre-Prohibition days, these dances got very rowdy, and the noise was deafening; cops got constant complaints about all the racket. And somehow, as happens with slang, the rackets and "racketeering" came to be a term not just for the dances themselves, but for the methods the gangs used to sell the tickets. In later years, the tickets being sold as part of the "numbers racket" weren't to a dance. The classic numbers racket was like a lottery. The bets could be on any set of numbers; one of the most common was what the last four numbers of the close of the Dow would be that day. People would bet small amounts, like a nickel, but when they won, they won big. It was a very lucrative business.

The fantasy was that everyone would just stop drinking if you made it illegal. It's the same waltz these days with cigarettes. And, in both cases, it's a dizzy dance in circles, because it's based on a false assumption. What really happens when you make something as popular as drinking illegal is that the average Joe loses respect for the law; most people would rather keep on drinking and break the law.

Mob bosses laid awake at night dreaming about this kind of situation. The Mafia and organized crime established itself as an empire because of Prohibition, making untold millions off America's thirst for beer and booze. They either made their liquor here, in hidden breweries and distilleries, or they imported the more expensive brand-name liquor, smuggling it in from Canada, Mexico, and Europe.

The infamous Chicago gangster Al Capone was fond of pointing out that there was nothing in the law about *drinking* liquor. This little catch was cleaned up with the passage of the Volstead Act, the federal Prohibition act that gave the government powers to enforce the Eighteenth Amendment.

Actually, the "speakeasies," the most common name for a hidden, illegal bar, had an enormous social impact on the period. Jazz, America's most important contribution to music, was born there. In some places speakeasies were called "blind pigs," because of a colorful way around the law against selling liquor that sprang up. The innkeeper charged you to see some sort of exhibit or unusual animal, then the booze was complimentary. The Irish sometimes called speakeasies "shebeens," which was the word in the old country for a pub that operated on the sly without a license. These places were lively and fun, and became the backbone of American social and clubbing life in the roaring 1920s.

Reprieve! Open up the taps

Franklin Roosevelt made himself beloved, not just to Democrats but to all Americans, when he finally got the 21st Amendment passed in 1933, the only time a constitutional amendment (the hated 18th) was repealed by another. Well, he made everyone happy except the gangsters, who saw untold millions going out the window with every legal bar and liquor store that opened.

Actually, many a rumrunner, even some of the most powerful of the gangsters, simply retired with the money or used it to open legitimate businesses. But for the hard-core Mafiosos, those millions would have to be replaced, and eventually of course, they were, by the traffic in heroin and other drugs.

The war between the wars

Between World War I and World War II, the period of the 1920s and the 1930s, several Mafia wars broke out in New York, as the money poured in, and dons of the various families began jockeying to be the *Capo dei capi,* more commonly the *Capo di Tutti Capi,* the Boss of Bosses, the most powerful and influential of the dons. There was so much money in bootlegging, that too many bosses wanted to run the whole show. Eventually it broke into two major factions: Salvatore Maranzano and Joe "the Boss" Masseria. (For much, much more on mob lingo, see the Cheat Sheet at the front of this book.)

It was called the Castellamarese War, a very bloody struggle between the older West Sicily families of the Castellamarese area represented by Maranzano and the Young Turks under Masseria. Maranzano felt he was the big boss, because he had ties to Don Vito Cascio Ferro in Sicily, the Boss of Bosses (69 arrests, no convictions), who'd helped to found the Black Hand in New York before being deported. As usual with Mafia wars, the hits and the retaliatory hits and the boomerang-back-at-you hits drug on for a couple of years, killing business for everyone.

Charles "Lucky" Luciano was of the Masseria faction, the biggest bootlegger in New York. He ran a class operation, with imported brand-name liquor, instead of bathtub gin and wood alcohol hooch. He felt the war had to stop. Boss Masseria was going paranoid, and he'd tried to have Luciano killed. So Luciano hit Masseria and made peace with Maranzano. But it didn't last long. The old man from Castellamarese was still itching for a fight, and when his close friend Meyer Lansky told Lucky that now *Maranzano* had a hit out on him, Lucky took him out, as well. Luciano found himself the last man standing, the *capo di tutti capi,* whether he wanted it or not.

No Luciano on the Marquee

Luciano decided there should never again be any such thing in New York as a "Boss of Bosses." There would be a new way, like the Cupola in Sicily, a board of families. It's true that none of the Five Families of New York ever bore the name of Luciano (see "The Big Five of the Commission," later in the chapter). Nevertheless, he was the man who founded them, leaving his mark on Mafia history.

The very phrase *Cosa Nostra,* the term for the Mafia preferred by insiders, was coined by Lucky Luciano. It simply means "our thing," or "our affair." The story goes that at the first meeting of the new five Mafia families, Lucky Luciano decreed that there would no longer be a "Boss of Bosses" — all the members would be equal. When he was asked what this new commission would be called, he shot back, "No names. Give it a name, and you give them something to come after. This is just our thing, our private thing." And so an infamous name, Cosa Nostra, was born. Luciano's two biggest allies within the Mafia were Frank Costello and Vito Genovese. Though the family founded by Luciano would be called the Genovese Family, Vito would not wrest control for many years from Frank Costello, the dapper and clever gangster called the Prime Minister of the Commission. But both men had been set up in business by Luciano. Outside of the Mafia, Lucky had two close friends, Bugsy Siegel, and his closest friend of all, Meyer Lansky, both of the Kosher mob. Luciano was making a staggering amount of money as a bootlegger, and he wasn't about to let another pointless war destroy his empire. He implemented ideas from many sources when he created the Commission, and though he was only one more member, it wasn't healthy to get in his way. Legend has it that Lanskey and Seigel set up for Luciano a contract killing firm, Murder, Incorporated, to get rid of any of Lucky's dangerous enemies (for more on Murder, Inc., see Chapter 12).

Some of America's most infamous Prohibition gangsters were *not* in the Mafia. That's why, as a whole, it was called organized crime. The Mafia was only interested in drafting young men with familiar bloodlines from the old country. And because Sicily had no more murderous sociopaths per capita than any other place on earth, they got to be pretty choosy. But America's most famous gangster of all, Al Capone, wasn't in the Mafia. He was an Italian, whose family hailed from Naples on the mainland, and he was a leader of *organized crime,* but not of the Mafia. Capone's operation was called the Chicago Outfit, and was sometimes allied with the New York Mafia. But Capone was an equal opportunity employer; he'd hire anyone for the Outfit, so long as they did their job well. In fact, he ran his empire a lot like Donald Trump, except that if you screwed up, he didn't fire you. He just beat you to death with a baseball bat. But still, he wasn't a Mafioso. Apart from the big Five Families, Luciano also pulled together 26 other families and organizations, like the Jewish mob, into a National Crime Syndicate, all working together for the good of the whole. Various other Mafia families were given other territories, like the Scarfos in Philadelphia, for example.

Lucky's connections

Lucky Luciano paid lip service to all the Sicilian mob stuff, but in truth had little patience with it. After all, he had a Jew as his closest friend; as boys, Luciano and Meyer Lansky had worked the streets together. The two met when Lucky and some of his gang tried to shake down the small and soft-spoken Lansky. His defiant and gutsy but unprintable reply endeared him to Luciano, and they became friends at once. It was the closest friendship in the history of the mob, and through it the Jewish Lansky would gain great power in the Mafia.

As Jews, Meyer Lansky and his partner in crime, Ben "Bugsy" Siegel, were forbidden membership in the Mafia, but they had their own smaller Jewish mob going. Their organization even had its own lingo; for example, their muscle enforcers weren't *piciotto;* they were *schtarka,* Yiddish for someone who's a climber. Even the word "shamus" for a private detective that was so popular with writers like Micky Spillane and Raymond Chandler, had its roots in the Yiddish word *shammus,* which was a caretaker in a synagogue. Later it came to mean a guard in the organization.

Luciano helped out their new gang and made friends with Siegel, although he found Bugsy's fits of temper unnerving; after all, the man was called "Bugsy" for being crazy as a bed bug. Prohibition made these three young toughs major underworld players. And Lucky Luciano was "the connection," the man who made it possible for his two closest cohorts, both outsiders, to be powers within the Mafia.

Luciano goes up the river

For Meyer Lansky, rising mob star, the toughest blow was when he ultimately lost Lucky Luciano. And the irony is that Luciano was put away by a man whose life he saved.

Thomas Dewey, "the Racket Buster," became fixated on putting Luciano, the big fish, behind bars. Dewey was a high-profile crime fighter, and he tried to nail one of Luciano's men, Dutch Schultz, on tax evasion. Despite getting off, Schultz became obsessed with killing Dewey. When nothing Luciano could do would stop him, he had no choice but to put out a hit on Schultz in order to save Dewey and keep the wrath of God from coming down on the Commission.

Dewey knew this fact. Yet, when he couldn't get Lucky on a legitimate charge, he finally nailed Luciano on a trumped-up charge of running a prostitution ring. Luciano was sentenced to 30 years in prison, which seems awfully harsh. Yet, it's said that he continued to run his empire from his prison cell, thanks to the loyalty of his friends on the Commission and his closer friends like Lansky outside of it. (After World War II, in gratitude for his services to the government during the war, the absurd 30-year sentence was commuted, and Luciano was deported to Sicily.)

The shift from booze to dice

Even with Luciano in jail, the plan remained the same — find new sources of income to take the place of bootlegging. And the idea for that source came from Saratoga Springs, in upstate New York. The mob often vacationed there in August, when the racetrack was open. The horsey high-society types loved it, and when the track closed at six, the gangsters rented the nearby grand Saratoga Lake homes and turned them into party-house casinos throughout the high-flying month. There was great food, star-studded floor shows, and gambling until the wee hours.

The Valachi Papers

Part of the inspiration for the RICO Act and bulletproof witness protection came out of the testimony of the first, and the most famous, Mafia rat of all time — Joe Valachi. His story spawned both a popular book and a movie. The Witness Protection Program was created because the FBI knew they would never be able to prosecute the bosses who gave the orders unless they could shatter the Omertà, the Code of Silence. In Valachi's case, the FBI used good old-fashioned head games. Godfather Vito Genovese, in a coup for the government, had been sent to a federal prison for heroin trafficking. Joe Valachi, one of his soldiers, was in the same jail with him. The FBI played a little game with Genovese — they kept calling Valachi in for long sessions of questioning, again and again. Valachi sat for two hours and more, saying nothing. But the ploy worked, because after awhile, nobody, including Vito Genovese, believed Valachi wasn't singing to the feds.

Finally, one day in the prison cafeteria, Genovese grabbed Valachi and gave him the "kiss of death," sealing his doom. Valachi, with nowhere else to turn, took the feds up on their offer. When Valachi testified before Congress on national television in 1963 for the McClellan hearings, the whole country was riveted by his stories of the rituals and secrets of la Cosa Nostra. It sent the FBI out on a 30-year crusade against organized crime that would be, for the most part, successful.

In Saratoga Springs, Lansky saw a vision of another kind of money pot. He noticed that, unlike the smoky back-room poker games and gambling dives of New York, here the men brought their wives and girlfriends, because there was so much for them to do. And the women started playing the tables, as well, meaning everybody stayed longer and bet more. The dream took hold of him of building a mob-owned palace in a mob-dominated place, somewhere far from racket-buster Thomas Dewey in New York, somewhere that gambling was legal year-round, where he could re-create this same atmosphere. The gambling had to be honest; nothing drove the big players away faster than any whiff of a "bust-out joint," where the games were fixed. And it had to be luxurious in feel, with great food and shows.

Both Lansky and Siegel were sent out to scout for gambling businesses. Lansky did it quietly and carefully, and Siegel did it with enough noise to be heard back in New York.

Cuban Pete with the rumba beat

Lansky started in Florida, in a few municipalities where gambling was legal. But Cuba soon beckoned. It was an easy destination, less than 100 miles off the Florida coast, and it was already a hotspot for playboy and Hollywood types. And best of all, not only was gambling legal in this American possession, but also the president, Fulgencio Batista, walked around with a big "For Sale" sign on his back. Cuban music was hot, and Cuba was often featured in the movies as an exotic locale.

The mob couldn't dump money into the Havana casinos fast enough. But it all came crashing down around their heads on New Year's Eve of 1958. Batista had been fighting the forces of the revolutionary Fidel Castro since early fall, but he'd blown it badly. That night, Castro came rolling into Havana, and the wise guys all hopped on the next plane back to Florida. Castro declared the casinos government property, and promptly made gambling illegal. (This mess was the cause of the most believable conspiracy theory concerning Sam Giancana, the Mafia, and the assassination of JFK. For more, see Chapter 5.)

Bugsy Siegel and the founding of modern Las Vegas

While Meyer Lansky was busy keeping a low profile and doing his job, Bugsy Siegel was making a splash in Hollywood. He ran with the "in" crowd, and his closest friend was superstar George Raft. The ladies loved Bugsy; he was the most charming and handsome psychopath to ever rat-a-tat-tat a Tommy gun. And when he met mob tramp and actress wannabee Virginia Hill, the romance caught fire. But Bugsy was still out West to do a job, and he'd fixed his eyes on a new potential source of gambling riches.

Nevada was the only state in the union that had legalized gambling. And way, *way* off the beaten track, was a little tourist trap called Las Vegas, with tiny casinos done up to look like the background for a Roy Rogers movie. Its location in the southernmost tip of Nevada made it very convenient to Los Angeles by air. The Chicago Outfit was already considering buying up some of these casinos, but Bugsy found a bigger dream, when he discovered that a gambler and builder named Billie Wilkerson was constructing a large, modern casino, but was out of cash. Bugsy muscled in, and the dream of the Flamingo was born.

Unfortunately, Bugsy was a great killer, but a lousy businessman. He was persistently being double and even triple billed, and costs were soaring, while the opening date loomed. Unwisely, he stuck by his announced Christmas Eve 1946 open, and it was a disaster. The rooms weren't finished, none of his big stars showed up because of a storm that kept them from flying, and all the shoddy construction kept causing problems for guests and staff. The whole thing was supposed to cost $1 million; Bugsy had already spent $4 million.

The last straw came when Bugsy and Virginia were caught skimming off the top. Mob casinos always took some off the top in the counting rooms, before the money was banked and seen by the IRS. But this glittering pair, apparently believing they could get away with anything, had skimmed a couple million for themselves. Bugsy had signed his own death warrant, and even Meyer Lansky couldn't stop it.

Siegel was gunned down through a plate glass window while staying in Virginia Hill's mansion in Beverly Hills. Virginia may have been warned not to be there. Even though he was shot from behind, the bullets, chillingly enough, came through his eyes, those deadly blue eyes that the ladies had found so irresistible.

What's in a name?

As with all Mafiosi, Joe Bonanno had a nickname, Joe "Bananas" Bonanno, and, as with all Mafiosi, he hated it. You didn't call Ben Siegel "Bugsy" to his face, not if you wanted to live through dinner. But the Mafia is very fond of saying that it's a business like any other. So, what if other businesses were like this? Would you have Bugsy "the Enforcer" Gates running Microsoft, or Steve "the Mechanic" Jobs at Apple? How about Dave "the Burnoose" Lesar at Halliburton, or Rex "the Valdez" Tillerson at Exxon. After all, Ted "Crackers" Turner of CNN once challenged Rupert "Crocodile Dundee" Murdoch to a public boxing match to settle their feud. Maybe corporate American isn't so different from the Mafia after all.

The FBI, RICO, and the Decline of the Mafia

With the death of Bugsy Siegel, much of the glamour went out of the Mafia. The last nail in that coffin came in 1951 with the Kefauver Senate hearings into organized crime. The godfathers didn't seem quite so distant and forbidding when they could be drug before a senate subcommittee by one little subpoena. By the 1970s, the FBI declared war on the Mafia, and the new federal anti-Mafia laws, particularly the RICO Act (Racketeer Influenced and Corrupt Organizations Act), made it awfully difficult for the mob to do business.

The RICO Act basically provides additional federal charges and gives stiffer sentences to those who persistently commit the same crime over the course of a ten-year period in what is deemed by the attorney general to be a "racketeering" pattern. Up until then, mobsters had defended themselves in court by declaring there was no such thing as organized crime. But after a RICO indictment, the government can seize the assets of this non-existent activity. Although it's been used on everyone from abortion protesters to stockbrokers, the law is written with the Mafia in mind. It's there to nail the godfathers, not just the soldiers. Wiretapping and patient surveillance were the FBI's chief weapons. As part of a one-two punch with the Witness Protection Program, the old days of the Mafia's way of doing business, at least in America, have been torpedoed.

The Big Five Families of the Commission

In this section, we cover the Five Families of the New York Mafia, families whose names live on, even in cases where the founder's bloodline is long dead. These Families were established by 1931, each one named for the *Capofamiglia,* the don of each Family.

Unfortunately, we don't have enough room in this single chapter for the juicy stories within each Family of wars for control, peaces brokered, and assassinations, not to mention the shifting alliances among the five. They played out like a Greek tragedy, more like a movie than real life. In other words, it's not surprising that five Mafia bosses, not to mention all their underbosses, would be in a constant state of plotting and scheming against one another in various combinations.

The Gambino Family

The Gambino family was founded by one Vincent Mangano, who had all the usual rackets: unions, loan sharking, gambling, and prostitution. Carlo Gambino and Paul Castellano were powerful lieutenants in the family. After a period of murder and mayhem, Carlo Gambino got rid of the biggest psychos and took over. He became the most powerful leader of the Five Families in the 1960s. At Gambino's death in 1976, control of the powerful family passed to his brother-in-law Paul Castellano. At this time, John Gotti was merely a comer, a muscle mobster under Castellano, but really on the crew of another faction of the family under a capo named Dellacroce, an enemy of Castellano's.

By the late 1970s, the FBI had targeted the Gambino Family big time. They bugged Castellano's house and caught him on tape discussing some highly illegal family business. In the early 1980s, he was up on charges, and it looked like the old man was going to the hoosegow. Castellano had already named his old friend and ally Thomas Gambino, Carlo's son, as his successor. But in 1983, the poop hit the fan when 13 of the Gambino Family were arrested by the FBI for drug trafficking, including John Gotti's brother Gene, and his best friend Angelo "Quack Quack" Ruggiero. (*Quack Quack?* Can you imagine getting the job of having to whack Quack Quack?) With the death from cancer of Castellano's main family rival, Aniello Dellacroce, Gotti saw the vacuum, and decided to act fast. On December 16, when Castellano was headed for a dinner meeting at Spark's Steak House, he was gunned down in the street by four men. Gotti was now head of the Gambino Family.

Unfortunately, Gotti was a new style Mafioso, all brash vanity and braggadocio. The FBI wanted him bad on that account. After a long and unprecedented battle and a series of trials, the FBI got Sammy "the Bull" Gravano, a long-time Gotti associate, to turn state's evidence, and the Teflon Don went to the slammer, where he died of cancer in 2002. John Junior took over for a time, until he was sent up the river, as well. The war against the FBI had turned the once-mighty Gambino Family to a shadow of its former self. What's left of it is presently being run, so it's said, jointly by Nicholas "Little Nick" Corozzo and John "Jackie Nose" D'Amico. They are both, needless to say, keeping a very low profile.

The Genovese Family

This is the family founded by Lucky Luciano and his close associate, Frank Costello, who ran it for many years until his retirement after an attempt on his life made by Vito Genovese. The family is named for Genovese, who had been one of the founders, with Frank Costello and Lucky Luciano. But in the 1930s, Genovese was indicted for murder and fled to Italy. Costello took over. Years later, after World War II, Vito Genovese returned, beat the murder rap, and began fighting to topple Costello, who by that time was just as happy to retire and hand it over to him. Along with the numbers rackets, one of the Gambino specialties was buying up politicians and judges. Longtime boss Frank Costello was called "the Prime Minister of the Underworld." He also put the Family into the legitimate liquor import business. In the style of their founder Luciano, the Genovese Family is probably the most tightly run in New York, and the one that draws the least press. Nevertheless, when Joe Valachi, a Genovese soldier, broke Omertà and testified before the McClellan hearings, it ratcheted up a 20-year FBI fever to bring the Family down. They've had a number of damaging successes. Genovese was nailed for drug dealing in 1959, and died in prison in 1969.

The most colorful boss of the later period was definitely Vincent "the Chin" Gigante, dubbed "the Oddfather." Like most Genoveses, he kept a high level of secrecy about operations. But his favorite trick for getting out of trouble with the Feds was to act as if he'd gone nuts. He was always pleading insanity. He liked to walk around Greenwich Village in his pajamas and slippers, pretending to talk to himself. It worked for years. The present don is probably Mario Gigante, brother of "the Chin," though he's in his 80s and probably at least semi-retired. If *he* wanders around in his PJs and talks to himself, there's a reason. Daniel Leo is probably the acting boss. No one knows for sure, because the Genoveses are keeping a very, very low profile.

The Colombo Family

The Colombo Family was founded by Joe Profaci and once known as the *Profaci Family.* Giuseppe "Joe" Profaci was an old-fashioned Sicilian Mafioso in the worst sense, hated by many for his heavy-handed use of taxes and tithes on family members. Those soldiers who didn't pay into his slush fund, which was supposedly for the families of dead or imprisoned family members, ended up dead themselves. Many dons lived surprisingly simple lives, but Profaci liked to live large, making himself a target. In the 1950s, the Feds went after him big time with their usual mob weapons, charges of tax evasion, and threats of deportation, but he died of liver cancer in 1962 before any punishments were inflicted.

Because Profaci was so hated, his family was often torn by internal strife and takeover attempts. After a 1961 internal war, Joe Colombo was named head of the new Colombo Family. He was young, only 41, and did several things to annoy his fellows on the Commission, including forming the Italian-American Civil Rights League. It made him far too public, and at a League event in 1971, he was shot as he stepped up to the podium. He lingered in a coma for eight years before he died. Internal strife weakened the family; it is now run from prison by Carmine Persico, one more casualty of the RICO Act.

The Lucchese Family

The Lucchese Family was founded by Gaetano "Tommy" Gagliano and his underboss Gaetano "Tommy Brown" Lucchese. After the death of Gagliano in 1953, his loyal underboss Lucchese took over. He had a reputation for making big money (including interests in trucking and the Teamsters) while keeping a low profile much admired by the Commission. In 44 years, he was never once charged with a crime. After his death, the Family wasn't so lucky, and several members went down over the infamous "French Connection" heroin busts. The next boss, Tony "Ducks" Corallo also fell victim to FBI bugs and the RICO laws. Once again, the family is officially being run by 72-year-old Don Vic Amuso from his prison cell, while his street boss Aniello Migliore attempts to bring some stability back to the operation.

The Bonanno Family

The Bonanno Family was founded by Joseph (Giuseppe) Bonanno, a Sicilian immigrant from the town of Castellammare del Golfo, in the westernmost region of Sicily called the province of Trapani. He left Sicily at the age of 26 during Mussolini's crackdown on the Mafia, taking his young wife and new-born son Salvatore (Bill) to America. Bill is often seen as a mythic figure, the conflicted Sicilian-American mobster who starting out wanting to run the legitimate end of the family business, and ended up being drawn into the Mafia by deep ties of honor and obligation. In 1956, he married the innocent young Rosalie Profaci, a royal Mafia marriage between the Bonanno and Colombo families.

We probably know more about the inner workings and personalities within the Bonanno Family than any other. First came Gay Talese's groundbreaking 1971 book, *Honor Thy Father,* which was the story of the Bonanno family and their everyday life. Then came the autobiography of Rosalie Bonanno, followed by autobiographies written in retirement by Bill Bonanno, and by his father Joseph, the *paterfamilias.* Code of Silence or no Code of Silence, this is a family that likes getting things off its collective chest.

Welcome to the Family! Mafia Rituals

A lot of hogwash has been written over the years about the rituals and initiation rites of the Mafia. But this section explains the real ritual of admission to the Mafia that's come to light slowly over the course of the last 40 years, ever since Joe Valachi made a few references to it in his testimony before Congress. Tommasso Buscetta added more details when he told the tale of his initiation to Sicilian mob-buster Giovanni Falcone after his extradition from Brazil. Minor differentiations exist, but the core of it remains the same, both in Sicily and America.

The hard part isn't the ritual itself; you don't have to memorize reams of ritual phrases and responses. The hard part is getting there. Generally, you have to bloody your hands, particularly if you weren't born into the family. Here's an outline of the general process:

1. **The candidate, or _neophyte_ (which is a phrase from Christian history for a man entering the faith), is brought to a darkened, candle-lit room, where the don of the family is sitting in dignified silence.**

2. **Depending on the time and the people involved, various symbolic items may be laid out on the table before him.**

   These items can include a knife and a gun, a photograph of the founder of the don's family, or other symbols important to the Big Guy.

3. **The neophyte is accompanied by at least three "men of honor" within the Family; the oldest of them reminds the candidate that he's been brought into the Family's house to protect the weak from the strong.** Right.

4. **The oldest man of honor cuts the finger of the neophyte (or sometimes the don does the cutting) and then presents him with a sacred image, usually a saint card.**

   The saint card was popular in the Catholic Church in the last century; they contained a representation of the saint, usually a reprint from one of the old masters, and the story of the saint on the back. This pricking of the finger is why the whole ceremony is sometimes called _Punciuto_, from the root for the verb _pricked_.

5. **The neophyte then smears the card with his blood and sets it on fire.**

   The candidate must hold the card in his hands as it burns. After the card turns to ashes, the neophyte swears before the silent don, "May my flesh burn like this saint if I fail to keep my oath."

   The oath he's speaking of is the oath of _Omertà_, which was explained in the opening of this chapter. This sacred oath of silence is the most important one a member of the Mafia will ever take. Even if you or your loved ones are the victims of someone within the Family, you will never betray its secrets, and you will _never_ cooperate with the authorities, or any other outsiders, in betraying what you know of the organization. It can be a heavy oath to bear. For example, if you're ratted out and sent to the slammer for a crime that someone else in the Family committed, you're expected to serve your time and keep your mouth shut. To break this sacred oath is a death sentence.

The mob bosses were devout Catholics in their fashion, and the records of their crimes are loaded with their idea of proof. Joe Colombo was given a jewel-studded crown stolen from a Brooklyn church. He ordered it returned, and when the thief kept three of the jewels, Colombo ordered him murdered, left with a rosary around his neck. Joe Profaci had two petty thieves tortured to death for robbing a Catholic donation box.

The Ongoing Struggle to Crush the Mafia

The great divide in dialects, culture, and economic wealth that separated Sicily from mainland Italy still resonates into the 21st century. Today Sicily is considered to be a part of Italy, although after the fall of Mussolini, in 1947, it was granted a special autonomous status, meaning that in many respects, it's now a country of its own. This left the problem of dealing with the dons to the local magistrates. They would soon discover that the code of Omertà combined with Mafia ruthlessness would make this a tall order.

As a magistrate, cop, or judge in Sicily, you were either on the Mafia's payroll, or you were in their gun sights. The hundreds of funerals for magistrates who didn't play by these rules that darkened the late 19th and early 20th century bore silent witness to the power of la Cosa Nostra.

Ever since 1903, police in New York and New Orleans have known there was an "Atlantic pipeline," a tie between Sicilian crime in the U.S. and Palermo. But what the Americans were too naïve to understand was the absolute power of the dons over Sicily. An American cop named Joe Petrosino famously walked right into Sicily without understanding this fact of life.

Taking the fight back to Sicily

As the Sicilian gang influence became powerful in New York (see the section, "Mafia and Organized Crime in America," earlier in this chapter), Joe Petrosino convinced his superiors that they needed a special Italian squad — officers who knew the language and the methods of the Mafia. It was created, and he was promoted to lieutenant in charge in 1908. He had many successes with solving murders and kidnappings. He even protected the world-renowned opera singer Enrico Caruso, when the Black Hand, the early Mafia, attempted to extort money from him.

Petrosino soon figured out that to bring down Sicilian gangs like the Black Hand in the U.S., he had to start at the source. And so, in March of 1909, he went to Sicily undercover to investigate. He arrived on March 9, and checked into a Palermo hotel under the name Guglielmo De Simini. On March 12, he was waiting, unarmed, to meet a contact in the Piazza Marina, when two men gunned him down in the street. He was killed instantly. For Americans, it was a shock and an outrage; in Palermo, there was hardly a ripple. For a Sicilian, this death was to be expected for someone who openly opposed the Mafia.

All through the 1960s, during the so-called First Mafia War in Sicily, it was open season on honest government officials. Even by the 1980s, there were two kinds of magistrates in Sicily: the Mafia ones, and the dead ones. This was the period of the Second Mafia War, when the Corleonese Family, who weren't even in the Cupola, tried to take over the heroin trade by literally declaring war on both the government and *all* the other Mafia families. It was a bloodbath. Led by a little maniac named Toto Riina, nicknamed "the Beast," the violence level reached an all-time high, both in numbers and in gruesomeness. No more bullet to the back of the head. Now it was chain saws and torture murders. No more leaving the family alone. Riina killed them all, and if he could get hold of their children, he killed them, too.

It seems strange that when director Francis Ford Coppola set out to make his classic *The Godfather,* he chose the name of "Corleone" for his character. Corleone is a real place, a small town in the Province of Palermo in northwestern Sicily. In fact, the family of the film's lead, Al Pacino, immigrated from there. But it's strange because, in the real history of the Sicilian Mafia, the *Corleonese* of Toto Riinawere brash outsiders who flooded Sicily in a sea of blood.

Two real "men of honor"

After the death of so many officials over the years, it might seem that the Sicilian people were shockproof, but it wasn't so. During this second period of bloody Mafia violence in the 1980s, a very brave Sicilian magistrate stepped up to the plate to take on the Cosa Nostra. His name was Giovanni Falcone, and he formed a task force of prosecutors to bring the Mafia down. His closest friend from childhood was named Paulo Borsellino, a fellow attorney, and Falcone drafted him into the battle as his second-in-command. For more than a decade, they had one spectacular success after another.

The most famous success was called "the Maxi Trial" for the incredibly large number of defendants. A staggering 474 defendants were put on trial; 119 of them, who'd escaped, were tried in absentia. Falcone finally got a mobster to turn informant — a powerful man extradited from Brazil named Tommaso Buscetta, who'd lost many close family members. Under Falcone's expert handling, Buscetta started to sing. The Maxi Trial was the result. Until that time, the very existence of the Mafia had been either denied or downplayed by officials who were in its pocket. Falcone was the first to name them openly for who and what they were.

The trial took two years to pull off. In the end, 360 of the defendants were convicted, a great victory for Italian justice. The state seemed to be winning the war. In fact, it was Falcone's naming of the Mafia as an organization, and his trying of them as a whole, rather than as individuals for individual crimes, that inspired U.S. officials in the same fight to draft the successful RICO Act. (See "The Valachi Papers" earlier in this chapter.)

In the beginning, the people around him held their breath, waiting for Falcone to be assassinated. But as the years passed, it seemed that a golden glow of good luck surrounded the man. On May 23, 1992, that luck ran out. Falcone landed at Palermo airport with his wife, and then drove in a caravan of three cars toward the capital city at high speed, in case of sniper attack. A Mafia lookout spotted them with binoculars outside Capaci and picked up a cell phone. Moments later, a shattering explosion from about 400 kegs of explosives laid into hidden roadside trenches and drain pipes took out a huge section of the highway. It left an enormous, debris-filled crater. Giovanni Falcone was killed, along with his wife, Francesca Morvillo, who was also a magistrate, as well as three of his police escort bodyguards.

Many Sicilian officials said that the only parallel in feeling in America would've been the death of JFK. The entire nation of Italy was steeped in mourning for its hero. But there would be no time to put away the black dresses and suits before they were needed again. On July 19, less than two months later, Falcone's successor, Paulo Borsellino, was killed. He went to ring the bell at his mother's apartment house in Palermo to pick her up for a doctor's appointment. At that pre-arranged signal, an enormous car bomb nearby exploded. The shock could be felt for miles — windows were broken in the apartment building 11 floors up. Borsellino was killed instantly, along with five of his bodyguards.

We're mad as hell, and we're not going to take it anymore!

The island of Sicily erupted, as grief turned to rage, and rage was taken to the streets. In many respects, from that moment, the Mafia's days were numbered, at least as a hidden society. No one was looking the other way anymore. The Italian government sent thousands of troops to help the Sicilian police and people wipe out the Mafia. Mafiosos fled the island like rats out of a flooded drain. Finally, in 1998, the troops went home. The Mafia was pronounced officially dead in Sicily.

So, is the Cosa Nostra really dead? It would seem that, apart from the new mafia organizations in Italy, Cosa Nostra is still breathing. The president of the Sicilian Region has been under investigation for Mafia ties, and another investigation is looking into Mafia infiltration of the Forza Italia political party. As Mark Twain said on reading his own obituary, "The reports of my death are greatly exaggerated."

Other Mafias, Lost and Found

"Mafia" is one of those words like "Kleenex" or "Coke," in that the product itself was long ago merged with the brand name in the public's perception. Yet, in the late 20th century, the word, which was coined by the international press, was well chosen, because these copycat criminal organizations were inspired by the Mafia, and often structured in the same pyramid pattern. There have been many mafias through the years, some lost to history and faded from memory. Others are relatively new, and are yet to achieve any fame, particularly in America.

Apart from often having an international reach, these groups generally share something else with the Mafia — their birth occurred during a time in which the government was weak or virtually non-existent. In many cases it's difficult for American intelligence to gauge who's really running the country — the government or the forces of organized crime.

Going Italian

There are quite a few new Italian-based mafias active in the United States; the FBI refers to them as a whole as "IOC," Italian Organized Crime. They're all involved in the same old Mafia-style operations: drug dealing, arms sales, counterfeiting, smuggling of both goods and people, illegal gambling, kidnapping, blackmail, and extortion. They use the classic Mafia methods to maintain their power base — bribery, terror, and assassination.

The scary part about all these new Italian mafias is that they have such chummy relations with all the other mafias in Russia, China, Eastern Europe, and just about anywhere else on the planet. Here are the major "other Italian mafias."

The Comorra

The Comorra reached its height of fame and power about the time the Mafia was getting big in Sicily, in the late 19th century. In fact, the Comorra became so powerful in the area around Naples that the Borbón monarchs drafted them into key positions in the police and the military, as well as the civil service. Although they shared much with the Mafia, from thievery and extortion to the code of Omertà, their big game was piracy.

Like the Mafia, the Comorra survived the attempts of dictator Benito Mussolini to stamp them out, but afterwards they were never again as powerful. In America, the Comorra was absorbed by the powerful Morello crime family early on, and so eventually into the American Mafia. However, it does make a point of interest that the Comorra may be more powerful in Italy today than it was a century ago. It seems that the Comorra muscled in on the garbage business in the Campanian region of Italy, for which Naples is the capital. Unfortunately, they ran it in typical Mafia fashion, ignoring laws about disposal, mixing in heavy metals and chemical waste with garbage that is supposed to be free of such things, and burning it when they were found out, causing very bad pollution problems in the area. The government, as this is being written, is attempting to bring the Comorra to heel over the problem, but it's no mean feat.

The 'Ndrangheta

The 'Ndrangheta (which means *The Honored Society*) is little-known in this country. They have ties to the Sicilian Mafia because of their geographic nearness — their central turf is in Calabria, the boot tip of Italy. Italian authorities estimate about 5,000 members in 100 'Ndrangheta clans around Calabria. For their small number they're remarkably wealthy, mostly from drug money, but also from quasi-legitimate businesses in restaurants, supermarkets, and of course, that old mafia standby, the construction business. (What is it about concrete and mobsters? Even Yasir Arafat was in the concrete business.)

They're often called mafiosi in the press, but they're known properly as *'ndrinu*. Occasionally 'Ndrangheta groups will pop up far from home; outposts have been discovered in Australia, France, Spain, and even Canada. But for the most part, they're a tighter-knit group than the Mafia, and they've done a better job of keeping a low profile.

The Sacra corona unita

The Sacra corona unita, or United Sacred Crown (aka the SCU), is a much newer mafialike organization in Apulia along the southern boot heel, especially in Brindisi and Lecce. They're principally smugglers, smuggling Albanians into Italy (and into prostitution), as well as smuggling cigarettes, drugs, and arms. There are about 50 clans and 2,000 members. They have ties to other mafia groups in Eastern Europe, as well as Russia and Columbia. They also may have extended into Florida, Illinois, and New York.

The Stidda

The Stidda is another new mafia, born on the southeast coast of Italy, but moving in on northern Italy, where mafia activity has historically been far less prevalent. The reign of terror on Sicily brought about a general disenchantment with Cosa Nostra, and many of the capos in this organization in particular are men who walked away during the Corleonese wars. For this reason, the bloodthirsty Toto Riina not only waged war on all the families of Cosa Nostra, but also on the Stidda, as well, killing over a thousand of them before he was finally put away. The fact that they remained standing has given them a great deal of respect as a mafia organization.

Stidda means "star" in the Sicilian dialect. Many members of the Stidda, the *stiddari,* have a tattoo of five green marks in a circle that look like a star, the symbol of their creed, *i punti della malavita,* or "the points of the criminal life." For this five-pointed symbol they're also sometimes called "the Fifth Mafia."

The Mala del Brenta

The Mala del Brenta, also called *la Mafia del Brenta* or *Malavita del Brenta,* is the Venetian version of the Mafia. It's a rare bird, being classified under Italian law as a mafia-type organization, despite being operated by northerners. Still, it was originally spawned in the south. For the last 20 years they've been operating in the Veneto region of northern Italy, moving as far northeast as Yugoslavia, Hungary, and other former Russian satellite nations.

But there are few areas of Italy more independent-minded than Venice; there is, in fact, a strong political party there in favor of achieving a breakaway status that has caused a lot of trouble in the last 20 years. So of course, the name "mafia" wasn't good enough; they had to have a name of their own for essentially the same organization.

Going International

The last four decades have proved one thing for certain — you don't have to be Italian to have a mafia. Everybody, it seems, wants to be Don Corleone. Below are the most prominent of the international mafia organizations:

- **Russia** should certainly get pride of place for the Russian *Mafyia* — also called *Bratva.* Probably the most powerful mafia in the world, because their emergence from the shadowy world of the Russian black market in 1991 occurred as the Soviet system was headed for a tumble. They are now a worldwide operation, and according to an FBI agent assigned to them, the Mafyia is far more ruthless than the American Mafia. Or, in his words, "These guys'll shoot you just to see if the gun works." Russia being a poor country, they like to live large, though at least they have a sense of humor about it — several have big American cars with a horn that plays the theme from *The Godfather.* The kingpins are never seen without a bodyguard almost always in the uniform of dark pants and a black leather bomber jacket. The Russian Mafyia's success spawned numerous mafias behind the former Iron Curtain, such as the Chechen mafia and Albanian mafia. Their yearly profits are in the hundreds of millions, and their economic strength probably outstrips that of the legitimate Soviet economy.

- **Great Britain** is overrun with London street gangs, some of whom have become very powerful. The good old Irish mob, which still has major teeth in Boston and New York, also operates there. Some of the mobs are referred to by family names, the Brindles or the Daleys, but the most powerful is purported to be the Adams Family, aka the Clerkenwell Syndicate or the A-Team. Despite the fact that their boss, Terry Adams, went to jail in 2007, and MI-5 is taking a page from the FBI playbook and monitoring every word they say, the A-Team is still a powerful underworld society.

✔ **France** is still known for its Unione Corse, or Corsican underworld. Like Napoleon, it was born on the island of Corsica of mostly Italian descent, but moved up into Marseilles (still its principal stronghold) and the rest of France. Unione Corse is most famous for its heroin trade, the infamous French Connection of 1940–1972.

✔ **Central America** has numerous gangs, but the most powerful are probably the remnants of the Colombian drug lords, like the Black Eagles or the Norte del Valle cartel, and the new kids on the block, called MS-13, a ruthless secret organization dealing in drugs, forced prostitution, and general nastiness that is moving up into the U.S.

✔ **The Chinese Triads** are very old underworld secret societies, initially formed as a group of revolutionaries who wanted to overthrow the Manchu Dynasty. When that task was completed, they had nothing else to occupy their time, and so turned to crime. In America, the infamous Chinese Tong considered themselves an offshoot of the Triads.

✔ **Japan** has one of the most colorful mafias, literally, with the *Yakuza,* the famous tattoo-covered Japanese mobsters, with rituals like *Yubitsume,* which is ritually cutting off a finger as penance. They deal in drugs, extortion, and forced prostitution, particularly in Southeast Asia.

✔ **Nigeria,** last but not least, has set upon the world the irritation of the Nigerian OC crime brotherhood, which has become a particular thorn in the side of Internet cruisers, because it's hard to move through the World Wide Web without being assaulted by one of their numerous scams to get their hands on your private banking information.

The Impact of the Mafia on Popular Culture

The mob and the movies have had a symbiotic relationship for longer than most people realize. And if you're wondering what a *symbiotic* relationship is, well, did you ever hear the story of the bird in Africa that rides around on a rhinoceros's back? The *tickbird* survives by eating ticks and other bugs off the rhino's back, and the rhino acts as the tickbird's great big bodyguard. This is a symbiotic relationship, and the mob has had one with the movies since the birth of them both in America.

In the early years of the 20th century, the era of silent films, new immigrants flocked to the movies — by 1907, roughly 200,000 of them attended one of New York's 500 movie houses every single day. Early gangsters loved going to the movies as much as any other immigrants, and rather than being offended by them, they loved gangster movies. They imitated the dress and the mannerisms of the actors who played them. And the movies loved to claim to be putting the real story of gangsterism in America on film, scouring newspaper stories for their plotlines, and making up the actors to look like newspaper photographs of real Black Hand or other gang members. *Musketeers of Pig Alley,* a D. W. Griffith film of 1912, was shot on location on the Lower East Side, and promoters claimed that real gangsters had been used as extras and bit players, and had even served as technical advisors on the film's big gunfight sequence.

Close to 80 percent of the silent movies ever made are lost to historians. That's because they were shot on something called *celluloid nitrate film stock,* which was, believe it or not, combustible. If you open up an old can of film, the smell that hits you is unforgettable, not to mention the orange acid all over the celluloid base that has literally eaten away the image. Occasionally, these stored cans of film would self-ignite, causing a fire that could wipe out hundreds of other films. Unfortunately, it wasn't until the 1970s that universities and fans started getting into the business of film preservation, and by that time, silent films were already lost.

Early gangster films

Despite the number of lost silents, the date on the oldest surviving gangster film is still impressive — 1906. It was a one-reeler (a reel of film lasted ten minutes) called *The Black Hand,* which tells the melodramatic tale of a shopkeeper in New York who goes head to head with the Black Hand and gets his little daughter kidnapped by them. It was based on newspaper reports at the time on the activities of the Black Hand in the Five Points, though of course, it has a happy ending, with a triumph of justice over lawlessness. It was so popular it was remade three times soon after. And the symbiotic relationship was already unfolding, because members of the Black Hand started dressing and wearing their hair like the classic "Mustache Pete" portrayed in the film.

By the early 1920s, movies were getting a little more sophisticated and less obsessed with a happy ending. When Lon Chaney played gangster Big Mike in the 1920's *Outside the Law,* real gangsters aped his mannerisms and looks. Yet the great age of movie gangsters didn't even occur until the arrival of the talkies. These gritty and hard-edged dramas came just on the heels of sound in 1929, and they were masterpieces still treasured today. It made stars out of some very unlikely Warner Brothers contract players, but the public couldn't get enough of Humphrey Bogart, Edward G. Robinson, and the ultimate gangster pinup, James Cagney. It's a testament to Cagney's talent that he was able to survive being typecast, because he defined the consummate American mobster in such films as *The Public Enemy, The Roaring Twenties,* and *White Heat.* The same was true of Edward G. Robinson, whose talent kept him from staying forever the bad guy after unforgettable performances at the dawn of sound in *Outside the Law, Little Caesar,* and a bit later in films like *The Last Gangster* and *Key Largo.*

The weird symbiosis continued as filmmakers struggled to do gangsters that were realistic, while the gangsters were picking up the clothing, slang, and mannerisms of the mobsters they saw on film.

The Godfather myth cycle

Joe Valachi appeared before Congress in 1963. Next came *The Valachi Papers* in 1968, the true story of the mob informant. The book was a very big hit. Then, on its heels, came Mario Puzo and *The Godfather,* in 1969. This was the smash novel of all time, and Mob mania was about to take hold of the country.

Puzo considered it a pity that his first book on the subject of Sicilian immigrants, *The Fortunate Pilgrim,* was respected, but not a hit. It was the story of his immigrant mother's struggle to make it in a new land, and in Puzo's opinion, it was a better, truer book than *The Godfather.* Personally, we think both books are great. A few Mafia films came along in the wake of Valachi and Mario Puzo, but none captured the public's imagination.

Then, when everybody in Hollywood said you couldn't recapture the glory days of the 1930s, and that the gangster film was as dead as the micro-mini skirt, the Queen Mother of all mob movies came looming up over the horizon, probably one of the ten greatest American films ever made — Francis Ford Coppola's *The Godfather.*

The Godfather was seared into the public consciousness, its images part of the fabric of our culture. In 1962, the public was aware of organized crime, but the Mafia was almost unheard of — even in Sicily they denied its existence. By 1972, the Mafia was as well known an American institution as baseball or hot dogs or Marilyn Monroe, an unbelievable about-face. Coppola's film also became one of America's leading exports, sending those indelible images around the world, until, from Russia to Venezuela, everybody wanted to be Don Corleone.

The Godfather was rich in characterization, in appearance, and in historical truth. Even Don Tommasso Buscetta, the most powerful Sicilian Mafia figure to ever turn state's evidence, said it was his favorite film (though he thought the business at the end with everyone kissing Michael Corleone's ring wasn't realistic). By the time Coppola had done two sequels to the film, it took on the appearance of an American myth cycle, something like a Wagnerian opera for a German.

And for good or ill, Coppola also unleashed on America a new onslaught of mob films, from *Goodfellas* to *The Sopranos,* still with us today, though they're far more violent and obscenity laced than any studio would have tolerated in the golden age of Cagney and Bogart and Robinson. Every major Hollywood director, it seems, has done his take on the mob, hoping for the same cash cow. This has only helped to create the glamorous aura surrounding the Mafia that's spread around the world.

Old Blue Eyes and the boys

Did Frank Sinatra really get an Oscar-winning part in *From Here to Eternity* because the producer woke up with a horse's head in his bed? Probably not. This colorful fiction was born in the mind of Mario Puzo in the novel *The Godfather,* which, in all fairness, was based on the stories Puzo had grown up hearing about the mob.

For Frank Sinatra, 1951 was a lousy year. He was going through a bitter and protracted divorce, while his career was literally in the toilet. Hollywood and music business trades were openly calling him a has-been, while the panting hordes of bobby soxers who'd once mobbed him wherever he went in 1942 were now long gone.

It was during this difficult period that he was called before the Kefauver Congressional Committee, the first Senate committee to investigate organized crime, which they generally called "the Syndicate." Sinatra's faded celebrity at least spared him the indignity of being dragged before the cameras in the committee room. He was allowed to give his testimony at four in the morning, in the private office of his attorney. But the ink still stuck, and for all his life his name would be associated with organized crime.

Sinatra had read James Jones's best-selling novel *From Here to Eternity,* and he knew that he was born to play the doomed soldier Maggio. But Harry Cohn, the head of Columbia Pictures, treated him with complete contempt, even demanding that Sinatra do a screen test, a humiliating thing for a man who'd already shown his natural acting gifts in several films. But Sinatra did the test, gladly, and the word on the lot was that he had the part, because the test was terrific. But Harry Cohn, who was a legendary boor, perhaps the most boorish of all the studio moguls of his day, still treated Sinatra with a "Don't call us, we'll call you" attitude. However, it's not likely that Sinatra got the part by having his friends in the Mafia put the squeeze on Cohn, no matter how colorful a story it makes. It's far more likely that Sinatra's wife, actress Ava Gardner, helped him get the part. She was the hottest actress in Hollywood at that moment, and Cohn wasn't likely to refuse her anything she agitated for.

Nevertheless, there's no denying that Sinatra's Mob ties had helped him in his early career. You didn't need to put a horse's head in anyone's bed; just mentioning that Lucky Luciano was your dear friend could get you nightclub work in the 1930s. The fact is that Sinatra, born in Brooklyn, had hung out on the Lower East Side and made friends with gangsters, friendships that would last his whole life. He was particularly close to Sam Giancana (notorious head of the Chicago Outfit), Lucky Luciano, and Willie Moretti, a high-ranking underboss of the Genovese Family. Sinatra was not a gangster, but a man who liked hanging out with gangsters. Or as one music critic put it, it was hard to tell whether Sinatra was a gangster groupie or the gangsters were Sinatra groupies. Ultimately, it was the durable talent of "the Voice" that made him an Oscar-winning actor and America's premiere pop singer of the 20th century.

Chapter 15

Banks and Super Committees: Knowing All, Owning All, Controlling All

In This Chapter

▷ Revealing evil bankers and their plots

▷ Understanding the committees and commissions of the past

*T*his chapter discusses the distrust of international bankers, and the origin of the notion of the Jewish Bankers who conspiracists believe control the world's banking. We follow that with the lineup of the most mentioned (and least trusted) one-world, one-government, New World Order committees — the Rhodes-Milner Round Table, Tri-Lats, CFRs, Bilderbergers, and the creepy outdoor rituals of the Bohemian Grove. Think of them all as the zoning commission for world domination.

Bankers and Nefarious Banking Plots

Much of 21st-century anti-Semitism harps on the subject of Jews as the "world's bankers," controlling the world's economy (as explained in Chapter 6). The old favorite was that "five Jew bankers" (most notably, the members of the Rothschild banking family — we'll get to them in this chapter) ran everything; now, modern conspiracists have upped the ante to eight Jewish bankers, and they run the U.S. Federal Reserve. But, what about the Rockefellers and the Morgans, the Goulds and the Fisks? They weren't Jewish. What about Cecil Rhodes? (They all get to Cecil Rhodes, sooner or later. And so do we.) He wasn't Jewish, either. How can it be said that the Jews run all the banks?

Well, according to some conspiracists, they still do; others say they don't. It depends on whose conspiracy magnum opus you're reading. Some subscribe to the theory of a tightly-knit, White Anglo-Saxon Protestant (WASP) group of financiers that really run things, their history generally dated from John D. Rockefeller, the Standard Oil giant straddling early-20th-century history, and America's first billionaire. For them, the nasty derogatory label isn't "Jew;" it's "banker." Others, who don't like to let go of the "five Jew bankers" theory, believe that Rothschild's money seeded these WASP empires, and that they were basically all in this together, because race and religion have nothing to do with it — money and power are the only things that matter.

However, one principle guides it all — international financiers control all historical events and get rich off them. They start all the wars, so they can loan money to both sides. They reap the benefit of boom years, but arrange busts, like the 1929 Stock Market Crash, so they have an excuse to use a time of devalued currency to snap up huge chunks of real estate and foreclosed property.

Why do the Jews get the banking blame?

Way back in the old days, the Catholic Church, based on a very small passage in Luke, forbade what they called usury, the practice of lending money. With the arrival of the Middle Ages, hatred of the Jews became part of the fabric of European culture. For that reason, Jews were banned from the powerful guilds, the labor unions that controlled most of the various jobs. Confined to the ghetto, cut off from society, there weren't that many ways to make a living left open to them. Not being Christian, and therefore not forbidden by the Catholic Church to lend money, it became easy for Jews to slip into both pawnbroking and moneylending.

Moneylending

The interest charged by Jewish moneylenders was high. This is one accusation of the Jew-baiters that's true. It could go as high as 50 percent, because the risk in loaning money to Christians was so high. See it from the lender's perspective; the next pogrom or the next mass expulsion of the nation's Jews might leave you holding the bag, not to mention the fact that powerful Christians often simply refused to pay back the loan, figuring the Jews had little legal recourse against them. Kings were often the worst offenders. They may have lived the high life, but most of them weren't good money managers, with some outstanding exceptions, and they were always on the mooch. So, they borrowed money to hire mercenaries, to build a new capital, or to put on a swell show for a visiting foreign king whose daughter was marrying their son.

There were other moneylenders in the Middle Ages; the bankers of Lombard, for example, being the most famous. Lombards were Northern Italians living in France (and elsewhere) who practiced a form of usury that slipped around the church by setting things up along the lines of a pawnshop; "Lombard Street" in a European city was usually where the pawnbrokers were.

Both Jews and Lombards became part of the "merchants and bankers" structure of finance in the early Middle Ages, using an idea that was a bit older. The Christian Knights Templar had been the largest bankers of Europe during the Crusades, issuing paper documents, like deposit slips, for money deposited in one of their thousands of preceptories. The slip could then be cashed at another preceptory. This made it easier for pilgrims making the long and dangerous voyage to the Holy Land, because they did not have to carry gold or valuables on their persons.

Medieval trade fairs picked up on the same idea. You could go to one fair, and a merchant would give you a bill of exchange, refundable at another fair, so you didn't have to hassle with actually carrying gold on buying trips.

This was really the beginning of banking in Europe. The Lombards were the biggest force in trade-fair banking, but the Jews did it, as well. By the 16th century, banking in London, for example, which had grown out of the money-lending going on in the London coffee houses, would lead to the founding by Queen Elizabeth I of the Royal Exchange, the famous center of the city's commerce.

The Court Jew

Eventually, the myth, or the truth, of Jewish prowess in banking (you've got to learn something after five centuries) was so great that a peculiar social phenomenon grew up in Europe — the "Court Jew." It started during the Renaissance, and was particularly popular in the courts of the petty Germanic kings of the Holy Roman Empire. Sometimes they were also called "court factors," or "chamber agents." These were men deemed especially knowledgeable about money. Occasionally they were Jewish moneylenders who had leant money to the duke or king. They were brought to court and kept close to the ruler to advise him in all money matters, and often came up with clever ideas, such as various lotteries and tontines, to make the ruler money as well.

Court Jews both enjoyed and suffered an odd status, neither fish nor fowl. They had certain social privileges in the Christian world, and of course prominence among other Jews. But there was also jealousy and bitter resentment from their fellow Jews, as well as dangers in the Christian world, not to mention being the ruler's favorite target for jokes, something of a royal stooge. The other dangers were more life threatening; if a petty king or prince owed his court Jew money, he might just whip up a pogrom, a persecution of the Jews, and quietly get rid of him. Court Jews could find themselves rising precariously high, sometimes even into diplomatic circles. But again, if things went wrong, they made the perfect scapegoat.

Protestantism changes the rules

As Protestantism began to arise, particularly in the states that are now modern Germany, the middle classes embraced it with open arms at least in part because Protestantism was tailor made for the man of business. There was no injunction against moneylending in the Protestant faith, and many businessmen of the great early Protestant states of the Netherlands and Germany and England got into this business, competing with and pushing aside the great Jewish moneylending families. Here was born the Protestant work ethic, and the pride, rather than Catholic shame, to be found in acquiring wealth from labor and business savvy. Still, Jewish competitors in this new, 16th- and 17th-century banking universe kept Protestants on their toes.

Still, the belief that banks were all in the hands of Jews became commonplace all over Europe and remained strong well into the 20th century and beyond. The most notorious Nazi propaganda film of all time, *Jew Süss,* fixed the image of the wily and usurious Jew banker in the public consciousness. It didn't matter that most of the greatest fortunes in the world were in the hands of Gentiles, like the Morgans and the Rockefellers and the Carnegies. The image was set in stone; the Jews ruled the banks, and the banks ruled the world.

The Rothschild banking family

Of all the boogeymen, all the disliked people of the conspiracy universe, there's none more universally suspected than the Rothschild family. Sooner or later, conspiracists from Texe Marrs to David Icke to Louis Farrakhan all get to the Rothschilds. To these guys, they're the very soul of evil.

The Rothschilds are a wealthy and powerful family. And when one looks at their history, it's easy to see that old Mayer Bauer Rothschild, the founder of their empire, was pretty smart, keeping all the banks family owned (as they still are today). It certainly made his empire elastic enough to survive one disaster after another, from Napoleon's victory at Austerlitz to the arrival of the Nazis.

Mayer Rothschild was a man who started with almost nothing, a Jewish pawnbroker in the city of Frankfort. He built his fortune out of his first big loan, to Wilhelm IX, Elector of Hesse-Cassel, holder of one of the largest private fortunes in Europe. Wilhelm discovered that Mayer Rothschild was dependable, shrewd, and scrupulously honest.

When Wilhelm was driven out of his country for several years during the Napoleonic Wars, as were many kings, he left his fortune in Mayer's hands. Mayer Rothschild would remain his closest advisor.

Frankfurt was the wheeling-and-dealing capital of European banking and stock speculation, a powerful center of the medieval trade fairs. In Mayer's day, Frankfurt was ruled by the Hapsburgs, and he learned one thing from them: Keep it in the family. That was how the Hapsburgs procreated and married their way into numberless branches of royalty, creating ruling houses of the Holy Roman Empire, the Austro-Hungarian Empire (Germany), Spain,

Portugal, Tuscany, Hungary, and more. It was even a Hapsburg princess who married Napoleon after he dumped the empress Josephine, in his obvious attempt to polish up his humble Corsican bloodline.

Mayer became like a mini-Habsburg, encouraging his sons to marry cousins or relations of some sort. He then set his five sons up in five banks across Europe, the cleverest move a financier ever made. If the House of Rothschild in Naples got in trouble, the House of Rothschild in Vienna or London could take up the slack. These five houses in five major capitals kept the family on top of every important development in politics that affected the world of finance. Consequently, Mayer Rothschild became the most powerful money-lender of the age. He was called a banker by then — a banker who walked with kings.

Remaining a family business, even today, has enabled the Rothschilds to maneuver more shrewdly, with more resilience. Their most recent reorganization and merger with their London branch has made Rothschild & Cie Banque, once again, the most important bank in France.

Perils of the Federal Reserve

Where pure banking conspiracism is concerned, it all arrives, sooner or later, at the U.S. Federal Reserve Bank, affectionately known as "the Fed." The essential structure of the Fed is so unusual that it leaves the door wide open for conspiracists to cry foul.

The Federal Reserve isn't really "federal" at all. The name is purposefully misleading. In fact, it's a consortium of *private* banks and holding companies that together form the core of the banking system of the United States. It was formed out of private interests in 1913 (the same year of the graduated personal income tax); however, it does have a governing board of presidential appointees, making it something of a shotgun wedding between a private and a public institution.

These "national banks" become members by buying stock in their district from the Federal Reserve and are required by law to jump through all sorts of hoops. The rules of the Fed determine how much they have to have in reserve, among other things. In theory, they don't operate for profit, and they can't sell off the stock they own in the Fed, any more than they can make loans based on their government-mandated reserves.

However, thanks to the system engineered by the Fed, those reserves are meaningless. At one time, paper money was literally a receipt for an equal amount of gold in the bank. Now that piece of paper is just, well, a piece of paper. It's only money because we *believe* it's money. But it's paper, and they print as much of it as they like, thereby causing an ever-spiraling devaluation of currency.

"I killed the Bank"

In the first struggling years of the United States, the nation didn't have much in the way of an international impact and didn't have any sort of federal bank. Alexander Hamilton, Secretary of the Treasury, was annoyed to no end. It was an article of faith for Alexander Hamilton that the federal government had to have a national bank, which would assume the debt of the states and control the federal debt. (There's a task.) He also founded the U.S. Mint and, finally, the First National Bank of the United States, in 1791.

At that time, America had only three banks. Unfortunately, it also had over 50 different kinds of currency, the most popular still being British pounds. But people were just as likely to pay for things with anything from a Spanish gold doubloon to a French bank note or a Portuguese real. It was economic chaos. A system of credit and a national coinage had to be established; Hamilton's bank achieved this.

But when the bank's 20-year charter from the Congress ran out in 1811, the Congress chose not to renew it, and the bank folded, which led to arguments aplenty, not to mention street riots, over the eventual establishment of the Second Bank of the United States, whose principal foe was President Andrew Jackson. It was rechartered in 1816, but Jackson declared war on it, refusing to deposit federal funds into a privately owned bank. It lost its federal charter in 1836.

Jackson routinely referred to all bankers (you know, the guys investing their private money into the future of the United States) as "vipers," and the bank as "subversive," though he did have a point when he said that it was, in some respects, a monopoly, one that had been caught in several financial scandals. Yet, all states had the right to charter banks anytime they wanted to. Jackson was so proud of this veto that the hero of the Creek Wars and the War of 1812, not to mention the president, had put on his tombstone "I killed the Bank." National banks wouldn't rear their head again in America until 1863, because, once again, there were too many different currencies out there, issued by individual states, that caused economic chaos and destabilization.

For many years, conspiracists have said that it isn't "Reagan's economy" or "Bush's economy" or "Clinton's economy" — it's Alan Greenspan's economy. And really, there's a great deal of truth in it. Despite political changes, Alan Greenspan remained chairman of the Fed for nearly 20 years. Current Fed chairman Ben Bernanke is a personal protégé of his. For conspiracists, this is more proof that political parties are all smoke and mirrors to keep the masses amused, but have nothing whatsoever to do with who's running things.

In the same way that your credit card company can keep you paying off just the interest for years, without ever touching the principle of the debt, that's all our government ever does with this complex web of bankers, making them ever richer. On the other hand, the bankers didn't have a gun in the back of the government forcing it to drive the nation further and further into debt. There is much chatter amongst conspiracists that this is a way for the wealthy to control the government, but it seems to us that this is a two-way street — it's also a way for the government to feed off its wealthiest citizens.

This is what Alexander Hamilton envisioned in his first national Bank of America: The nation's wealthiest men buy shares in the future of America, in the same way that a man buys shares in a company, and the government uses that money to build the nation. Hamilton understood something that a lot of clever businessmen will still tell you today; whenever possible while buying something, use somebody else's money to do it with.

Supersecret Committees

In this section you will find what many conspiracists fear most — the alleged supersecret committees that meet privately around the world and decide the destiny of the rest of us poor, clueless "sheeple." In truth, virtually all these groups have meetings that issue reports, Web sites that publicize their activities, and even lists of their members and guests. But it's the closed doors and the importance of their participants that raise the nervous hackles on investigators and the perennially suspicious. Worried about the undue influence of the United Nations on national sovereignty? Mere pikers, compared to these groups.

Cecil Rhodes and the Rhodes-Milner Round Table

You have undoubtedly heard of academic brain boxes known as Rhodes scholars (see the "Rhodes scholarships" sidebar), but you may not have heard of the man who they're named for — Cecil John Rhodes. Rhodes is a regular in the Rogues Gallery of conspiracism, and his name gets attached to a passing parade of secret "world government" New World Order groups. There's a reason for that. He was the founder of the De Beers diamond company, which at one time controlled 90 percent of the diamonds sold around the world, and still about 60 percent these days. A diamond is forever, indeed.

Rhodes was born in England in 1853, but made his fortune on the African continent. He was a sickly child and was sent from England to live with his brother in the healthier climate of Cape Colony (what's now South Africa) in 1870. Diamonds were discovered nearby in Kimberley, and Rhodes became a prospector. By the time he was just 19, he'd already made a tidy fortune in the diamond business. He went back home to study at Oxford between 1873 and 1881, but returned to Africa where he spent the rest of his life.

Rhodes was a staunch advocate of British colonialism, from which he profited handsomely. He wasn't shy about using powerful friends in English government to exact mineral rights and mining claims across the colonies in Africa. In 1888, he founded De Beers Consolidated Mines Ltd. and monopolized the diamond business across much of what's now South Africa, Zambia, Zimbabwe, and Botswana.

In honor of his activities and prestige, the region of Zambia and Zimbabwe were named Rhodesia. And how did Rhodes manage to afford to snap up all the major and minor diamond mining in southern Africa? By a massive loan from his friend Lord Nathan Mayer Rothschild and the London House of Rothschild.

Rhodes had his own peculiar brand of colonial philosophy. He believed that the English "race" was the most "civilizing" on Earth, and that British colonialism would raise up the "inferior" people of the world. Cape Colony, Australia, New Zealand, and Canada (what he thought of as the "white" colonies of Britain) would extend the Empire to new heights of greatness, and of course improve the lot of those miserable darker natives. Of course, what was really going on was the wholesale plundering of natural resources, along with large-scale destruction of all those insignificant folks who'd lived there first. The time between 1880 and the outbreak of World War I was known as the Mad Scramble for Africa, as European nations carved up the African continent for themselves. Eventually, Rhodes was convinced that the British, Germans, and Americans would eventually rule the Earth.

Rhodes and the Society of the Elect

Rhodes struggled with lousy health all his life, and he rewrote his will at least six times. It was worth rewriting, because at the time he was the richest man in the world. It is the first of his six wills, written when he was just 23, before he had much in the way of money, that generally raises eyebrows in conspiracy camps. It stated, in part, that he wanted to provide "for the establishment, promotion and development of a Secret Society, the true aim and object whereof shall be for the extension of British rule throughout the world . . . the furtherance of the British Empire and the bringing of the whole uncivilized world under British rule, for the recovery of the United States, for the making the Anglo-Saxon race but one Empire."

Rhodes became a Freemason as a young man, but was unimpressed with it, at first. He believed that Freemasonry (covered in Chapter 9) was missing the boat by not using its worldwide reach and influence to really change the world. He wrote, "I see the wealth and power they possess, the influence they hold and I think over their ceremonies and I wonder that a large body of men can devote themselves to what at times appear to be the most ridiculous and absurd rites with no object, with no end."

Naturally this all sets off alarm bells that Rhodes set up his secret society and set about his plan to fill all the continents of the world with red telephone

---

Rhodes scholarships

Rhodes did die quite young, at 42, in 1902, and his sixth will and testament prevailed. Because he believed in the genetic, economic, and philosophic superiority of the British, German, and American people, when he died, he left the overwhelming bulk of his incredible wealth to set up the Rhodes scholarship program. The scholarship provides for studies at England's Oxford University.

Of course, he included the United States as an ulterior motive — he wanted to foster the growth of a new breed of "philosopher kings" who would eventually come to their collective senses and compel America to rejoin the British Empire.

Ultimately, he believed that by bringing American and German students to Oxford, greater understanding and war prevention between the countries would be fostered. That said, Germans were written out of the scholarship from 1914 to 1932, and again from 1939 through 1970. Women were permitted to apply after 1975.

Notable U.S. recipients of the Rhodes scholarship have been Supreme Allied Commander Wesley Clark, former secretary of labor Robert Reich, Supreme Court Justice David Souter, former president Bill Clinton, singer songwriter Kris Kristofferson, and Louisiana governor Piyush Jindal.

---

boxes, double-decker buses, Beefeaters, and cars with the steering wheel on the wrong side. If Rhodes had his way, everyone would be eating bangers and mash, bubble and squeak, boiled steaks, and spotted dick. Moreover, the accusation has long been made that Rhodes eventually warmed up to the Masons, in which he was a life member, and eventually co-opted them for his plan to spread his world domination scheme.

Some researchers make the claim that Rhodes did in fact succeed at forming his own secret society, the *Society of the Elect*. He and *Pall Mall Gazette* editor William T. Stead met in 1891 and hammered out the details of such a group, which included himself as the *General* of the Society, with Stead and Lord Nathan Mayer Rothschild as his immediate underlings. Next came a level called the *Junta of Three,* followed by a *Circle of Initiates,* and finally the rank and file *Association of Helpers.* Important members of the British peerage and notable members of government were named to many of the higher positions, but it has never been proved that any of this ever got beyond the talking stage. Author Carroll Quigley claimed in his 1966 book *Tragedy and Hope* that the Society of the Elect was absolutely real, and that the members of the Association of Helpers were eventually organized as the *Rhodes-Milner Round Table.*

Again, we come back to Rhodes's various wills. By his fifth and sixth ones, the references to his secret society idea stopped, to be replaced by his plan for the Rhodes scholarships (see the "Rhodes scholarships" sidebar). There's no evidence that the Society of the Elect ever existed. It is only Carroll Quigley's allegation, with no proof.

Rhodes-Milner Round Tables

Here's where the cast increases and the plot thickens. Rhodes was not alone in his beliefs that the English were superior and destined to rule the world. High Commissioner Alfred Lord Milner became an incredibly influential statesman during this period and was a kindred soul to Rhodes's way of thinking. While he'd been born in Germany, Milner considered himself English, and like Rhodes, he had a dream for the Empire. Milner's vision was that all the major British colonies would have their own governments, with an Imperial Parliament in London that handled the overarching affairs of the Empire itself. The colonies would be represented in the Imperial government, which would handle defensive issues and international trade agreements, but the colonies would remain largely independent.

The United States was the best example of this kind of state/federal system, and Milner saw an Imperial Federation as the only way to extend and preserve the Empire, while encouraging white Englishmen to go forth, be fruitful, multiply, and be prosperous. Otherwise, he reasoned, sooner than later, the local, native populations (and previous owners) would rebel and demand independence. Which is exactly what happened.

While in Cape Colony after the end of the second Boer War (which led to the union of four different colonies into the nation of South Africa), Milner surrounded himself with a group of young civil service officers and administrators whom he influenced with his grand scheme, and they were branded as Milner's Kindergarten. Even though Milner and his like-minded friends attained very important and influential positions in the British government over the next few decades, his Imperial Federation idea never came to be.

In 1910, the group founded the *Round Table* magazine to discuss these ideas, and the group (which actually called itself "Moot" — *Round Table* was only the name of the magazine) still exists today. They have a Web site at www.moot.org.uk.

At the end of World War I, U.S. president Woodrow Wilson's closest advisor, Edward M. House, met in Paris with the Round Table group, and it's believed by some researchers that the New York–based Council on Foreign Relations was formed, based on that meeting. The allegation is that Americans wouldn't listen to such an Anglo-centric organization, so they spawned the CFR (see the section "Council on Foreign Relations").

Council on Foreign Relations

The *Council on Foreign Relations (CFR)* is a think tank, a nonpartisan organization made up of American and global leaders dedicated to educating policymakers, journalists, businesspeople, and students about international cultures, economies, policies, and defense issues.

First started as an informal group in 1917, the Council consisted of 150 history and political scholars (mostly from New York) assembled by President Woodrow Wilson. Their mission was to provide Wilson with guidance about post–World War I foreign policy, so he could negotiate halfway intelligently at the Paris Peace talks. While Wilson had originally envisioned a British and American group of academics and diplomats, the Council eventually consisted of just over 100 New York manufacturers, attorneys, and bankers and was presided over by Nobel Peace Prize–winner and then secretary of state Elihu Root.

The Council was officially formed in 1921, and was quickly dominated by financiers, many with connections to J. P. Morgan. The Rockefeller family also became major players in the Council, providing funding and donating a New York mansion as its headquarters. David Rockefeller became a director of the Council in 1949, and its chairman between 1970 and 1985. He remains its honorary chairman today.

CFR study groups had great, if secret, influence on the government of Franklin Delano Roosevelt during WWII, and on post-WWII policies. It is believed that the Marshall Plan, NATO, and the Cold War policy of Soviet "containment" all came from CFR study groups. CFR members were important members of the Eisenhower administration, and Nixon's national security advisor Henry Kissinger was a longtime CFR member and contributor to its study groups. Critics have nervously pointed out that between 1945 and 1972 more than 500 top government officials were CFR members. Half of the U.S. presidents since WWII have been CFR members.

The CFR today has more than 4,300 members. How secret a group can that be? It publishes *Foreign Affairs* magazine, and their Web site (www.cfr.org) lists dates and locations. Its self-proclaimed goal is to increase America's understanding of the world, and to contribute ideas to U.S. foreign policy. Annual reports on a wide array of topics are available to anyone.

Notable members include former president Bill Clinton, former secretary of state Colin Powell, former Fed chairman Alan Greenspan, former NBC anchorman Tom Brokaw, and actress Angelina Jolie. For the nervous folks on the Right, there's Move-On.org investor George Soros. For the nervous on the Left, Henry Kissinger is still kicking it. Their lofty goals are regarded with great suspicion by conspiracists, who believe that the CFR, like the other groups mentioned in this section, is creating the policies that will lead to a one-world government — the New World Order.

Their Web site is at www.cfr.org.

The Trilateral Commission

The Trilateral Commission is a nongovernment think tank of some 300 members. Membership is drawn from North America, Europe, the Pacific Asia, and Australia, because these places are considered the dominant areas of industrialized democracy in the world. (Or they were at the time of its founding in 1973 at the behest of Chase Manhattan Bank's David Rockefeller.) The goal of the Commission is to promote international cooperation, and members are business leaders and former government and United Nations officials. Naturally, that makes them suspected candidates for architects of the New World Order.

The Tri-Lats, as they're better known, became objects of suspicion in 1980 when three presidential contenders during the primaries — Jimmy Carter, George H. W. Bush, and third-party candidate John Anderson — were all members of the Commission, along with Carter's vice president, Walter Mondale. Carter had appointed 26 Tri-Lats as senior members of his administration in the late '70s, and suddenly the Commission found itself at the center of election-year mudslinging. The far-right John Birch Society went ballistic. And even though nonmember Ronald Reagan won the 1980 election, he did make Tri-Lat Bush his vice-presidential running mate.

If powerful bankers worry you, it should be noted that Paul Volker and Alan Greenspan were both founding members of the Trilateral Commission. Both eventually became head of the U.S. Federal Reserve.

Members meet regularly and publish the papers presented at their gatherings, frequently on issues of expanding democracy. Far from being secret, you're free to contact the group for a list of its approximately 350 members. Annual meeting reports are publicly available online. However, the evil, world takeover plots don't seem to be available on their Web site: www.trilateral.org.

The Bilderberg Group

The Bilderberg Group was started during the Cold War to increase understanding between world leaders of Europe and the United States. The group was created in 1954 by Prince Bernhard in Oosterbeek, Netherlands, and is named after the hotel that they met in that first year. The theory goes that the World Wars that had started in Europe could be averted in the future if leaders of those countries had a chance to meet and get to know each other in an informal setting. Each year, 100 government, economic, and business leaders are invited to meet and talk freely without the interference of the news media (or their own constituents). The list of attendees is made public, and members of the press may attend, but may not report on proceedings. Minutes are kept, but they don't contain the names of who said what, only what was spoken.

The buzz among conspiracists is that no one can become President of the United States without being a Bilderberger. Both President Bushes, John Kerry, John Edwards, Bill Clinton, Bill Gates, Henry Kissinger, Donald Rumsfeld, Steven Spielberg, as well as Tony Blair and a list of equally well-placed European notables, have attended past meetings. The group is undeniably an elite collection of movers and shakers, and what they say behind closed doors is kept a secret. Conspiracy addicts see this as an evil plot for one-world government, yet the group proposes no legislation, issues no policy statements, and takes no votes. The participants regard it as an opportunity to chat informally with people who are their international peers without every word being scrutinized on the nightly news.

All these similarly designed groups bring up an important conundrum. On the one hand, democratic societies don't like closed door sessions of powerful people, under any circumstances. Without public input and the vigilance of public watchdogs, secret "star chambers" of rich or influential power brokers can plan evil doings, or at least hatch remarkably bad ideas. On the other hand, national and international leaders need to share ideas and concerns just like professional associations of doctors, real estate agents, and school-teachers do, without always having to screen every word they say with a camera rolling. As for the connection between groups like the Bilderbergers, the Trilateral Commission, and the Council on Foreign Relations, and members who go on to become presidents, prime ministers, and CEOs of multinational companies, it's a small world when you get to that level. The conspiracy allegation is that these councils and commissions tell these influential wannabees what to do, on their way to creating some creepy, universal, "Zionist-dominated," global-controlled, New World Order.

Bohemian Club and Bohemian Grove

In 2007, former president Bill Clinton was making a speech and was interrupted by a "9/11 Truther" who shouted allegations about the 9/11 attacks being a hoax, followed by a reference to Clinton and Bohemian Grove. As the guy was dragged out of the auditorium, Clinton quipped, "That's where all those rich Republicans go up and stand naked against redwood trees right? I've never been to the Bohemian Club but you oughta go. It'd be good for you. You'd get some fresh air."

Word on the street is that the boyish fun at the campouts of the Bohemian Grove, the world's most star-studded Scout troop, includes Satanic rituals, rapes, outdoor S&M, public urination "swordfights," and setting fire to a great big owl. We'll tell you right from the start. The owl stuff is true. So is the public urination.

San Francisco's Bohemian Club was started in 1872 as a private men's club by a group of journalists who were looking for a little culture, along with attracting *avant garde* artists, musicians, actors, and writers, known in those days as *Bohemians.* The trouble with trying to form an exclusive men's club with a bunch of starving, off-kilter, and unusual, artsy types is that most of them were broke. So, the club had to also admit a few rich patrons, just to keep the lights on.

The result was that the rich men stayed and quickly crowded out most of the starving artists. The membership quickly became dominated by financial titans, famous politicians, and other powerful figures (overwhelmingly Republicans). Yet, the bylaws required that a certain number of members still be writers and other artists. Authors like Mark Twain, Jack London, and Ambrose Bierce were early members.

In the late 1800s, the Bohemian Club held regular summer camp outs in several locations in the forests outside of San Francisco. The feeling was that the club had become too socially conscious, too clubby, too cushy, and had lost the Bohemian spirit of unconventional living. So, in 1899, the group established a permanent campground on an isolated, 2,700-acre, redwood-filled property known as *Bohemian Grove,* near the tiny town of Monte Rio. Every July since then, the Grove has been the location of an annual outdoor, two-week celebration of Bohemian life. And because of the many influential members and guests of the club, along with rumors of certain activities, a growing suspicion has developed over their carryings-on.

Retreat for the ruling class

The Grove itself is a massive compound made up of different themed camps, sort of like a rural Disneyland. These days, some 1,500 members and guests attend. Each area has its own cabins and dining area, and the more than 100 campsites all have their own names like Valhalla, Mandalay, Cave man, Pink Onion, Woof, Jungle, and Dragons (William F. Buckley, Jr., George H. W. Bush, and Astronaut Frank Borman hang out at the Hillbilly Camp). Throughout the 16 days of the Grove, there are lectures, plays, and music, along with great food, cigars, and endlessly flowing booze. The Lakeside Speakers are an annual lineup of the world's most powerful guest speakers who address the campers throughout the session (many aspiring Republican presidential candidates have tried out their stump speeches here). But if an attendee wants to go swim nude in the Russian River, that's his business. Women are not allowed on the property during these summer festivities.

Remember that the Bohemian Club has a mandated group of members who are actors, writers, musicians, and artists, so the entertainment is nonstop — annual events are the Lo-Jinx musical comedy show and a more serious Grove Play. The Clubhouse back in San Francisco has a 600-seat auditorium in the basement for putting on plays throughout the year, and for rehearsing shows headed for the Grove. The "Men of Talent" are often given reduced membership fees, in return for their work on Club shows, which are presented in the Clubhouse every Thursday night from October to May. Mark Twain would work all year on phony Elizabethan poems and suggestive fishing songs involving the size of a man's cod, to be presented at the Grove.

Member Herman Wouk, author of *The Winds Of War,* said of the Grove, "Men can decently love each other; they always have, but women never quite understand." Still, not everyone thinks highly of the Grove and its antics. Member Richard Nixon once called it, "the most faggy goddamn thing that you would ever imagine." Interestingly, even though past presidents and presidential hopefuls are regular attendees, the Grove has a rule that sitting presidents may not give speeches during the event. Nevertheless, members and guests are a stunning array of business and political leaders, which is what makes the decidedly lowbrow, high-schoolish level of pranks, name calling, theatrical drag acts, and fart jokes seem so out of place for these otherwise dour men of power. And then there's all that public urinating.

Yes, the Grove is a freewheeling place where guys like George Schultz, Henry Kissinger, and Newt Gingrich can pee on a tree and not have some reporter from *The Inquirer* plaster it on the cover. The Grove isn't a place where world domination is planned; it's where the men who already dominate the world go to relax. They aren't worshiping Satan; they aren't sacrificing orphaned children to the ancient god Moloch. They are doing what the rest of us can do privately without having cameras and microphones thrust at us while we're sitting in a boat, baiting a hook and drinking a beer. They drink nonstop, joke with each other, and act like big kids for a couple of weeks a year. The Grove's meetings have been infiltrated many times, and the overwhelming conclusion is that there's nothing sinister going on. Unfortunately, that doesn't sell books and DVD exposés to a breathless public who believes otherwise.

The Cremation of Care

For over 100 years, the opening of the Grove's annual outdoor session has been a dramatic, overproduced, and slightly bizarre ceremony called the *Cremation of Care.* The centerpiece of the Grove's central gathering area is an outdoor amphitheater, with a pond and a 45-foot-tall concrete owl — a symbol of wisdom and the Bohemian Club's mascot and logo.

The point of the ceremony is that the majority of attendees at the Grove may be the movers and shakers of the financial and political world, but while they are in the Grove, they are to put the cares and worries of the outside world aside. And they do this by burning them. Well, not literally, even though conspiracist Alex Jones thinks otherwise. The ceremony begins with a boat slowly crossing the pond carrying an effigy that represents Dull Care. This dreaded reminder of the outside world mocks the attendees, and shouts at them over the booming PA system, "Fools! Fools! Fools!" The Bohemians have the last laugh, as hooded, vaguely Druidic-looking Grovers take Dull Care out of the boat, put it on an altar, and set it on fire, to the happy cheers of the crowd, which are accompanied by triumphant music and fireworks. And the voice of the Owl during the ceremony? Former CBS news anchorman Walter Cronkite. Of course, Alex Jones believes this is a live body they burn every year. His clandestine video of the event is all over the Internet.

The point being made goes along with the Bohemian Club's motto: "Weaving spiders come not here" (a line taken from Shakespeare's *A Midsummer Night's Dream*). It means don't come and make plots or transact business or bring the evil cares of the outside world in here.

The Committee of 300

Also referred to in some circles as *The Olympians,* the Committee of 300 is such a super-duper secret organization, that only one man in the whole world has ever discovered anything about it. Conspiracist Dr. John Coleman, in his book *Conspirators Hierarchy: The Story of the Committee of 300,* describes an organization supposedly made up of top political, military, and business leaders. This one is allegedly led by Britain's Queen Elizabeth II.

Coleman, who claims to be a former British MI6 intelligence officer, alleges the Committee is responsible for "phony drug wars" in the United States that allow government to confiscate property of otherwise innocent citizens (we don't question that this goes on only that Coleman is pointing to the wrong group). But the real aim of the Committee is population control to save natural resources. It was allegedly formed by Cecil Rhodes (see "Cecil Rhodes and the Rhodes-Milner Round Table") to organize a one-world government. The usual suspects of Rockefellers and Rothschilds are named as possible members.

Coleman goes on to allege that the Tavistock Institute of Human Relations in London has been brainwashing citizens for decades, while developing mind-control programs for the CIA and other agencies. These techniques, so the tale goes, are used to modify public opinion and behavior and render everyone helpless to oppose world dictatorship. And of course to keep the "sheeple" from ever discovering the truth about the mysterious Committee of 300.

A few words about order

To quote Howard Johnson in the movie *Blazing Saddles,* "You know, Nietzsche said 'Out of chaos comes order.'" Well, it might eventually, but it doesn't without any help. We're going to say it without beating around the bush. The committees, councils, commissions, clubs, and societies mentioned in the last part of this chapter really *are* out to rule the world.

There. Cat's out of the bag. It's a nasty, filthy, and frequently dangerous job, but for crying out loud, *somebody* has to do it. They are made up of the richest and/or the most powerful people in the free world, so there's little in it for them to engineer more power or more money for themselves. Most important, they are the most successful at their chosen professions, and they have lots of collective experience. And who are you going to consult about international monetary policy and the effects of political destabilization — your dentist?

What all these groups are ultimately after is the same thing: They want to keep some 6.6 billion selfish, greedy, single-minded, uneducated, tribalistic Neanderthals from murdering, robbing, spending, starving, or exploding each other into oblivion. When you get right down to it, that's all any of them, and a whole raft of others, are after — from the World Trade Organization, the G7, the World Social Forum, and the Project for the New American Century, to the United Nations, the International Monetary Fund, Greenpeace, and whatever crazy bunch Ted Turner is pimping this week. They all have a different solution to the problems that plague the world, some dumber than others. But the people involved in them, whether you agree or disagree with their ideas, are the people who have studied the world's problems far more closely than most

of us who sit in bars and wag our fingers in the air, believing we have all the answers to all the troubles in the world.

Groups like the CFR, the Trilateral Commission, the Bilderbergers, and even the Bohemian Grovers peeing on old-growth trees in the redwood forest are not summoning forth Satan, electing the Antichrist, or sacrificing kidnapped third-world babies to pagan gods on pyres lit with Saudi oil. Their influential members may own a lot and control a lot, but they don't own and control it all; the world is too unpredictable a place, and there are still elections held like clockwork in the democratic parts of the world. Conspiracy mongers who spread these accusations are little more than modern-day Barnums bilking a gullible public into having a peek at the alligator woman.

Like it or not, civilization comes to a grinding halt and order descends right back into chaos when we all refuse to trust anyone anymore. The old Cold War saying about nuclear weapons negotiation was, "Trust and verify." Likewise with the people who step up to try to bring a little order to central Africa, downtown Cleveland, or a New England town hall meeting. It should never be blind trust — trust and verify, hold them to the highest standards, and demand transparency. But we have to trust the people we put in charge of our businesses, neighborhoods, and nations. They can't all be crooks and thieves and evildoers and schemers, because if they are, that means no one can be trusted, anywhere, anytime. That's no way to live, and the alternative is lousy, because no anarchist will ever let you keep your Chevy Tahoe parked in the driveway for long.

Part IV
The Part of Tens

The 5th Wave   By Rich Tennant

CENTRAL INTELLIGENCE AGENCY

Enter Here

"Enter here? That's what they want you to believe."

In this part . . .

A *For Dummies* book wouldn't feel right without a few lists of ten. In this part, we serve up ten conspiracy theories that really turned out to be true; ten conspiracy theories that skirted the edge of madness; and ten of the drop-dead weirdest secret societies of all time.

Chapter 16

Ten Conspiracy Theories That Skirt the Edge of Madness

In This Chapter

▶ Hijacking the throne of Peter

▶ Exposing supposed space program skullduggery

▶ Plotting for and against the government

*E*xploring conspiracy theories can be fun or frightening, depending on your point of view. But there are some theories that are just *too* crazy, and in a few cases, some folks are just crazy enough to attempt to pull them off. And at least one of the conspiracy theories presented in this chapter has caused a great deal of harm on a global scale (see the section, "Polio Epidemic Spread by a Conspiracy Theory"). Following are ten conspiracy theories that just plain defy rational thought.

There's More than One Pope

In 1962, Pope John XXIII announced that it was time to "throw open a window" so that the church could look out at the world and the world could look in. That year, he assembled the first of four annual sessions of what became known as the Second Vatican Council, or in more Hollywood sequel-esque terms, *Vatican II* (Vatican I had been held a century before, but was interrupted by a revolution in Italy and never reconvened). Pope John's purpose with Vatican II was to drag the Catholic Church, screaming and kicking, into the 20th century. He wouldn't live to see the end result — he died of cancer in 1963. But his successor, Pope Paul VI, continued with the council meetings and subsequent reforms.

The changes made to the church in the mid-1960s were massive:

▸ The Mass would be said in the vernacular of the country rather than liturgical Latin, so the congregation could actually understand what was being said.

- The altar was turned around so parishioners could see what was going on.

- The church admitted the possibility of eternal salvation for believers of other faiths.

- Jews, who'd historically been held responsible as a race for the killing of Christ, were ordered to be held blameless — individuals had been responsible, not the Jews as a people.

- Catholics didn't even have to eat fish on Fridays anymore.

For lifelong Catholics, Vatican II, for good or ill, was a shock to the system, and those who regarded it as heretical abandonment began to sniff a blasphemous rat. Breakaway groups of "traditionalist Catholics," who believe that Vatican II was a Masonic conspiracy to destroy the church and that Popes John XXIII and Paul VI were responsible, have formed over the last 40 years. In fact, some of these groups say that Paul VI was actually kidnapped and replaced by an actor. Others simply say that all popes since John XXIII have been illegally elected.

In the light of this vacuum of legal and proper spiritual leadership, somebody just had to step in. In fact, there have even been a few who've stepped to their own balconies, sent up a little white smoke, and proclaimed *"Habemus papem"* *(We have a pope)*. As of this writing, there are perhaps a dozen worldwide (including a Popette, Gregoria XVIII in Quebec). Here are the best known:

- David Allen Bawden was elected pope on July 16, 1990, and took as his papal name Pope Michael I. Bawden isn't an ordained priest, because his election was held in his family's store in Belvue, Kansas. While all Catholics from around the world were invited to attend the election and vote, only six showed up, including Bawden, his parents, and his girl-friend (who has since withdrawn her support and proclaimed Pope Michael a heretic). The latest estimate of Catholics who believe the Holy See is situated in Kansas is less than 50.

- While Kansas's Pope Michael I disses the Roman pretenders ever since Paul VI, some traditional Catholics think even Pope John XXIII was bogus. Such a contrarian is Father Lucian Pulvermacher, known to his flock as Pope Pius XIII. Pulvermacher believes that John XXIII's election was illegal because, according to some, Pope John had become a Freemason in 1935 while in Turkey. Masonic membership among Catholics can be an excom-municable offense, which rendered Pope John's election void, according to some traditionalists (even though his Masonic membership has never been proved). Pulvermacher was elected pope on October 24, 1994, in a conclave held in rural Montana. Unfortunately, because all electors had trouble getting to the location, some of the voting was done by telephone. Nevertheless, he won by unanimous vote and was consecrated at a local hotel the next year, taking the name of Pius XIII, while surrounded by an enthusiastic throng of 28. He has since moved the Vatican to a rural location in Springdale, Washington.

- The Palmarian Catholic Church in Spain took the step of simply pro-claiming Clemente Dominguez y Gomez as Pope Gregory XVII in 1978.

Gomez believed Vatican II's real Pope Paul VI had been drugged and kidnapped by Communists and Freemasons. Gomez died in 2005 while saying Easter Mass and was made Saint Gregory the *Very* Great. He was succeeded by Manuel Alonso Corral, who calls himself Pope Peter II.

Space Shuttle Columbia's "Deliberate" Destruction

On February 1, 2003, the Space Shuttle *Columbia* mission STS-107 was headed for a routine Florida landing after 16 days in space. Suddenly, just 16 minutes away from the Cape Canaveral runway, the shuttle, traveling at Mach 18, broke up in the skies 203,000 feet above Texas. The crash killed all seven members of the crew. Debris rained down on the area around Palestine, Texas, and almost immediately, the conspiracists saw something far more sinister than just a simple accident.

Conspiracist Alex Jones had "predicted" some kind of disaster several days before it happened, with the hypothesis that the U.S. government may stage some kind of tragedy as a way to either divert the public's attention from war activities, or to justify a much larger war in the Middle East. Of course, Jones regularly "predicts" this kind of thing, so he's always ready for any major event. The tragedy brought a shameless pack of conspiracy theories front and center:

- **The Jews did it:** Ilan Ramon was an Israeli colonel who'd taken part in the bombing of an Iraqi nuclear facility back in 1981 and the first Israeli to be launched into space. With an Israeli on board, such a high profile attack on the American spacecraft would've been a major publicity and ideological coup. Rumors circulated that Ramon had been making atmospheric and photographic studies of Iraq from space for biological warfare use, and that his "martyrdom" was intentionally staged to gin up support for Israeli military action in Lebanon, the Palestinian territories, and eventually, Iraq.

- **The U.S. Military did it:** The military, alleged by "investigator" Sherman Skolnick, shot down the shuttle using a sophisticated particle beam weapon (an as yet unverifiable technology). But most who ascribed to the notion that it was deliberately destroyed by the government figured it was just a boring old missile attack. Naturally, because the shuttle disintegrated over Texas, home of President George W. Bush and his big spread in Crawford, Bush was immediately implicated in either having prior knowledge, or even having ordered the "attack."

- **The Chinese did it:** This particular Columbia mission was the first to receive its own Internet address and satellite connection to the Web. It was over this connection, so the story goes, that the onboard computer was hacked and infected with a virus or worm from China that managed to cause some sort of reentry maneuver that resulted in its destruction. An alternate enemy named was North Korea. Curiously, this particular theory came from an unusual source — the Russian news service PRAVDA.

✔ **The hand of God did it:** The Islamic press claimed the disaster was the hand of Allah punishing both the Americans and the Jews, as well as a message from God that Jews weren't welcome in space. Christian fundamentalists saw portentous symbolism in the death of an Israeli and the debris falling on the town of Palestine, Texas, while Palestinians in the Middle East regarded it as an anti-Israeli message. Doomsayers claimed it was the first sign of the Apocalypse, and as proof, pointed to a small scroll of the Torah that Ramon carried into space with him that read: "Has any nation ever heard the voice of God speaking out of the midst of the fire, as you have, and yet lived?" (Deuteronomy 4:33).

White supremacist Richard Barrett saw the shuttle's destruction as a cautionary message from God exacting his vengeful wrath against insidious "diversity" — out of the seven crew members, only three had been white, American men.

A NASA investigation concluded that the accident had been caused by a piece of insulating foam from the orbiter's external fuel tank falling off and destroying several insulating tiles from the shuttle's left wing. Heat during reentry caused the unprotected area to burn through and tear the wing apart. Conspiracists disagree.

Richard Hoagland and the Face on Mars

In July 1976, NASA's Viking I spacecraft orbited the planet Mars and sent back photos of a region known as *Cydonia Mensae,* a portion of the planet's surface in between the smooth northern plains and the heavily pockmarked, crater-covered area in the south. Upon close examination of one photo taken from directly overhead, the combination of sun and shadow made the surface of a large mesa appear to have the vague features of eyes, a nose, a mouth, and a squared-off helmet or hair line.

"The Face on Mars!" quickly became the stuff of supermarket tabloid head-lines. Author Richard Hoagland and others believe the photo is "evidence" of a Martian race of creatures. Hoagland sees a ruined city, and even pyramids, around the "face." Subsequent photos with far better resolution have shown that the "face" is really nothing more than a lumpy bit of geology, combined with an out of focus photo taken when the sun was low on the Martian horizon to create what amounts to an interplanetary Rorschach test. But somehow those conspiracy theorists who believe in NASA's fuzzy first photos, *disbelieve* that same agency's more detailed photographic evidence. Hoagland and other true believers continue to allege that NASA is covering up the truth about evidence of extraterrestrial life on Mars.

Polio Epidemic Spread by a Conspiracy Theory

In the 1990s, an international campaign began to wipe out polio worldwide, once and for all. By 2000, virtually all parts of the world had been made polio free. But beginning in 2003, a conspiracy theory gripped the Muslim world, and the result was deadly.

It started in Nigeria. The president of Nigeria's Supreme Council for Islamic Sharia Law, Doctor Ibrahim Datti Ahmed, announced that Americans had poisoned polio vaccinations with an infertility drug to sterilize Muslim children. According to Dr. Ahmed, Americans were the "worst criminals on Earth." Ibrahim Shekarau, governor of Kano, one of the three Nigerian states that outlawed the vaccines, said that it was preferable for a few children to die than to risk rendering thousands of their girls infertile. Angry villagers chased health workers, assaulting and threatening them so badly that they simply dumped the vaccines.

By the next year, the conspiracy theory had spread to India, and by 2005, in countries where polio cases had all but disappeared, the disease came back with a vengeance. Sixteen nations reported major outbreaks, and the disease shot like wildfire through mostly Muslim countries — strains spread from Nigeria by pilgrims making the annual *hajj* to Mecca. Despite pleas from the World Health Organization (WHO), Muslim governments have been uncooperative about confronting the conspiracy theory, as well as unsupportive with money for the vaccination project.

David Icke, Reptilian Humanoids, and the Babylonian Brotherhood

There's a certain brand of conspiracist who goes so far overboard, who seems to have such a large deficiency of marbles, that you have to admire the sheer boldness, inventiveness, and wackiness of their theories. The pinnacle of this P. T. Barnum style of conspiracy peddling is British writer David Icke (rhymes with "Yike!" — not "sick" or "icky").

In 1991, Icke, a former English soccer goalie, sports commentator, and Green Party activist, claimed to have been given a special message from the spirit world. He began wearing only turquoise-colored clothes and announced that he was the Son of God. Since then, he has written 20 books that weave a tangled haze combining New Age spiritualism, apocalyptic doom, and a bizarre take on the Masonic–Jewish–New World Order global domination theory.

Icke spouts the standard stuff about the Illuminati and the vast Global Elite that "runs everything," but he does it with a twist. Because, you see, according to his book, *The Biggest Secret,* Icke believes the real power on Earth is a race of shape-shifting alien lizards from Alpha Draconis, known as the Babylonian Brotherhood. By night, behind closed doors, they are 12 feet tall and they drink blood, nibble on rodents, molest children, and sacrifice humans in an alien Satanic ceremony. But by day, their bodies change size and shape and they become Queen Elizabeth II, Prince Charles and his two sons, Hillary Clinton, both George Bushes, Tony Blair, William F. Buckley, Jr., Bob Hope, Billy Graham, Kris Kristofferson, and even country singer Boxcar Willie, just to name a few.

According to Icke, he was told about the royal family's alien lizard lineage by Princess Diana, and it was, apparently, the Royal lizards who had her rubbed out. (We thought the most exotic alien place the Windsor's came from was Saxe-Coburg-Gotha.) And the reason that England's royal family has a massive estate in Scotland is because it guards the entrance to their vast subterranean lizard city.

Further, the Global Elite answers to what Icke calls the Luciferic Consciousness of the Fourth Dimension. The Babylonian Brotherhood supposedly uses alien technology to change weather patterns on Earth, and are using "global warming" as a cover story. They also created the New Age movement to prepare the Earth for a "vibrational change."

Of course, Icke drinks in ridicule like mother's milk. His speaking engagements are very well attended, and his rambling books sell well. But in addition, he regularly writes extensively about the *Protocols of the Elders of Zion* (see Chapter 6), a phony "exposé" of a supposed board of Jewish elders outlining their plan for world takeover.

The Anti-Defamation League (ADL), founded in 1913 to help stop anti-Jewish hate speech, has since branched into all forms of activism against prejudice. Needless to say, when Icke launches off on his typical "the Roshschilds start all the wars so they can loan money to both sides, and the Protocols is a true document of the plot by the Aryan Brotherhood to take over the world" rant, the ADL gets a little testy. The problem is, with all due respect to the ADL and the work that they do, we think they just don't get it here. When Icke says that the Rothschilds and their minions are lizards, "lizards" isn't a code word for "Jews." No, he really *means* lizards.

Icke has classified a long list of different lizard races that are vying for supremacy on Earth: Grays, Troglodytes, Crinklies, Tall Robots, Tall Blondes (!), Elderbarians (they make crop circles), Zebra Repticulars, Annunaki (which include the Bush presidents), the Interdimensional Sasquatch . . . it's quite a list.

Naturally, the more he's mocked, the more Icke and his fans believe he's really on to the tricks and the truth of the reptilian Illuminati. And the reason that the famous folks he has "outed" as Satanic, baby-eating alien reptiles have never sued him? Because they really *are* 12-foot lizards, of course. *Boxcar Willie?!*

The "Murder" of Princess Diana

On August 31, 1997, Diana, Princess of Wales and former wife of England's prince Charles, died after a high-speed car accident in the Pont d'Alma tunnel in Paris. Diana was traveling in a black Mercedes S280 with Dodi Al-Fayed (son of billionaire Mohamed Al-Fayed, owner of Harrod's department store in London and the Hotel Ritz in Paris). In the front seats were bodyguard Trevor-Rees Jones and the Hotel Ritz's acting security manager, Henri Paul, who'd been ordered to shake the cars and motorcycles packed with paparazzi that were chasing the famous couple. Paul crashed into a support column (portentously, the 13th one) in the tunnel, and eventually all but Jones died from their injuries.

Almost immediately, Dodi's famous father came out swinging. He claimed that Diana was murdered by the English Crown to hide the fact that the couple was about to be engaged, and that Diana was pregnant with her Egyptian boyfriend's child, a scandal that Britain's royal family wouldn't stand for. French authorities investigated the case and judged it an accident, caused by driver Henri Paul's reckless driving while under the influence of antidepressants and too much booze (three times the legal limit in France).

Al-Fayed was relentless, and wild charges were made over the years (not to mention the fact that the eccentric billionaire turned his equally eccentric take on the once dignified Harrod's into a virtual altar of Dodi-Diana worship, with gaudy full-scale statuary that makes the Vatican look like minimalist architecture):

- The late Henri Paul was accused of being in the paid service of the British, French, or U.S. intelligence communities (it varied, depending on who was telling the tale).
- French investigators were accused of swapping Paul's blood samples with a drunken suicide victim (later debunked by DNA records).
- Britain's MI5 and MI6 security services were implicated, as were Prince Charles and Queen Elizabeth's husband Prince Phillip.

Other claims bubbled to the surface. One especially lunatic one was that Diana's well-publicized campaign against the use of landmines had cut into the business of unscrupulous landmine manufacturers, so she had to be snuffed by the military-industrial complex.

Conspiracy whack-job David Icke (see "David Icke, Reptilian Humanoids, and the Babylonian Brotherhood") got in the game, claiming that Diana had seen

Queen Elizabeth transform herself into a 12-foot-tall alien lizard, a secret so devastating that she had to be murdered.

As for the pregnancy claims, Diana had never said anything to anyone about it, and blood tests, in fact, revealed no sign of pregnancy, though an early stage of pregnancy in a late post-mortum is apparently difficult to determine. Reports that Dodi had purchased an engagement ring turned out to be false. As for Feyed's notion that the couple had been murdered out of some racist motivation, Diana had just ended a two-year liaison with a Pakistani Muslim that the Royal Family seemed to have no objections to her marrying, if she'd been so inclined.

In January 2004, London's Metropolitan Police began its own inquiry, *Operation Paget,* led by then commissioner Lord John Stevens, with a team that would eventually include 14 officers. (Your tax pounds at work!) After nearly three years and a cost of £3.7 million (more than US $7 million), the initial 832-page report was issued in December 2006 saying that *every single one of the conspiracy theories* were without foundation, and that Diana hadn't been murdered.

The Bombing of New Orleans's Levees

The destruction and aftermath of Hurricane Katrina across Alabama, Mississippi, and Louisiana was the source of a rapidly spread conspiracy theory in 2006, making it the first tropical depression with a conspiratorial agenda. Nation of Islam Minister Louis Farrakhan quickly alleged that the government had intentionally blown up a levee to allow floodwaters to destroy poor parts of New Orleans's 9th Ward, inhabited by African Americans. Some breathless believers embellished the story with Coast Guard cutters supposedly ramming the earthen dikes or even shelling them with artillery to flood black neighborhoods and lower the floodwaters of white suburbs.

It's true that at least one river barge broke free from its moorings in the aftermath of the storm and busted through a levee in the lower 9th Ward (lest anyone forget that a powerful hurricane had just passed through). The massive barge wound up coming to rest in a residential neighborhood, but it's a whale of a stretch to allege that it was deliberately piloted there to destroy the levee and take out the neighborhood. Some said they heard as many as seven "explosions" attributed to the levee story, but such sounds would be common as millions of gallons of water tore through the barriers, or as loose barges slammed into them.

Filmmaker Spike Lee repeated the story on television interview programs, saying on *Real Time with Bill Maher,* "Presidents have been assassinated. So why is that so far-fetched?" It's far-fetched because it presupposes that no white people in local, state, and federal government have any sense of moral right and wrong; it presupposes that any African-Americans in the government (of which there were many, including the mayor) would go along and shut up about such a genocidal plan; and it presupposes that members of the Army Corps of Engineers, the Coast Guard, FEMA, and the Department of Homeland Security would all be willing accomplices.

The same kinds of allegations were made in the very same neighborhood during Hurricane Betsy's hit on New Orleans in 1965. Design changes to breeched levees during Betsy were made by the Army Corps of Engineers to make them taller and stronger, but these "improved" designs failed during Katrina.

Hurricane Katrina was one of the five deadliest in American history, the sixth strongest hurricane *ever recorded* in the Atlantic, and the third strongest to hit the U.S. It didn't just devastate New Orleans, but also Biloxi, Pascagoula, Pass Christian, Long Beach, Gulf Port, and Ocean Springs. The final death toll of 1,836 people was the worst from a hurricane in America since 1928. There's no question that the federally built flood protection levees experienced a total meltdown. But it's also true that, when Mother Nature gets that cranky, all you can do is get out of the way.

Scientology and the IRS

The Church of Scientology was created in the 1950s by California science fiction author L. Ron Hubbard, as the "religious" extension of his self-help method *Dianetics*. Because of the psychological basis of Scientology's methods, the religion is adamant about its followers refusing psychiatric care from the mainstream medical community. Depending on which source you read, it costs as low as $30,000 or as high as $360,000 to enter into the higher levels of the religion, and members are forbidden to discuss their progress or the materials they've studied, even with each other. Presumably, only after you've lost enough free will, common sense, and cash are you ready for the awesome revelations about mankind's role in an intergalactic space opera.

For 25 years, the Internal Revenue Service regarded Scientology's various operations as a commercial enterprise and not a church worthy of tax-exempt status. So, in the 1970s, Scientology went on the attack against 136 government agencies, foreign embassies, and organizations critical of the church, in what they called *Operation Snow White*.

Using as many as 5,000 church members as agents worldwide, Scientologists went on the warpath, especially against the IRS in order to steal or destroy reports and records critical of the church, and to pressure the Feds into granting the church tax-exempt status as a bona fide religion. Scientologists infiltrated the IRS and other agencies, and engaged in theft of government documents, wiretapping, and conspiring to create smear campaigns against government employees.

While Scientology founder L. Ron Hubbard avoided prosecution as an "un-indicted co-conspirator," his wife Mary Sue didn't, and she did hard jail time for following his orders. Eleven church officials were convicted in U.S. Federal court in 1979 and seven more in Canada in 1996.

Nevertheless, the scheme worked. In 1993, the IRS changed its mind and granted tax-exempt status to the Church of Scientology and its various connected entities, along with complaining to foreign countries that didn't follow suit. Belgium and Germany both continue to fight the well-financed forces of Scientology, and both countries regard the church as a for-profit business that illegally makes medical claims while financially fleecing its flock.

The Pentagon Cruise Missile of 9/11

One of the most insane accusations of the so-called 9/11 "Truth Movement" (see Chapter 8) is that the Pentagon wasn't hit by an airplane, but by a U.S. Navy cruise missile, intentionally fired to simulate a terrorist attack, in order to create popular support for granting the government unheard-of powers in a phony "war on terror." Whew.

The "evidence" of this accusation begins with a series of time-lapse photographs released by the Pentagon of a security camera pointed at a parking lot guard shack immediately adjacent to the crash site. Because the photos are taken several seconds apart, the first image shows nothing, the second shows a blur, and the third shows a massive explosion. Bear in mind that the images were from a security camera, taking one frame per second, of a plane traveling at 780 feet per second.

Conspiracists say that the hole punched in the side of the Pentagon was far too small to have been made by a plane, and that no wreckage was found from a jetliner. The 16-foot diameter hole punched into the interior walls of the Pentagon was too small to be made by a 757, but the fuselage of that plane is, in fact, 16 feet in diameter. Photos of the aftermath clearly show a 90-foot-wide section of the building smashed in, with further damage beyond that width — clear evidence of the wings' impact.

Of all the claims made by 9/11 "Truthers," this is without question the most insane in our opinion. The Pentagon was hit by American Airlines Flight 77, a Boeing 757. Literally hundreds of drivers stuck in morning rush hour traffic on the roads that densely surround the Pentagon saw it fly into the side of the massive military administration building, regardless of what doesn't show up on security camera tapes. There were passengers aboard the plane talking on their cell phones when it hit, and their bodies were found in the wreckage. The plane's black box recorders were both recovered.

Deniers of the Holocaust

World War II was a meat grinder in which 70 million people died. An assessment by the Russian government after the fall of Communism puts their losses alone at a staggering 26 million human beings. And the concentration camps were equal opportunity destroyers — nearly 18 million civilians were killed by the Nazis.

It wasn't only the Jews who got sent to the camps; they got Freemasons, Jehovah's Witnesses, homosexuals, unruly priests and nuns, Slavs, evangelical Christians, gypsies, communists, labor organizers, criminals, malcontents, and publishers of anti-Nazi materials of any sort.

Yet, there are revisionists who say that the Holocaust, the common term for the targeted extermination of nearly 6 million of Europe's Jews by Adolph Hitler and his Nazi regime, never really happened.

There are all sorts of Holocaust deniers out there, but the lynchpin of the movement is a small group of "scholars" who call themselves, with due modesty, the "Institute for Historical Review." Along with the fancy name, they publish a quarterly, off and on, between lawsuits, called the *Journal of Historical Review*. It is not, needless to say, a normal, peer-reviewed academic historical publication. Nevertheless, since the 1970s, this motley crew of pseudo-historians has attempted to wrap themselves in the trappings of a legitimate scholarly organization.

Because the evidence is so unbelievably overwhelming, there are certain points that most deniers concede:

- The Jews were subjected by the Nazis to a systematic oppression throughout the 1930s that led to their expulsion from society.
- Their belongings were confiscated.
- They were confined in concentration camps.
- Tens or hundreds of thousands of Jews were either worked to death in these labor camps or died of hunger and disease in either the camps or the ghettos.
- Mass shootings of Jews occurred (some concede) on the eastern front as Hitler's army moved into Soviet Russia. But they don't concede that the Nazis built concentration camps that gassed the Jews, or anyone else.

In 1941, SS *Gruppenfuhrer* Reinhard Heydrich presided over the Wannsee Conference, a high-level meeting of Nazi officials to plan for the ultimate extermination of 11 million Jews across Europe and the Soviet Union. The standard method of simply rounding up Jews from villages, taking them to the edge of town, and shooting and burying them in trenches was deemed inefficient and cruel to the soldiers required to carry out such killings. Mobile vans that pumped exhaust into sealed compartments filled with victims were expensive, time consuming, and didn't kill enough people at one time.

So, by 1942, a string of death camps was designed and built to murder Jews and other undesirables with factorylike efficiency and to dispense with their bodies in massive incinerators. By the end of the war, Adolf Eichmann, head of the Gestapo's department on Jewish Affairs, estimated that 2 million Jews had been killed in mobile vans and other methods, and 4 million in the death camps (mostly located in Poland). The methodical, detail-obsessed Nazis left a fact-filled paper trail of their activities, despite the fact that, after the Allied invasion, an order came down called "Aktion 1005," to dismantle and destroy all evidence of mass murder.

None of the major players in the Nazi party, while on trial for war crimes, ever denied that the Final Solution, the program of methodical destruction of the Jewish race, had happened. Eichmann, who was hanged by the Israelis in 1962, never once denied that the liquidation of the Jews had taken place. He fell back on the same old line as every war criminal — the laws of his country had decreed it to be proper, and he was obeying those laws. He was proud of his role. But he never *denied* that it happened.

Yet, Holocaust deniers do. They claim that men like Eichmann were simply bragging. They claim poisonous gas like Zyclon B was only used in camps to delouse clothes, and that the gas chambers weren't designed in such a way that anyone could've been killed in them. They were simply rigged to look that way later, for the tourists.

For Holocaust deniers, the contention goes something like this: When the Jews who survived WWII decided to take up Zionism and refound a new Israel in British-held Palestine, they schemed that they could get what they wanted by guilting the world into giving it to them if they could invent a story that millions more Jews died at the hands of the Nazis than really did. Zionists could also get more money that way, because in the 1950s the German government paid out some funds in reparation to Israel to help settle Holocaust survivors. Overestimating the loss by 3 or 4 or even 5 million people would be financially advantageous to the new Jewish nation.

Some of these Holocaust deniers are just plain curmudgeonly contrarians, who'll argue with anyone over anything, and the Internet has suddenly provided them with a worldwide soapbox to shout their opinions from. They're a tiny fringe group, to be sure. But if as a culture, we allow the Holocaust deniers to hijack this most horrible of all inhuman crimes, then there's no more anchor on the boat. It can drift anywhere.

So, maybe mass murderer Ted Bundy was innocent, after all. Maybe Charles Manson really was the reincarnation of Jesus Christ. Maybe American Southerners never really kept slaves. And maybe Stalin never had millions of people killed. In the final analysis, this "revisionist" train ride can't take you anywhere but a dead end.

Chapter 17

Ten Conspiracies That Were Absolutely True

In This Chapter

▶ Revealing America's wannabe kings

▶ Designing doctors and calculating corporations

▶ Gaming in the CIA: Tripping out and building assassins

*H*istorians can be a bit like scientists in the way they think — "show me the evidence" is their motto — though they have to be imaginative enough to look at the evidence and form a viable conclusion. Still, we're a bit pragmatic by nature.

So, there may have been times in this book that we've seemed to be more con than pro on conspiracy theories because too many of them are way too short on empirical evidence. But take this chapter as our *mea culpa* and sincere apology. Because the truth is that sometimes, yesterday's conspiracy theory is proven by the passing of time to have been not theory, but fact.

These ten tales of conspiracy meander through history, from 19th-century France to 1940s Los Angeles. Some entries are far longer than others, because of the level of complexity involved. But each plot and each intrigue has been proven true. So, these aren't conspiracy theories anymore. These are ten dark and scary instances of conspiracy fact.

The Aaron Burr Conspiracy

In the summer of 1806, America's third president, Thomas Jefferson, received a long and disturbing letter out of Nashville from Andrew Jackson, who would one day be president himself. Jefferson's mail pouch had been bulging for more than a year with ominous letters warning him about his former vice president, Aaron Burr. There were rumors of his plots to create a new empire carved out of the Western territories, including the newly acquired lands of the Louisiana Purchase, with Burr himself as its emperor. Some of the letters had been signed, and some had been anonymous, but all of them were disturbing. The letter from Jackson finally got Jefferson's full attention.

Aaron Burr had been Jefferson's first-term vice president, but it hadn't been a happy marriage. The presidential election of 1800 changed history. It was the first and last tie in a run for the presidency — Burr and Jefferson, both Republicans, had gotten *exactly* the same number of votes. John Adams came in third. In those days, America had an electoral college, as we have today. It's a complex system that gets a lot of flak; each state has the number of electors that is the same total as their representatives in the Congress. Today there is a total of 538 of them, and the election isn't official until they meet and vote, which is why the popular election is in November but the swearing-in is in January. People get appointed to be electors in all sorts of ways, because states have their own laws, but think of it this way: When you mark your ballot for your choice for president, you're really voting for the *electors* from your state who elect the president. The problem was that in 1800, the electors could only vote for president — the vice president was automatically the man who came in second. Apart from George Washington, of course, all our presidents up to that time had served as a vice president first, and so this was becoming the norm, like the preparation for the big job. It was therefore understood that former vice president Jefferson would be president, and Burr vice president. But it was a gentlemen's agreement, not a law. When Burr got the same number of votes, he decided to make a bold grab for the presidency. After all, there was no law against it. This whole mess took a long time (and a lot of ballots) to sort out, and the whole time Burr never did the gentlemanly thing, and simply refuse the office. Jefferson never forgave him.

The Constitution was amended to get rid of the president/vice president popularity vote problem in time for the 1804 elections, and Jefferson ran for a second term, this time dumping Burr as his running mate.

Along with being dumped by Jefferson (they barely spoke during Jefferson's first term), Burr finished off his political career with his infamous duel in 1804 with Alexander Hamilton. The two men were political rivals, and when Hamilton was killed, public opinion came down against Burr. It was a fatal one-two punch, and politically, Burr was finished in the East.

In the spring of 1805, Aaron Burr traveled to Pittsburgh, built himself a very comfortable flatboat, and headed 2,200 miles down the Ohio and Mississippi to New Orleans. Initially he traveled incognito, under the *nom de treason* Aaron King. That last name says it all. Burr had decided that the real golden opportunities were in the West. But he had no intention of starting over again at the bottom. In fact, what Aaron Burr had in mind was to start at the top — *all* the way at the top. From what historians can gather, Burr had three plans:

1. While still vice president, Burr told England's king George through the British ambassador that he would betray the U.S. if Britain would give him money and a few warships to help him steal the West from the U.S. government. As time passed, it was clear that Britain's king either wasn't really interested or didn't trust him. (Gosh, how could you not trust him?)

2. Burr had a plot to get cozy with the Spanish and set up an alliance where he'd get to be emperor over a new kingdom carved out of the Mississippi Valley, in exchange for being their solid ally against the constant encroachments of the new American nation into remaining Spanish holdings.

3. Burr would enlist the aid of the Spanish before betraying them and leading his hardy band of frontiersmen into either Florida or the West to carve out a new empire for himself. It was clear he'd take either place, Florida or the Mississippi Valley, or even the far West, so long as he got to be king of it.

Nashville, Andrew Jackson's home, was a common jumping-off point from land to river traffic. Burr was popular in the territories, and while in Nashville he spoke airily of taking over the West, as if it were a done deal, and then of turning his army about to invade and take Washington, D.C. He even spoke of assassinating Thomas Jefferson. Andrew Jackson had welcomed Burr at first, but this sort of thing turned Jackson, and prompted his letter to the president. In it, he brilliantly outlined all Burr's potential plans in great detail, based mostly on intelligent guesswork. He also mentioned a "certain general," never by name, as being Burr's henchman in the plot. Everyone knew he was talking about General James Wilkinson, a close friend of Burr's since they had fought together in the Revolutionary War, who was at that time both the commanding general of America's army and the governor of the northern Louisiana Territory.

In fact, Wilkinson had been a spy in the pay of the Spanish government for years. And, he and Burr had been plotting this scheme about the West for nearly as long, sending coded letters to one another, meeting in the dark of night, and in general shopping around for just the right opportunity. But by the late autumn of 1806, General Wilkinson found himself in a prickly position. He had pledged his loyalty to the United States government, to the King of Spain, and to Aaron Burr. And there he sat, upriver from New Orleans, facing a force of Spanish soldiers on the eastern side of the Sabine River, the side that supposedly belonged to America. They were obviously getting ready for a showdown over the border, perhaps even an attempt to take territory that the U.S. bought in the Louisiana Purchase. Wilkinson was ordered from Washington to stop them by force if they tried, this Spanish army whose possessions in America he'd sworn to protect. But Wilkinson was *also* supposed to wait where he was for Aaron Burr's forces, gathering on Blennerhassett Island in Virginia to make their trip down the Ohio and Mississippi to meet up with him. Then they would cross the lines to meet the Spanish officers with whom Wilkinson had remained chummy, and together they would invade New Orleans, cutting the heart out of the Louisiana Purchase, and betraying Jefferson.

Yet, Burr's constant delays, for lack of funds, had given Wilkinson too much time to get cold feet. When Burr's letter came proclaiming that the attack wasn't some far distant dream date, but *now,* Wilkinson decided to rethink the matter. If he betrayed Aaron Burr and gave him up to the president, he would have the government's eternal thanks. And if he made out to the Spanish that Burr had been planning to double-cross them, that *Burr* had been their real enemy all along, but on-the-ball Wilkinson had been there to stop him from stealing Spanish territory, he'd be a hero with his Spanish paymasters, as well. This seemed like a better idea all the way around.

So, Wilkinson betrayed his friend and brother-in-arms, and wrote to Jefferson to tell him all about it. Of course, he had to be a little vague, because if he wrote too much, someone might have had the common sense to ask, "Hey, how do *you* know so much about it?" He gave over just enough information about the "widespread conspiracy" of which he'd been a part to finally propel Jefferson to take action. The president sent the Virginia militia to go downriver and arrest Burr and his men.

Burr's trial took place that summer in Richmond, Virginia. By another simple twist of fate, Aaron Burr ended up with the most subtle legal mind of the century sitting the bench in his case — Chief Justice of the Supreme Court John Marshall. Marshall was a first cousin to President Jefferson, but they despised one another politically. Of course, this didn't mean Burr was automatically going to walk; Justice Marshall was too honorable for that. Also, Burr happened to be the murderer of Marshall's close political ally and friend, Alexander Hamilton. None of these factors entered into Marshall's performance on the bench.

With a dream team for both the prosecution and the defense, both sides spent days on end arguing subtle legal points, with famous lawyers drafted into jury duty who interrupted to ask questions of their own. The crowd was so large that the trial had to be moved to the House of Delegates in the Capital building. John Marshall, always calm and controlled, didn't let any of the sideshow throw him. His instructions to the jury interpreting the Constitution stated that he saw no evidence of an "overt act" of treason, nor had the state produced the necessary two witnesses to such an act. Therefore, he didn't see that Burr could be convicted of "levying war" against the United States, as the law was written.

The jury agreed, and declared Burr not guilty, with a little addendum that the charge was "not proven," a leftover verdict available under the old British common law system. In other words, "we think he did it, but the prosecution didn't prove it." Burr was a free man. Jefferson, of course, was livid, but he had his share of satisfaction. Burr would never again hold public office, and for the rest of his life would be marked a traitor.

The Tuskegee Study of Untreated Syphilis in the Negro Male

The Tuskegee Study of Untreated Syphilis in the Negro Male was a clinical study conducted in Tuskegee, Alabama, from 1932 to 1972, funded by the Public Health Department with the support of the prestigious Tuskegee Institute and its hospital. The study was patterned after a similar one in Oslo, Norway, on white men. A total of 399 black men with syphilis were studied over the course of 40 years, with a control group of 201 healthy black men. These men were mostly illiterate sharecroppers in the rural South, and it was easy for the doctors running the show to mislead them.

In 1929, when the study was proposed, there was no viable cure for syphilis, and very legitimate questions were being raised about the medications used to treat it. These "treatments" consisted of caustic and poisonous substances like arsenic and mercury, that were probably doing the patients more harm than good. That's why, originally, there was nothing cruel about the structure of the experiment, except perhaps for the fact that it involved black men only. But the argument for using black men was that syphilis was a particular plague in that community: That's why the Tuskegee Institute was involved with it. Tuskegee was founded by a former slave, Booker T. Washington, and a former slave owner, who came together in the post–Civil War South to create a "normal school," a teaching college to improve scholastic opportunities for freed slaves.

But two decades later, in 1947, this legitimate medical study turned into a nightmare of abuse. That's because in 1947, the wonder drug penicillin became widely available. One shot of penicillin stomped syphilis flat. So, of course, you'd think that the researchers would simply cure their patients with syphilis, right? Wrong. These doctors went right on lying to these men, allowing the syphilis to run its painful and potentially deadly course, just to see what would happen. At every turn, they tried to keep the men in the trials unaware that there was a cure out there for them now. The horrors of syphilis are absolutely biblical, starting with boils and fevers, then blindness or crippling loss of muscle control, and ending years later in an excruciatingly painful death. But these "doctors" stood back and watched, just to see and record what would happen.

Finally, a venereal disease investigator named Peter Buxtun discovered what was going on, and the story broke in 1972 in the *Washington Star* and *The New York Times*. The public was appalled. This event has since gone down in history as the most notorious medical experiment ever conducted in the United States, and many new laws were enacted to protect the rights of sick people taking part in medical studies.

The General Motors Streetcar Conspiracy

The reason that the major streets of America have no charming streetcars running down the main thoroughfares is quite simply because General Motors, Standard Oil, Firestone Tire Company, and Phillips Petroleum all got together in a massive conspiracy to destroy the streetcar. They used every trick in the book to do it.

The four companies, all tied hand and foot to the growth of the automobile, formed a holding company called National City Lines (NCL). All throughout the 1940s and early 1950s, the NCL traveled all over the country, buying up more than 100 electric interurban systems in 45 cities. And then they junked them, replacing them with buses.

General Motors had been working for some time to eliminate competition from streetcars, and Standard Oil practically invented the sort of "sink the competition at any price" tactics that had caused many antitrust and fair-trade laws to be passed. Together, especially after they got people, like the Interstate Highway Commission, on their side, they ensured that the days of the streetcar were numbered. Eventually General Motors was prosecuted under the Sherman Anti-Trust Act, but the judge thought the case lacked merit, and the company was fined a measly $5,000.

Project MKULTRA — The CIA's Mind Control and LSD Experiments

Project MKULTRA was the CIA's attempt to use LSD and other drugs to interrogate enemy agents, and, more ominously, to attempt to discover the inner secrets of the buzzword of the day, "brainwashing." They dreamed of a "Manchurian Candidate" effect, using LSD to create mind-controlled assassins. The entire project was an absurd waste of time, money, and worst of all, human lives.

The same thing was going on in other countries, but within MKULTRA, the most unethical part of the study was the general lack of informed consent. Various people, soldiers and civilians, were drugged with LSD by the CIA without their knowledge, just so they could play mind games with them to see the effects of the drug. Several of these subjects suffered permanent mental damage, some went literally mad, and a few even committed suicide.

Throughout the early 1970s, the CIA was pressured from all sides to reveal the facts of MKULTRA. But many of the records for the project had been destroyed. Still, thanks to the Freedom of Information Act, the papers that have survived are pretty damning.

Although it's impossible to tie all the incidents of madness, addiction, and suicide to MKULTRA without a shadow of doubt, the project paperwork makes plausible deniability difficult to achieve. Clinical research eventually proved that LSD not only caused temporary or recurring psychosis, but that in roughly 4 in 1,000 users, it caused a permanent state of psychosis.

When ex-CIA director William Colby was subpoenaed to testify about the reopened MKULTRA case in 1993, he was found a few days later face down in the river near his vacation home. The death was ruled to have been accidental. Those who are cynical have our sympathy.

The Ford Pinto Memorandum

The Pinto was marketed by Ford from 1971 to 1980 to try to feed the new American appetite for smaller cars. With its dinkster four-cylinder engine, the Pinto was battling the Volkswagon Beetle and the Toyota Corolla for the hearts and minds of those who wanted sewing-machine engines under their hoods.

Up until the first gas crisis of the 1970s, Americans were used to 30-cent-a-gallon gasoline. So American engineers weren't quite used to this business of dropping weight wherever possible in order to increase gas mileage. Consequently, the Pinto contained a major and potentially dangerous design flaw — the car had no classic, heavyweight bumper, as well as little reinforcement between the rear panel and the gas tank. When a Pinto got rear-ended, it was far too easy, even in a relatively minor accident, for the fuel tank to be ruptured, or worse, driven into the differential and punctured by the large bolts that held it in place. On top of this flaw, the doors could very easily jam after an accident, again due to the cracker-box construction that caused the metal to be so easily twisted and compressed. In other words, the Pinto was a deathtrap on four wheels.

Now the conspiracy begins. Ford was fully aware of all these construction problems. However, people didn't know that, until *Mother Jones* magazine published a stolen copy of an infamous memo that was sent out to all senior management at the Ford Motor Company.

Here are the highlights of the memo on the altar worshipping the Almighty buck:

1. With expected unit sales of 11 million Pintos, and a total cost per unit to modify the fuel tank of $11, a recall would have cost Ford $121 million.

2. But, using mathematical formulations of a probable 2,100 accidents that might result in 180 burn deaths, 180 seriously burned victims, and 2,100 burned-out vehicles, the "unit cost" per accident, assuming an out-of-court settlement, came to a probable $200,000 per death, $67,000 per serious injury, and $700 per burned-out vehicle, leaving a grand total of $49.53 million.

3. Allowing the accidents to occur represented a net savings of nearly $70 million.

4. Therefore, a human life was mathematically proven to be worth less than an $11 part.

Ford continued to build and market the Pinto without modifications. Or so they thought, until news of the memo broke. It led to criminal charges, an avalanche of lawsuits, and a recall of all Pintos; the mess went on for years. Not to mention the fact that Ford got some of the worst press an American car company has ever received. Later studies indicated that the Pinto may not have been any more prone to blowing up on contact than any other car, but by that time the damage was done.

The FDR Putsch Conspiracy

Though it's long forgotten today, the FDR Putsch Conspiracy was a serious threat to the presidency. This theory has also been called the Business Plot, but we just love the word *putsch,* the German term for an attempt to over-throw a government. This potential putsch was revealed to the American public during the hearings of the McCormack-Dickstein Committee, which was a precursor to HUAC, or the House Un-American Activities Committee.

The purpose of the hearings was to look for influence of Nazis and Nazi propa-ganda in American culture. What they got was an unexpected face-full from a retired Marine Corps major general named Smedley Butler. He was a highly decorated military officer (he won the Medal of Honor twice) and was greatly respected by the common soldiery, but he could also be a teeny-weeny bit of a loose cannon.

Smedley Butler was asked to testify before the committee, and he informed them that a shadowy group of men had come to him with a plan to overthrow President Roosevelt and take over the government. He claimed that these men were being funded by an organization called the American Liberty League, and that the organization had approached him through their strong contacts in the American Legion. Butler said they offered him half a million men, $30 million, and terrific conscience balm, because they weren't *exactly* going to get rid of Roosevelt. They would simply install one of their own in a newly created office, and he would keep Roosevelt in line, as a pampered and protected figurehead.

More than any other president in U.S. history, Roosevelt used the power of his personality, combined with the disaster of the Great Depression that had gotten him elected, to completely restructure the capitalist system as well as the power of the federal government. For Roosevelt's enemies, his ever-tight-ening grip on the office proved that if he wasn't a dictator, he was the next best thing. Those enemies would grow bitter over the years, as Roosevelt was elected to an unprecedented four terms. Only death had the power to get him out of the Oval Office.

The congressional committee investigated and then corroborated Smedley Butler's story, as well as dug up a couple of other officers who claimed that they'd been approached. Basically their final report said that they believed him. So why wasn't anyone arrested? Maybe the White House didn't think there was enough evidence to prove treason, like the Burr case discussed earlier in this chapter. Or maybe FDR just wanted to have something great to hang over the heads of his Wall Street enemies to keep them in line.

The P2 Masonic Lodge Conspiracy

The P2 Masonic Lodge Conspiracy is still going on and is still considered Italy's most lethal political plot since the days of the old Roman Empire. It involved the Vatican, the Mafia, the Freemasons, and a collection of very shady power-brokers. New revelations about this vast banking conspiracy are still coming out, more than 20 years after the scandal first broke.

In 1877, a Masonic lodge was chartered by the Grand Orient of Italy, called *Propaganda Due* (pronounced *doo-ay,* Italian for "two"). Propaganda Due Lodge over the years became a meeting place for dirty-dealing Italian businessmen, as well as government and military officials, many of whom had Mafia connections. By 1976, it had become so notorious that the Grand Master of the Grand Orient of Italy finally ordered it shut down. He pulled its charter, and expelled its members as well as its Worshipful Master, Licio Gelli. In response, Gelli simply collected up the mailing lists of his 1,000 or so members and went right back into business. He called the group P2 Lodge and still ran it like a Masonic lodge. Never mind that it was illegal, unrecognized, and unsanctioned by any Masonic body.

Two of Gelli's cohorts were Roberto Calvi, a Milan bank chairman who was secretly smuggling cash out of the country, and Michele "the Shark" Sindora, a banker who was in the employ of the Mafia. Sindora and Calvi were both in charge of managing the investments of the Vatican, and it appeared they were using Vatican accounts to launder Mafia heroin money. In 1981, police raided Gelli's offices of the P2 Lodge and made some jaw-dropping discoveries:

- P2 was literally a state within a state, the ultimate gray eminence.
- The list of over 1,000 P2 members was a who's who of anyone with power and money in Italy.
- There was ample evidence of Robert Calvi's money laundering within his Banco Ambrosiano, which seemed to be a sort of P2 private bank.

An audit was immediately called for the bank. It revealed that nearly 1.3 billion dollars had gone missing. Oops!

Banco Ambrosiano collapsed. Roberto Calvi was tried and sentenced to four years. However, he was released on bail pending a new trial, and went merrily on working at the bank, now cleverly renamed the Nuovo (New) Banco Amrosiano. The bank shut down its off-shore banking, and while everyone argued over who would take the losses, the Vatican quietly replaced the money.

The darkest aspect of the tangle of conspiracies behind the P2 Lodge is the possibility of their involvement in the murder of "the Smiling Pope," Pope John Paul I. He was a reformer, and he'd begun looking into the affairs of the Vatican Bank. He died on September 28, 1978, a shocking 33 days after his election, and the cause of his death has been much debated. First it was said to have been a myocardial infarction, a type of heart attack, though his long-time physician said he had no history of heart trouble. It's traditional not to perform an autopsy on a pope, although it had been done once before. But even more shocking was the fact that his body was embalmed within four hours of his death, thereby effectively destroying any proof that he could have been poisoned.

After the P2 scandal, the government fell in May of 1982. In July, Italy outlawed all secret societies. Meanwhile, Roberto Calvi fled to London, where he thought he'd be safe. He wasn't. On June 18, 1982, Calvi was found twisting at the end of a rope under Blackfriar's Bridge, his pockets stuffed with bricks, and his feet dangling in the Thames River.

NATO, Nazis, and the Gehlen Conspiracy

It's not pleasant to report a conspiracy between Americans and Nazis, but the truth is still the truth. It happened.

After World War II, most fleeing Nazi officers were terrified of being caught by the Russians, and practically groveled to get into gentler American hands. But Major General Reinhard Gehlen sauntered into Bavaria and announced he would only surrender to American intelligence. He then told them that buried in the Alps, in various locations that only he knew, were microfilmed copies in watertight containers of all the intelligence paperwork the Nazis possessed on Russia; her weapons and officers, her military structure, and her battlefield tactics. Needless to say, he got what he wanted. Gehlen and a small corps of his closest officers were given forged documents, put into American uniforms, and flown to the United States, where they went to work for us.

Working with the CIA, Gehlen helped to set up an entire network of what were called "stay behind" armies, paramilitary groups funded by the American government and given weapons. They were to be made operational either in the case of a Soviet invasion, or the less likely but possible victory of the communists at the polls, which was a major fear in Italy. These various stay behind armies operated under the CIA and NATO (the *North Atlantic Treaty Organization,* a union of Western nations protecting Europe from the Russians) for over 40 years, and they employed not only ex-Nazis, but a whole laundry list of undesirable types, from Mafiosos, to terrorists, to all-purpose thugs.

The CAN Coverup

The *Cult Awareness Network (CAN)* was a place for families to turn to when their kids had become involved in religious cults that might be dangerous. CAN kept records on the status and practices of over 200 mind-control organizations. It was founded by Patricia Ryan, daughter of Congressman Leo Ryan, who was assassinated in Guyana by members of Jim Jones's People's Temple cult. According to a *Time* magazine article from 1991, CAN got more concerned phone calls about Scientology than any other single organization. To quote the Chicago chapter's executive director, "Scientology is quite likely the most ruthless, the most classically terroristic, the most litigious, and the most lucrative cult the country has ever seen. No cult extracts more money from its members."

That's what made it so ironic that in the end, it was Scientology that would pervert the Cult Awareness Network. Scientology keeps a veritable coven of lawyers on call, and anyone who criticizes them, in any way, finds himself deluged by lawsuits. After the magazine article quoted above was released, they turned their guns full facing on the CAN:

1. First, they filed 50 civil lawsuits against them all over the U.S.

2. Next, they filed dozens of frivolous discrimination complaints against CAN with state-level human rights commissions. By 1994, CAN, which had an annual budget of about $300,000 a year, had been dumped by its insurers and owed tens of thousands of dollars to attorneys.

3. At the same time, Scientologists infiltrated CAN with employees who spied on the organization's day-to-day operations.

These were all the same ruthlessly successful tactics that the Church of Scientology used in order to take their pride of place as the only organization in American history to take on the IRS and come out the winner. Even Al Capone couldn't pull that one off. Despite the fact that many European nations refuse to grant Scientology the status of a religion, the church enjoys a special status with the IRS not granted to any other organization.

CAN did go down fighting. After some insulting remarks about the organization, CAN filed a few countersuits, but it was David and Goliath, and this David got creamed. The Scientologists drove CAN into bankruptcy, and all CAN's records ended up in the hands of the Church of Scientology. Then, once CAN had been driven into receivership, the Scientologists bought the Cult Awareness Network! They didn't change the name, or the supposed purpose. And so now, when a frightened wife or husband or parent calls looking for help because someone they love has been sucked into a cult, the person answering the phone is a Scientologist. Worse, the caller will not be informed of this fact. So, despite the fact that to many people around the world, Scientology is itself a cult, they remain the friendly folks behind the "Cult Awareness Network."

The Dreyfus Affair

The Dreyfus Conspiracy, what came to be known as *L'affair Dreyfus,* or the Dreyfus Affair, scared the French government out of 100 years' growth. Literally. It happened in the late 19th century, and it went on for 12 nightmarish years — one of the ugliest and longest-running conspiracies of all time. And the fact is, the French still don't like to talk about it.

The year was 1894. The French nation's particular enemy at that time was Germany; the last German invasion of France had occurred in 1868, in a war that the French lost. With the defeat at the hands of Germany still fresh in everyone's mind, someone in the French Ministry of War was selling artillery secrets to the Germans. When this fact was discovered, an innocent young captain in the Ministry, Alfred Dreyfus, was the perfect fall guy, made to order, because he was Jewish.

Dreyfus's sudden and unexpected arrest came with the discovery of the infamous *bordereau* (a memorandum or a list). This bordereau was a torn-up note describing the new French 120mm field howitzer. The piece of paper was found in a wastebasket in the German Embassy in Paris, in the office of the German military attaché, by a maid in the service of French intelligence. Naturally, an artillery officer would be suspected, because of the specifics of the note. And because the handwriting on it was somewhat similar to Dreyfus's, he was arrested.

In an irregular and scandalously short court-martial, with no evidence apart from the note (a note that Dreyfus and his counsel weren't allowed to see), Dreyfus was convicted and sentenced to life imprisonment on the Devil's Island penal colony off the coast of French Guiana in South America — a hell on earth if ever there was one.

The Ministry thought it had everything neatly tucked away. But though Dreyfus was gone, he wasn't forgotten. Unfortunately, anyone who tried to reexamine the case ended up sharing his fate. The defender of truth who suffered most was Lieutenant-Colonel Georges Picquart. The Dreyfus court-martial had always smelled funny to him, and when he was promoted to the office of Chief of Army Intelligence in 1896, it didn't take him long to discover who the real traitor was; one Major Ferdinand Walsin Esterhazy, who had already been accused, in 1892, of having become too chummy with the German military attaché. His handwriting was a far better match than Dreyfus's had been.

But the War Ministry wouldn't back down, even when Colonel Picquart completely exposed Esterhazy as a spy. Unbelievably, despite the mountain of evidence against him, Esterhazy was acquitted in a closed-door court-martial in 1898. As for Picquart, he was demoted from his position and accused of having written the bordereau himself; he was promptly arrested and jailed, to await court-martial.

After Dreyfus was found guilty of treason, he was officially stripped of his military honors on January 5, 1895. In this ancient ceremony of being degraded, or *cashiered,* Dreyfus was displayed to the public in a cobbled courtyard. His epaulets and buttons were torn from his military coat, his sword broken in two. There was a large crowd to witness the degradation of the "Jew traitor." Two very important people were standing there in that crowd. They would soon extend the effect of this tragic moment in history far and away beyond Paris or the French military. These men were:

- **Theodore Herzl:** A Viennese attorney and newspaperman working in France as a foreign correspondent. Like many Jews of his day, Herzl thought of himself as a "modern" Jew, and he believed that the best way to defeat anti-Semitism was through *assimilation,* which meant being a German or a Frenchman or whatever first, and a Jew second. Dreyfus, the first Jew in the War Ministry, was the ideal for assimilation. But when Herzl covered the Dreyfus trial, when he witnessed Dreyfus's degradation, as well as the bloody anti-Semitic riots that came after it, he did a complete about-face. It was Theodore Herzl who conceived the idea of "Zionism," meaning that Jews should have a homeland of their own. His work would bear fruit in 1948, with the establishment of the state of Israel in the former British Palestine.

- **Emile Zola:** France's greatest living writer. He believed in the innocence of Dreyfus, and, furious over Dreyfus's degradation and Picquart's "coverup" arrest, he wrote the greatest single newspaper essay of all time, on January 13, 1898: "J'accuse," French for "I accuse." It was written in the form of an open letter to the president and the French government, sharply firing off one accusation after another. He definitely named names.

Eventually Zola was brought to trail for criminal libel. A month after the absurd acquittal of Esterhazy, Zola was found guilty, whereupon he hot-footed it to England. But the government had underestimated the firestorm created by the publication of Zola's newspaper essay — "J'accuse" sold 200,000 copies the first day. After Colonel Picquart was jailed and Zola driven out of France, no one was talking about anything else. The whole country was splitting into two parties, the "Dreyfusards," and the "anti-Dreyfusards."

Finally, the New Minister of War, Godfrey Cavaignac, decided to find out once and for all what was going on. One of Zola's charges was that many of the documents that condemned Dreyfus and Picquart were forged. Cavaignac set one of his men to work to examine the documents, and a startling discovery was made on the very first one; it was a sneaky composite of two different documents that were two years apart. Eventually Cavaignac's men discovered one forgery after another, phony telegrams, wires, and departmental paperwork, most of it the work of a Major Joseph Henry, a chief witness against Dreyfus in the original 1894 court-martial. The whole house of cards collapsed around the conspirators with stunning speed. Major Henry was arrested and held for questioning, after which the spy Esterhazy fled the country. Major Henry then slit his throat with his shaving razor.

Unlike Esterhazy, who would die in exile in England, Zola came back within a year to see the fall of the government he'd accused. He was then offered a pardon. It wasn't an exoneration, but he'd achieved what he wanted and so didn't really care.

Dreyfus faced the same choice. In June of 1899, he was finally released from Devil's Island to face a new court-martial. Unfortunately, the government also offered him a pardon instead if he chose, meaning he could go free and not have to face either the new court-martial or a return to Devil's Island — but he would still be considered guilty. A physically shattered Dreyfus accepted the pardon, certain that a return to Devil's Island would mean his death.

Finally, in 1906, the French Supreme Court completely exonerated Dreyfus. Within the week he was formally re-instated in the army as a major, and was given France's highest award, the Legion of Honor. The noble Picquart's name was cleared as well, and he became a brigadier general and eventually the Minister of War.

And for anyone who thinks all the bitterness ended there, it didn't. The hatred lived on for years — someone even tried to assassinate Dreyfus at Zola's funeral. And in 1986, a statue of Dreyfus, titled *1986,* was commissioned to stand before the prestigious Ecole Militaire, France's military academy and Dreyfus's alma mater. The officers and students refused point blank to allow it on the grounds. It's spent the years since then being carted from place to place all over Paris, like some sort of party game where the last guy holding the statue has to take his pants off and sing the *Marseillaise* while balancing a beer stein on his head. The French may like to gripe about Americans being "warmongers," but they still get really testy if you mention the Dreyfus Affair. Perhaps this is understandable, because in the century since this massive conspiracy to imprison two innocent men was uncovered, not one person has ever been tried, or even charged, over their part in the plot.

Chapter 18

Ten Weirdest Secret Societies of All Time

In This Chapter

▷ Exploring extremely extreme secret societies

▷ Bellying up to bastions of the bizarre

*W*e've all known that kid in school who was weird just for the sake of being weird. In fact, we'll fess up and just let you know right now, both of us were that sort of oddball. Chris was, anyhow. Well, there have been thousands of secret societies over the centuries, and more than a few have been abnormal, eccentric, unorthodox, and more than a little strange. This chapter covers a collection of secret societies that run the gamut from mostly harmless to truly dangerous, and all points in between — but all of them are truly bizarre.

Bohemian Grove

The Bohemian Grove is actually more like the summer camp for a creepy, world-dominating secret society. It's the name of the massive country retreat of San Francisco's Republican, male-only Bohemian Club, but it's more commonly used as a term used to describe their lakeside gathering of the world's most influential business and political figures. This getaway is a retreat from reporters, advisors, wives, and other pests, and an opportunity to dress like slobs (or occasionally in drag), and the chance to drink like Jimmy Buffet fans on steroids.

The centerpiece of the annual Bohemian Grove festivities is the Cremation of Care ceremony, where a statue representing cares, woes, and responsibility is burned in a lavish pyrotechnic display by men dressed as priests in front of a large owl sculpture, which is the symbol of the Grove. Detractors have claimed the "body" used is actually a real human sacrifice. As impressive as that would be if it were true, the chief obsession of participants, from Henry Kissinger and George H. W. Bush to the most famous captains of business, seems to be, as we reveal in far more detail in Chapter 15, the freedom to urinate on trees without paparazzi photographing their shortcomings, if you get our drift.

Carnation-Painted Eyebrows Society

In spite of the seemingly precious-sounding name, the *Carnation-Painted Eyebrows Society* was one of the most feared secret societies of first-century China. It was a period of raging anarchy in China, as the Han dynasty briefly lost control of the throne to the usurper Wang Mang, and secret groups of bandits were carving up the country.

This group in particular rose to power and was named for the manner in which they painted their faces before a battle. The story goes that they came close to seizing the throne but were crushed by a cunning military strategy — troops loyal to the emperor painted their faces the same way as the society to confuse society members during the battle. It worked and the society was defeated. Seemed sort of obvious. Okay, so they didn't think it through.

E Clampus Vitus

Because of the wild popularity of secret societies — especially the Freemasons (see Chapter 9) and the Odd Fellows (see Chapter 13) — in the 1800s, inevitably parody groups arose. One such group was *E Clampus Vitus,* a Latin name that meant, well, absolutely nothing. It isn't even real Latin. The group's motto, the *Credo Quia Absurdium,* hints to the society's ultimate goal: Take nothing seriously unless it's absurd.

In 1848, only 2,000 people lived in California. After the discovery of gold at Sutter's Mills in 1849, 53,000 greed-crazed '49ers poured into the territory within just one year. Many from the East were looking for, or founded, lodges like they had back home. Others decided on a different path for their fraternalism.

E Clampus Vitus seems to have been brought to the California Gold Rush village of Hangtown (now more delicately called Placerville) by Joseph H. Zumwalt from Virginia in 1850. Zumwalt founded the first "lodge" in Mokelumne Hill, and the group quickly spread throughout Western mining towns and camps. Members were called Clampers, or Clamperers, depending on whom you ask, and the head of the organization was the Sublime Noble Grand Humbug. Officers included the Grand Iscutis, the Grand Gyascutis, the Clamps Petrix, the Clamps Matrix, and the Royal Platrix.

This group's "secret" sign of recognition was to extend the palms vertically, facing out on either side of the head, stick the thumbs in each ear, and madly waggle their fingers. They occasionally marched in parades with the other fraternal organizations, carrying their banner — a ladies' hoop skirt, festooned with the message, "This is the flag we fight under."

Meetings were held in "Halls of Comparative Libations" (saloons). The initiation ceremony was essentially designed to give far more enjoyment to the members of the club than to the new candidate and involved the sort of serious horseplay that only a crowd of drunken miners tormenting a poor dope in a blindfold can cook up. Hauled in "The Expungent's Chair" (a wheelbarrow full of wet sponges) across the rungs of a ladder on the floor, the candidate "crossed the rugged road to Dublin." He was often tossed onto a saddle that was attached to ropes looped over ceiling rafters for the ride of his life. And sometimes lack of imagination simply knocked him in the head and flattened him into a pile of horse dung. The point was to make it so raucous and unpleasant that the new recruit kept the tradition alive, if only to seek revenge on the next initiate.

Fils d'Adam (Sons of Adam)

The Fils d'Adam were — and presumably still may very well be — a peculiar group of necrophiliacs who hired prostitutes to do themselves up as corpses, climb into coffins or graves, and do the dirty deed with them — lying absolutely still, of course.

According to Alan Axelrod's exhaustive *International Encyclopedia of Secret Societies & Fraternal Orders* (Checkmark Books), this group's other rites have included a ritual involving sexual intercourse between females and snakes, supposedly to atone for original sin. The group seems to be confined to France.

The Khlysty

There's sometimes a very fine line between secret societies and religious sects, and sometimes a sect becomes a secret society because of its clash with the accepted norm. This is true of the *Khlysty,* a sect that emerged within the Russian Orthodox Church in the 1600s with a Russian peasant named Daniil Filippovich, when the group immediately started getting in hot water. And no wonder.

Khlysts didn't much care for priests or saints or the Bible. They believed that communion with God was a purely psychic communication with the Holy Spirit, who could appear in human form. Christ was a mortal reincarnation of

God on Earth, but Christ's story wasn't an isolated incident. Humans were constantly being born with the Holy Spirit in them, and it could happen to anyone. The name they actually gave themselves was Khristovery, meaning "Christ-believers."

Like many other religious groups, they believed in self-flagellation, and the term Khlysty actually comes from the Russian word *khlyst,* meaning "whip." But here's where it gets a little kooky. Their reasoning went that people who tried to lead virtuous lives were too prideful. Only someone who'd sinned a lot could be worthy of being saved by repenting and becoming reincarnated as God. A whole lotta sin was the path to salvation. So sin they did. Their ritual ceremonies, called *radenyi,* frequently turned into wild, noisy orgies. Members weren't allowed to be married, because sex between legal spouses was an abomination. Go figure.

The concept of this group then became popular all across Russia. Before the Russian Revolution in 1917, roughly 40,000 to 65,000 members existed in the countryside, secretly sinning their way to salvation. It's not surprising that the mad monk Rasputin was a member, what with all those orgies. To keep themselves hidden from church officials, Khlysts were encouraged to show almost fanatical devotion to the Russian Orthodox Church on the outside, while secretly practicing the beliefs and rituals of their sect.

It's believed that cells of Khlysts exist today. Some claim that they're in possession of Rasputin's infamously preserved sexual anatomy, which is revered as a sacred relic.

Los Hermanos Penitentes

The practice of whipping oneself (known as *self-flagellation*) as part of religious adoration has a long history, especially among a handful of zealous Christians who do it to symbolize Christ's suffering on the Way of the Cross. The Catholic Church, as a rule, was never wild about the practice, and many groups of religious fanatics over the centuries were described as sacrilegious by the church because of their excessive enthusiasm over it. Within Catholicism, penance is one thing, but big, noisy, bloody, public processions of the faithful ripping their backs to shreds with a cat o' nine tails is just too much.

That hasn't stopped the group, *Hermanos Penitentes* (the Penitent Brotherhood). They grew out of the Spanish society in what is now Colorado and New Mexico. While the Spaniards brought Catholicism to their American colonies, they also brought their rigid social class structure. The Spanish colonists were on top. Next came the native Pueblo Indians.

Slavery was permitted by Spanish law, but slaves could only be held for 10 to 20 years, after which they were freed. Unfortunately, this created a cultural purgatory for former slaves, who lived the rest of their lives as neither free nor slave, neither Spaniard nor Indian. They were known as *genizaros,* and were essentially noncitizens. They lived apart from the rest of the society and formed communities, customs, and a language of their own. They did the same with their religion, and combined Catholicism — especially the teachings of Franciscan friars — with native beliefs.

When Mexico gained its independence in 1821, the Spanish religious orders (Dominicans, Jesuits, and Franciscans) fled, or were removed, from the country, and villages all over Mexico were reduced to little more than a weekly visit by a traveling priest for their religious guidance. In the vacuum of more traditional influences, the genizaros developed their own practices.

Initiation into the male order is done during Holy Week. The candidate is conducted to the council house *(morada),* where he's stripped to the waist, asked a series of questions, and prays for the forgiveness of his sins. He then washes the feet of all present. Anyone he has offended may whip him during this part of the ceremony (the whip is called a *discipline*). Then comes the true test of his faith. A series of slices are made in his back, just below the shoulders, in the shape of crosses.

Initiates are led into the street where they publicly whip themselves, while some drag crucifixes through the street. In chapters that do things the old-fashioned way, one man is picked to actually be crucified in front of the village church, and more than a few have died over the years as a result.

This group's beliefs combine 19th-century Catholicism with a Christian mysticism that seems similar to the study of Kabbalah. Their ritual has much in common with Masonic and Rosicrucian terminology:

- Candidates seek "light."
- The group is constituted as a brotherhood and agrees to help each other.
- Charity is a strong aspect of the order.

While the groups exist today throughout the southwestern U.S., there's no official central authority. The Hermanos Penitentes came into conflict with American Catholic officials in the early 1900s and went underground as a secret society. Some say they have reconciled since the end of World War II, while others disagree. Some groups function openly, using statues instead of people for the scourging and crucifixions. Others clearly remain secret.

Order of the Peacock Angel

The mysterious author of the 1961 book *Secret Societies Yesterday and Today* (later reissued as *A History of Secret Societies,* published by Citadel) went by the pseudonym of "Arkon Daraul." To this day no one really knows who he was, although many believe the author was really 1960's mystic, Idries Shah.

In the book, Daraul described a secret society called the *Order of the Peacock Angel* that he came across in the posh suburbs of London. Their meetings were distinguished by ecstatic, whirling dances to the beat of a drum, in front of an 8-foot-tall stone statue of a large peacock.

According to Daraul, the group was brought to Britain by a Syrian expatriate in 1913. It's ritual seems to be based on Kabbalah and sacred numbers, and apparently is meant to "enlighten" members into finding their true vocation and life path. Their lodges are called *halkas,* and must consist of at least seven members.

Daraul claims the real origin of this group is in Mosul, Iraq, among the Kurdish tribes, much like the famed "whirling Dervishes."

The Skoptzy

The Skoptzy (meaning "the castrated") first came to the attention of Russian authorities in the 1770s. They seem to be the inverse opposite of the Khlysts (see the "The Khlysty" section earlier in this chapter), who existed at the same time. While the Khlysty were sinning their way to salvation, the Skoptzy were all about removing any vestiges of sin whatsoever.

The Skoptzy believed that Adam and Eve, when they were thrown out of Eden, attached the Garden's forbidden fruit to their bodies, which became the male's phallus and testicles and the female's breasts. We're only reporting here.

What pushes the Skoptzy over the edge was their remedy to this problem. Their most dedicated members had themselves, let's just say, surgically altered, in order to return their bodies to the state of grace before the stain of Adam and Eve's Original Sin. Female breasts and labia were removed, and males were either castrated (known as the "lesser seal") or removed the entire set of organs (known as the "great seal") so they more resembled a GI Joe out of uniform. Just to add the proper amount of sacrifice, the tool used was often a hot poker, so the subject was truly "baptized by fire." Over the years, to prove their courage, members used cut glass or smashed their hated organs between two bricks. Membership was secret, and accepted members dressed all in white at their meetings, referring to themselves as "white doves."

Members were severely punished and publicly humiliated whenever the Tsar's police found them, but it's estimated that there were close to 6,000 of these folks in the 1870s. Some were deported to Siberia and others to Romania, but these schemes had little effect on dissuading new recruits. The Skoptzy believed that Christ would return to Earth after they'd achieved the mystical membership goal of 144,000 (an apocalyptic number mentioned three times in the Bible's Book of Revelation). They never did, and the sect seems to have died off by about 1930.

The Vril Society

The *Vril Society* is a troublesome topic, because there's no authentic proof that such a group really existed, even though there's no shortage of people who claim that it did. What makes the alleged Vril Society really weird is that it started out as a science fiction story and from an author who is rarely connected these days with anything short of a joke.

Edward Bulwer-Lytton was a Victorian-era author whose books like *The Last Days of Pompeii* made him a household name (see the sidebar "A dark and stormy night"). In 1870 he published a science fiction novel, *The Power of the Coming Race*. It described an underground race of superhuman angel-like creatures and their mysterious energy force, *Vril,* an "all-permeating fluid" of limitless power. The story goes that the people, called *Vril-ya,* are able to control this energy source with their minds, both to do good, as well as to destroy. And, so the story goes, they're filling up the inside of the earth and are about to come out onto the Earth's surface looking for new real estate. And of course, before they can build their terrestrial civilization, the pesky humans will have to be destroyed.

The book was a huge success, and was partially responsible for a wave of speculation that the earth was indeed hollow and filled with aliens. The Vril-ya were supposed to be the descendants of Atlantis who crawled into the Earth's core to escape the deluge that supposedly destroyed the legendary city, and the novel became a favorite among true Atlantis believers. More important, the term Vril became widely used as a description of "life-giving elixir."

In 1935, German rocket scientist and science fiction author Willy Ley fled Nazi Germany and came to the U.S. In an article two years later, he mentioned that there was a group called *Wahrheitsgesellschaft* (Society for Truth) that formed to look for the real existence of Vril, in order to build a perpetual motion machine, among other goals. Based on Ley's mention of the group, other researchers began making claims that a real Vril Society did exist in Germany, before and after World War II.

In 1960, Jacques Bergier and Louis Pauwels published their speculative (and largely silly) book, *Morning of the Magicians,* in which they made claims about the Vril Society in Berlin being the precursor to the Thule Society and the Nazi Party. Others have built upon their somewhat sandy foundation to claim that the Society did indeed manage to communicate with the Vril-ya and that the Nazis built a Vril-powered flying saucer, the V-7, that made a flight to Prague in 1945. At the end of the war, the Vril Society, so the story goes, packed up its kit, took its flying saucers, and flew to a secret underground base in Antarctica. It has also been claimed that Vril technology allowed the Nazis to land on the Moon in 1942, where they built an underground base that still exists today — which sounds to us like one giant leap of delusional fantasy for mankind.

Worshippers of the Onion

More properly known by their French name, *Les Adorateurs de l'Oignon,* the *Worshippers of the Onion* were inspired by the writings of François Thomas, who marveled that the onion was a perfect symbol of "conservation of energy." The organization was started in 1929 after François had an epiphany in a vegetable stand in Paris. He took the name "Brother Thomas" and went in search of disciples.

The Worshippers were organized as a society that advocated sexual abstinence, and used the noble onion as the pinnacle of their adoration.

According to Thomas, the miracle of the bulb is that if planted in rich earth, it will grow. If a stem is broken to prevent it from going to seed, it becomes a poor eunuch — and yet still manages to germinate and grow again. He wrote, "Prevented from having children, it becomes a child again itself. . . . Thus, year by year, the onion is renewed in a body better than that which it had the year before. It strives for perfection and will always live."

Frankly, we never gave this noble vegetable that much thought, although it's troubling to think of a eunuch on your hamburger. But ultimately, that a society that didn't believe in sex could be born in France is weird beyond description.

Index

• *Numerics* •

3rd secret of Fatima, 102–103
9/11 conspiracy theories
  according to "Truthers," 139–140
  Al-Qaeda, 142
  debunkation, 152
  examining most common, 141–156
  origins of, 137–140, 326
  Pearl Harbor Syndrome, 140
  Truth Movement, 140–141
14/14 Words secret code, 244
19th Century Occult Societies. *See* Occult
  Societies, 19th Century
20th Century Occult Societies. *See* Occult
  Societies, 20th Century
88 (Heil Hitler) secret code, 244
311 (KKK) secret code, 244

• *A* •

Abraham, Larry, 16, 30
Acacia fraternity, 256
Adams, Douglas, 183
Adams, Terry, 293
ADL (Anti-Defamation League), 322
African Americans
  AIDS epidemic, 114
  CIA, cocaine and, 113–114
  COINTELPRO, 108–109
  King Alfred Plan, 109–110
  Memorandum 46, 111–112
  Tuskegee Study of Untreated Syphilis, 333
  Willie Lynch letter, 110–111
Ahmed, Ibrahim David, 321
AIDS epidemic, 106, 114
Al-Qaeda
  activities, 265–266
  Gulf War (1990), 263–264
  organization of, 264–265
  overview, 142, 263
Aldrin, Buzz, 133–136
Alien Autopsy (film), 121

Allen, Carl Meredith (pseudonym: Carlos
  Allende), 54
Allen, Gary, 16, 30, 217
Alumbrados, 208. *See also* Illuminati
Ancestral Heritage Research and Teaching
  Society, 206
Ancient Accepted Scottish Rite, 170
Ancient and Mystical Order Rosae Crucis
  (AMORC), 189
Ancient Order of Hiberneans, 251
Anderson, Gerald, 121
Andrae, Johann Valentin, 186–187
Angelou, Maya, 113
Angels and Demons (Brown), 207, 217
animinism, 39
Anti-Defamation League (ADL), 322
anti-semitism, 96–98, 297–298
Apollo I, 133–136
apophenia behavior, 23
*April, 1865 – The Month That Saved
  America* (Winik), 84
Area 51, 124–127
Areopagites secret society, 209–210
Ariosophy philosophy, 203
Armageddon, 115–116
Armstrong, Neil, 133–136
Arnold, Kenneth, 119
Arthur, Chester A., 90–91
Aryan Brotherhood, 202, 246
Aryan Nation, 202, 246
As-Sahab Foundation for Islamic Media
  Publication, 265
Ashmole, Elias, 165
Assassins
  Hassan as Sabbah, 222–224
  Ismailism, 223
  methods and targets, 224–226
  Old Man of the Mountain, 222, 224
  overview, 219, 221
  tactics, 223–224
Atlantis, The Vril Society, 349–350
Atzerodt, George, 89
Axelrod, Alan, 345

• B •

Babylonian Brotherhood, 319–323
Balsiger, David, 12
Banister, Guy, 75
banking
  Alexander Hamilton, 302, 303
  Andrew Jackson, 302
  Court Jew, 299
  Federal Reserve, 301–303
  Jews, 298–300
  moneylending, 298–299
  Protestantism, 299–300
  Rothschild family, 300–301
Baraka, Amiri, 154
Barkun, Michael, 21
Barrett, Richard, 320
Barruel, Abbé, 100, 174–175, 212
Barruel, Augustin de, 28–29
Bastille prison, 27
Bawden, David Allen, 318
Bay of Pigs, 71, 72
Bees. *See* Illuminati
behaviorists, 23–24
Bell, Alexander Graham, 91
Belnap, Jerry, 76
Bergier, Jacques, 350
Berlitz, Charles, 30, 55
Bermuda Triangle, The (Berlitz), 30
Bible Code, The (Drosnin), 188
Bickley, George W. L., 258–259
Biggest Secret, The (Icke), 322
Bilderberg Group, 308–309
Birth of a Nation (film), 235–236
Bishop James Madison Society, 215
Black Hand, The (film), 294
Black Hand gang, 273, 275
Black Panther Party, 247
black supremacism, 246–247
Blavatsky, Helena Petrovna, 199–202
Blood & Honour hate group, 248
B'Nai Brith, 251, 253
Bogart, Humphrey, 294
Bohemian Club/Bohemian Grove, 309–312,
  343–344
Bohme, Jacob, 191
Bonanno family, 285
Bonaparte, Napoleon, 27–28, 269
Booth, John Wilkes, 82–85

Borsellino, Paulo, 288–289
Bower, Doug, 134
Boylan, Richard, 126
Brazel, Mac, 119–120
Brewer, Bob, 259
Brock, Robert L., 247
Brookings Report, 132
Brown, Dan, 207, 217
Brown, John, 84
Brownsville Boys, 231–233
Brzezinski, Zbigniew, 111
Buchalter, Louis "Lepke," 231–233
Buckley, William F., 257
Bulwer-Lytton, Edward, 349
Burnett, Thom, 10
Burr, Aaron, 329–332
Buscetta, Tommasso, 286
Bush, George, 153–154, 179
Bush, George W., 179, 256
Business Plot to overthrow FDR, 336–337
Butler, Smedley, 336–337
Buxtun, Peter, 333

• C •

Cadet de Gassicourt, Charles Louis, 28, 174
Cagney, James, 294
Calvi, Roberto, 337–338
CAN (Cult Awareness Network), 339–340
Capone, Al, 276, 278
Capricorn One (film), 135
Carnation-Painted Eyebrows Society, 344
Carter, Jimmy, 111–112
Caruso, Enrico, 287–288
Case Closed (Posner), 73
Castellamarese War, 277
Castellano, Paul, 283
Castro, Fidel, 281
Catholic conspiracy theories
  3rd secret of Fatima, 102–103
  Freemasons, 167–168
  Los Hermanos Penitentes, 346–347
  multiple Popes, 317–319
  overview, 101–102
  P2 Masonic Lodge Conspiracy, 337–338
  Pope Pius XII and the Nazis, 104
  Vatican Islam, 105
Cause of World Unrest, The (Webster), 215
Cavaignac, Godfrey, 342

Cavendish-Bestinck, William, 228
Central Intelligence Agency (CIA), 113–114, 334–335, 338–339
CFR (Council on Foreign Relations), 306–307
Chaney, James, 243
Chanfray, Richard, 62
Chariots of the Gods? (Von Däniken), 30
Cheney, Dick, 56
Chick, Jack, 105
Chinese Triads, 293
Chorley, Dave, 134
Church of Scientology, 37, 325–326, 339–340
Church's Fried Chicken, 112
CIA (Central Intelligence Agency), 113–114, 334–335, 338–339
Citizen's Committee to Investigate the FBI, 109
Civil Rights Movement, 235, 243
Claiborne, Liz, 112–113
Clansman, The (Dixon), 235
Clement XIV, Pope, 209
Code of Silence (Omertà), 269, 280, 286
Cohn, Harry, 296
COINTELPRO (Counter Intelligence Program), 108–109
Colby, William, 335
Coleman, John, 312
Colombo family, 284–285, 287
Columbia (Space Shuttle) conspiracy theory, 319–320
Committee of Independent Workers, 205
Committee of 300, 312
Communist Manifesto (Marx), 214
Communist Party of the United States, 14
Comorra mafia, 290–291
Condon Committee, 131
Congress of Wilhelmsbad, 211
conspiracism
  birth of 20th-century U.S., 14–16
  conspiracist thought processes, 22–23
  overview, 10, 20–21
  peak of, 15
  recognizing, 20
  secret societies and, 21–22
  U.S. historical events, 13–14
Conspiracy Encyclopedia (Burnett), 10
conspiracy literature, 28–30
Conspiracy (Pipes), 22

conspiracy theories
  9/11, 141–156, 326
  Abraham Lincoln assassination, 81–90
  African Americans and, 108–115
  apocalyptic, 115–116
  author's view of, 1–2
  Catholic, 101–105, 317–319
  chemtrails, 50
  Church of Scientology, 325–326
  consideration and skepticism of, 9–13, 17–18
  Count de St. Germain, 62
  David Icke, 321–323
  Denver International Airport, 57–59
  Elvis Presley, 59–61
  Face on Mars, 320
  flouridated water, 48–49
  Freemason, 178–182
  HAARP, 52–53
  Holocaust, 327–328
  hot dogs, 65–66
  Islamic, 106–107
  James Garfield assassination, 90–91
  Jews, 95–101
  JFK assassination, 68–80
  New Orleans, 324–325
  particle beam weapon, 52
  Paul McCartney, 61–63
  Philadelphia Experiment, 53–55
  polio epidemic, 321
  Princess Diana, 323–324
  science fiction, 117–129, 132–136
  September 11, 2001, 141–156, 326
  Space Shuttle *Columbia*, 319–320
  subliminal advertising, 63–65
  Tesla Coils, 51–52
  true, 329–342
  types of, 24–25
  underground bunkers, 55–57
  William McKinley, 91–93
conspiracy theorists, 23–24, 31–32
Conspirators Hierarchy: The Story of the Committee of 300 (Coleman), 312
Copperheads, 258–260
Coppola, Francis Ford, 295–296
Corday, Charlotte, 28
Cosa Nostra, 270–271, 278
Cosa Nostra (Dickie), 267
Costello, Frank, 278, 284

Council on Foreign Relations (CFR), 306–307
The Creativity Movement, 246
Cremation of Care, 311–312
crop circles, 134
Crossfire: The Plot That Killed Kennedy (Marrs), 73
Crowley, Aliester, 193, 195–198, 214
Cuban Missile Crisis, 71, 72
Cult of Bacchus, 42–43
Culture of Conspiracy, A (Barkun), 21
Czolgosz, Leon Frank, 91–93

• D •

"Daraul, Arkon," 348
Dark Alliance (Webb), 113
Davis, Jefferson, 85–86
Death Angels, 247
Debunking 9/11 Myths (Meigs), 152
Dennis, Glenn, 121
Denver International Airport conspiracy theory, 57–59
Dewey, Thomas, 233, 279
Dialogues in Hell between Machiavelli and Montesquieu (Joly), 100
Diana, Princess of Wales, 323–324
Dickie, John, 267
Dionysiac Mysteries, 39
Dixon, Thomas, 235
Dominguez y Gomez, Clemente, 318–319
Dreyfus Conspiracy, 340–342
Drosnin, Michael, 188

• E •

E Clampus Vitus, 344–345
Eastland, Bernard, 53
Edward I, King of England, 225
Egyptian secret societies, 38
Eichmann, Adolf, 328
88 (Heil Hitler) secret code, 244
Eisenschiml, Otto, 88
Eisner, Will, 101
Eleusinian Mysteries, 40
Enlightenment period
  Freemasons, 166–168
  French Revolution, 26–27
  Hermeticism, 184–185

Illuminati, 208
  Rosicrucian societies, 187
esotericism, 183
Esterhazy, Ferdinand Walsin, 341–342
Eulogian Club. *See* Skull and Bones
European secret societies, 43
Exorcist, The (film), 63

• F •

Face on Mars conspiracy theory, 320
Falcone, Giovanni, 288–289
Fard, Wallace D., 107
Farrakhan, Louis, 246, 247, 324
"Fatima Crusader, The" (newsletter), 103
Fawkes, Guy, 102
Fayed, Mohamed Al-, 323–324
FBI X-files, 128
FCC (Federal Communications Commission), 64
FDR Putsch Conspiracy, 336–337
Federal Reserve, 301–303
FEMA (Federal Emergency Management Administration), 56
Fenian Brotherhood, 260–261
Ferrie, David, 74, 75
Filippovich, Daniil, 345
Fils d'Adam (Sons of Adam), 345
Final Call, The (newspaper), 107
Fitz-End, David, 143
Five Points gang, 272–273
Flying Saucer Working Party (FSWP), 133
FOI (Freedom of Information Act), 122
Force Acts (1870), 235
Ford, Henry, 100–101
Ford Pinto Memorandum, 335–336
Foreign Affairs (magazine), 307
Forrest, Nathan Bedford, 234–235, 238
Fortunate Pilgrim, The (Puzo), 295
Franklin, Benjamin, 216
fraternalism
  benevolence, 254
  birth of fraternalism, 250–254
  colleges, 251–252, 255–257
  fun orders, 253–254
  initiation secrets, 252–253
  military orders, 255
  overview, 249–250
  women and, 254

Frederick II, King, 268
Freedom of Information (FOI) Act, 122
Freemasons
    Ancient Accepted Scottish Rite, 170
    Andrew Michael Ramsay, 169, 172
    Augustin de Barruel, 29–30
    conspiracy theories, 178–182
    degrees of membership, 161, 168–169
    distrust of, 170–171
    Enlightenment period, 166–168
    Illuminati, 173, 180
    Jews, 173–175, 179
    Karl Gotheif, Baron Von Hund, und Alten-
        Grotkau, 170
    Knights Templar, 172–173
    leaders of, 175–176
    Lodges, 165
    methods and memberships, 166–170
    Mormons and, 177–178
    origin of, 159–165
    P2 Masonic Lodge Conspiracy, 337–338
    public perception of, 170–171
    real plots, 176–178
    Rite of Memphis-Mizraim, 195–196
    Rite of Strict Observance, 170
    Scottish Rite 32nd degree, 182
    secrets of, 161–162
    suspicions regarding, 167–168
    symbols, 163
    Templars, Illuminati, and Jews, 171–178
    York Rite degrees, 170
Freemasons For Dummies (Hodapp), 160
French Revolution, 26–28, 212
From Here to Eternity (Jones), 296
FSWP (Flying Saucer Working Party), 133

Gagliano, Gaetano "Tommy," 285
Gambino family, 283
Garfield, John, 90–91
Garrison, Jim, 73–79
Gehlen, Reinhard, 338
Gehlen Conspiracy, 338–339
Gelli, Licio, 337
General Motors Streetcar Conspiracy, 334
Génération Kémi Séba (KGS) hate group, 248
Genovese family, 278, 280, 284
gentlemen's clubs, 42

German Nazi party. *See* Nazis
German occultism, 203–205
German Worker's Party, 205
Germanenorden, 204
Germer, Karl, 198
Getler, Warren, 259
Giancana, Sam, 73
Gigante, Vincent "the Chin," 284
Godfather, The (film), 295–296
Goebbels, Joseph, 263
Goldstein, Martin "Bugsy," 232
Golovinsky, Mathieu, 100
Good Shepherd, The (film), 257
Goodman, Andrew, 243
Gotheif, Baron Von Hund, und Alten-
    Grotkau, Karl, 170
Gotti, John, 283
Grand Army of the Republlic (GAR), 255
Grant, Ulysses S., 235
Gravano, Sammy "the Bull," 283
Great White Brotherhood, 200
Greater Mysteries degrees, 211
Greece, 38–40
Griffith, D. W., 235–236, 294
Guido von List Society, 203
Guiteau, Charles Julius, 90
Gulf War (1990), 263–264

HAARP (High Frequency Active Auroral
    Research Program) conspiracy theory,
    52–53
Hamilton, Alexander, 302, 303, 330, 332
Hapsburgs, 300–301
hashasshim. *See* Assassins
Henry, Joseph, 342
Hermetic Order of the Golden Dawn,
    193–194
Hermeticism, 184–185
Herold, David, 89
Herzl, Theodore, 341
Heydrich, Reinhard, 327–328
Hidden Persuaders, The (Packard), 64
High Armenian Order, 203
Hilfiger, Tommy, 113
Hill, Virginia, 281
Himmler, Heinrich, 205–206
History of Magic, A (Eliphas), 214

Hitchhiker's Guide to the Galaxy, The (Adams), 183
Hitler, Adolph, 101
Hoagland, Richard, 320
Hodapp, Christopher, 29, 102, 160, 173
Holocaust conspiracy theory, 327–328
Honor Thy Father (Talese), 267, 285
Hoover, J. Edgar, 128, 244
Hubbard, L. Ron, 198, 325–326
Hynek, J. Allen, 132

● *I* ●

Icke, David, 321–323
Ickstatt, Johann Adam, 209
Illuminati
  Adam Weishaupt, 209
  American, 213–214
  Areopagites, 209–210
  Augustin de Barruel, 29–30
  Congress of Wilhelmsbad, 211
  Dan Brown, 217
  David Icke, 218
  degree structure, 210–211
  Enlightenment period, 208
  Freemasons, 173, 180
  French Revolution, 212
  John Birch Society, 216–217
  Masons, 210–211
  modern theories, 216–218
  movement dies, 212–213
  Nesta Webster, 215–216
  occult and, 214
  origin of, 207–208
  Spartacus, 209–210
  Texe Marrs, 218
  Thomas Jefferson, 215
  ZOG, 218
Illustrations of Masonry (Morgan), 177
Imperial Klans of America, 245
Independent Order of Odd Fellows, 250
International Encyclopedia of Secret Societies & Fraternal Orders (Axelrod), 345
International Flat Earth Society, 135
Internet. *See* Web sites
IOC (Italian Organized Crime), 290
Irish Republican Brotherhood (IRB), 260–261

IRS (Internal Revenue Service), 325–326
Iscariot, Judas, 221
Isis Revealed (Blavatsky), 201
Islamic conspiracy theories, 106–107
Ismail, Hazem Sallah Abu, 106

● *J* ●

"J'accuse" (Zola), 341
Jack the Ripper, 178–179
Jackson, Andrew, 302, 329–330, 331
James, Jesse, 260
Jefferson, Thomas, 174, 215, 255, 329–330
Jennings, Peter, 79
Jesuits, 28–29
Jewish conspiracy theories
  banking and, 298–300
  conspiracy theories and, 96–101, 106, 215
  Freemasons and, 173–175, 179
Jewish Defense League (JDL) hate group, 248
JFK (film), 73–79
John Birch Society, 216–217, 308
John Paul I, Pope, 338
Johnson, Andrew, 86–87
Johnson, Lyndon, 69, 70, 72
Joly, Maurice, 100
Jones, Alex, 141, 319
Jones, James, 296
Jones, Jim, 339
Journal of Historical Review, 327
Judge, William Quan, 200–202

● *K* ●

Kabbalah For Dummies (Kurzweil), 188
Kaufman, Frank, 121
Kefauver Senate hearings, 282, 296
Kellner, Carl, 195–196
Kennedy, John F.
  Bay of Pigs, 71
  books, 73
  Clay Shaw prosecution, 73–74
  conspiracy theories regarding assassination of, 70–73, 75–79
  Cuban Missile Crisis, 71
  facts, 67–69
  Jack Ruby, 70, 72, 80

Jim Garrison, 73–79
Lee Harvey Oswald, 69–70, 72, 75–79
Lyndon Johnson, 69, 70, 72
quote on secrecy and secret societies, 15
Warren report, 70
Kennedy, Robert F., 72
Kerry, John, 256
Key, Wilson Bryan, 64
Khan, Aly, 225
Khlysty, The, 345–346
KIGY (Klansman, I Greet You) secret
    code, 244
King Alfred Plan, 109–110
Knigge, Adolf Franz Friederich, 210–213
Knightly Order, 205–206
Knights of Columbus, 251, 253, 255
Knights of Mary Phagan, 237
Knights of Pythias, 255
Knights of the Ku Klux Klan, 234
Knights of the White Kamelia, 245
Knights Templar, 172–173, 255
Know Nothings, 252
Ku Klux Klan
  Bayou Knights, 245
  Birth of a Nation film, 235–236
  Civil Rights Movement and, 243
  cross burning, 243
  decline of, 242
  FBI and, 244
  fear of Catholicism, 242
  hate groups spawned by, 245–246
  lodges and officers, 238–239
  membership, 243
  modern, 245
  origin of, 234–235
  rebirth of, 235–236, 239
  Stephenson, David Curtiss (Steve),
      239–242
  underground, 243–244
  wardrobe, 238
  white supremacist movement codes, 244
Kubrick, Stanley, 135
Kurzweil, Arthur, 188

• *L* •

Lansky, Meyer, 231, 278–281
Lanz, Adolf Josef, 203–204
Late Great Planet Earth, The (Lindsey), 30
Lazar, Robert, 126
Lee, Robert E., 84–85
Lee, Spike, 112–113, 324
LeFranc, 28
Lévi, Eliphas, 189, 214
Lewis, Harvey Spencer, 189, 197
Ley, Willy, 349
Lincoln, Abraham
  assassination conspiracy theories, 82–83,
      85–88
  David Herold, 89
  George Atzerodt, 87, 89
  John Wilkes Booth, 82–85, 89–90
  Knights of Pythias, 250
  Lewis Paine, 88–89
  Mary Surratt, 88
  overview, 81–82
  Robert E. Lee, 84–85
  Samuel Mudd, 89–90
Lincoln Conspiracy, The (Balsiger &
    Sellier), 12
Lindsey, Hal, 30
List, Guido von, 203
literature on conspiracies, 28–30
Little, Robert Wentworth, 190
Liuzzo, Viola Gregg, 243
Lodge Theodore of Good Council, 210
Loose Change (video), 155–156
Los Hermanos Penitentes, 346–347
Lower Mysteries degrees, 211
LSD and Project MKILTRA, 334–335
Lucchese family, 285
Luce, Henry, 257
Luciano, Charles "Lucky," 277–279, 284
Lynch, William, 110–111

• *M* •

Madison, James, 215
Mafia
  American, 272–273
  attempts to destroy, 287–290
  birth of Cosa Nostra, 270–271
  Black Hand, 275
  Bonanno family, 285
  Castellamarese War, 277
  Charles "Lucky" Luciano, 277–279

Mafia *(continued)*
  Code of Silence (Omertà), 269, 280, 286
  Colombo family, 284–285
  Cupola, 271
  decline of, 282
  ethnic lines, 274
  Gambino family, 283
  Genovese family, 284
  impact on popular culture, 293–296
  Irish, 273
  Italian, 290–292
  Jewish, 274–275
  Joe Valachi, 280
  Lucchese family, 285
  nicknames, 282
  origins of, 270
  prohibition, 275–281
  Rackets, 275–281
  rituals, 286–287
  Sicily, 268–269
  vendettas, 271–272
  wars, 277
Magdalene, Mary, 102
Majestic-12 Committee, 124
Malavita del Brenta, 292
Man Who Cried I Am, The (Williams), 109
Manga For Dummies (Okabayashi), 231
Mangano, Vincent, 283
Maranzano, Salvatore, 277
Marat, Jean-Paul, 27–28
Marcel, Jesse, 120, 121
Marrc, Texe, 218
Marrs, Jim, 73
Marshall, John, 332
Martinism, 191–192
Marx, Karl, 214
Masonry degrees, 211
Masons and Masonic Temple. *See* Freemasons
Masseria, Joe "the Boss," 277
Maxi Trial, 288–289
McCartney, Paul, 61–63
McClellan hearings, 284
McKinley, William, 91–93
McMurtry, Grady, 198
Meigs, James B., 152

Memoirs Illustrating the History of Jacobinism (Barruel), 29, 100, 174–175, 212
Memorandum 46, 111–112
Metzger, Tom, 247
Military Industrial Complex, 72
Milner, Alfred Lord, 306
Moore, William, 55
Moray, Robert, 165
Morgan, William, 176–177
Mormons, 177–178
Morning of the Magicians (Bergier & Pauwels), 350
Morris, S. Brent, 180
Mother Jones (magazine), 335
Mount Weather bunker, 56
Mudd, Samuel, 89–90
Muhammad, Khalid Abdul, 247
Murder, Incorporated, 231–233
Musketeers of Pig Alley (film), 294
Muslim American Society, 107
Muslim conspiracy theories, 106–107
Mussolini, Benito, 269, 287

• *N* •

Nation of Islam (NOI), 107, 246
Nation of Yahweh, 247
National Socialist German Worker's Party. *See* Nazis
NATO (North Atlantic Treaty Organization), 338–339
Nazarenos, the Brotherhood of the Passion, 238
Nazi LowRiders (NLR), 246
Nazis
  FDR Putsch Conspiracy, 336–337
  Gehlen Conspiracy, 338–339
  German occultism, 203–205
  Pope Pius XII and, 104
  Vril Society, 349–350
'Ndrangheta, The (The Honored Society), 291
Neuwabians, The, 247
New Black Panther Party, 247
New World Airport Commission, 58
Nilus, Sergei, 100
ninjas, 228–231

Nixon, Richard, 60, 73, 311
NOI (Nation of Islam), 107, 246
None Dare Call It Conspiracy (Allen & Abraham), 16, 30, 217
North Atlantic Treaty Organization (NATO), 338–339

• *O* •

Oberholtzer, Madge, 241–242
Occult Societies, 19th Century
  Hermetic Order of the Golden Dawn, 193–194
  Ordo Templi Orientis (OTO), 195–198
  overview, 192
  Spiritualism, 194–195
Occult Societies, 20th Century
  German, 203–206
  Great White Brotherhood, 200
  Helene Petrovna Blavatsky Theosophical Society, 199–202
  overview, 198–199
Ockham's Razor maxim, 25
O'Hair, Madalyn Murray, 136
Okabayashi, Kensuke, 231
Olcott, Henry Steel, 200–202
Old Man of the Mountain, 222, 224
The Olympians, 312
On the Trail of the Assassins (Garrison), 73
Operation High Dive, 123
Operation Paget, 324
Operation Werwolf, 262–263
Operation Whitecoat, 115
Order of the Oriental Templars, 195–198
Order of the Peacock Angel, 348
Order of the Temple of the East, 195–198
Ordere Martinist schools, 191
Ordo Novi Templi, 203–204
Ordo Rosae Rubeae et Aureae Crucis, 193
Ordo Templi Orientis (OTO), 195–198
ORION (Our Race Is Our Nation) secret code, 244
OStara (magazine), 204
Oswald, Lee Harvey, 69–70, 72, 75–79
Our Lady of Fatima, 102
Outside the Law (film), 294

• *P* •

P2 Masonic Lodge Conspiracy, 337–338
Packard, Vance, 64
Paine, Lewis, 88–89
Parker, John, 82–83
Passover Plot, The (Schonfield), 30
Patriarchs Militant, 255
Pauwels, Louis, 350
Pearl Harbour Syndrome, 140
Penn, Lemuel, 243
The Pentagon Papers, 15
People's Temple cult, 339
Perfectabilists. *See* Illuminati
Petrosino, Joe, 287–288
Phagan, Mary, 237
Phi Beta Kappa, 255
Philadelphia Experiment: Project Invisibility, The (Berlitz & Moore), 55
Picquart, George, 340–342
Pipes, Daniel, 22
Pius XII, Pope, 104
Plot: The Secret Story of the Protocols of the Elders of Zion, The (Eisner), 101
Pohl, Hermann, 204–205
Politician, The (Welch), 216
Posner, Gerald, 73
Power of Prophecy ministry, 218
Power of the Coming Race, The (Bulwer-Lytton), 349
Presley, Elvis, 59–61
Profaci, Giuseppe "Joe," 284–285, 287
Profiles in Courage (Kennedy), 86
prohibition
  Al Capone, 276
  Ben "Bugsy" Siegel, 281
  Charles "Lucky" Luciano, 277–279
  Cuba, 280–281
  Franklin Roosevelt, 277
  Joe Valachi, 280
  Las Vegas, 281
  overview, 275–276
  rackets, 276
  shift from alcohol to gambling, 279–280
  speakeasies, 276
Project Blue Book, 129–131
Project for the New American Century, 153

Project Grudge, 128
Project MKULTRA, 334–335
Project Mogul, 123
Project Sign, 127
Proofs of a Conspiracy Against All the Religions and Governments of Europe Carried on in the Secret Meetings of Freemasons (Robison), 28, 174, 212, 213
Proposed Implications of Peaceful Space Activities For Human Affairs, 132
Protestantism, 299–300
Prutzman, Hans-Adolf, 262–263
public perception of Freemasons, 168, 170–171
Pulvermacher, Lucian, 318
Puzo, Mario, 295–296

• *Q* •

Quigley, Carroll, 305

• *R* •

Ragdsale, Jim, 122
RAHOWA (Racial Holy War) secret code, 244
Ramon, Ilan, 319
Ramsay, Andrew Michael, 169, 172
Reconstruction Trilogy, The (Dixon), 235
Regius Manuscript, 165
Reles, Abe "Kid Twist," 232–233
religious groups. *See specific groups*
Remy, Will, 242
Reuss, Theodore, 196, 197, 214
Revelation, 115–116
REX-84 (Readiness Exercise 1984), 110
Rhodes, Cecil John, 303–306, 312
RICO Act (Racketeer Influenced and Corrupt Organizations Act), 282
Rite of Memphis-Mizraim, 195–196
Rite of Strict Observance, 170
Rivera, Alberto Magno Romero, 105
ROA (Race Over All) secret code, 244
Robb, Thom, 245
Robertson Commission, 130
Robinson, Edward G., 294–295
Robison, John, 28, 174, 212, 213
Rockefeller family, 298, 307, 308
Roman secret societies, 40–43

Roosevelt, Clinton, 213–214
Roosevelt, Franklin Delano, 140, 277, 336–337
Rosen, Joe, 233
Rosenkratz, Christian, 186
Rosicrucianism
  birth of societies, 187
  Christian Rosenkratz, 186
  Freemasons and, 189–190
  Hermeticism compared to Enlightenment, 184–185
  Johann Valentin Andrae, 186–187
  Kabbalah, 188
  masonic related groups, 190
  modern, 188–189
  overview, 183–184, 185–186
  symbol, 185–186
Roswell Incident
  Majestic-12 committee, 124
  Operation High Dive, 123
  overview, 119–120
  Project Mogul, 123
  Roswell Report,
  witness testimonies, 121–122
Rothschild family, 300–301, 305
Round Table (magazine), 306
The Royal Society of London For The Improvement of Natural Sciences, 165
Rozier, Robert, 247
Ruby, Jack, 70, 80
Ruppelt, Edward J., 129–130
Russell, William Huntington, 256
Ryan, Patricia, 339

• *S* •

Saint-Martin, Louis-Claude de, 191
Santos, Lucia, 102–103
Schonfield, Hugh Joseph, 30
Schulgen, George F., 118
Schultz, Dutch, 279
Schwerner, Michael, 243
Science of Government Founded on Natural Law (Roosevelt), 213–214
Scottish Rite 32nd degree, 182
Sebottendorf, Rudolf Glandeck von, 204
Secret Doctrines, The (Blavatsky), 202

secret societies
  ancient Egyptian, 38
  ancient European, 43
  ancient Greek, 38–40
  ancient Roman, 40–43
  author's view of, 1–2
  Bohemian Grove, 343–344
  Carnation-Painted Eyebrows Society, 344
  conspiracism and, 21–22
  E Clampus Vitus, 344–345
  early United States, 43–44
  Fils d'Adam (Sons of Adam), 345
  Khlysty, 345–346
  Los Hermanos Penitentes, 346–347
  murderous, 221–245
  new interest, 44
  Order of the Peacock Angel, 348
  overview, 9–11, 33–34
  religious cults compared to, 35–37
  revolutionary, 258–266
  Skoptzy, 348–349
  Vril Society, 349–350
  Worshippers of the Onion, 350
Secret Societies Yesterday and Today
  ("Daraul"), 348
Sellier, Charles E., 12
September 11, 2001 attacks. *See* 9/11
  conspiracy theories
Shadows of the Sentinel (Getler &
  Brewer), 259
Shaw, Clay, 73–75
Shears, Billy, 61–62
Shield Society, 261–262
shinobi. *See* ninjas
Shriners, 253
Sicarii, 220–221
Sicily, 268–269
Siegel, Ben "Bugsy," 231, 278–279, 281
Sigma Mu Sigma, 256
Silverstein, Larry, 150–151
Simmons, William J., 236–239
Sinatra, Frank, 296
Sindora, Michele "the Shark," 337–338
Site R underground bunker, 56
skinhead movement, 245
Skolnick, Sherman, 319
Skoptzy, The, 348–349
Skull and Bones, 179, 256–257

Skulls, The (film), 257
Smith, Joseph, 177–178
Societas Rosicruciana in Anglia (SRIA), 190
Societas Rosicruciana in Civitatibus
  Foederatis (SRICF), 190
Society of the Elect, 304–305
Soldiers of Woodcraft, 255
Somebody Blew Up America (Amiri), 154
Sons of Liberty, 258
Space Shuttle *Columbia* conspiracy theory,
  319–320
Spartacus, 209–210
Spiritualism, 194–195
Square and Compass, 256
St. Germain, Count de, 62
Stanton, Edwin, 87–88
Stead, William T., 305
Stephenson, David Curtiss (Steve), 239–242
Stewart, Payne, 147
Stidda mafia, 291–292
Stone, Oliver, 22, 73
streetcar conspiracy, 334
Subliminal Seduction (Key), 64
Sue, Eugène, 100
Surratt, Mary, 88
Synarchy, 192

• T •

Taft, William Howard, 257
Talese, Gay, 267, 285
Tannenbaum, Alfred, 233
Templar Code For Dummies, The (Hodapp
  & Von Kannon), 29, 102, 173
Tesla, Nikola, 51–52
Teutonic Order, 204
Thelema religion, 197
Theosophical Society, 200–201
Thomas, François, 350
Thugee and Dacoity (bandit)
  Department, 228
Thugs, 226–228
Thule Gesellschaft, 205
Tippit, J.D., 69
Tomb of Jacques Molay, The (Cadet de
  Gassicourt), 28, 174
Tragedy and Hope (Quigley), 305
Trilateral Commission, 308

Truman, Harry, 124
"Truth Movement" (9/11), 140–141
Truthers, 137
Turks, 224
Tuskegee Study of Untreated Syphilis in
    the Negro Male, 333
20th Century Occult Societies. *See* Occult
    Societies, 20th Century

• *U* •

UFO Experience: A Scientific Study, The
    (Hynek), 132
UFOs, 118–119, 127–133
urban legends, 112–113
U.S. Air Force Office of Special
    Investigations (AFOSI), 129
USS *Cole* bombing, 142
USS *Eldredge* (destroyer), 53–55

• *V* •

Valachi, Joe, 280, 284, 286, 295
Vatican Islam conspiracy theory, 105
Veil Withdrawn, The (LeFranc), 28
Vestal Virgins, 42
Vicary, James, 64
Volksfront hate group, 248
Von Däniken, Erich, 30
Von Kannon, Alice, 29, 102, 173
Vril Society, 349–350

• *W* •

Wallace, George, 244
Walvater of the Holy Grail, 204
WAR (White Aryan Resistance), 246
Wardenclyffe Tower, 52
Warren Report, 70
Washington, Booker T., 333
Washington, George, 173, 180, 213
Watchmen On The Walls hate group, 248
Web sites
    Council on Foreign Relations (CFR), 307
    Elvis Sighting Society, 61

JFK assassination facts and allegations, 79
Project Blue Book, 131
Round Table, 306
Trilateral Commission, 308
Webster, Nesta, 215–216
Weishaupt, Adam, 208–213
Welch, Robert F., 216
White Aryan Resistance (WAR), 246
Why Lincoln Was Murdered (Eisenschiml), 88
Wilkinson, James, 331–332
Williams, John A., 109
Wilson, Woodrow, 307
Winds of War, The (Wouk), 311
Winik, Jay, 84
women and fraternalism, 254–255
Woodford, A.F.A., 193
Woodmen of America, 236
World Church of the Creator, 246
Worshippers of the Onion (Les Adorateurs
    d l'Oignon), 350
Wouk, Herman, 311
WPWW (White Pride World Wide) secret
    code, 244

• *Y* •

Y2K, 115–116
Yahweh ben Yahweh (pseudonym: Hulon
    Mitchell, Jr.), 247
Yale University, 256–257
York, Malachi Z., 247
York Rite, 170
Yukio Mishima, 261–262

• *Z* •

Zealots, 220–221
Zimmerman, Johann Jacob, 187
Zionism, 218, 341
ZOG (Zionist Occupied Government), 218
Zola, Emile, 341, 342
Zumwalt, Jospeh H., 344

BUSINESS, CAREERS & PERSONAL FINANCE

0-7645-9847-3

0-7645-2431-3

Also available:
- Business Plans Kit For Dummies
  0-7645-9794-9
- Economics For Dummies
  0-7645-5726-2
- Grant Writing For Dummies
  0-7645-8416-2
- Home Buying For Dummies
  0-7645-5331-3
- Managing For Dummies
  0-7645-1771-6
- Marketing For Dummies
  0-7645-5600-2

- Personal Finance For Dummies
  0-7645-2590-5*
- Resumes For Dummies
  0-7645-5471-9
- Selling For Dummies
  0-7645-5363-1
- Six Sigma For Dummies
  0-7645-6798-5
- Small Business Kit For Dummies
  0-7645-5984-2
- Starting an eBay Business For Dummies
  0-7645-6924-4
- Your Dream Career For Dummies
  0-7645-9795-7

HOME & BUSINESS COMPUTER BASICS

0-470-05432-8

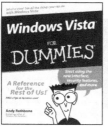

0-471-75421-8

Also available:
- Cleaning Windows Vista For Dummies
  0-471-78293-9
- Excel 2007 For Dummies
  0-470-03737-7
- Mac OS X Tiger For Dummies
  0-7645-7675-5
- MacBook For Dummies
  0-470-04859-X
- Macs For Dummies
  0-470-04849-2
- Office 2007 For Dummies
  0-470-00923-3

- Outlook 2007 For Dummies
  0-470-03830-6
- PCs For Dummies
  0-7645-8958-X
- Salesforce.com For Dummies
  0-470-04893-X
- Upgrading & Fixing Laptops For Dummies
  0-7645-8959-8
- Word 2007 For Dummies
  0-470-03658-3
- Quicken 2007 For Dummies
  0-470-04600-7

FOOD, HOME, GARDEN, HOBBIES, MUSIC & PETS

0-7645-8404-9

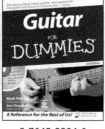

0-7645-9904-6

Also available:
- Candy Making For Dummies
  0-7645-9734-5
- Card Games For Dummies
  0-7645-9910-0
- Crocheting For Dummies
  0-7645-4151-X
- Dog Training For Dummies
  0-7645-8418-9
- Healthy Carb Cookbook For Dummies
  0-7645-8476-6
- Home Maintenance For Dummies
  0-7645-5215-5

- Horses For Dummies
  0-7645-9797-3
- Jewelry Making & Beading For Dummies
  0-7645-2571-9
- Orchids For Dummies
  0-7645-6759-4
- Puppies For Dummies
  0-7645-5255-4
- Rock Guitar For Dummies
  0-7645-5356-9
- Sewing For Dummies
  0-7645-6847-7
- Singing For Dummies
  0-7645-2475-5

INTERNET & DIGITAL MEDIA

0-470-04529-9

0-470-04894-8

Also available:
- Blogging For Dummies
  0-471-77084-1
- Digital Photography For Dummies
  0-7645-9802-3
- Digital Photography All-in-One Desk Reference For Dummies
  0-470-03743-1
- Digital SLR Cameras and Photography For Dummies
  0-7645-9803-1
- eBay Business All-in-One Desk Reference For Dummies
  0-7645-8438-3
- HDTV For Dummies
  0-470-09673-X

- Home Entertainment PCs For Dummies
  0-470-05523-5
- MySpace For Dummies
  0-470-09529-6
- Search Engine Optimization For Dummies
  0-471-97998-8
- Skype For Dummies
  0-470-04891-3
- The Internet For Dummies
  0-7645-8996-2
- Wiring Your Digital Home For Dum
  0-471-91830-X

* Separate Canadian edition also available
† Separate U.K. edition also available

SPORTS, FITNESS, PARENTING, RELIGION & SPIRITUALITY

0-471-76871-5

0-7645-7841-3

Also available:
- Catholicism For Dummies
  0-7645-5391-7
- Exercise Balls For Dummies
  0-7645-5623-1
- Fitness For Dummies
  0-7645-7851-0
- Football For Dummies
  0-7645-3936-1
- Judaism For Dummies
  0-7645-5299-6
- Potty Training For Dummies
  0-7645-5417-4
- Buddhism For Dummies
  0-7645-5359-3

- Pregnancy For Dummies
  0-7645-4483-7 †
- Ten Minute Tone-Ups For Dummies
  0-7645-7207-5
- NASCAR For Dummies
  0-7645-7681-X
- Religion For Dummies
  0-7645-5264-3
- Soccer For Dummies
  0-7645-5229-5
- Women in the Bible For Dummies
  0-7645-8475-8

TRAVEL

0-7645-7749-2

0-7645-6945-7

Also available:
- Alaska For Dummies
  0-7645-7746-8
- Cruise Vacations For Dummies
  0-7645-6941-4
- England For Dummies
  0-7645-4276-1
- Europe For Dummies
  0-7645-7529-5
- Germany For Dummies
  0-7645-7823-5
- Hawaii For Dummies
  0-7645-7402-7

- Italy For Dummies
  0-7645-7386-1
- Las Vegas For Dummies
  0-7645-7382-9
- London For Dummies
  0-7645-4277-X
- Paris For Dummies
  0-7645-7630-5
- RV Vacations For Dummies
  0-7645-4442-X
- Walt Disney World & Orlando
  For Dummies
  0-7645-9660-8

GRAPHICS, DESIGN & WEB DEVELOPMENT

0-7645-8815-X

0-7645-9571-7

Also available:
- 3D Game Animation For Dummies
  0-7645-8789-7
- AutoCAD 2006 For Dummies
  0-7645-8925-3
- Building a Web Site For Dummies
  0-7645-7144-3
- Creating Web Pages For Dummies
  0-470-08030-2
- Creating Web Pages All-in-One Desk
  Reference For Dummies
  0-7645-4345-8
- Dreamweaver 8 For Dummies
  0-7645-9649-7

- InDesign CS2 For Dummies
  0-7645-9572-5
- Macromedia Flash 8 For Dummies
  0-7645-9691-8
- Photoshop CS2 and Digital
  Photography For Dummies
  0-7645-9580-6
- Photoshop Elements 4 For Dummies
  0-471-77483-9
- Syndicating Web Sites with RSS Feeds
  For Dummies
  0-7645-8848-6
- Yahoo! SiteBuilder For Dummies
  0-7645-9800-7

NETWORKING, SECURITY, PROGRAMMING & DATABASES

0-471-74940-0

Also available:
- Access 2007 For Dummies
  0-470-04612-0
- ASP.NET 2 For Dummies
  0-7645-7907-X
- C# 2005 For Dummies
  0-7645-9704-3
- Hacking For Dummies
  0-470-05235-X
- Hacking Wireless Networks
  For Dummies
  0-7645-9730-2
- Java For Dummies
  0-470-08716-1

- Microsoft SQL Server 2005 For Dummies
  0-7645-7755-7
- Networking All-in-One Desk Reference
  For Dummies
  0-7645-9939-9
- Preventing Identity Theft For Dummies
  0-7645-7336-5
- Telecom For Dummies
  0-471-77085-X
- Visual Studio 2005 All-in-One Desk
  Reference For Dummies
  0-7645-9775-2
- XML For Dummies
  0-7645-8845-1

HEALTH & SELF-HELP

0-7645-8450-2

0-7645-4149-8

Also available:
- Bipolar Disorder For Dummies
  0-7645-8451-0
- Chemotherapy and Radiation
  For Dummies
  0-7645-7832-4
- Controlling Cholesterol For Dummies
  0-7645-5440-9
- Diabetes For Dummies
  0-7645-6820-5* †
- Divorce For Dummies
  0-7645-8417-0 †

- Fibromyalgia For Dummies
  0-7645-5441-7
- Low-Calorie Dieting For Dummies
  0-7645-9905-4
- Meditation For Dummies
  0-471-77774-9
- Osteoporosis For Dummies
  0-7645-7621-6
- Overcoming Anxiety For Dummies
  0-7645-5447-6
- Reiki For Dummies
  0-7645-9907-0
- Stress Management For Dummies
  0-7645-5144-2

EDUCATION, HISTORY, REFERENCE & TEST PREPARATION

0-7645-8381-6

0-7645-9554-7

Also available:
- The ACT For Dummies
  0-7645-9652-7
- Algebra For Dummies
  0-7645-5325-9
- Algebra Workbook For Dummies
  0-7645-8467-7
- Astronomy For Dummies
  0-7645-8465-0
- Calculus For Dummies
  0-7645-2498-4
- Chemistry For Dummies
  0-7645-5430-1
- Forensics For Dummies
  0-7645-5580-4

- Freemasons For Dummies
  0-7645-9796-5
- French For Dummies
  0-7645-5193-0
- Geometry For Dummies
  0-7645-5324-0
- Organic Chemistry I For Dummies
  0-7645-6902-3
- The SAT I For Dummies
  0-7645-7193-1
- Spanish For Dummies
  0-7645-5194-9
- Statistics For Dummies
  0-7645-5423-9

Get smart @ dummies.com®

- **Find a full list of Dummies titles**
- **Look into loads of FREE on-site articles**
- **Sign up for FREE eTips e-mailed to you weekly**
- **See what other products carry the Dummies name**
- **Shop directly from the Dummies bookstore**
- **Enter to win new prizes every month!**

* Separate Canadian edition also available
† Separate U.K. edition also available

Available wherever books are sold. For more information or to order direct: U.S. customers visit www.dummies.com or call 1-877-762-2974.
U.K. customers visit www.wileyeurope.com or call 0800 243407. Canadian customers visit www.wiley.ca or call 1-800-567-4797.

Printed in the USA
CPSIA information can be obtained
at www.ICGtesting.com
JSHW052032270124
56033JS00007B/76

9 780470 184080